Lecture Notes in Artificial Intelligence　　1216

Subseries of Lecture Notes in Computer Science
Edited by J. G. Carbonell and J. Siekmann

Lecture Notes in Computer Science

Edited by G. Goos, J. Hartmanis and J. van Leeuwen

Springer
Berlin
Heidelberg
New York
Barcelona
Budapest
Hong Kong
London
Milan
Paris
Santa Clara
Singapore
Tokyo

Jürgen Dix   Luís Moniz Pereira
Teodor C. Przymusinski (Eds.)

Non-Monotonic Extensions
of Logic Programming

Second International Workshop, NMELP '96
Bad Honnef, Germany, September 5-6, 1996
Selected Papers

 Springer

Series Editors

Jaime G. Carbonell, Carnegie Mellon University, Pittsburgh, PA, USA
Jörg Siekmann, University of Saarland, Saarbrücken, Germany

Volume Editors

Jürgen Dix
Institut für Informatik, Universität Koblenz-Landau
Rheinau 1, D-56075 Koblenz, Germany
E-mail: dix@mailhost.uni-koblenz.de

Luís Moniz Pereira
Departamento de Informática, Universidade Nova de Lisboa
P-2825 Monte da Caparica, Portugal
E-mail: lmp@fct.unl.pt

Teodor C. Przymusinski
Department of Computer Science, University of California
Riverside, CA 92521, USA
E-mail: teodor@cs.ucr.edu

Cataloging-in-Publication Data applied for

Die Deutsche Bibliothek - CIP-Einheitsaufnahme

Non-monotonic extensions of logic programming : selected papers /
Second International Workshop NMELP '96, Bad Honnef, Germany,
September 5 - 6, 1996. Jürgen Dix ... (ed.). - Berlin ; Heidelberg ;
New York ; Barcelona ; Budapest ; Hong Kong ; London ; Milan ;
Paris ; Santa Clara ; Singapore ; Tokyo : Springer, 1997
  (Lecture notes in computer science ; Vol. 1216 : Lecture notes in
  artificial intelligence)
  ISBN 3-540-62843-6 kart.

CR Subject Classification (1991): I.2.3, F.4.1, D.1.6

ISBN 3-540-62843-6 Springer-Verlag Berlin Heidelberg New York

Typesetting: Camera ready by author
SPIN 10549412   06/3142 – 5 4 3 2 1 0   Printed on acid-free paper

Preface

This book is the outcome of the compilation of extended and revised versions of selected papers presented at the workshop on *Non-Monotonic Extensions of Logic Programming* held in Bad Honnef, Germany, on September 5–6, 1996. A total of 18 papers were submitted, 9 of which were finally accepted and published in this volume.

The impressive research progress of the last few years as well as the significant advances made in logic programming implementation techniques now provide us with a great opportunity to bring to fruition computationally efficient implementations of the recent extensions to logic programming and their applications. The resulting programming systems must not only ensure the increased expressiveness and declarative transparency of the evolving paradigm of logic programming, but should also be suitable to serve as inference engines for other non-monotonic reasoning formalisms and deductive databases, as well as specification languages for software engineering.

This workshop was the sixth in a series of workshops held in conjunction with Logic Programming conferences (NACLP '90, ILPS '91, ILPS '93, ICLP '94, and ICLP '95) and dealt with all three aspects of extended logic programming: *theory*, *applications* and *implementation*. As a result, the collected papers are naturally divided into three sections

- Semantics
- Applications
- Computation.

This volume starts with a short overview of the presented papers, and an article entitled *"Prolegomena to logic programming for non-monotonic reasoning"*. This article was written by the editors, and its purpose was to provide an introduction to and motivation for the area of extended logic programming.

We would like to thank the members of the program committee and the additional reviewers listed below.

February 1997

Jürgen Dix, Koblenz
Luís Moniz Pereira, Lisboa
Teodor C. Przymusinski, Riverside

Organization

Previous Workshops

1990 WS at NACLP '90, U.S.A.   1991 WS at ILPS '91, U.S.A.
1993 WS at ILPS '93, U.S.A.   1994 WS at ICLP '94, Italy
1995 WS at ICLP '95, Japan   1996 WS at JICSLP '96, Germany

Sponsors

Compulog Network of Excellence, University of Koblenz.

Organizing Committee

Jürgen Dix   University of Koblenz
Luís Moniz Pereira   Universidade Nova de Lisboa
Teodor Przymusinski   University of California at Riverside

Program Committee

Rachel Ben-Eliyahu   Technion Haifa, Israel
Jürgen Dix   University of Koblenz, Germany
Michael Gelfond   University of Texas at El Paso, U.S.A.
Anthony Kakas   University of Cyprus, Cyprus
Wiktor Marek   University of Kentucky at Lexington, U.S.A.
Jack Minker   University of Maryland, U.S.A.
Luís Moniz Pereira   Universidade Nova de Lisboa, Portugal
Teodor Przymusinski   University of California at Riverside, U.S.A.
V. S. Subrahmanian   University of Maryland, U.S.A
Chiaki Sakama   University of Wakayama, Japan
David S. Warren   SUNY at Stony Brook, U.S.A.

Additional Referees

J. J. Alferes, C. Aravindan, C. V. Damásio, Y. Dimopoulos, K. Inoue, V. Lifschitz, C. Ruiz, M. L. Sapino and M. Truszczyński.

Table of Contents

Introduction

Semantics

Applications

Computation

Papers in this Book

In order to facilitate reading of this volume, we now present a brief overview of the content of the presented papers. We follow our classification of papers into three categories: *semantics*, *applications* and *computation*.

Semantics

While Bochman and Pearce are concerned with characterizations of classical semantics, the other two papers deal with *aggregation* (Osorio/Jayaraman), and *constraints* (Wang/You/Yuan).

A. Bochman: In his paper *"On Logics and Semantics for General Logic Programs"* the author introduces a 4-valued monotonic logic which, when augmented with a non-monotonic operator of minimization (or circumscription), allows us to obtain, depending on the additional assumptions about the logic, various semantics of logic programs. In this way, differences between many proposed semantics for logic programs are reduced to the differences between the underlying monotonic logics while the non-monotonic part, namely circumscription, remains the same.

In this sense, Bochan's paper is similar to Przymusinski's formalism of *Autoepistemic Logic of Knowledge and Beliefs* [Prz94,Prz95] in which the underlying modal logic is also monotonic. After being augmented with a minimal belief operator it leads, depending on the additional logical axioms, to the characterization of different semantics for logic programs.

D. Pearce: The paper "A New Logical Characterization of Stable Model" is devoted to a characterization of the stable model semantics. It introduces a non-monotonic logic, called the "equilibrium logic", which is the least constructive extension of the modal logic "here-and-there", and shows that on logic programs it coincides with the stable model semantics. However, the proposed formalism applies to all first-order theories. Moreover, as opposed to the original definition of stable models or its characterization via autoepistemic expansions, it does not involve any fixed-point definition.

M. Osorio and B. Jayaraman: The paper *"Aggregation and WFS$^+$"* considers the problem of representing aggregate operations, such as taking maximum or minimum over a given set of values, by means of normal logic programs. The main result of the paper is the description of a natural translation of partial-order programs with aggregate operations into normal logic programs which transforms any cost-monotonic partial-order program into a stratified normal program so that their respective semantics are preserved. As a result, aggregate operations present in the original program do not explicitly appear in the translated normal program.

X. Wang, J.-H. You and L.-Y. Yuan: In their paper titled *"Nonmonotonic Reasoning by Monotonic Inferences and Priority Constraints"* the authors introduce a a non-monotonic formalism called "priority logic" and based on a combination of a monotonic logic coupled with priority constraints. They show that well known non-monotonic formalisms, such as default logic and defeasible inheritance networks, can be recast in this new logic. They also argue that such an approach has many advantages, including the fact that it allows us to represent knowledge by means of purely monotonic rules while achieving its non-monotonic behavior by superimposing priorities which often form a natural part of commonsense knowledge.

Applications

The paper, by Baldoni, Giordani, Martelli and Patti, is concerned with *abduction* and reasoning about actions. The two papers of Alferes and Pereira and Bidoit/Maabout discuss *update-programs* and *revision-programs*.

J. J. Alferes and L. M. Pereira: In the first part of the paper *"Update-- programs Can Update Programs"* the authors extend the notion of a revision program, introduced in [MT94], by allowing partial revisions (for the sake of consistency with the established terminology, the authors propose to use the term *update* rather than revision) thus ensuring that consistent updates exist for a much wider class of update programs. Such an extension can also be obtained by using partial stable semantics (instead of stable semantics) in the translation of update programs into logic programs described in [PT95]. In the second part of the paper, the authors describe a mechanism for automatic transformation of logic programs into updated logic programs. Previous approaches were essentially restricted to the description of the set of models that the updated logic program should satisfy but they did not provide any direct way of construction of such a program.

M. Baldoni, L. Giordano, A. Martelli and V. Patti: In their paper *"Abductive Proof Procedure for Reasoning about Actions in Modal LP"* the authors investigate a modal approach to reasoning about actions. The proposed base language is a standard modal language with Kripke semantics. However, in order to deal with non-monotonic aspects of reasoning about actions, such as the frame problem, they augment their logic with an abductive semantics based on Dung's argumentation framework. They also define a sound and goal-directed procedure for answering queries in the abductive semantics.

N. Bidoit and S. Maabout: The paper *"Update Rule Programs Versus Revision Programs"* proposes a new approach to interpretation update via logic-program-type rules. As does Alferes and Pereira's paper, it extends and modifies the approach proposed by Marek and Truszczynski [MT94] (revision programs) in two ways. On the one hand, it adds premises of update rules which allow us to distinguish between facts holding in the interpretation that is being updated and those facts which are to be updated (either removed or added to the interpretation). On the other hand, it bases the whole update process on the well-founded semantics rather than on the stable semantics. In the process, it also reinterprets the heads of update (revision) rules by forcing them to intuitively mean that some facts cannot be true (false) rather than to be true (false) in the updated interpretation. This is an important consideration given the fact that the updates are usually partial models.

Computation

Both Brass, Zukowski and Freitag as well as Dix and Stolzenburg present computational frameworks for normal and disjunctive programs that are currently being implemented.

S. Brass, S. Zukowski and B. Freitag: The paper *"Transformation-Based Bottom-Up Computation of the WFS"* is devoted to the study of bottom-up methods of computation of the well-founded semantics (WFS). Its main result is the introduction of a rather simple and yet polynomial bottom-up method of computing the WFS of normal programs. The work builds upon previous approaches, such as SLG-resolution and the notion of residual programs, but it introduces a significant number of new elements. In some sense, the proposed method combines the good features of the residual approach and the alternating fixed-point approach, while avoiding their known efficiency problems.

J. Dix and F. Stolzenburg: The paper *"Computation of Non-Ground Disjunctive WFS with Constraint LP"* addresses the issue of computation of answers to queries to disjunctive programs with variables and functions, as opposed to dealing with instantiated, propositional programs only. While for semantic considerations, usually it suffices to consider instantiated programs, due to efficiency problems, such an approach is completely unsuitable for the purpose of general query answering. The authors attempt to solve the problem by introducing a calculus of transformations defined on disjunctive programs which extends the calculus developed earlier by Brass and Dix for ground programs [BD95]. The calculus, which is also proved to be confluent, in principle allows us to transform arbitrary disjunctive programs with variables and functions into much simpler, residual programs for which query answering is greatly simplified.

References

[BD95] Stefan Brass and Jürgen Dix. Disjunctive Semantics based upon Partial and Bottom-Up Evaluation. In Leon Sterling, editor, *Proceedings of the 12th Int. Conf. on Logic Programming, Tokyo.* MIT, June 1995.

[MT94] W. Marek and M. Truszczyński. Revision specifications by means of revision programs. In *Logics in AI. Proceedings of JELIA '94.* Lecture Notes in Artificial Intelligence. Springer-Verlag, 1994.

[Prz94] T. C. Przymusinski. A knowledge representation framework based on autoepistemic logic of minimal beliefs. In *Proceedings of the Twelfth National Conference on Artificial Intelligence, AAAI-94, Seattle, Washington, August 1994,* pages 952–959, Los Altos, CA, 1994. American Association for Artificial Intelligence, Morgan Kaufmann.

[Prz95] T. C. Przymusinski. Autoepistemic logic of knowledge and beliefs. (In preparation), University of California at Riverside, 1995. (Extended abstract appeared in 'A knowledge representation framework based on autoepistemic logic of minimal beliefs' In *Proceedings of the Twelfth National Conference on Artificial Intelligence, AAAI-94, Seattle, Washington, August 1994,* pages 952-959,

Los Altos, CA, 1994. American Association for Artificial Intelligence, Morgan Kaufmann.).

[PT95]   T. C. Przymusinski and Hudson Turner. Update by means of inference rules. In A. Nerode, editor, *Proceedings of the Third International Conference on Logic Programming and Non-Monotonic Reasoning, Lexington, KY*, pages 156–174. LPNMR'95, Springer Verlag, 1995.

Prolegomena to Logic Programming for Non-monotonic Reasoning

Jürgen Dix[1] and Luís Moniz Pereira[2] and Teodor Przymusinski[3]

[1] Dept. Computer Science, University of Koblenz
Rheinau 1, D-56075 Koblenz, Germany
dix@mailhost.uni-koblenz.de
[2] Dept. Computer Science and CENTRIA, Universidade Nova de Lisboa
2825 Monte da Caparica, Portugal
lmp@di.fct.unl.pt
[3] Dept. Computer Science, University of California at Riverside
Riverside, CA 92521, USA
teodor@cs.ucr.edu

Abstract. The present prolegomena consist, as all indeed do, in a critical discussion serving to introduce and interpret the extended works that follow in this book. As a result, the book is not a mere collection of excellent papers in their own specialty, but provides also the basics of the motivation, background history, important themes, bridges to other areas, and a common technical platform of the principal formalisms and approaches, augmented with examples.

In the introduction we whet the reader's interest in the field of logic programming and non–monotonic reasoning with the promises it offers and with its outstanding problems too. There follows a brief historical background to logic programming, from its inception to actuality, and its relationship to non–monotonic formalisms, stressing its semantical and procedural aspects.

The next couple of sections provide motivating examples and an overview of the main semantics paradigms for normal programs (stable models and well–founded) and for extended logic programs (answer–sets, e–answer–sets, Nelson's strong negation, and well–founded semantics with pseudo and with explicit negation).

A subequent section is devoted to disjunctive logic programs and its various semantical proposals.

To conclude, a final section on implementation gives pointers to available systems and their sites.

We leave out important concerns, such as paraconsistent semantics, contradiction removal, and updates. Hopefully they will be included in the next book in this series. But an extensive set of references allows the reader to delve into the specialized literature.

For other recent relevant complementary overviews in this area we refer to [AP96,BDK97,BD96b,Min96,Dix95c].

1 Introduction

One of the major reasons for the success story (if one is really willing to call it a success story) of human beings on this planet is our ability to invent tools that help us improve our — otherwise often quite limited — capabilities. The invention of machines that are able to do interesting things, like transporting people from one place to the other (even through the air), sending moving pictures and sounds around the globe, bringing our email to the right person, and the like, is one of the cornerstones of our culture and determines to a great degree our everyday life.

Among the most challenging tools one can think of are machines that are able to handle knowledge adequately. Building smart machines is at the heart of Artificial Intelligence (AI). Since such machines will need tremendous amounts of knowledge to work properly, even in very limited environments, the investigation of techniques for representing knowledge and reasoning is highly important.

In the early days of AI it was still believed that modeling general purpose problem solving capabilites, as in Newell and Simon's famous GPS (General Problem Solver) program, would be sufficient to generate intelligent behaviour. This hypothesis, however, turned out to be overly optimistic. At the end of the sixties people realized that an approach using available knowledge about narrow domains was much more fruitful. This led to the expert systems boom which produced many useful application systems, expert system building tools, and expert system companies. Many of the systems are still in use and save companies millions of dollars per year[1].

Nevertheless, the simple knowledge representation and reasoning methods underlying the early expert systems soon turned out to be insufficient. Most of the systems were built based on simple rule languages, often enhanced with ad hoc approaches to model uncertainty. It became apparent that more advanced methods to handle incompleteness, defeasible reasoning, uncertainty, causality and the like were needed.

This insight led to a tremendous increase of research on the foundations of knowledge representation and reasoning. Theoretical research in this area has blossomed in recent years. Many advances have been made and important results were obtained. The technical quality of this work is often impressive.

On the other hand, most of these advanced techniques have had surprisingly little influence on practical applications so far. To a certain degree this is understandable since theoretical foundations had to be laid first and pioneering work was needed. However, if we do not want research in knowledge representation to remain a theoreticians' game, more emphasis on computability and applicability seems to be needed. We strongly believe that the kind of research presented in this book, that is research aiming at interesting combinations of ideas from logic programming and non–monotonic reasoning, and its implementation, provides an important step into this direction.

---

[1] We refer the interested reader to the recent book [RN95] which gives a very detailed and nice exposition of what has been done in AI since its very beginning until today.

Research in the area of logic programming and non-monotonic reasoning makes a significant contribution not only towards the better understanding of relations existing between various formalizations of non-monotonic reasoning, and, hopefully, towards the eventual discovery of deeper underlying principles of non-monotonic reasoning and logic programming, but, perhaps more importantly, towards the eventual development of relatively efficient inference engines based on the techniques originating in logic programming. Needless to say, the problem of finding efficient inference mechanisms, capable of modelling human common-sense reasoning, is one of the major research and implementation problems in AI. Moreover, by incorporating the recent theoretical results, the next qualitative leap in logic programming systems is well under way.

In fact, during the last decade a truly impressive body of knowledge has been accumulated, providing us with a better understanding of semantic issues in logic programming and the nature of its relationship to non-monotonic formalisms. New, significantly improved, semantics for logic programs have been introduced and thoroughly investigated and their close relationship to major non-monotonic formalisms has been established. A number of fundamental results describing ways in which non-monotonic theories can be translated into logic programs have been obtained. Entirely new computational mechanisms for the new, greatly improved, semantics have been introduced and several very promising implementations of logic programming systems based on these semantics have been developed.

In spite of these unquestionable successes some major problems remain:

1. Standard logic programs are not sufficiently expressive for the representation of large classes of knowledge bases. In particular, the inability of logic programs to deal with disjunctive information proved to be a major obstacle to using them effectively in various knowledge domains, in particular, it constitutes a major obstacle to using logic programming as a declarative specification language for software engineering. The problem of extending of the logic programming paradigm to the class of disjunctive programs and deductive databases turned out to be a difficult one, as evidenced by a large number of papers, the book [LMR92] and several workshops ([Wol94,DLMW96]) devoted to this issue. It is well known that disjunctive programs are significantly more expressive than normal programs.

2. In recent years, several authors have underscored the importance of extending logic programming by introducing different types of negation (explicit, strong or classical negation) which proved essential for knowledge representation and are indispensable for the effective use of integrity constraints. This important enhancement of logic programming immediately leads, however, to the new basic problem of how to deal with contradiction in such extended logic programs. The proper definition of declarative and procedural semantics for contradiction removal is particularly crucial in applications of logic programming to diagnosis, database updates, and declarative debugging.

3. The existing logic programming systems suffer from an important procedural limitation of being unable to deal with non-ground negative queries.

This well-known phenomenon, known as the *floundering problem*, severely restricts the usefulness of logic programs for knowledge representation. Several major attempts have been made recently to deal with this problem but much more work is still needed.

4. In spite of the unquestionable progress obtained during the last decade or so, insufficient attention has been paid to the study of various applications of the new logic programming paradigm and to the actual testing and experimentation with the new systems in various application domains. Extensive experimentation will allow us to better understand and evaluate their potential value for knowledge representation, at the same time exposing their possible weaknesses and inadequacies.

5. While several promising implementations of logic programming systems have been developed recently, much more effort has to be devoted to this issue during the next several years if we are to come up with a truly practical and efficient alternative to the currently existing logic programming paradigm. These efforts must include implementations which are capable, among others, to deal with disjunctive information, contradiction removal and constructive negation. More work is also needed towards the development of object-oriented logic programming systems.

In short, the advent of low cost multiprocessor machines, impressive research progress of the past decade as well as significant advances in logic programming implementation techniques now provide us with a great opportunity to bring to fruition computationally efficient implementations of extended logic programming. The resulting programming system must not only ensure the increased expressivity and declarative clarity of the new paradigm of logic programming but it should also be suitable to serve as an inference engine for other non-monotonic reasoning formalisms and deductive databases and as a specification language for software engineering.

This book is the successor of [DPP95] and the next in a series addressing such issues. To facilitate access to the book, and to this research area, we decided to provide here an introduction and motivation for (extended and disjunctive) logic programming, which is commonly used as a basis for knowledge representation and non–monotonic reasoning, and applications. Other more specific developments, such as belief revision or updates, are deliberately left out. The reader is referred to the collection of papers in this book and the references therein for such topics.

2 Brief historical logic programming background

Computational Logic arose from the work begun by logicians since the midfifties. The desire to impart the computer with the ability to reason logically led to the development of automated theorem proving, which took up the promise of giving logic to artificial intelligence. This approach was fostered in the 1970's by Colmerauer et al. [CKPR73] and Kowalski [Kow74,Kow79] as Logic Programming (and brought on the definition and implementation of *Prolog* [CKPR73]).

It introduced to computer science the important concept of *declarative* – as opposed to *procedural* – programming. Ideally, a programmer should need only to be concerned with the declarative meaning of his program, while the procedural aspects of program's execution are handled automatically. The Prolog language became the privileged vehicle approximating this ideal. The first Prolog compiler [WPP77] showed that it could be a practical language and helped disseminate it worldwide.

Clearly, this ideal cannot possibly be fulfilled without a precise definition of proper declarative semantics of logic programs and, in particular, of the meaning of negation in logic programming. Logic programs, however, do not use classical logical negation, but rely instead on a non-monotonic operator, often referred to as "negation by failure" or "negation by default". The non-monotonicity of this operator allows us to view logic programs as special non-monotonic theories, and thus makes it possible to draw from the extensive research in the area of non-monotonic reasoning and use it as guidance in the search for a suitable semantics for logic programs.

On the other hand, while logic programs constitute only a subclass of the class of all non-monotonic theories, they are sufficiently expressive to allow formalizations of many important problems in non-monotonic reasoning and provide fertile testing grounds for new formalizations. Moreover, since logic programs admit relatively efficient computational mechanisms, they can be used as inference engines for non-monotonic formalisms.

The development of formal foundations of logic programming began in the late 1970s, especially with the works [EK76,Cla78,Rei78b]. Further progress in this direction was achieved in the early 1980's, leading to the appearance of the first book on the foundations of logic programming [Llo87]. The selection of logic programming as the underlying paradigm for the Japanese Fifth Generation Computer Systems Project led to the rapid proliferation of various logic programming languages.

In parallel, starting at about 1980, *non–monotonic Reasoning* entered into computer science and began to constitute a new field of active research. It was originally initiated because *Knowledge Representation* and *Common-Sense Reasoning* using classical logic came to its limits. Formalisms like classical logic are inherently monotonic and they seem to be too weak and therefore inadequate for such reasoning problems.

In recent years, independently of the research in logic programming, people interested in knowledge representation and non–monotonic reasoning also tried to define declarative semantics for programs containing *default* or *explicit* negation and even *disjunctions*. They defined various semantics by appealing to (different) intuitions they had about programs.

Due to logic programming's declarative nature, and amenability to implementation, it quickly became a prime candidate for knowledge representation. Its adequateness became more apparent after the relationships established in the mid 1980's between logic programs and deductive databases [Rei84,GMN84,LT85], [LT86,Min88].

The use of both logic programming and deductive databases for knowledge representation is based on the so called *"logical approach to knowledge representation"*. This approach rests on the idea of providing machines with a logical specification of the knowledge that they possess, thus making it independent of any particular implementation, context–free, and easy to manipulate and reason about.

Consequently, a precise meaning (or semantics) is associated with any logic program in order to provide its declarative specification. The performance of any computational mechanism is then evaluated by comparing its behaviour to the specification provided by the declarative semantics. Finding a suitable declarative semantics for logic programs has been acknowledged as one of the most important and difficult research areas of logic programming.

From the implementational point of view, for some time now programming in logic has been shown to be a viable proposition. As a result of the effort to find simple and efficient theorem proving strategies, Horn clause programming under SLD resolution was discovered and implemented [KK71,CKPR73].

However, because Horn clauses admit only positive conclusions or facts, they give rise to a monotonic semantics, i.e. one by which previous conclusions are never questioned in spite of additional information, and thus the number of derived conclusions cannot decrease – hence the monotonicity.

Horn clause programming augmented with the NOT operator (i.e. Prolog), under the SLDNF derivation procedure [Llo87], does allow negative conclusions; these, however, are only drawn by default (or implicitly), just in case the corresponding positive conclusion is not forthcoming in a finite number of steps, taking the program as it stands. This condition also prevents, by definition, the appearance of any and all contradictions, and so does not allow for reasoning about contradictory information.

The NOT form of negation is capable of dealing with incomplete information, by assuming false exactly what is not true in a finite manner – hence the Closed World Assumption (CWA) [Rei78a] or completion semantics given to such programs [Cla78]. However, irrespective of other problems with this semantics, there remains the issue of the proper treatment of non-terminating computations, even for finite programs.

To deal with the difficulties faced by the completion semantics, a spate of semantic proposals were set forth from the late eigthies onwards, of which the well–founded semantics of [GRS91] is an outcome. It deals semantically with non-terminating computations, by assigning them the truth value "undefined", thereby giving semantics to every program. Moreover, it enjoys a number of desirable structural properties [Dix92a,Dix92b,Dix91,Dix95a,Dix95b,BD96a].

However, the well–founded semantics deals solely with normal programs, i.e. those with only negation by default, and thus it provides no mechanism for explicitly declaring the falsity of literals. This can be a serious limitation. In fact, recently several authors have stressed and shown the importance of including in logic programs a symmetric form of negation, denoted ¬, with respect to default negation [APP96], for use in deductive databases, knowledge representation, and non–monotonic reasoning [GL91,GL92,Ino91,Kow90,KS90,PW90,PAA91b,AP96], [PAA92,PDA93,Wag91,PAA91c]. This symmetric negation may assume several garbs and names (*classical, pseudo, strong, explicit*) corresponding to different properties and distinct applicability. Default and symmetric negation can be related: indeed some authors uphold the *coherence principle*, which stipulates the latter entails the former.

So-called *extended* logic programs, those which introduce a symmetric form of negation, both in the body and conclusion of rules, have been instrumental in bridging logic programming and non–monotonic reasoning formalisms, such as *Default Logic*, *Auto–Epistemic Logic*, and *Circumscription*: non–monotonic reasoning formalisms provide elegant semantics for logic programming, in particular in what regards the meaning of negation as failure (or by default); non–monotonic reasoning formalisms help one understand how logic programming can be used to formalize and solve several problems in AI. On the other hand, non–monotonic reasoning formalisms benefit from the existing procedures of logic programming; and, finally, new problems of non–monotonic reasoning are raised and solved by logic programming.

Of course, introducing symmetric negation conclusions requires being able to deal with contradiction. Indeed, information is not only normally incomplete but contradictory to boot. Consequently, not all negation by default assumptions might be made, but only those not partaking of contradiction. This is tantamount to the ancient and venerable logical principle of "reductio ad absurdum": *if an assumption leads to contradiction withdraw it.* One major contribution of work on extended logic programming is that of tackling this issue.

Whereas default negation, and the revision of believed assumptions in the face of contradiction, are the two non–monotonic reasoning mechanisms available in logic programming, their use in combination with symmetric negation adds on a qualitative representational expressivity that can capture a wide variety of logical reasoning forms, and serve as an instrument for programming them. The application domains facilitated by extended logic programming include for example taxonomies with exceptions and preferences, reasoning about actions, model based diagnosis, belief revision, updates, and declarative debugging.

It should be noted that symmetric negation differs from classical negation. In particular, the principle of the excluded middle is not adopted, and so neither is case analysis, whereby if p if q, and if p if $\neg q$, then p. Indeed, propositions are not just true or false, exclusively. For one, they may be both true and false. Moreover, once contradiction is removed, even so a proposition and its negation may both remain undefined. In fact, truth in logic programming should be taken in an auto-epistemic sense: truth is provability from an agent's knowledge, and possibily neither a proposition nor its negation might be provable from its present knowledge – their truth-value status' might be undefined for both. Hence case analysis is not justified: p may rest undefined if q or $\neg q$ are undefined.

This is reasonable because the truth of q is not something that either holds or not, inasmuch as it can refer to the agent's ability to deduce q, or some other agent's view of q. For that matter, the supposition that either q holds or does not hold might be contradictory with the rest of the agent's knowledge in either case.

Also, the procedural nature of logic programming requires that each conclusion be supported by some identifiable rule with a true body whose conclusion it is, not simply by alternatively applicable rules, as in case analysis. Conclusions must be procedurally grounded on known facts. This requirement is conducive to a sceptical view of derived knowledge, which disallows jumping to conclusions when that is not called for.

Next we make a short technical overview of the main results in the last 15 years in the area of logic program's declarative semantics. This overview is divided into four sections. In the first we review some of the most important semantics of normal logic programs while in the second we motivate the need of extending logic programming with a second kind of negation, and overview recent semantics for such extended programs. The third and forth section are very compact and not as detailed as the previous ones. In the third section we treat disjunctive logic programming and in the fourth section we give an overview of implemented systems and where they can be obtained.

3 Normal logic programs

Several recent overviews of normal logic programming semantics can be found in the literature (e.g. [She88,She90,PP90,Mon92,AB94,Dix95c,BD96b]). Here, for the sake of this text's self–sufficiency and to introduce some motivation, we distill a brief overview of the subject. In some parts we follow closely the overview of [PP90].

The structure of this section is as follows: first we present the language of normal logic programs and give some definitions needed in the sequel. Then we briefly review the first approaches to the semantics of normal programs and point out their problems. Finally, we expound in greater detail two of the more recent and important proposals, namely stable models and well–founded semantics.

3.1 Language

By an alphabet $\mathcal{A}$ of a language $\mathcal{L}$ we mean a (finite or countably infinite) disjoint set of constants, predicate symbols, and function symbols. In addition, any alphabet is assumed to contain a countably infinite set of distinguished variable symbols. A *term* over $\mathcal{A}$ is defined recursively as either a variable, a constant or an expression of the form $f(t_1, \ldots, t_n)$, where f is a function symbol of $\mathcal{A}$, and the t_i are terms. An atom over $\mathcal{A}$ is an expression of the form $p(t_1, \ldots, t_n)$, where p is a predicate symbol of $\mathcal{A}$, and the t_is are terms. A literal is either an atom A or its negation *not* A. We dub default literals those of the form *not* A.

A term (resp. *atom, literal*) is called *ground* if it does not contain variables. The set of all ground terms (resp. atoms) of $\mathcal{A}$ is called the *Herbrand universe* (resp. base) of $\mathcal{A}$. For short we use $\mathcal{H}$ to denote the Herbrand base of $\mathcal{A}$.

A *normal* logic program is a finite set of rules of the form:

$$H \leftarrow L_1, \ldots, L_n \qquad (n \geq 0)$$

where H is an atom and each of the L_is is a literal. In conformity with the standard convention we write rules of the form $H \leftarrow$ also simply as H.

A normal logic program P is called *definite* if none of its rules contains default literals. We assume that the alphabet $\mathcal{A}$ used to write a program P consists precisely of all the constants, and predicate and function symbols that explicitly appear in P. By Herbrand universe (resp. base) of P we mean the Herbrand universe (resp. base) of $\mathcal{A}$.

By *grounded version* of a normal logic program P we mean the (possibly infinite) set of ground rules obtained from P by substituting in all possible ways each of the variables in P by elements of its Herbrand universe.

In this work we restrict ourselves to Herbrand interpretations and models[2]. Thus, without loss of generality (cf. [PP90]), we coalesce a normal logic program P with its grounded version.

3.2 Interpretations and models

Next we define 2 and 3–valued Herbrand interpretations and models of normal logic programs. Since non–Herbrand interpretations are beyond the scope of this work, in the sequel we sometimes drop the qualification Herbrand.

Definition 1 (Two–valued interpretation). A 2–valued interpretation I of a normal logic program P is any subset of the Herbrand base $\mathcal{H}$ of P.

Clearly, any 2–valued interpretation I can be equivalently viewed as a set

$$T \cup not\ F \ ^3$$

where $T = I$ and is the set of atoms which are true in I, and $F = \mathcal{H} - T$ is the set of atoms which are false in I. These interpretations are called 2–valued because in them each atom is either true or false, i.e. $\mathcal{H} = T \cup F$.

As argued in [PP90], interpretations of a given program P can be thought of as "possible worlds" representing possible states of our knowledge about the meaning of P. Since that knowledge is likely to be incomplete, we need the ability to describe interpretations in which some atoms are neither true nor false but rather undefined, i.e. we need 3–valued interpretations:

Definition 2 (Three–valued interpretation). By a 3–valued interpretation I of a program P we mean a set

$$T \cup not\ F$$

---

[2] For the subject of semantics based on non–Herbrand models, and solutions to the problems resulting from always keeping Herbrand models see e.g. [Kun87,Prz89c,GRS91].

[3] Where $not\ \{a_1, \ldots, a_n\}$ stands for $\{not\ a_1, \ldots, not\ a_n\}$.

where T and F are disjoint subsets of the Herbrand base $\mathcal{H}$ of P.

The set T (the T-part of I) contains all ground atoms true in I, the set F (the F-part of I) contains all ground atoms false in I, and the truth value of the remaining atoms is unknown (or undefined).

It is clear that 2–valued interpretations are a special case of 3–valued ones, for which $\mathcal{H} = T \cup F$ is additionally imposed.

Proposition 3. *Any interpretation $I = T \cup not\ F$ can equivalently be viewed as a function $I : \mathcal{H} \to V$ where $V = \{0, \frac{1}{2}, 1\}$, defined by:*

$$I(A) = \begin{cases} 0 & \text{if } not\ A \in I \\ 1 & \text{if } A \in I \\ \frac{1}{2} & \text{otherwise} \end{cases}$$

Of course, for 2–valued interpretations there is no atom A such that $I(A) = \frac{1}{2}$. Models are defined as usual, and based on a truth valuation function:

Definition 4 (Truth valuation). If I is an interpretation, the truth valuation $\hat{I}$ corresponding to I is a function $\hat{I} : C \to V$ where C is the set of all formulae of the language, recursively defined as follows:

- if A is a ground atom then $\hat{I}(A) = I(A)$.
- if S is a formula then $\hat{I}(not\ S) = 1 - \hat{I}(S)$.
- if S and V are formulae then

  - $\hat{I}((S, V)) = min(\hat{I}(S), \hat{I}(V))$.
  - $\hat{I}(V \leftarrow S) = 1$ if $\hat{I}(S) \leq \hat{I}(V)$, and 0 otherwise.

Definition 5 (Three–valued model). A 3–valued interpretation I is called a 3–valued model of a program P iff for every ground instance of a program rule $H \leftarrow B$ we have $\hat{I}(H \leftarrow B) = 1$.

The special case of 2–valued models has the following straightforward definition:

Definition 6 (Two–valued model). A 2–valued interpretation I is called a 2–valued model of a program P iff for every ground instance of a program rule $H \leftarrow B$ we have $\hat{I}(H \leftarrow B) = 1$.

Some orderings among interpretations and models will be useful:

Definition 7 (Classical ordering). If I and J are two interpretations then we say that $I \leq J$ if $I(A) \leq J(A)$ for any ground atom A. If $\mathcal{I}$ is a collection of interpretations, then an interpretation $I \in \mathcal{I}$ is called minimal in $\mathcal{I}$ if there is no interpretation $J \in \mathcal{I}$ such that $J \leq I$ and $I \neq J$. An interpretation I is called least in $\mathcal{I}$ if $I \leq J$ for any other interpretation $J \in \mathcal{I}$. A model M of a program P is called minimal (resp. least) if it is minimal (resp. least) among all models of P.

Definition 8 (Fitting ordering). If I and J are two interpretations then we say that $I \leq_F J$ [Fit85] iff $I \subseteq J$. If $\mathcal{I}$ is a collection of interpretations, then an interpretation $I \in \mathcal{I}$ is called F-minimal in $\mathcal{I}$ if there is no interpretation $J \in \mathcal{I}$ such that $J \leq_F I$ and $I \neq J$. An interpretation I is called F-least in $\mathcal{I}$ if $I \leq_F J$ for any interpretation $J \in \mathcal{I}$. A model M of a program P is called F-minimal (resp. F-least) if it is F-minimal (resp. F-least) among all models of P.

Note that the classical ordering is related with the amount of true atoms, whereas the Fitting ordering is related with the amount of information, i.e. nonundefinedness.

3.3 Clark's and Fitting's Semantics

As argued above, a precise meaning or semantics must be associated with any logic program, in order to provide a declarative specification of it. Declarative semantics provides a mathematically precise definition of the meaning of a program, which is independent of its procedural executions, and is easy to manipulate and reason about.

In contrast, procedural semantics is usually defined as a procedural mechanism that is capable of providing answers to queries. The correctness of such a mechanism is evaluated by comparing its behaviour to the specification provided by the declarative semantics. Without the latter, the user needs an intimate knowledge of the procedural aspects in order to write correct programs.

The first attempt to provide a declarative semantics to logic programs is due to [EK76], and the main motivation behind their approach is based on the idea that one should minimize positive information as much as possible, limiting it to facts explicitly implied by a program, making everything else false. In other words, their semantics is based on a natural form of *"closed world assumption"* [Rei78a].

Example 9. Consider program P :

$$able\_mathematician(X) \leftarrow physicist(X)$$
$$physicist(einstein)$$
$$president(soares)$$

This program has several (2–valued) models, the largest of which is the model where both Einstein and Soares are at the same time presidents, physicists and able mathematicians. This model does not correctly describe the intended meaning of P, since there is nothing in P to imply that Soares is a physicist or that Einstein is a president. In fact, the lack of such information should instead indicate that we can assume the contrary.

This knowledge is captured by the least (2–valued) model of P :

$$\{physicist(einstein), able\_mathematician(einstein), president(soares)\}$$

The existence of a unique least model for every definite program (proven in [EK76]), led to the definition of the so called *"least model semantics"* for definite programs. According to that semantics an atom A is true in a program P iff it belongs to the least model of P; otherwise A is false.

It turns out that this semantics does not apply to programs with default negation. For example, the program $P = \{p \leftarrow not\ q\}$ has two minimal models, namely $\{p\}$ and $\{q\}$. Thus no least model exists.

In order to define a declarative semantics for normal logic programs with negation as failure[4], [Cla78] introduced the so-called *"Clark's predicate completion"*. Informally, the basic idea of completion is that in common discourse we often tend to use "if" statements when we really mean "iff" ones. For instance, we may use the following program P to describe the natural numbers:

$$natural\_number(0)$$
$$natural\_number(succ(X)) \leftarrow natural\_number(X)$$

This program is too weak. It does not imply that nothing but $0, 1, \ldots$ is a natural number. In fact what we have in mind regarding program P is:

$$natural\_number(X) \Leftrightarrow (X = 0 \vee (\exists Y \mid X = succ(Y) \wedge natural\_number(Y)))$$

Based on this idea Clark defined the completion of a program P, the semantics of P being determined by the 2–valued models of its completion.

However Clark's completion semantics has some serious drawbacks. One of the most important is that the completion of consistent programs may be inconsistent, thus failing to assign to those programs a meaning. For example the completion of the program $\{p \leftarrow not\ p\}$ is $\{p \Leftrightarrow not\ p\}$, which is inconsistent.

In [Fit85], the author showed that the inconsistency problem for Clark's completion can be elegantly eliminated by considering 3–valued models instead of 2–valued ones. This led to the definition of the so–called *"Fitting semantics"* for normal logic programs. In [Kun87], Kunen showed that this semantics is not recursively enumerable, and proposed a modification.

Unfortunately, "Fitting's semantics" inherits several problems of Clark's completion, and in many cases leads to a semantics that appears to be too weak. This issue has been extensively discussed in the literature (see [She88,Prz89c,GRS91], [Dix95c,BD96b]). Forthwith we illustrate some of these problems with the help of examples:

Example 10. Consider[5] program P :

$$edge(a, b)$$
$$edge(c, d)$$
$$edge(d, c)$$
$$reachable(a)$$
$$reachable(X) \leftarrow reachable(Y), edge(X, Y)$$

---

[4] Here we adopt the designation of *"negation by default"*. Recently, this designation has been used in the literature instead of the more operational *"negation as failure"*.

[5] This example first appeared in [GRS91].

that describes which vertices are reachable from a given vertice a in a graph.

Fitting semantics cannot conclude that vertices c and d are not reachable from a. Here the difficulty is caused by the existence of the symmetric rules $edge(c, d)$, and $edge(d, c)$.

Example 11. Consider P :

$$bird(tweety)$$
$$fly(X) \leftarrow bird(X), not\ abnormal(X)$$
$$abnormal(X) \leftarrow irregular(X)$$
$$irregular(X) \leftarrow abnormal(X)$$

where the last two rules just state that "irregular" and "abnormal" are synonymous.

Based on the fact that nothing leads us to the conclusion that tweety is abnormal, we would expect the program to derive *not abnormal(tweety)*, and consequently that it flies. But Clark's completion of P is:

$$bird(X) \Leftrightarrow X = tweety$$
$$fly(X) \Leftrightarrow bird(X), not\ abnormal(X)$$
$$abnormal(X) \Leftrightarrow irregular(X)$$

from which it does not follow that tweety isn't abnormal.

It is worth noting that without the last two rules both Clark's and Fitting's semantics yield the expected result.

One possible explanation for such a behaviour is that the last two rules lead to a loop. This explanation is procedural in nature. But it was the idea of replacing procedural programming by declarative programming that brought about the concepts of logic programming in first place and so, as argued in [PP90], it seems that such a procedural explanation should be rejected.

The problems mentioned above are caused by the difficulty in representing transitive closure using completion. In [Kun90] it is formally showed that both Clark's and Fitting's semantics are not sufficiently expressive to represent transitive closure.

In order to solve these problems some model–theoretic approaches to declarative semantics have been defined. In the beginning, such approaches did not attempt to give a meaning to every normal logic program. On the contrary, they were based on syntactic restrictions over programs, and only program complying with such restrictions were given a semantics. Examples of syntactically restricted program classes are stratified [ABW88], locally stratified [Prz89c] and acyclic [AB91], and examples of semantics for restricted programs are the perfect model semantics [ABW88,Prz89c,Gel89b], and the weakly perfect model semantics [PP88]. Here we will not review any of these approaches. For their overview, the reader is referred to e.g. [PP90].

3.4 Stable model semantics

In [GL88], the authors introduce the so–called *"stable model semantics"*. This model–theoretic declarative semantics for normal programs generalizes the previously referred semantics for restricted classes of programs, in the sense that for such classes the results are the same and, moreover, for some non–restricted programs a meaning is still assigned.

The basic ideas behind the stable model semantics came from the field of non–monotonic reasoning formalism. There, literals of the form *not A* are viewed as default literals that may or may not be assumed or, alternatively, as epistemic literals $\sim\!\mathcal{B}A$ expressing that A is not believed.

Informally, when one assumes true some set of (hypothetical) default literals, and false all the others, some consequences follow according to the semantics of definite programs [EK76]. If the consequences completely corroborate the hypotheses made, then they form a stable model. Formally:

Definition 12 (Gelfond–Lifschitz operator). Let P be a normal logic program and I a 2–valued interpretation. The GL–transformation of P modulo I is the program $\frac{P}{I}$ obtained from P by performing the following operations:

- remove from P all rules which contain a default literal *not A* such that $A \in I$;
- remove from the remaining rules all default literals.

Since $\frac{P}{I}$ is a definite program, it has a unique least model J. We define $\Gamma(I) = J$.

It turns out that fixed points of the Gelfond–Lifschitz operator Γ for a program P are always models of P. This result led to the definition of stable model semantics:

Definition 13 (Stable model semantics). A 2–valued interpretation I of a logic program P is a stable model of P iff $\Gamma(I) = I$.

An atom A of P is true under the stable model semantics iff A belong to all stable models of P.

One of the main advantages of stable model semantics is its close relationship with known non–monotonic reasoning formalisms:

As proven in [BF88], the stable models of a program P are equivalent to Reiter's default extensions [Rei80] of the default theory obtained from P by identifying each program rule:

$$H \leftarrow B_1, \ldots, B_n, not\ C_1, \ldots, not\ C_m$$

with the default rule:

$$\frac{B_1, \ldots, B_n\ :\ \sim C_1, \ldots, \sim C_m}{H}$$

where $\sim$ denotes classical negation.

Moreover, from the results of [Gel87], it follows directly that stable models are equivalent to Moore's autoepistemic expansions [Moo85] of the theory obtained by replacing in P every default literal $not\ A$ by $\sim\!\mathcal{B}A$ and then reinterpreting the rule connective $\leftarrow$ as material implication.

In spite of the strong relationship between logic programming and non–monotonic reasoning, in the past these research areas were developing largely independently of one another, and the exact nature of their relationship was not closely investigated or understood.

The situation has changed significantly with the introduction of stable models, and the establishment of formal relationships between these and other non–monotonic formalisms. In fact, in recent years increasing and productive effort has been devoted to the study of the relationships between logic programming and several non–monotonic reasoning formalisms. As a result, international workshops have been organized, in whose proceedings many works and references to the theme can be found [NMS91,PN93,MNT95,DFN97].

Such relationships turn out to be mutual beneficial. On the one hand, non–monotonic formalisms provide elegant semantics for logic programming, specially in what regards the meaning of default negation (or negation as failure), and help one understand how logic programs can be used to formalize several types of reasoning in Artificial Intelligence. On the other hand, those formalisms benefit from the existing procedures of logic programming, and some new issues of the former are raised and solved by the latter. Moreover, relations among non–monotonic formalisms themselves have been facilitated and established via logic programming.

3.5 Well–founded semantics

Despite its advantages, and of being defined for more programs than any of its predecessors, stable model semantics still has some important drawbacks:

- First, some programs have no stable models. One such program is $P = \{a \leftarrow not\ a\}$.
- Even for programs with stable models, their semantics do not always lead to the expected intended results. For example consider program P :

$$a \leftarrow not\ b$$
$$b \leftarrow not\ a$$
$$c \leftarrow not\ a$$
$$c \leftarrow not\ c$$

  whose only stable model is $\{c, b\}$. Thus b and c are consequences of the stable model semantics of P. However, if one adds c to P as a lemma, the semantics of P changes, and b no longer follows. This issue is related with the property of *cumulativity* ([Dix95a]).
- Moreover, it is easy to see that it is impossible to derive b from P using any derivation procedure based on top–down (SL–like) rewriting techniques.

This is because such a procedure, beginning with the goal $\leftarrow b$ would reach only the first two rules of P, from which b cannot be derived. This issue is related with the property of *relevance* ([Dix95b]).

- The computation of stable models is NP–complete [MT91] even within simple classes of programs, such as propositional logic programs. This is an important drawback, specially if one is interested in a program for efficiently implementing knowledge representation and reasoning.
- Last but not least, by always insisting on 2–valued interpretations, stable model semantics often lack expressivity.

The well–founded semantics was introduced in [GRS91], and overcomes all of the above problems. This semantics is also closely related to some of the major non–monotonic formalisms ([AP96]).

Many different equivalent definitions of the well–founded semantics exist (e.g. [Prz89a,Prz89b,Bry89,PP90,Dun91,Prz91a,BS91,Mon92,Dix95b,BD97b]). Here we use the definition introduced in [PP90] because, in our view, it is the one more technically related with the definition of stable models above[6]. Indeed, it consists of a natural generalization for 3–valued interpretations of the stable model semantics. In its definition the authors begin by introducing 3–valued (or partial) stable models, and then show that the F–least of those models coincides with the well–founded model as first defined in [GRS91].

In order to formalize the notion of partial stable models, Przymusinski first expand the language of programs with the additional propositional constant $\mathbf{u}$ with the property of being undefined in every interpretation. Thus they assume that every interpretation I satisfies:

$$\hat{I}(\mathbf{u}) = \hat{I}(not\ \mathbf{u}) = \frac{1}{2}$$

A non–negative program is a program whose premises are either atoms or $\mathbf{u}$. In [PP90], it is proven that every non–negative program has a 3–valued least model. This led to the following generalization of the Gelfond–Lifschitz Γ–operator:

Definition 14 (Γ^*–operator). Let P be a normal logic program, and let I be a 3–valued interpretation. The extended GL–transformation of P modulo I is the program $\frac{P}{I}$ obtained from P by performing the operations:

- remove from P all rules which contain a default literal $not\ A$ such that $I(A) = 1$;
- replace in the remaining rules of P those default literals $not\ A$ such that $I(A) = \frac{1}{2}$ by $\mathbf{u}$;
- remove from the remaning rules all default literals.

Since the resulting program is non–negative, it has a unique 3–valued least model J. We define $\Gamma^*(I) = J$.

---

[6] For a more practical introduction to the well–founded semantics the reader is referred to [PAA91a]. A detailed exposition based on abstract properties is given in [BD96b].

Definition 15 (Well–founded semantics). A 3–valued interpretation I of a logic program P is a partial stable model of P iff $\Gamma^*(I) = I$.

The well–founded semantics of P is determined by the unique F–least partial stable model of P, and can be obtained by the (bottom–up) iteration of Γ^* starting from the empty interpretation.

An alternative equivalent definition, by means of the squared Γ operator, is given as a special case in the section on well–founded semantics with explicit negation below.

4 Extended logic programs

Recently several authors have stressed and shown the importance of including, beside default negation, a symmetric second kind of negation ¬ in logic programs [APP96], for use in deductive databases, knowledge representation, and non–monotonic reasoning [GL91,GL92,Ino91,Kow90,KS90,PW90,PAA91b,PAA91c], [PAA92,PDA93,Wag91]. This symmetric form of negation may assume several garbs and names (*classical, pseudo, strong, explicit*) corresponding to different properties and distinct applicability. Default and symmetric negation can be related: indeed some authors uphold the *coherence principle*, which stipulates that the latter entails the former.

In this section we begin by reviewing the main motivations for introducing this kind of symmetric negation in logic programs. Then we define an extension of the language of programs to two negations, and briefly overview the main proposed semantics for these programs.

4.1 Motivation

In normal logic programs the negative information is implicit, i.e. it is not possible to explicitly state falsity, and propositions are assumed false if there is no reason to believe they are true. This is what is wanted in some cases. For instance, in the classical example of a database that explicitly states flight connections, one wants to implicitly assume that the absence of a connection in the database means that no such connection exists.

However this is a serious limitation in other cases. As argued in [PW90,Wag91], explicit negative information plays an important rôle in natural discourse and commonsense reasoning. The representation of some problems in logic programming would be more natural if logic programs had some way of explicitly representing falsity. Consider for example the statement:

"Penguins do not fly"

One way of representing this statement within logic programming could be:

$$no\_fly(X) \leftarrow penguin(X)$$

or equivalently:

$$fly'(X) \leftarrow penguin(X)$$

as suggested in [GL89].

But these representations do not capture the connection between the predicate $no\_fly(X)$ and the predication of flying. This becomes clearer if, additionally, we want to represent the statement:

"Birds fly"

Clearly this statement can be represented by

$$fly(X) \leftarrow bird(X)$$

But then, no connection whatsoever exists between the predicates $no\_fly(X)$ and $fly(X)$. Intuitively one would like to have such an obvious connection established.

The importance of these connections grows if we think of negative information for representing exceptions to rules [Kow90]. The first statement above can be seen as an exception to the general rule that normally birds fly. In this case we really want to establish the connection between flying and not flying.

Exceptions expressed by sentences with negative conclusions are also common in legislation [Kow89,Kow92]. For example, consider the provisions for depriving British citizens of their citizenship:

40 - (1) Subject to the provisions of this section, the Secretary of State may by order deprive any British citizen to whom this subsection applies of his British citizenship if [...].

(5) The Secretary of State shall not deprive a person of British citizenship under this section if [...].

Clearly, *40 (1)* has the logical form "P if Q" whereas *40 (5)* has the form "¬ P if R". Moreover, it is also clear that *40 (5)* is an exception to the rule of *40 (1)*

Above we argued for the need of having a symmetric negation in the head of rules. But there are also reasons that compel us to believe symmetric negation is needed also in their bodies. Consider the statement[7]:

" A school bus may cross railway tracks under the condition that there is no approaching train"

It would be wrong to express this statement by the rule:

$$cross \leftarrow not\ train$$

The problem is that this rule allows the bus to cross the tracks when there is no information about either the presence or the absence of a train. The situation is different if symmetric negation is used:

$$cross \leftarrow \neg train$$

---

[7] This example is due to John McCarthy, and was published for the first time in [GL91].

Then the bus is only allowed to cross the tracks if the bus driver is sure that there is no approaching train. The difference between *not p* and ¬*p* in a logic program is essential whenever we cannot assume that available positive information about *p* is complete, i.e. we cannot assume that the absence of information about *p* clearly denotes its falsity.

Moreover, the introduction of symmetric negation in combination with the existing default negation allows for greater expressivity, and so for representing statements like:

" *If the driver is not sure that a train is not approaching then he should wait*"

in a natural way:

$$wait \leftarrow not \ \neg train$$

Examples of such combinations also appear in legislation. For example consider the following article from "The British Nationality Act 1981" [HMS81]:

> (2) *A new-born infant who, after commencement, is found abandoned in the United Kingdom shall acquire british citizenship by section 1.2 if it is not shown that it is not the case that the person is born [...]*

Clearly, conditions of the form "it is not shown that it is not the case that *P*" can be expressed naturally by *not* ¬*P*.

Another motivation for introducing symmetric negation in logic programs relates to a desired symmetry between positive and negative information. This is of special importance when the negative information is easier to represent than the positive one. One can first represent it negatively, and then say that the positive information corresponds to its complement.

In order to make this clearer, take the following example [GL91]:

Example 16. Consider a graph description based on the predicate $arc(X,Y)$, which expresses that in the graph there is an arc from vertice X to vertice Y. Now suppose that we want to determine which vertices are terminals. Clearly, this is a case where the complement information is easier to represent, i.e. it is much easier to determine which vertices are not terminal. By using symmetric negation in combination with negation by default, one can then easily say that terminal vertices are those which are not nonterminal:

$$\neg terminal(X) \leftarrow arc(X,Y)$$
$$terminal(X) \leftarrow not \ \neg terminal(X)$$

Finally, another important motivation for extending logic programming with symmetric negation is to generalize the relationships between logic programs and non-monotonic reasoning formalisms.

As mentioned in section 3.3, such relationships, drawn for the most recent semantics of normal logic programs, have proven of extreme importance for both sides, giving them mutual benefits and clarifications. However, normal logic programs just map into narrow classes of the more general non–monotonic formalisms. For example, simple default rules such as (where "$\sim$" is classical negation):

$$\frac{\sim a \; : \; \sim b}{c} \qquad\qquad \frac{a \; : \; b}{c} \qquad\qquad \frac{a \; : \; b}{\sim c}.$$

cannot be represented by a normal logic program. Note that not even normal nor semi–normal default rules can be represented using normal logic programs. This is so because these programs cannot represent rules with negative conclusions, and normal rules with positive conclusions have also positive justifications, which is impossible in normal programs.

Since, as shown below, extended logic programs also bear a close relationship to non–monotonic reasoning formalisms, they improve on those of normal programs as extended programs map into broader classes of theories in non-monotonic formalisms, and so more general relations between several of those formalisms can now be made via logic programs.

One example of such an improvement is that the introduction of symmetric negation into logic programs makes it possible to represent normal and semi–normal defaults within logic programming. On the one side, this provides methods for computing consequences of normal default theories. On the other, it allows for the appropriation in logic programming of work done using such theories for representing knowledge.

4.2 Language of extended programs

As for normal logic programs, an atom over an alphabet $\mathcal{A}$ is an expression of the form $p(t_1, \ldots, t_n)$, where p is a predicate symbol, and the t_is are terms. In order to extend our language with a second kind of negation, we additionally define an objective literal over $\mathcal{A}$ as being an atom A or its symmetric negation $\neg A$. We also use the symbol $\neg$ to denote complementary literals in the sense of symmetric negation. Thus $\neg\neg A = A$. Here, a literal is either an objective literal L or its default negation $not\ L$. We dub default literals those of the form $not\ L$.

By the extended Herbrand base of $\mathcal{A}$, we mean the set of all ground objective literals of $\mathcal{A}$. Whenever unambiguous we refer to the extended Herbrand base of an alphabet, simply as Herbrand base, and denote it by $\mathcal{H}$.

An extended logic program is a finite set of rules of the form:

$$H \leftarrow L_1, \ldots, L_n \qquad (n \geq 0)$$

where H is an objective literal and each of the L_is is a literal. As for normal programs, if $n = 0$ we omit the arrow symbol.

By the extended Herbrand base $\mathcal{H}$ of P we mean the extended Herbrand base of the alphabet consisting of all the constants, predicate and function symbols that explicitly appear in P.

Interpretation is defined as for normal programs, but using the extended Herbrand base instead.

Whenever unambigous, we refer to extended logic programs simply as logic programs or programs. As in normal programs, a set of rules stands for all its ground instances.

4.3 Answer–sets semantics

The first semantics defined for extended logic programs was the so–called *"answer-sets semantics"* [GL91]. There the authors defined for the first time the language of logic programs with two kinds of negation – default negation *not* and what they called "classical" negation ¬, which is symmetric with respect to *not* .

The answer–sets semantics is a generalization of the stable model semantics for the language of extended programs. Roughly, an answer–set of an extended program P is a stable model of the normal program obtained from P by replacing objective literals of the form $\neg L$ by new atoms, say $\neg\_L$.

Definition 17 (The Γ–operator). Let P be an extended logic program and I a 2–valued interpretation. The GL–transformation of P modulo I is the program $\frac{P}{I}$ obtained from P by:

- first denoting every objective literal in $\mathcal{H}$ of the form $\neg A$ by a new atom, say $\neg\_A$;
- replacing in both P and I, these objective literals by their new denotation;
- then performing the following operations:
  - removing from P all rules which contain a default literal *not* A such that $A \in I$;
  - removing from the remaning rules all default literals.

Since $\frac{P}{I}$ is a definite program it has a unique least model J.

If J contains a pair of complementary atoms, say A and $\neg\_A$, then $\Gamma(I) = \mathcal{H}$.

Otherwise, let J' be the interpretation obtained from J by replacing the newly introduced atoms $\neg\_A$ by $\neg A$. We define $\Gamma(I) = J'$.

Definition 18 (Answer–sets semantics). A 2–valued interpretation I of an extended logic program P is an answer–set model of P iff $\Gamma(I) = I$.

An objective literal L of P is true under the answer–sets semantics iff L belongs to all answer–sets of P; L is false iff $\neg L$ is true; otherwise L is unknown.

In [GL91], the authors showed that the answer–sets of an extended program P are equivalent to Reiter's default extensions of the default theory obtained from P by identifying each program rule:

$$H \leftarrow B_1, \ldots, B_n, \neg C_1, \ldots, \neg C_m, not\ D_1, \ldots, not\ D_k, not\ \neg E_1, \ldots, not\ \neg E_j$$

with the default rule:

$$\frac{B_1, \ldots, B_n, \sim C_1, \ldots, \sim C_m\ :\ \sim D_1, \ldots, \sim D_k, E_1, \ldots, E_j}{H'}$$

where $H' = H$ if H is an atom, or $H' =\sim L$ if $H = \neg L$.

4.4 e–answer–sets semantics

Another semantics generalizing stable models for the class of extended programs is the e–answer–sets semantics of [KS90]. There, the authors claim that "classically" negated atoms in extended programs play the rôle of exceptions. Thus they impose a preference of negative over positive objective literals.

The e–answer–sets semantics is obtainable from the answer–sets semantics after a suitable program transformation. For the sake of simplicity, here we do not give the formal definition of e–answer–sets, but instead show its behaviour on an example:

Example 19. Consider program P :

$$fly(X) \leftarrow bird(X)$$
$$\neg fly(X) \leftarrow penguin(X)$$
$$bird(X) \leftarrow penguin(X)$$
$$penguin(tweety)$$

This program allows for both the conclusions $fly(tweety)$ and $\neg fly(tweety)$. Thus its only answer–sets is $\mathcal{H}$.

In e–answer–sets semantics, since conclusions of the form $\neg L$ are preferred over those of the form L, $\neg fly(tweety)$ overrides the conclusion $fly(tweety)$, and thus

$$\{penguin(tweety), bird(tweety), \neg fly(tweety)\}$$

is an e–answer–set of P.

The rationale for this overriding is that the second rule is an exception to the first one.

4.5 Well–founded semantics with pseudo negation

In [Prz90], the author argues that the technique used in answer–sets for generalizing stable models is quite general. Based on that he defines a semantics which generalizes the well–founded semantics for the class of extended programs[8], as follows:

Definition 20 (Well–founded semantics with pseudo negation). A 3–valued interpretation I is a partial stable model of an extended logic program P iff I' is a partial stable model of the normal program P', where I' and P' are obtained respectively from I and P, by replacing every objective literal of the form $\neg A$ by a new atom, say $\neg\_A$.

The well–founded semantics with pseudo negation of P is determined by the unique F–least partial stable model of P.

---

[8] In the sequel we refer to this semantics as *"well–founded semantics with pseudo negation"*.

4.6 Nelson's strong negation semantics

Based on the notions of vivid logic [Lev86] and strong negation [Nel49], [Wag91] presents an alternative definition of the answer–sets semantics. There, the author claims that the ¬–negation of extended logic programs is not classical negation but rather Nelson's strong negation.

In fact, consider the following program P :

$$b \leftarrow a$$
$$b \leftarrow \neg a$$

If *real* classical negation were used then b would be a consequence of P, because for classical negation $a \vee \neg a$ is a tautology. However, in neither of the above mentioned semantics b follows from P.

4.7 Well–founded semantics with explicit negation

Many semantics for extended logic programs view default negation and symmetric negation as unrelated. To overcome this situation a new semantics for extended logic programs was proposed in [PA92,AP96]. Well-founded Semantics with Explicit Negation (WFSX for short) embeds a "coherence principle" providing the natural missing link between both negations: if $\neg L$ holds then *not L* should too (similarly, if L then *not $\neg L$*). More recently, a paraconsistent extension of this semantics ($WFSX_p$) has been proposed in [ADP95,Dam96] via an alternating fixpoint definition that we now recapitulate.

As usual, for the sake of simplicity and without loss of generality, we will restrict the discussion to (possibly infinite) propositional, or to ground, programs. A non-ground program stands for its fully instantiated version, i.e. the set of all ground instances of its rules. The alphabet of the language of the programs is the set of atoms At. Atoms can be negated by juxtaposing them with the explicit negation symbol "¬" thereby obtaining the explicitly negated literals. The explicit complement of a set $A = \{a_1, a_2, \ldots\}$ is $\neg A = \{\neg a_1, \neg a_2, \ldots\}$. The set of objective literals is $OLit = At \cup \neg At$. Default literals are of the form *not a* and *not ¬a*, where a is an atomic proposition in the language's alphabet. The set of all literals is $Lit = OLit \cup not\ OLit$, where default negation of a set of objective literals stands for the set comprised of the default negation of each one.

Definition 21. An extended logic program is a set of rules of the form

$$L_0 \leftarrow L_1, \ldots, L_m, not\ M_1, \ldots, not\ M_n \qquad (m, n \geq 0)$$

where L_i $(0 \leq i \leq m)$ and M_j $(1 \leq j \leq n)$ are objective literals.

We begin by recalling the definition of Gelfond-Lifschitz Γ operator, used in the alternating fixpoint definition of *WFS* [Gel89a], *WFSX*, and *WFSX_p*.

To impose the coherence requirement Alferes and Pereira resort to the semi-normal version of an extended logic program.

Definition 22. [PA92,AP96] The semi-normal version P_s of a program P is obtained from P by adding to the (possibly empty) *Body* of each rule $L \leftarrow Body$ the default literal $not \neg L$, where $\neg L$ is the complement of L with respect to explicit negation.

The semi-normal version of a program introduces a new anti-monotonic operator: $\Gamma_{P_s}(S)$. Below we use $\Gamma(S)$ to denote $\Gamma_P(S)$, and $\Gamma_s(S)$ to denote $\Gamma_{P_s}(S)$.

Theorem 23. [ADP95] *The operator $\Gamma\Gamma_s$ is monotonic, for arbitrary sets of literals.*

Consequently every program has a least fixpoint of $\Gamma\Gamma_s$. This defines the semantics for paraconsistent logic programs. It also ensures that the semantics is well-defined, i.e. assigns meaning to every extended logic program.

Definition 24. [ADP95] Let P be an extended logic program and T a fixpoint of $\Gamma\Gamma_s$, then $T \cup not\ (\mathcal{H}_P - \Gamma_s T)$ is a paraconsistent partial stable model of P (PSM_p). The paraconsistent well-founded model of P, $WFM_p(P)$, is the least PSM_p under set inclusion order.

To enforce consistency on the paraconsistent partial stable models Alferes and Pereira need only insist the extra condition $T \subseteq \Gamma_s T$ be verified, which succintly guarantees that for no objective literal, L and $not\ L$ simultaneously hold. So it automatically rejects contradictory models where L and $\neg L$ are both true because, by coherence, they would also entail $not\ L$ and $not\ \neg L$. Therefore $WFSX_p$ generalizes $WFSX$, as it does not impose this additional condition. Furthermore, for normal logic programs, it coincides with WFS, which is definable as the least fixpoint of $\Gamma\Gamma$.

Example 25. Let P be the extended logic program:

$$a \leftarrow not\ b. \quad b \leftarrow not\ c. \quad b \leftarrow not\ \neg c. \quad c. \quad \neg c. \quad d \leftarrow not\ d.$$

The sequence for determining the least fixpoint of $\Gamma\Gamma_s$ of program P is:

$$
\begin{aligned}
I_0 &= \{\} \\
I_1 &= \Gamma\Gamma_s\{\} &&= \Gamma\{a,b,c,\neg c,d\} = \{c,\neg c\} \\
I_2 &= \Gamma\Gamma_s\{c,\neg c\} &&= \Gamma\{a,d\} &&= \{a,b,c,\neg c\} \\
I_3 &= \Gamma\Gamma_s\{a,b,c,\neg c\} &&= \Gamma\{d\} &&= I_2
\end{aligned}
$$

Thus $WFM_p(P) = \{a,b,c,\neg c, not\ a, not\ \neg a, not\ b, not\ \neg b, not\ c, not\ \neg c, not\ \neg d\}$.

One of the distinguishing features of $WFSX_p$ is that it does not enforce default consistency, i.e. a and $not\ a$ can be simultaneously true, in contradistinction to all other semantics. In the above example this is the case for literals a, b, c and $\neg c$. It is due to the adoption of the coherence principle: for instance, because a and $\neg a$ hold then, by coherence, $not\ \neg a$ and $not\ a$ must hold too.

5 Disjunctive Logic Programs

Recently, considerable interest and research effort[9] has been given to the problem of finding a suitable extension of the *logic programming paradigm* beyond the class of normal logic programs. In particular, considerable work has been devoted to the problem of defining natural extensions of logic programming that ensure a proper treatment of *disjunctive information* . However, the problem of finding a suitable semantics for disjunctive programs and databases proved to be far more complex than it is in the case of normal, non-disjunctive programs[10].

There are good reasons justifying this extensive research effort. In natural discourse as well as in various programming applications we often use *disjunctive statements*. One particular example of such a situation is *reasoning by cases*. Other obvious examples include:

- *Null values:* for instance, an age "around 30" can be 28, 29, 30, 31, or 32;
- *Legal rules:* the judge always has some freedom for his decision, otherwise he/she would not be needed; so laws cannot have unique models;
- *Diagnosis:* only at the end of a fault diagnosis do we know exactly which part of some machine was faulty but while we are searching, different possibilities exist;
- *Biological inheritance:* if the parents have blood groups A and 0, the child must also have one of these two blood groups (example from [Lip79]);
- *Natural language understanding:* here there are many possibilities for ambiguity and they are represented most naturally by multiple intended models;
- *Conflicts in multiple inheritance:* if we want to keep as much information as possible, we should assume disjunction of the inherited values [BL93].

As [EGM93,EG93,EGM94] have shown, formalisms promoting disjunctive reasoning are more *expressive* and they are also more *natural to use* since they permit direct translation of disjunctive statements from natural language and from informal specifications. The additional expressive power of disjunctive logic programs significantly simplifies the problem of *translation* of non-monotonic formalisms into logic programs, and, consequently, facilitates using logic programming as an *inference engine* for non-monotonic reasoning. Moreover, extensive recent work devoted to theoretic and algorithmic foundations of disjunctive programming, suggests that there are good prospects for *extending the logic programming paradigm* to disjunctive programs.

What then should be viewed as an "extension of logic programming"? We believe that in order to demonstrate that a class of programs can be justifiably called an *extension of logic programs* one should be able to argue that:

---

[9] It suffices just to mention several recent workshops on *Extensions of Logic Programming* specifically devoted to this subject ([DPP95,DHSH96,Wol94,DLMW96]).

[10] The book by Minker et. al. [LMR92] provides a detailed and well-organized account of the extensive research effort in this area. See also [Dix95c,Min93].

- the proposed *syntax* of such programs resembles the syntax of logic programs but it applies to a significantly broader class of programs, which includes the class of disjunctive logic programs as well as the class of logic programs with "classical" (or symmetric) negation;
- the proposed *semantics* of such programs constitutes an intuitively natural extension of the semantics of normal logic programs, which, when restricted to normal logic programs, coincides with one of the well-established semantics of normal logic programs;
- there exists a reasonably simple procedural mechanism allowing, at least in principle, to compute the semantics[11].

It would be also desirable for the proposed class of programs and their semantics to be a special case of a more general non-monotonic formalism which would clearly link it to other well-established non-monotonic formalisms.

Several approaches to the semantics of disjunctive logic programs have been recently proposed and studied in the literature, e.g. [LMR92,Ros92,RT88,GL91], [Dix92b], [BD94,BD97b,BD97a,BD96a,EG93,EGM93,BLM90,Prz91b,Prz95b], and [Prz95a,BDNP97,BDP96]. Since a more thorough discussion of disjunctive programming is beyond the scope of this brief introduction, we refer the reader to those papers, as well as to papers published in this volume, for more details.

6 Implementations

In this section we give a rough overview of what semantics have been implemented so far and where they are available.

It should be noted, that the first-order versions of all semantics investigated here are undecidable. Nevertheless it is an important task to have running systems that *can handle programs with free variables*, and *are Goal-Oriented*. To ensure *completeness* (or *termination*) we need then additional requirements like *allowedness* (to prevent floundering), and no function symbols.

Although these restrictions ensure the Herbrand-universe to be finite (and thus we are really considering a propositional theory) we think that such a system has great advantages over a system that can just handle ground programs. For a language $\mathcal{L}$, the fully instantiated program can be quite large and difficult to handle effectively.

The goal-orientedness (or *Relevance* as mentioned above) is also important — after all this was one reason for the success of SLD-Resolution. As noted above, such a goal-oriented approach is not possible for the stable semantics.

There are various commercial PROLOG-systems that perform variants of SLDNF-Resolution. But in what follows, we concentrate in the following on extensions of semantics introduced in this paper.

---

[11] Observe that while such a mechanism cannot even in principle be efficient, due to the inherent NP-completeness of the problem of computing answers to just positive disjunctive programs, it can be efficient when restricted to specific subclasses of programs and queries and it can allow efficient approximation methods for broader classes of programs.

Currently, a library of implemented logic programming systems and interesting test-cases for such systems is collected as a project of the artificial intelligence group at Koblenz. We refer to <http://www.uni-koblenz.de/ag-ki/LP/>.

6.1 Non-Disjunctive Semantics

There are many theoretical papers that deal with the problem of implementation ([BD93,KSS91,DN95,FLMS93]) but only a few running systems. The problem of handling and representing ground programs given a non-ground one has also been addressed [KNS94,KNS95,EGLS96].

In [BNNS93,BNNS94] the authors showed how the problem of computing stable models can be transformed to an Integer-Linear Programming Problem. This has been extended in [DM93] to disjunctive programs.

Inoue et. al. show in [IKH92] how to compute stable models by transforming programs into propositional theories and then using a model-generation theorem prover.

In Bern, Switzerland, a group around G. Jäger is building a non-monotonic reasoning system which incorporates various monotonic and non-monotonic logics. We refer to http://lwbwww.unibe.ch:8080/LWBinfo.html.

Extended logic programs under the well-founded semantics are considered by Pereira and his colleagues: [PAA93,ADP95,AP96]. The REVISE system, which deals with contradiction removal pro paraconsistent programs in this semantics, can be found in <http://www.uni-koblenz.de/ag-ki/LP/> too.

[NS96] describes an implementation of WFS and STABLE with a special eye on complexity.

The most advanced system has been implemented by David Warren and his group in Stony Brook based on OLDT-algorithm of [TS86]. They first developed a meta-interpreter (SLG, see [CW96]) in PROLOG and then directly modified the WAM for a direct implementation of WFS (XSB). They use tabling-methods and a mixture of top-Down and bottom-up evaluation to detect loops. Their system is complete and terminating for non-floundering DATALOG. It also works for general programs but termination is not guaranteed. This system is described in [CW93,CSW95,CW95], and is available by anonymous ftp from ftp.cs.sunysb.edu/pub/XSB/.

6.2 Disjunctive Semantics

There are theoretical descriptions of implementations that have not yet been implemented: [FM95,MR95,CL95].

Here are some implemented systems. Inoue et. al. show in [IKH92] how to compute stable models for extended disjunctive programs in a bottom-up-fashion using a theorem prover. The approach of Bell et. al. ([NNS91]) was used by Dix/Müller [DM93,DM92,Mül92] to implement versions of the stationary semantics of Przymusinski ([Prz91c].

Brass/Dix have implemented both D-WFS and DSTABLE for allowed DAT-ALOG programs ([BD95][12]). An implementation of static semantics ([Prz95b]) is described in [BDP96][13].

Seipel has implemented in his DisLog-system various (modified versions of) semantics of Minker and his group. His system is publicly available at the URL http://sunwww.informatik.uni-tuebingen.de:8080/dislog/dislog.tar.Z.

Finally, there is the DisLoP project undertaken by the Artificial Intelligence Research Group at the University of Koblenz and headed by J. Dix and U. Furbach ([DF96,ADN97]). This project aims at extending certain theorem proving concepts, such as restart model elimination [BF94] and hyper tableaux [BFN96] calculi, for disjunctive logic programming. Information on the DisLoP project and related publications can be obtained from the WWW page <http://www.uni-koblenz.de/ag-ki/DLP/>.

Acknowledgements

We wish to thank our colleagues José Júlio Alferes, Stefan Brass, Gerhard Brewka, Carlos Damásio, and Halina Przymusinska for our use of material from joint publications. Luís Moniz Pereira acknowledges also the support of JNICT/PRAXIS and its funding of the project MENTAL (#2/2.1/TIT/1593/95).

References

[AB91]   K. Apt and M. Bezem. Acyclic programs. *New Generation Computing*, 29(3):335–363, 1991.

[AB94]   Krysztof R. Apt and Roland N. Bol. Logic Programming and Negation: A Survey. *Journal of Logic Programming*, 19-20:9–71, 1994.

[ABW88]   K. Apt, H. Blair, and A. Walker. Towards a theory of declarative knowledge. In J. Minker, editor, *Foundations of Deductive Databases and Logic Programming*, pages 89–142. Morgan Kaufmann, 1988.

[ADN97]   Chandrabose Aravindan, Jürgen Dix, and Ilkka Niemelä. The DisLoP-project. Technical Report TR 1/97, University of Koblenz, Department of Computer Science, Rheinau 1, January 1997.

[ADP95]   J. J. Alferes, C. V. Damásio, and L. M. Pereira. A logic programming system for non-monotonic reasoning. *Journal of Automated Reasoning*, 14(1):93–147, 1995.

[AP96]   Jose Julio Alferes and Luiz Moniz Pereira, editors. *Reasoning with Logic Programming*, LNAI 1111, Berlin, 1996. Springer.

[APP96]   J. J. Alferes, L. M. Pereira, and T. Przymusinski. "Classical" negation in non monotonic reasoning and logic programming. In H. Kautz and B. Selman, editors, *4th Int. Symposium on Artificial Intelligence and Mathematics*, Fort Lauderdale, USA, January 1996. Florida Atlantic University.

[BD93]   Roland N. Bol and L. Degerstedt. Tabulated resolution for well-founded semantics. In *Proc. Int. Logic Programming Symposium'93*, Cambridge, Mass., 1993. MIT Press.

---

[12] ftp://ftp.informatik.uni-hannover.de/software/index.html

[13] ftp://ftp.informatik.uni-hannover.de/software/static/static.html

[BD94]   Stefan Brass and Jürgen Dix. A disjunctive semantics based on unfold-
           ing and bottom-up evaluation. In Bernd Wolfinger, editor, *Innovationen
           bei Rechen- und Kommunikationssystemen*, (IFIP '94-Congress, Workshop
           FG2: Disjunctive Logic Programming and Disjunctive Databases), pages
           83–91, Berlin, 1994. Springer.

[BD95]   Stefan Brass and Jürgen Dix. A General Approach to Bottom-Up Compu-
           tation of Disjunctive Semantics. In J. Dix, L. Pereira, and T. Przymusinski,
           editors, *Nonmonotonic Extensions of Logic Programming*, LNAI 927, pages
           127–155. Springer, Berlin, 1995.

[BD96a]   Stefan Brass and Jürgen Dix. Characterizing D-WFS: Confluence and
           Iterated GCWA. In L.M. Pereira J.J. Alferes and E. Orlowska, editors,
           Logics in Artificial Intelligence (JELIA '96), LNCS 1126, pages 268–283.
           Springer, 1996. (Extended version will appear in the *Journal of Automated
           Reasoning* in 1997.).

[BD96b]   Gerhard Brewka and Jürgen Dix. Knowledge representation with logic pro-
           grams. Technical report, Tutorial Notes of the 12th European Conference
           on Artificial Intelligence (ECAI '96), 1996. Also appeared as Technical
           Report 15/96, Dept. of CS of the University of Koblenz-Landau. Will ap-
           pear as Chapter 6 in *Handbook of Philosophical Logic*, 2nd edition (1998),
           Volume 6, Methodologies.

[BD97a]   Stefan Brass and Jürgen Dix. Characterizations of the Disjunctive Stable
           Semantics by Partial Evaluation. *Journal of Logic Programming*, forth-
           coming, 1997. (Extended abstract appeared in: Characterizations of the
           Stable Semantics by Partial Evaluation *LPNMR, Proceedings of the Third
           International Conference, Kentucky*, pages 85–98, 1995. Springer.).

[BD97b]   Stefan Brass and Jürgen Dix. Semantics of Disjunctive Logic Programs
           Based on Partial Evaluation. *Journal of Logic Programming*, accepted for
           publication, 1997. (Extended abstract appeared in: Disjunctive Semantics
           Based upon Partial and Bottom-Up Evaluation, *Proceedings of the 12-th
           International Logic Programming Conference, Tokyo*, pages 199–213, 1995.
           MIT Press.).

[BDK97]   Gerd Brewka, Jürgen Dix, and Kurt Konolige. *Nonmonotonic Reasoning:
           An Overview*. CSLI Lecture Notes 73. CSLI Publications, Stanford, CA,
           1997.

[BDNP97]   Stefan Brass, Jürgen Dix, Ilkka Niemelä, and Teodor. C. Przymusinski.
           Comparison and Efficient Computation of the Static and the Disjunctive
           WFS. Technical report, University of Koblenz, Department of Computer
           Science, Rheinau 1, January 1997. submitted to a conference. Preliminary
           version appeared as Technical Report 2/96.

[BDP96]   Stefan Brass, Jürgen Dix, and Teodor. C. Przymusinski. Super Logic Pro-
           grams. In L. C. Aiello, J. Doyle, and S. C. Shapiro, editors, *Principles of
           Knowledge Representation and Reasoning: Proceedings of the Fifth Inter-
           national Conference (KR '96)*, pages 529–541. San Francisco, CA, Morgan
           Kaufmann, 1996.

[BF88]   N. Bidoit and C. Froidevaux. General logic databases and programs: default
           logic semantics and stratification. *Journal of Information and Computa-
           tion*, 1988.

[BF94]   P. Baumgartner and U. Furbach. Model Elimination without Contrapos-
           itives and its Application to PTTP. *Journal of Automated Reasoning*,

13:339–359, 1994. Short version in: Proceedings of CADE-12, Springer LNAI 814, 1994, pp 87–101.

[BFN96] Peter Baumgartner, Ulrich Furbach, and Ilkka Niemelä. Hyper tableaux. In L.M. Pereira J.J. Alferes and E. Orlowska, editors, *Logics in Artificial Intelligence (JELIA '96)*, LNCS 1126, pages 1–17. Springer, 1996.

[BL93] Stefan Brass and Udo W. Lipeck. Bottom-up query evaluation with partially ordered defaults. In Stefano Ceri, Katsumi Tanaka, and Shalom Tsur, editors, *Deductive and Object-Oriented Databases, Third Int. Conf., (DOOD'93)*, number 760 in LNCS, pages 253–266, Berlin, 1993. Springer.

[BLM90] Chitta Baral, Jorge Lobo, and Jack Minker. Generalized Disjunctive Well-founded Semantics for Logic Programs: Procedural Semantics. In Z.W. Ras, M. Zemankova, and M.L Emrich, editors, *Proceedings of the 5th Int. Symp. on Methodologies for Intelligent Systems, Knoxville, TN, October 1990*, pages 456–464. North-Holland, 1990.

[BNNS93] Colin Bell, Anil Nerode, Raymond T. Ng, and V. S. Subrahmanian. Implementing Stable Semantics by Linear Programming. In Luis Moniz Pereira and Anil Nerode, editors, *Logic Programming and Non-Monotonic Reasoning, Proceedings of the Second International Workshop*, pages 23–42, Cambridge, Mass., July 1993. Lisbon, MIT Press.

[BNNS94] Colin Bell, Anil Nerode, Raymond T. Ng, and V. S. Subrahmanian. Mixed Integer Programming Methods for Computing Non-Monotonic Deductive Databases. *Journal of the ACM*, 41(6):1178–1215, November 1994.

[Bry89] François Bry. Logic programming as constructivism: A formalization and its application to databases. In *Proc. of the Eighth ACM SIGACT-SIGMOD-SIGART Symposium on Principles of Database Systems (PODS'89)*, pages 34–50, 1989.

[BS91] C. Baral and V. S. Subrahmanian. Dualities between alternative semantics for logic programming and nonmonotonic reasoning. In A. Nerode, W. Marek, and V. S. Subrahmanian, editors, *LP & NMR*, pages 69–86. MIT Press, 1991.

[CKPR73] A. Colmerauer, H. Kanoui, R. Pasero, and P. Roussel. Un système de communication homme-machine en français. Technical report, Groupe de Intelligence Artificielle Universite de Aix-Marseille II, 1973.

[CL95] Stefania Costantini and Gaetano A. Lanzarone. Static Semantics as Program Transformation and Well-founded Computation. In J. Dix, L. Pereira, and T. Przymusinski, editors, *Nonmonotonic Extensions of Logic Programming*, LNAI 927, pages 156–180. Springer, Berlin, 1995.

[Cla78] Keith L. Clark. Negation as Failure. In H. Gallaire and J. Minker, editors, *Logic and Data-Bases*, pages 293–322. Plenum, New York, 1978.

[CSW95] Weidong Chen, Terrance Swift, and David S. Warren. Efficient Top-Down Computation of Queries under the Well-Founded Semantics. *Journal of Logic Programming*, 24(3):219–245, 1995.

[CW93] Weidong Chen and David S. Warren. A Goal Oriented Approach to Computing The Well-founded Semantics. *Journal of Logic Programming*, 17:279–300, 1993.

[CW95] Weidong Chen and David S. Warren. Computing of Stable Models and its Integration with Logical Query Processing. *IEEE Transactions on Knowledge and Data Engineering*, 17:279–300, 1995.

[CW96] Weidong Chen and David S. Warren. Tabled Evaluation with Delaying for General Logic Programs. *Journal of the ACM*, 43(1):20–74, January 1996.

[Dam96]   C. V. Damásio. *Paraconsistent Extended Logic Programming with Constraints*. PhD thesis, Universidade Nova de Lisboa, October 1996.

[DF96]   J. Dix and U. Furbach. The DFG-Project DisLoP on Disjunctive Logic Programming. *Computational Logic*, 2:89–90, 1996.

[DFN97]   J. Dix, U. Furbach, and A. Nerode, editors. *Logic Programming and Non-monotonic Reasoning*, LNAI to appear, Berlin, 1997. Springer.

[DHSH96]   Roy Dyckhoff, Heinrich Herre, and Peter Schroeder-Heister, editors. *Extensions of Logic Programming*, LNAI 1050, Berlin, 1996. Springer.

[Dix91]   J. Dix. Classifying semantics of logic programs. In A. Nerode, W. Marek, and V. S. Subrahmanian, editors, *LP & NMR*, pages 166–180. MIT Press, 1991.

[Dix92a]   J. Dix. A framework for representing and characterizing semantics of logic programs. In B. Nebel, C. Rich, and W. Swartout, editors, *3rd Int. Conf. on Principles of Knowledge Representation and Reasoning*. Morgan Kaufmann, 1992.

[Dix92b]   Jürgen Dix. Classifying Semantics of Disjunctive Logic Programs. In K. R. Apt, editor, *LOGIC PROGRAMMING: Proceedings of the 1992 Joint International Conference and Symposium*, pages 798–812, Cambridge, Mass., November 1992. MIT Press.

[Dix95a]   Jürgen Dix. A Classification-Theory of Semantics of Normal Logic Programs: I. Strong Properties. *Fundamenta Informaticae*, XXII(3):227–255, 1995.

[Dix95b]   Jürgen Dix. A Classification-Theory of Semantics of Normal Logic Programs: II. Weak Properties. *Fundamenta Informaticae*, XXII(3):257–288, 1995.

[Dix95c]   Jürgen Dix. Semantics of Logic Programs: Their Intuitions and Formal Properties. An Overview. In Andre Fuhrmann and Hans Rott, editors, *Logic, Action and Information – Essays on Logic in Philosophy and Artificial Intelligence*, pages 241–327. DeGruyter, 1995.

[DLMW96]   Jürgen Dix, Donald Loveland, Jack Minker, and David. S. Warren. Disjunctive Logic Programming and databases: Nonmonotonic Aspects. Technical Report Dagstuhl Seminar Report 150, IBFI GmbH, Schloß Dagstuhl, 1996.

[DM92]   Jürgen Dix and Martin Müller. Abstract Properties and Computational Complexity of Semantics for Disjunctive Logic Programs. In *Proc. of the Workshop W1, Structural Complexity and Recursion-theoretic Methods in Logic Programming, following the JICSLP '92*, pages 15–28. H. Blair and W. Marek and A. Nerode and J. Remmel, November 1992. also available as Technical Report 13/93, University of Koblenz, Department of Computer Science.

[DM93]   Jürgen Dix and Martin Müller. Implementing Semantics for Disjunctive Logic Programs Using Fringes and Abstract Properties. In Luis Moniz Pereira and Anil Nerode, editors, *Logic Programming and Non-Monotonic Reasoning, Proceedings of the Second International Workshop*, pages 43–59, Cambridge, Mass., July 1993. Lisbon, MIT Press.

[DN95]   Lars Degerstedt and Ulf Nilsson. Magic Computation of Well-founded Semantics. In J. Dix, L. Pereira, and T. Przymusinski, editors, *Non-monotonic Extensions of Logic Programming*, LNAI 927, pages 181–204. Springer, Berlin, 1995.

[DPP95]   J. Dix, L. Pereira, and T. Przymusinski, editors. *Non-Monotonic Extensions of Logic Programming*, LNAI 927, Berlin, 1995. Springer.

[Dun91]   P. M. Dung. Negation as hypotheses: An abductive framework for logic programming. In K. Furukawa, editor, *8th Int. Conf. on LP*, pages 3–17. MIT Press, 1991.

[EG93]   Thomas Eiter and Georg Gottlob. Propositional Circumscription and Extended Closed World Reasoning are Π_2^P-complete. *Theoretical Computer Science*, 144(2):231–245, Addendum: vol. 118, p. 315, 1993, 1993.

[EGLS96] T. Eiter, G. Gottlob, J. Lu, and V. S. Subrahmanian. Computing Non-Ground Representations of Stable Models. Technical report, University of Maryland, 1996.

[EGM93]   Thomas Eiter, Georg Gottlob, and Heikki Mannila. Expressive Power and Complexity of Disjunctive DATALOG. In *Proceedings of Workshop on Logic Programming with Incomplete Information, Vancouver Oct. 1993, following ILPS' 93*, pages 59–79, 1993.

[EGM94]   Thomas Eiter, Georg Gottlob, and Heikki Mannila. Adding disjunction to datalog. In *Proc. of the Thirteenth ACM SIGACT-SIGMOD-SIGART Symposium on Principles of Database Systems (PODS'94)*, pages 267–278, 1994.

[EK76]   M. Van Emden and R. Kowalski. The semantics of predicate logic as a programming language. *Journal of ACM*, 4(23):733–742, 1976.

[Fit85]   M. Fitting. A Kripke-Kleene semantics for logic programs. *Journal of LP*, 2(4):295–312, 1985.

[FLMS93] J. A. Fernández, J. Lobo, J. Minker, and V.S. Subrahmanian. Disjunctive LP + Integrity Constraints = Stable Model Semantics. *Annals of Mathematics and Artificial Intelligence*, 8(3-4), 1993.

[FM95]   J. A. Fernández and J. Minker. Bottom-Up Computation of Perfect Models for Disjunctive Theories. *Journal of Logic Programming*, 25(1):33–51, 1995.

[Gel87]   M. Gelfond. On stratified autoepistemic theories. In *AAAI'87*, pages 207–211. Morgan Kaufmann, 1987.

[Gel89a] A. Van Gelder. The alternating fixpoint of logic programs with negation. In *8th Symposium on Principles of Database Systems*. ACM SIGACT-SIGMOD, 1989.

[Gel89b] A. Van Gelder. Negation as failure using tight derivations for general logic programs. *Journal of LP*, 6(1):109–133, 1989.

[GL88]   M. Gelfond and V. Lifschitz. The stable model semantics for logic programming. In R. Kowalski and K. A. Bowen, editors, *5th Int. Conf. on LP*, pages 1070–1080. MIT Press, 1988.

[GL89]   Michael Gelfond and Vladimir Lifschitz. Compiling Circumscriptive Theories into Logic Programs. In Reinfrank, de Kleer, Ginsberg, and Sandewall, editors, *Non-Monotonic Reasoning*, LNAI 346, pages 74–99, Berlin, January 1989. Springer.

[GL91]   Michael Gelfond and Vladimir Lifschitz. Classical Negation in Logic Programs and Disjunctive Databases. *New Generation Computing*, 9:365–387, 1991. (Extended abstract appeared in: Logic Programs with Classical Negation. *Proceedings of the 7-th International Logic Programming Conference, Jerusalem*, pages 579–597, 1990. MIT Press.).

[GL92]   M. Gelfond and V. Lifschitz. Representing actions in extended logic programs. In K. Apt, editor, *Int. Joint Conf. and Symp. on LP*, pages 559–573. MIT Press, 1992.

[GMN84]   H. Gallaire, J. Minker, and J. Nicolas. Logic and databases: a deductive approach. *ACM Computing Surveys*, 16:153–185, 1984.

[GRS91]   A. Van Gelder, K. A. Ross, and J. S. Schlipf. The well-founded semantics for general logic programs. *Journal of the ACM*, 38(3):620–650, 1991.

[HMS81]   HMSO. *British Nationality Act.* Her Majesty's Stationery Office, 1981.

[IKH92]   Katsumi Inoue, M. Koshimura, and R. Hasegawa. Embedding negation-as-failure into a model generation theorem prover. In Deepak Kapur, editor, *Automated Deduction — CADE-11*, number 607 in LNAI, Berlin, 1992. Springer.

[Ino91]   K. Inoue. Extended logic programs with default assumptions. In Koichi Furukawa, editor, *8th Int. Conf. on LP*, pages 490–504, Cambridge, Mass., 1991. MIT Press.

[KK71]   R. Kowalski and D. Khuener. Linear resolution with selection function. *Artificial Intelligence*, 5:227–260, 1971.

[KNS94]   Vadim Kagan, Anil Nerode, and V. S. Subrahmanian. Computing Definite Logic Programs by Partial Instantiation. *Annals of Pure and Applied Logic*, 67:161–182, 1994.

[KNS95]   Vadim Kagan, Anil Nerode, and V. S. Subrahmanian. Computing Minimal Models by Partial Instantiation. *Theoretical Computer Science*, 155:157–177, 1995.

[Kow74]   R.A. Kowalski. Predicate logic as a programming language. In *Proceeedings IFIP' 74*, pages 569–574. North Holland Publishing Company, 1974.

[Kow79]   R. Kowalski. Algorithm = logic + control. *Communications of the ACM*, 22:424–436, 1979.

[Kow89]   R. Kowalski. The treatment of negation in logic programs for representing legislation. In *2nd Int. Conf. on AI and Law*, pages 11–15, 1989.

[Kow90]   R. Kowalski. Problems and promises of computational logic. In John W. Lloyd, editor, *Computational Logic*, Basic Research Series, pages 1–36, Berlin, 1990. Springer.

[Kow92]   R. Kowalski. Legislation as logic programs. In *Logic Programming in Action*, pages 203–230. Springer–Verlag, 1992.

[KS90]   R. Kowalski and F. Sadri. Logic programs with exceptions. In Warren and Szeredi, editors, *7th Int. Conf. on LP*, Cambridge, Mass., 1990. MIT Press.

[KSS91]   David B. Kemp, Peter J. Stuckey, and Divesh Srivastava. Magic Sets and Bottom-Up Evaluation of Well-Founded Models. In Vijay Saraswat and Kazunori Ueda, editors, *Proceedings of the 1991 Int. Symposium on Logic Programming*, pages 337–351. MIT, June 1991.

[Kun87]   Kenneth Kunen. Negation in Logic Programming. *Journal of Logic Programming*, 4:289–308, 1987.

[Kun90]   Kenneth Kunen. Some Remarks on the completed Database. *Fundamenta Informaticae*, XIII:35–49, 1990.

[Lev86]   H. Levesque. Making believers out of computers. *Artificial Intelligence*, 30:81–107, 1986.

[Lip79]   W. Lipski, Jr. On semantic issues connected with incomplete information databases. *ACM Transactions on Database Systems*, 4:262–296, 1979.

[Llo87]   John W. Lloyd. *Foundations of Logic Programming*. Springer, Berlin, 1987. 2nd edition.

[LMR92]   Jorge Lobo, Jack Minker, and Arcot Rajasekar. *Foundations of Disjunctive Logic Programming*. MIT-Press, 1992.

[LT85]   John W. Lloyd and Rodney W. Topor. A basis for deductive database systems. *The Journal of Logic Programming*, 2:93–109, 1985.

[LT86]   John W. Lloyd and Rodney W. Topor. A basis for deductive database systems II. *The Journal of Logic Programming*, 3:55–67, 1986.

[Min88]   Jack Minker. *Foundations of Deductive Databases*. Morgan Kaufmann, 95 First Street, Los Altos, CA 94022, 1st edition, 1988.

[Min93]   Jack Minker. An Overview of Nonmonotonic Reasoning and Logic Programming. *Journal of Logic Programming, Special Issue*, 17, 1993.

[Min96]   Jack Minker. Logic and databases: A 20 year retrospective. In Dino Pedreschi and Carlo Zaniolo, editors, *Proceedings of the International Workshop on Logic in Databases (LID)*, LNCS 1154, pages 3–58. Springer, Berlin, 1996.

[MNT95]   W. Marek, A. Nerode, and M. Truszczyński, editors. *Logic Programming and Nonmonotonic Reasoning*, LNAI 928, Berlin, 1995. Springer.

[Mon92]   L. Monteiro. Notes on the negation in logic programs. Technical report, Dep. of Computer Science, Univerdade Nova de Lisboa, 1992. Course Notes, 3rd Advanced School on AI, Azores, Portugal, 1992.

[Moo85]   R. Moore. Semantics considerations on nonmonotonic logic. *Artificial Intelligence*, 25:75–94, 1985.

[MR95]   Jack Minker and Carolina Ruiz. Computing stable and partial stable models of extended disjunctive logic programs. In J. Dix, L. Pereira, and T. Przymusinski, editors, *Nonmonotonic Extensions of Logic Programming*, LNAI 927, pages 205–229. Springer, Berlin, 1995.

[MT91]   W. Marek and M. Truszczynski. Autoepistemic logics. *Journal of the ACM*, 38(3):588–619, 1991.

[Mül92]   Martin Müller. Examples and Run-Time Data from KORF, 1992.

[Nel49]   D. Nelson. Constructible falsity. *JSL*, 14:16–26, 1949.

[NMS91]   A. Nerode, W. Marek, and V. S. Subrahmanian, editors. *Logic Programming and Non-monotonic Reasoning: Proceedings of the First Int. Ws.*, Washington D.C., USA, 1991. The MIT Press.

[NNS91]   Anil Nerode, Raymond T. Ng, and V.S. Subrahmanian. Computing Circumscriptive Deductive Databases. CS-TR 91-66, Computer Science Dept., Univ. Maryland, University of Maryland, College Park, Maryland, 20742, USA, December 1991.

[NS96]   Ilkka Niemelä and Patrik Simons. Efficient implementation of the well-founded and stable model semantics. In M. Maher, editor, *Proceedings of the Joint International Conference and Symposium on Logic Programming*, pages 289–303, Bonn, Germany, September 1996. The MIT Press.

[PA92]   L. M. Pereira and J. J. Alferes. Well founded semantics for logic programs with explicit negation. In B. Neumann, editor, *European Conf. on AI*, pages 102–106. John Wiley & Sons, 1992.

[PAA91a]   L. M. Pereira, J. J. Alferes, and J. N. Aparício. A practical introduction to well founded semantics. In B. Mayoh, editor, *Scandinavian Conf. on AI*. IOS Press, 1991.

[PAA91b]   L. M. Pereira, J. N. Aparício, and J. J. Alferes. Counterfactual reasoning based on revising assumptions. In Ueda and Saraswat, editors, *Int. LP Symp.*, pages 566–577. MIT Press, 1991.

[PAA91c]   L. M. Pereira, J. N. Aparício, and J. J. Alferes. Nonmonotonic reasoning with well founded semantics. In Koichi Furukawa, editor, *8th Int. Conf. on LP*, pages 475–489. MIT Press, 1991.

[PAA92]   L. M. Pereira, J. N. Aparício, and J. J. Alferes. Logic programming for nonmonotonic reasoning. In *Applied Logic Conf.* Preproceedings by ILLC, Amsterdam, 1992. To appear in Springer–Verlag LNAI.

[PAA93]   L. M. Pereira, J. N. Aparício, and J. J. Alferes. Non-Monotonic Reasoning with Logic Programming. *Journal of Logic Programming*, 17:227–264, 1993.

[PDA93]   L. M. Pereira, C. Damásio, and J. J. Alferes. Diagnosis and debugging as contradiction removal. In L. M. Pereira and A. Nerode, editors, *2nd Int. Ws. on LP & NMR*, pages 316–330, Cambridge, Mass., 1993. MIT Press.

[PN93]   L. M. Pereira and A. Nerode, editors. *Logic Programming and Non-monotonic Reasoning: Proceedings of the Second Int. Ws.*, Lisboa, Portugal, 1993. MIT Press.

[PP88]   H. Przymusinska and T. Przymusinski. Weakly perfect model semantics. In R. Kowalski and K. A. Bowen, editors, *5th Int. Conf. on LP*, pages 1106–1122. MIT Press, 1988.

[PP90]   H. Przymusinska and T. Przymusinski. Semantic issues in deductive databases and logic programs. In R. Banerji, editor, *Formal Techniques in AI, a Sourcebook*, pages 321–367. North Holland, 1990.

[Prz89a] T. Przymusinski. Every logic program has a natural stratification and an iterated fixed point model. In *8th Symp. on Principles of Database Systems*. ACM SIGACT-SIGMOD, 1989.

[Prz89b] T. Przymusinski. Three–valued non–monotonic formalisms and logic programming. In R. Brachman, H. Levesque, and R. Reiter, editors, *1st Int. Conf. on Principles of Knowledge Representation and Reasoning*, pages 341–348. Morgan Kaufmann, 1989.

[Prz89c] Teodor Przymusinski. On the declarative and procedural Semantics of logic Programs. *Journal of Automated Reasoning*, 5:167–205, 1989.

[Prz90]   T. Przymusinski. Extended stable semantics for normal and disjunctive programs. In Warren and Szeredi, editors, *7th Int. Conf. on LP*, pages 459–477, Cambridge, Mass., 1990. MIT Press.

[Prz91a] T. Przymusinski. Autoepistemic logic of closed beliefs and logic programming. In A. Nerode, W. Marek, and V. S. Subrahmanian, editors, *LP & NMR*, pages 3–20. MIT Press, 1991.

[Prz91b] Teodor Przymusinski. Stable Semantics for Disjunctive Programs. *New Generation Computing Journal*, 9:401–424, 1991. (Extended abstract appeared in: Extended stable semantics for normal and disjunctive logic programs. *Proceedings of the 7-th International Logic Programming Conference, Jerusalem*, pages 459–477, 1990. MIT Press, Cambridge, Mass.).

[Prz91c] Teodor Przymusinski. Stationary Semantics for Normal and Disjunctive Logic Programs. In C. Delobel, M. Kifer, and Y. Masunaga, editors, *DOOD '91, Proceedings of the 2nd International Conference*, Berlin, December 1991. Muenchen, Springer. LNCS 566.

[Prz95a] Teodor Przymusinski. Semantics of normal and disjunctive logic programs: A unifying framework. In J. Dix, L. Pereira, and T. Przymusinski, editors, *Proceedings of the Workshop on Non-Monotonic Extensions of Logic Programming at the Eleventh International Logic Programming Conference, ICLP'94, Santa Margherita Ligure, Italy, June 1994*, pages 43–67. Springer, 1995.

[Prz95b] Teodor Przymusinski. Static Semantics For Normal and Disjunctive Logic Programs. *Annals of Mathematics and Artificial Intelligence*, 14:323–357, 1995.

[PW90]   D. Pearce and G. Wagner. Reasoning with negative information I: Strong negation in logic programs. In L. Haaparanta, M. Kusch, and I. Niiniluoto, editors, *Language, Knowledge and Intentionality*, pages 430–453. Acta Philosophica Fennica 49, 1990.

[Rei78a] R. Reiter. On closed–world data bases. In H. Gallaire and J. Minker, editors, *Logic and DataBases*, pages 55–76. Plenum Press, 1978.

[Rei78b]	Raymond Reiter. On closed world data bases. In Hervé Gallaire and Jack Minker, editors, *Logic and Data Bases*, pages 55–76, New York, 1978. Plenum.
[Rei80]	Raymond Reiter. A Logic for Default-Reasoning. *Artificial Intelligence*, 13:81–132, 1980.
[Rei84]	R. Reiter. Towards a logical reconstruction of relational database theory. In M. Brodie and J. Mylopoulos, editors, *On Conceptual Modelling*, pages 191–233. Springer–Verlag, 1984.
[RN95]	Stuart Russel and Peter Norvig. *Artificial Intelligence — A Modern Approach*. Prentice Hall, New Jersey 07458, 1995.
[Ros92]	Kenneth A. Ross. A procedural semantics for well-founded negation in logic programs. *Journal of Logic Programming*, 13:1–22, 1992.
[RT88]	Kenneth A. Ross and Rodney A. Topor. Inferring negative Information from disjunctive Databases. *Journal of Automated Reasoning*, 4:397–424, 1988.
[Sak89]	Chiaki Sakama. Possible Model Semantics for Disjunctive Databases. In Won Kim, Jean-Marie Nicolas, and Shojiro Nishio, editors, *Deductive and Object-Oriented Databases, Proceedings of the First International Conference (DOOD89)*, pages 1055–1060, Kyoto, Japan, 1989. North-Holland Publ.Co.
[She88]	John C. Shepherdson. Negation in Logic Programming. In Jack Minker, editor, *Foundations of Deductive Databases*, chapter 1, pages 19–88. Morgan Kaufmann, 1988.
[She90]	J. Shepherdson. Negation as failure, completion and stratification. In *Handbook of AI and LP*, 1990.
[SI93]	Chiaki Sakama and Katsumi Inoue. Negation in Disjunctive Logic Programs. In D. Warren and Peter Szeredi, editors, *Proceedings of the 10th Int. Conf. on Logic Programming, Budapest*, Cambridge, Mass., July 1993. MIT Press.
[SS95]	Chiaki Sakama and Hirohisa Seki. Partial Deduction of Disjunctive Logic Programs: A Declarative Approach. In *Logic Program Synthesis and Transformation – Meta Programming in Logic*, LNCS 883, pages 170–182, Berlin, 1995. Springer. Extended version to appear in *Journal of Logic Programming*.
[TS86]	H. Tamaki and T. Sato. OLD Resolution with Tabulation. In *Proceedings of the Third International Conference on Logic Programming, London*, LNAI, pages 84–98, Berlin, June 1986. Springer.
[Wag91]	G. Wagner. A database needs two kinds of negation. In B. Thalheim, J. Demetrovics, and H-D. Gerhardt, editors, *Mathematical Foundations of Database Systems*, LNCS 495, pages 357–371, Berlin, 1991. Springer.
[Wol94]	Bernd Wolfinger, editor. *GI-Fachgespräch 2:* Disjunktive logische Programmierung und disjunktive Datenbanken, pages 51–100. Springer, Berlin, 1994.
[WPP77]	D. H. Warren, L. M. Pereira, and F. Pereira. Prolog: The language and its implementation compared with Lisp. In *Symp. on AI and Programming Languages*, pages 109–115. ACM SIGPLAN-SIGART, 1977.

On Logics and Semantics
for General Logic Programs

Alexander Bochman

e-mail: bochman@bimacs.cs.biu.ac.il

Abstract. We suggest a general logical formalism for Logic Programming (called a *biconsequence relation*) based on a four-valued inference. We show that it forms a proper setting for representing logic programs of a most general kind and for describing logics and semantics that characterize their behavior. In this way we also extend the connection between Logic and Logic Programming beyond positive programs.

A uniform representation of various semantics for logic programs is presented. The main conclusion from this representation is that the distinction between these semantics can be largely attributed to the difference in their underlying (monotonic) logical systems. Moreover, in most cases the difference can even be reduced to that of the *language*, that is, to the difference in the logical connectives allowed for representing derivable information. In addition, it allows us to see a reasoning about logic programs as a most simple kind of nonmonotonic reasoning in general.

1 Introduction

In this study we suggest a general logical framework for Logic Programming based on a four-valued inference. The formalism employs Belnap's interpretation of the four truth-values [2] according to which a four-valued interpretation amounts to a pair of independent interpretations assigning, respectively, truth and falsity to propositions. This interpretation has been widely used in the literature, mainly in order to give a representation of reasoning in presence of incomplete and inconsistent information (see, e.g., [3, 14, 22]). What we are going to show here is that it also forms a proper setting for representing logic programs of a most general kind and for describing logics and semantics that characterize their behavior.

At its beginning, Logic Programming was based on an idea that the language of (classical) logic can be used directly as a programming language preserving at the same time the declarative meaning of the logical connectives. Thus, the rules of positive (Horn) programs can be also seen as ordinary logical formulas with the usual interpretation of the connectives involved. However, for program clauses involving negation as failure this correspondence between logical and procedural interpretation has been lost, since the latter cannot already be interpreted as classical logical formulas. What we are going to show, however, is that there is a logical interpretation of such program clauses that agrees with their procedural interpretation. To be more exact, we will see that they can be viewed as logical formulas of a certain four-valued logic. In this way the lost connection between Logic and Logic Programming is restored.

Our formalism will also bring us another important benefit, namely a clear separation between logical and nonmonotonic aspects of reasoning about logic programs. A most surprising general conclusion of this study obtained on the basis of this separation is that the distinction between various semantics for logic programs can be largely attributed to the difference in their underlying (monotonic) logical systems. In other words, most of these formalisms use the same nonmonotonic principle of 'jumping to conclusions', and the only difference between them consists in the logic used for deriving monotonic consequences. Moreover, in many cases the difference can even be reduced to that of the *language*, that is, to the difference in the connectives allowed for representing derivable information.

The connection between logic programming and nonmonotonic reasoning is usually established in the form of translation of logic programs into different nonmonotonic formalisms, such as default logic, circumscription or modal nonmonotonic logics. From the viewpoint of our framework, however, the connection between these two fields turns out to be even closer. On our approach program clauses can be directly identified with rules of our formalism, and in this way the reasoning about logic programs and their semantics can be seen as a (most simple) kind of nonmonotonic reasoning in general.

2 Biconsequence Relations and Four-Valued Inference

A logical formalism we suggest for representing logic programs is based on a four-valued entailment. More exactly, we are primarily interested in a four-valued inference based on a particular interpretation of the four truth-values suggested by Belnap in [2]. It amounts to their identification with the *subsets* of the set of classical truth-values $\{t, f\}$, allowing propositions to be not only true or false, but also neither true nor false or both true and false. The four truth-values $\top, \mathbf{t}, \mathbf{f}, \bot$ are identified, respectively, with $\{t, f\}, \{t\}, \{f\}$ and $\emptyset$. Thus, $\top$ means that a proposition is both true and false (i.e., contradictory), $\mathbf{t}$ means that it is 'classically' true (that is, true without being false), $\mathbf{f}$ means that it is classically false (without being true), while $\bot$ means that it is neither true nor false (undetermined). This interpretation allows us to see any 4-assignment as a *pair* of ordinary classical assignments, corresponding, respectively, to assignments of truth and falsity to propositions. To be more exact, for any 4-assignment ν (under the above interpretation) and any proposition A we can define the following two assignments:

$$\nu \models A \quad \text{iff} \quad t \in \nu(A) \qquad \nu \dashv A \quad \text{iff} \quad f \in \nu(A)$$

Clearly, the source 4-assignment can be restored from the above two valuations. This means that the "binary" representation is fairly general and does not restrict the set of possible four-valued interpretations. However, this representation has a significant heuristic power. In fact, it provides a natural connection, noticed already by Belnap, between four-valued reasoning and 'real' problems of commonsense reasoning and thereby the main reason for using a four-valued formalism in studying it.

2.1 Biconsequence Relations

Taking into account the above interpretation of the four truth-values, a four-valued reasoning in general can be seen as reasoning about truth and falsity of propositions, the only distinction from classical reasoning being that the assignments of truth and falsity are independent of each other. This leads us to the following construction that will provide a syntactic counterpart of such a reasoning.

By a *bisequent* we will mean a rule of the form $a : b \Vdash c : d$, where a, b, c, d are finite sets of propositions. The intended interpretation of such rules is

"If all propositions from a are true and all propositions from b are false, then one of the propositions from c is true or one of the propositions from d is false".

Accordingly, propositions from a and b will be called, respectively, *positive* and *negative premises*, while that from c and d - *positive* and *negative conclusions*. The following definition provides a primary characterization of such bisequents in accordance with their intended interpretation.

Definition 1. A *biconsequence relation* is a set of bisequents that is closed with respect to the following rules:

(Monotonicity) $\quad \dfrac{a : b \Vdash c : d}{a' : b' \Vdash c' : d'},\quad$ if $a \subseteq a', b \subseteq b', c \subseteq c', d \subseteq d'$.

(Pos. Reflexivity) $\qquad\qquad\qquad A : \Vdash A :$

(Neg. Reflexivity) $\qquad\qquad\qquad : A \Vdash : A$

(Pos. Cut) $\qquad \dfrac{a : b \Vdash A, c : d \quad A, a : b \Vdash c : d}{a : b \Vdash c : d}$

(Neg. Cut) $\qquad \dfrac{a : b \Vdash c : A, d \quad a : A, b \Vdash c : d}{a : b \Vdash c : d}$

A biconsequence relation can be seen as a 'doubled' version of an ordinary sequent calculus reflecting the independence of the truth and falsity assignments. As in the latter, we can extend the notion of a bisequent to arbitrary sets of propositions by accepting the following *compactness condition*:

(Compactness) $\qquad u : v \Vdash w : z \quad$ iff $\quad a : b \Vdash c : d,$

for some finite sets a, b, c, d such that $a \subseteq u, b \subseteq v, c \subseteq w$ and $d \subseteq z$.

The following definition describes 'canonical models' of biconsequence relations.

Definition 2. A pair of sets of propositions (u, v) is a *bimodel* of a biconsequence relation $\Vdash$ if

$$u : \overline{v} \nVdash \overline{u} : v.$$

It is easy to show that the above condition is equivalent to the closure requirement, given below. The requirement describes the sense in which our bimodels are *closed* with respect to the rules of a biconsequence relation.

If $a : b \Vdash c : d$ and $a \subseteq u, b \subseteq \bar{v}$, then either $c \cap u \neq \emptyset$ or $d \cap \bar{v} \neq \emptyset$.

Notice that any bimodel (u, v) can be identified with a four-valued interpretation by taking u to be the set of true propositions and v the set of propositions that are not false. Accordingly, a bimodel (u, v) will be called *consistent* if $u \subseteq v$, *complete* if $v \subseteq u$ and *classical* if $u = v$.

The following Representation Theorem can be used to show that biconsequence relations are adequate for their intended four-valued interpretation.[1]

Theorem 3 (Representation Theorem). *$a : b \Vdash c : d$ iff, for any bimodel (u, v), if $a \subseteq u$ and $b \subseteq \bar{v}$, then either $c \cap u \neq \emptyset$ or $d \cap \bar{v} \neq \emptyset$.*

Now we will consider the relation between biconsequence relations and logic programs. To begin with, bisequents will serve as direct representations of logic programming rules of a most general kind, namely ones involving disjunction and negation in their heads (see, e.g., [15] for a use of such rules). Thus, a rule

$$\textbf{not } D_1 \vee \ldots \vee \textbf{not } D_k \vee C_1 \vee \ldots \vee C_l \leftarrow A_1 \wedge \ldots A_m \wedge \textbf{not } B_1 \wedge \cdots \wedge \textbf{not } B_n$$

will be represented by a bisequent

$$A_1, \ldots, A_m : B_1, \ldots, B_n \Vdash C_1, \ldots, C_l : D_1, \ldots, D_k.$$

Note that the formalism also allows us to represent *constraints*, that is, program rules without heads.

If S is a set of bisequents corresponding to program clauses, then we will denote by $\Vdash_S$ the least biconsequence relation containing S. This biconsequence relation can be considered as a *logical theory* corresponding to a logic program. Clearly, this identification makes sense only if the rules characterizing biconsequence relations do not change the meaning of a program. In the case of normal programs, for example, if a rule $A \leftarrow B \wedge \textbf{not } C$ belongs to a program, then neither the rule $A \leftarrow B \wedge D \wedge \textbf{not } C$ nor the rule $A \leftarrow B \wedge \textbf{not } C \wedge \textbf{not } D$ should change the meaning of the program when added to it (as is required by Monotonicity). Similarly, we should always be able to add the rules of the form $A \leftarrow A$ to a program[2]. Note that the latter condition excludes, in fact, semantics based on Clark's completion as representing the meaning of a logic program. We will show, however, that for the majority of other semantics suggested for logic programs, this condition will hold.

Another question posed by this representation is whether the connectives $\wedge$, $\vee$, **not** and $\leftarrow$ appearing in program rules can be treated as logical connectives of some kind. A positive answer to this question will follow from the results stated below.

---

[1] The implication from right to left below is a suitable adaptation of 'Lindenbaum Lemma' for a four-valued case.

[2] See the normalform requirements in [13]. Cf. also [10].

2.2 Introducing Connectives

To begin with, note that our formalism, unlike the majority of other formalisms for many-valued reasoning, does not depend, as such, on a particular choice of four-valued connectives. Moreover, any such connective is expressible in it via introduction and elimination rules as in ordinary sequent calculi, the only distinction being that we have a pair of introduction rules and a pair of elimination rules corresponding to two premise sets and two conclusion sets, respectively (see [7] for details). In this study, however, we are not interested in a four-valued reasoning in its generality. Rather, we will be primarily interested in *what information such a reasoning can give us about ordinary, classical truth and falsity*, that is about **t** and **f**. In accordance with this, our first restriction will amount to the requirement that a four-valued reasoning must agree with a classical one in cases when the context does not involve inconsistent or incomplete information. As a precondition, we should restrict our attention to connectives that are *classical* in the sense that they give classical values when their arguments receive classical values **t** or **f**.

It turns out that there are four connectives that are jointly sufficient for defining all classical four-valued connectives.

$$
\begin{array}{ll}
\nu \models A \vee B \quad \text{iff} \quad \nu \models A \text{ or } \nu \models B & \nu \mathbin{=\!\!\mid} A \vee B \quad \text{iff} \quad \nu \mathbin{=\!\!\mid} A \text{ and } \nu \mathbin{=\!\!\mid} B \\
\nu \models {\sim} A \quad \text{iff} \quad \nu \mathbin{=\!\!\mid} A & \nu \mathbin{=\!\!\mid} {\sim} A \quad \text{iff} \quad \nu \mathbin{=\!\!\mid} A \\
\nu \models \neg A \quad \text{iff} \quad \nu \not\models A & \nu \mathbin{=\!\!\mid} \neg A \quad \text{iff} \quad \nu \not{\mathbin{=\!\!\mid}} A \\
\nu \models \mathbf{L} A \quad \text{iff} \quad \nu \models A & \nu \mathbin{=\!\!\mid} \mathbf{L} A \quad \text{iff} \quad \nu \not\models A
\end{array}
$$

The first is a well-known disjunction connective. Next, there are two unary connectives that can be seen as natural 'extensions' of a classical negation to the four-valued setting. Note that these are the only connectives that coincide with the classical negation on the classical truth-values and satisfy the Double Negation rule. The difference between the two is that the first one 'switches' the context between truth and falsity, while the second one retains the context. Accordingly, we will call $\sim$ and $\neg$ a *switching negation* and a *local negation*, respectively. Note also that each of them can be used together with the disjunction to define a natural *conjunction* connective:

$$A \wedge B \equiv {\sim}({\sim}A \vee {\sim}B) \text{ (or, equivalently, } \neg(\neg A \vee \neg B))$$

Finally, the unary connective **L** can be seen as a kind of a modal operator. It determines a (rudimentary) modal logic definable in the four-valued setting.

As has been said, all these connectives can be characterized syntactically using appropriate introduction and elimination rules.

It can be shown that all these connectives can be characterized using suitable introduction and elimination rules, given below. Just as in the classical case, the rules are easily discernible from the above definitions given the intended interpretation of the premises and conclusions of a bisequent.

Rules for disjunction

$$\frac{a, A : b \Vdash c : d \quad a, B : b \Vdash c : d}{a, A \vee B : b \Vdash c : d} \qquad \frac{a : b \Vdash c, A, B : d}{a : b \Vdash c, A \vee B : d}$$

$$\frac{a : b \Vdash c : d, A \quad a : b \Vdash c : d, B}{a : b \Vdash c : d, A \vee B} \qquad \frac{a : b, A, B \Vdash c : d}{a : b, A \vee B \Vdash c : d}$$

Rules for $\sim$

$$\frac{a, A : b \Vdash c : d}{a : \sim\! A, b \Vdash c : d} \qquad \frac{a : A, b \Vdash c : d}{a, \sim\! A : b \Vdash c : d}$$

$$\frac{a : b \Vdash c, A : d}{a : b \Vdash c : \sim\! A, d} \qquad \frac{a : b \Vdash c : A, d}{a : b \Vdash c, \sim\! A : d}$$

Rules for $\neg$

$$\frac{a, A : b \Vdash c : d}{a : b \Vdash \neg A, c : d} \qquad \frac{a : A, b \Vdash c : d}{a : b \Vdash c : \neg A, d}$$

$$\frac{a : b \Vdash c, A : d}{a, \neg A : b \Vdash c : d} \qquad \frac{a : b \Vdash c : A, d}{a : b, \neg A \Vdash c : d}$$

Rules for **L**

$$\frac{a, A : b \Vdash c : d}{a, \mathbf{L}A : b \Vdash c : d} \qquad \frac{a : b \Vdash A, c : d}{a : \mathbf{L}A, b \Vdash c : d}$$

$$\frac{a : b \Vdash A, c : d}{a : b \Vdash \mathbf{L}A, c : d} \qquad \frac{A, a : b \Vdash c : d}{a : b, A \Vdash c : \mathbf{L}A, d}$$

Just as for classical logic, the above rules can be used to show that any bisequent involving four-valued connectives is reducible, ultimately, to a set of bisequents containing atomic propositions only. We will call such bisequents *basic* ones. More generally, for any given language containing only 'truth-functional' four-valued connectives there is a one-to-one correspondence between biconsequence relations and their restrictions to the basic bisequents. Note that the latter can be considered as biconsequence relations on their own right, namely as biconsequence relations in the language without connectives. Such biconsequence relations will be also called *basic*.

Having the above connectives at our disposal, we can transform bisequents into more familiar rules.

For any set of propositions u, we will denote by $\sim\! u$ the set $\{\sim\! A \mid A \in u\}$. The notation $\neg u$ will have a similar meaning. In addition, for a finite set of propositions a, we will denote by $\bigvee(a)$ the disjunction of all propositions from a.

Lemma 4. *Any bisequent* $a : b \Vdash c : d$ *is equivalent to each of the following:*

(1) $$a, \sim b : \Vdash c, \sim d :$$

(2) $$\Vdash \bigvee(\neg a \cup \neg \sim b \cup c \cup \sim d) :$$

Bisequents of the form (1) can be considered as ordinary rules with multiple consequents. Moreover, since the set of positive conclusions can be replaced by their disjunction, we can transform bisequents into usual 'Tarski-type' rules using only the switching negation and disjunction. As is shown by Belnap and others, the resulting system will coincide with a (flat) theory of *relevant entailment*. Finally, using a local negation we can transform each bisequent into a formula (2) as in the classical sequent calculus. Moreover, it is easy to see that the disjunction and a local negation behave in an entirely classical way in this context. In this way a standard Hilbert type axiomatization of our logic can be constructed. This logic can be seen as an extension of the classical logic in the language $\{\vee, \neg\}$ by two new connectives, $\sim$ and **L** (see [7] for details).

The above transformation of bisequents into logical formulas shows, in particular, that if our representation of program clauses by bisequents is justified, then the connectives involved in program clauses can indeed be considered as *logical connectives* of our four-valued logic. To be more exact, $\vee$ and $\wedge$ can be seen, respectively, as four-valued disjunction and conjunction, $\leftarrow$ corresponds in this sense to material implication, while **not** can be identified with the switching negation $\sim$. In this way, logic program clauses can, after all, be considered as logical formulas.

Remark. According to the view advocated in this work, a common understanding of **not** as 'negation by failure' does not reflect the *meaning* of the connective, but rather a particular (nonmonotonic) mechanism of obtaining negative assumptions, a mechanism that we will describe in subsequent sections. In other words, on our view the *logical* (declarative) meaning of **not** is given by its four-valued interpretation, while the 'negation by failure' principle says, roughly, that if a certain procedure of proving A fails, then we should assume **not** A 'by failure'.

3 Biconsequence Relations Circumscribed

In this section we will give a description of the nonmonotonic construction providing a mechanism for 'jumping to conclusions' in the context of biconsequence relations. The basic idea behind the construction is the well-known *minimization principle* according to which truth and falsity of a proposition should be determined on the basis of *minimal* models satisfying a given body of knowledge or beliefs. This principle of nonmonotonic reasoning has already a long history that begins with McCarthy's Circumscription, Reiter's Closed World Assumption and

Minker's Generalized CWA. A modification of the principle appropriate to our 'bicomponent' context was suggested, in fact, by Teodor Przymusinski in [20] and subsequent papers (see also [25]), though our description will be somewhat different from that given there. It amounts to a relativization of the principle with respect to negative information.

The notion of a minimal model used by the minimization principle is based on the ordering of models with respect to inclusion with respect to propositional *atoms* that hold in them. Consequently, in the rest of this section we will consider only basic biconsequence relations. Note, however, that this does not restrict the generality of our approach, since, as we said earlier, any biconsequence relation containing four-valued connectives is equivalent to some basic biconsequence relation.

A bimodel (u, v) of a basic biconsequence relation will be called *positively minimal* if there is no bimodel (u_1, v) such that $u_1 \subset u$. Now a *Positive Minimization Principle* says that only positively minimal models should matter in determining truth-values of propositions. Accordingly, the *circumscription* of a biconsequence relation $\Vdash$ will be defined as a biconsequence relation $\Vdash^c$ determined by positively minimal bimodels of $\Vdash$.

Definition 5. $a : b \Vdash^c c : d$ iff $c \cap u \neq \emptyset$ or $d \cap \overline{v} \neq \emptyset$, for any positively minimal bimodel (u, v) of $\Vdash$ such that $a \subseteq u$ and $b \subseteq \overline{v}$.

The following proposition (proved in [7]) provides a syntactic characterization of circumscription.

Theorem 6. *If $\Vdash^c$ is a circumscription of $\Vdash$, then $a : b \Vdash^c c : d$ if and only if $: b, b' \Vdash c, c' : d, d'$, for any b', c', d' such that $: b' \Vdash c', \bigwedge a : d'$.*

As can be seen, the circumscription of a biconsequence relation is uniquely determined by bisequents without positive premises that belong to it. Moreover, it is shown in [7] that $\Vdash^c$ can even be characterized as the greatest biconsequence relation having the same bisequents of such form as $\Vdash$.

Finally, note that if $\Vdash$ is represented using the corresponding logical formulas, then $\Vdash^c$ can be described as a result of circumscribing $\Vdash$ with respect to atomic propositions that are not in the scope of $\sim$ (see [20]). In other words, $\Vdash^c$ can be seen as a result of a *parameterized* circumscription that does not vary negative propositions.

3.1 Circumscription and GPPE

As we said, the circumscription of a biconsequence relation is uniquely determined by bisequents without positive premises that belong to it. We will show now that this feature of the circumscribed biconsequence relation constitutes a logical basis of the *partial deduction (or evaluation) principle* for logic programs (see [10, 23]).

The *Generalized Principle of Partial Evaluation (GPPE)* can be easily formulated for biconsequence relations in general and amounts to the following:

If S is a set of bisequents, replace a bisequent $A, a : b \Vdash c : d$ by a set of bisequents $a, a_i : b, b_i \Vdash c, c_i : d, d_i$, for every bisequent $a_i : b_i \Vdash c_i, A : d_i$ from S containing A among its positive conclusions.

GPPE can be used to eliminate bisequents containing positive premises. It has been shown to be valid for a number of semantics for logic programs. It will also turn to be valid for all the semantics generated by our general construction. This is due to the following result showing that GPPE preserves generated circumscribed biconsequence relations.

Theorem 7. *If S is a set of bisequents and S' is obtained from S by an application of GPPE, then $\Vdash_S^c = \Vdash_{S'}^c$.*

The semantic construction described later in this paper is based on a certain extension of the circumscribed biconsequence relation corresponding to a program. Consequently, programs generating the same circumscribed biconsequence relation will be always assigned the same semantics. In fact, GPPE can be seen as a general syntactic principle characterizing this feature of semantics for logic programs, a clear sign that a semantics is constructed 'on top' of the circumscribed program.

3.2 Finite Case

Our next result shows that in the case of *finite* biconsequence relations only bisequents of the 'constraint' form $a : b \Vdash : d$ need to be added to a biconsequence relation in order to produce its circumscription[3].

Theorem 8. *If $\Vdash$ is a finite biconsequence relation, then $\Vdash^c$ is the least biconsequence relation containing $\Vdash$ and all bisequents of the form $a : b \Vdash : d$ from $\Vdash^c$.*

The above result can be further strengthened for particular kinds of biconsequence relations. Thus, the circumscription of *disjunctive* biconsequence relations, that is, biconsequence relations generated by bisequents without negative conclusions, is determined only by bisequents of the form $a : \Vdash : d$ and $: b \Vdash c :$.

Corollary 9. *If $\Vdash$ is a finite disjunctive biconsequence relation, then $\Vdash^c$ is the least biconsequence relation containing all bisequents of the form $a : \Vdash : d$ and $: b \Vdash c :$ from $\Vdash^c$.*

If a biconsequence relation is *quasi-normal* (that is, corresponds to a normal program with constraints), then it can be shown that its circumscription is already determined by adding bisequents of the form $A : \Vdash : d$. The following results give the conditions for including such bisequents into the circumscription.

---

[3] A suitable counterexample can be produced (see [7]) showing that the finiteness restriction is essential for this result.

Corollary 10. *1. For a quasi-normal biconsequence relation* $\Vdash$, *A* $:\Vdash^c:$ *d if and only if* $: b \Vdash$ *or* $b \cap d \neq \emptyset$, *for any b such that* $: b \Vdash A:$.

2. If $\Vdash$ *is a normal biconsequence relation, then A* $:\Vdash^c:$ *d if and only if* $: \overline{d} \nVdash A:$.

The above results suggest a general method of circumscribing a finite biconsequence relation. To this end we must find all bisequents without positive premises that belong to $\Vdash$ and add to them all bisequents of an appropriate constraint type that do not change the former set of bisequents. A procedure of constructing circumscription along these lines, based on generalized Clark's completion, is described in [8].

4 Coherence

Belnap's interpretation of the truth-values can help us once more, this time in determining some further plausible constraints on biconsequence relations.

The main benefit of Belnap's interpretation of the four truth-values is that it allows us to use four-valued reasoning as a general framework for logical reasoning in the presence of inconsistent or incomplete information. However, though it may sound paradoxically, this generality has a weak side in that it completely ignores the distinction between ordinary truth and falsity, on the one hand, and inconsistency and incompleteness, on the other. All the four truth-values have an equal status in the context of such a reasoning. Consequently, what seems to be missing is a principle that would allow us to infer 'classical' information in the framework of biconsequence relations.

The relevant principle is provided by a requirement that *provable truth and refutability must coincide with provable classical truth and falsity*. If this condition holds for a biconsequence relation, the information we can *infer* using it will be of a usual classical kind.

Biconsequence relations satisfying this requirement will be called coherent. The strength of the requirement, however, can vary depending on what propositional formulas are susceptible to coherence. Generally speaking, the more expressive the language is, the more strong is the corresponding constraint imposed by the requirement.

In what follows, by a *language* $\mathcal{L}$ we will mean a subset of classical connectives and by $\mathcal{L}$-propositions propositions constructed from atoms using connectives from $\mathcal{L}$. Then a rule that holds for a biconsequence relation will be called *logical in a language* $\mathcal{L}$ if it does not involve explicit occurrences of connectives, but is valid for substitutions of arbitrary $\mathcal{L}$-propositions for propositional atoms.

Definition 11. A biconsequence relation will be called $\mathcal{L}$-*coherent* if it satisfies the following two logical rules with respect to $\mathcal{L}$:

$$(PT) \quad \frac{\Vdash A:}{:A \Vdash} \qquad\qquad (PnT) \quad \frac{A:\Vdash}{\Vdash: A}$$

The influence of the underlying language $\mathcal{L}$ amounts to imposing language restrictions on the applicability of the coherence rules. As we will see, various semantics for logic programs can be obtained by varying these restrictions.

5 Nonmonotonic Completion and Nonmonotonic Semantics

Finally we have all we need in order to describe a nonmonotonic entailment and semantics generated by a given biconsequence relation. In fact, both arise from a combination of the two reasoning principles described earlier, namely coherence and circumscription. To be more exact, we will consider a biconsequence relation obtained from $\Vdash$ by first circumscribing it and then adding the coherence rules. As we will see, the resulting biconsequence relation embodies all information that can be nonmonotonically inferred from the latter.

Definition 12. 1. A *nonmonotonic $\mathcal{L}$-completion* of a biconsequence relation $\Vdash$ (denoted by $^c\Vdash^c$) is the least $\mathcal{L}$-coherent biconsequence relation containing $\Vdash^c$.

2. A *nonmonotonic $\mathcal{L}$-semantics* of a biconsequence relation $\Vdash$, $SEM_{\Vdash}^{\mathcal{L}}$, is a pair of sets of propositions in the language $\mathcal{L}$ that are, respectively, provable and refutable in the nonmonotonic $\mathcal{L}$-completion:

$$SEM_{\Vdash}^{\mathcal{L}} = \langle \{A \mid {}^c\Vdash^c A : \}, \{A \mid A : {}^c\Vdash^c \} \rangle.$$

Note that propositions that belong to the first component of SEM are both provably true and provably non-false in the nonmonotonic completion (that is classically true), while that from the second component will be provably classically false.

'Historical' note. As a matter of fact, the above construction of the nonmonotonic completion and semantics have arisen as a certain modification of Teodor Przymusinski's earlier, non-modal construction of stationary completion and semantics, suggested in [20]. Actually, the very formalism used by Przymusinski in that paper was very similar to that of a four-valued logic (see below). The relevant modifications made to Przymusinski's construction could be summarized as follows:

- The underlying language was allowed to vary in order to characterize alternative semantics for logic programs (in Przymusinski's construction such a variation was achieved through a change in non-monotonic principles used).
- The fixed-point construction of the stationary completion was 'splitted' into two consecutive stages: circumscription and coherence. As a result, the fixed-point characterization of the completion was replaced by coherence closure of the circumscribed consequence relation. This idea of performing circumscription 'in one step' with subsequent closure with respect to coherence rules was 'borrowed', in fact, from [25].

Recall that for a set of bisequents S, $\Vdash_S$ denotes the least biconsequence relation containing S. The latter represents a logical theory corresponding to S. Now for all semantics we will consider in this study, S and $\Vdash_S$ (viewed as a set of bisequents) will have the same semantics. Consequently we will use SEM_S to denote $SEM_{\Vdash_S}$.

6 General Case: WFS, D-WFS and Static Semantics

If our language contains no connectives, the coherence rules are reducible to the case of singular atomic premises or conclusions. Even in this case the resulting semantics gives us the well-founded semantics for normal logic programs.

The following theorem holds for the language without connectives, that is for the case when the coherence rules (and the nonmonotonic semantics!) are restricted to atomic propositions. This theorem is actually a consequence of more general representation results given later in the paper.

Proposition 13. *Let S be a set of 'normal' basic bisequents of the form $a : b \Vdash A :$. Then $SEM_S^\emptyset$ coincides with the well-founded semantics of S.*

Though appropriate for normal logic programs, such a semantics is surely too weak for disjunctive programs, since it ignores, in effect, a disjunctive information. Hence, a natural step is to extend the language at least by adding disjunction.

If the language contains disjunction, the coherence PT is already equivalent to the following structural rule (see [7]):

$$\frac{\Vdash a :}{: a \Vdash}$$

though PnT is still reducible to its singular variant. It turns out that for disjunctive programs the resulting semantics will coincide with the semantics D-WFS suggested by Brass and Dix [11].

D-WFS is definable as the least semantics that is invariant under a number of "Reduction & Elimination" transformations of a disjunctive program. It turns out that these transformations correspond to appropriate rules and conditions in our construction:

- *Elimination of Tautologies*: elimination of program clauses containing common atoms in heads and bodies. This transformation can be seen as a 'reductive' version of the Reflexivity axiom for biconsequence relations.
- *Elimination of Non-Minimal Rules*: if a rule $a \leftarrow b, \text{not } c$ belongs to a program, then all rules of the form $a, a' \leftarrow b, b', \text{not } c, \text{not } c'$ can be eliminated. This is a reductive version of the Monotonicity rule for biconsequence relation.
- The *Generalized Principle of Partial Evaluation* (GPPE) allows to eliminate positive premises in bodies of program rules. As we mentioned above, the justification of this principle lies in the fact that the circumscription of a biconsequence relation is determined only by bisequents without positive premises, so the relevant transformation preserves the resulting nonmonotonic completion.
- *Positive Reduction*: if an atom A does not belong to heads of clauses of a program, then all occurrences of A in negative premises can be eliminated. It is easy to see that this principle is a consequence of the coherence rule PnT.

– *Negative Reduction*: If $a_0 \leftarrow$ belongs to a program, then all rules of the form $a \leftarrow b, \mathbf{not}\, c$ such that $a_0 \subseteq c$ can be eliminated. Clearly, this principle is a consequence of the above 'disjunctive' coherence rule.

The above correspondences provide a basis for the equivalence result stated below.

Theorem 14. *If S is a set of bisequents of the form $a : b \Vdash c :$, then $SEM_S^{\vee}$ coincides with the Disjunctive Well-Founded Semantics (D-WFS) of S.*

Brass and Dix have shown that the construction of the D-WFS can be given in the form of a *confluent calculus* in which the above reduction rules can be applied in any order. It turns out that the construction of the nonmonotonic $\vee$-completion satisfies a similar confluence property, that is, the coherence rules can be applied both before and 'in the course of' circumscription. As a result of the correspondence between D-WFS and the $\vee$-completion of a program, the relevant reduction calculus of Brass and Dix can be used as a method of computing this semantics. In other words, this reduction calculus provides a fairly general way of transforming our purely declarative description into a computation procedure.

The above semantics can be also shown to be closely connected with Przymusinski's *static semantics* of general logic programs [21] (cf. [12]). In an accompanying paper [9] we present a detailed description of this semantics. It is shown there that the static semantics of general logic programs can also be represented as an instance of our general construction, namely as a closure of a circumscribed biconsequence relation with respect to the following 'coherence' rule:

$$\frac{a^1 :\Vdash c :}{: c \Vdash : a^1}$$

where a^1 is either empty or contains one proposition only. As can be easily seen, the above rule is stronger than $\vee$-coherence, but is weaker than $\{\vee, \neg\}$-coherence (see below). Still, it does not correspond to some $\mathcal{L}$-coherence rule in our sense.

The following example from [21] is especially interesting in analyzing expressive capabilities and restrictions of the static semantics.

$$Goto\_Australia \vee Goto\_Europe$$
$$Goto\_Both \leftarrow Goto\_Australia \wedge Goto\_Europe$$
$$Save\_Money \leftarrow \mathbf{not}\, Goto\_Both$$
$$Cancel\_Reservation \leftarrow \mathbf{not}\, Goto\_Australia$$
$$Cancel\_Reservation \leftarrow \mathbf{not}\, Goto\_Europe$$

The following bisequent is obtained by circumscription:

(*) $Goto\_Australia \wedge Goto\_Europe : \Vdash,$

while the next bisequent is a consequence of the last two clauses of the program:

$: Goto\_Australia \wedge Goto\_Europe \Vdash Cancel\_Reservation :$

However, the 'static' coherence rule is inapplicable to (*), because the relevant formula contains a conjunction. Consequently, both the static semantics and D-WFS say that we are not going to both Europe and Australia (and hence will save money), but still do not say that we should cancel reservation, as is predicted, for example, by the perfect semantics for this (stratified) program. As can be seen, this is because these semantics do not use a negative conjunctive information. The situation can be compared with the distinction between GCWA and Extended GCWA (see [17]), where the latter, while not the former, allows to infer new negative disjunctive clauses (negations of conjunctions). More expressive semantics, described below, allow to overcome this limitation.

7 Stationary Semantics and Stable Classes

Adding conjunction to the language of formulas susceptible to coherence gives a stronger, 'multiple' variant of the negative coherence rule PnT:

$$\frac{a : \Vdash}{\Vdash : a}$$

In this way we arrive at Przymusinski's stationary semantics for logic programs. In fact, in order to account for this semantics in its different versions, we only need to extend the class of formulas admissible for coherence rules. Without going into details at this point, we will mention only the main correspondences.

- $\{\wedge, \vee\}$-completion corresponds to the notion of a stationary completion from [20] without the Disjunctive Inference Rule, DIR. This language restriction corresponds to Przymusinski's 'official' definition that involved only *pure* positive or negative disjunctions[4]. In fact, the formalism used by Przymusinski in that paper is almost identical with the four-valued logic in the language $\{\vee, \neg, \sim\}$, the only addition being that our switching negation $\sim$ (that corresponds to **not** in Przymusinski's formalism) satisfies the rule of double negation. Actually, the language of [20] does not allow for iterations of **not** at all and treats formulas of the form **not** A (where A is a classical proposition in the language $\{\vee, \neg\}$) as new propositional atoms.

- $\{\vee, \wedge, \mathbf{L}\}$-completion roughly corresponds to the version of the stationary semantics from [20] that includes the Disjunctive Inference Rule. In particular, the two versions of the rule DIR used in [18] to define the stationary semantics

$$\frac{\Vdash a, b :}{: a \Vdash b :} \qquad \frac{a, b : \Vdash}{a : \Vdash : b}$$

turn out to be equivalent to the two coherence rules in the language $\{\vee, \wedge, \mathbf{L}\}$.

- $\{\vee, \neg\}$-coherence will give us a version of stationary semantics described in [21] using a modal representation. The two coherence rules in the language $\{\vee, \neg\}$ are already equivalent, and each of them amounts to the following structural rule:

$$\frac{a : \Vdash c :}{: c \Vdash : a}$$

---

[4] Unfortunately, Przymusinski's claim that this restriction is unnecessary turns out to be incorrect (see below).

As the following example shows, this semantics is stronger than the $\{\vee, \wedge\}$-semantics even for disjunctive programs.

$$
\begin{array}{ll}
\Vdash A, C : & : A, C \Vdash D : \\
: C \Vdash A : & : A, D \Vdash A, D : \\
: A \Vdash C : & : A, D \Vdash B, D : \\
: A, C \Vdash B : & : A, B \Vdash D :
\end{array}
$$

In the $\{\vee, \wedge\}$-completion of this biconsequence relation the following sets of propositional atoms form positive parts of bimodels: $\{C\}, \{C, D\}, \{A\}, \{A, B, C\}$. On the other hand, the $\{\vee, \neg\}$-completion has only two bimodels, $(\{A\}, \{A\})$ and $(\{C, D\}, \{C, D\})$ (and hence coincides with the full classical completion – see below). As a result, the $\{\vee, \neg\}$-completion of the corresponding biconsequence relation contains $\Vdash A, D$: and B : $\Vdash$, though neither belong to the relevant $\{\vee, \wedge\}$-completion. Hence the former semantics is more informative both positively and negatively.

Surprisingly enough, the language $\{\vee, \neg\}$ turns out to be also appropriate for a semantics of *stable classes* for normal programs suggested by Baral and Subrahmanian [1].

Stable classes are defined as sets of sets of propositional atoms S satisfying the following condition:

$$
S = \{\mathbf{F}(s) \mid s \in S\},
$$

where $\mathbf{F}$ is a *Gelfond-Lifschitz operator* giving the least model of the corresponding Gelfond-Lifschitz transformation of a normal program. The above condition is equivalent to the following two:

(i) If $s \in S$, then $\mathbf{F}(s) \in S$;
(ii) IF $s \in S$, then there exists $u \in S$ such that $s = \mathbf{F}(u)$.

The correspondence between stable classes and our construction is based on an easily established fact (cf. [4]) that a pair (u, v) is a positively minimal bimodel of a normal program if and only if $u = \mathbf{F}(v)$. In addition, the above rule of $\{\vee, \neg\}$-coherence amounts to a semantic requirement that a negative part of any bimodel should be also a positive part of some bimodel, that is, if (u, v) is a bimodel, then there exists w such that (v, w) is also a bimodel. It is easy to see that applying this requirement to positively minimal bimodels, we obtain precisely the above condition (ii). In other words, stable classes can be considered as generated by sets of positively minimal bimodels satisfying the above semantic requirement. This allows to establish a one-to-one correspondence between stable classes of a normal program and $\{\vee, \neg\}$-coherent biconsequence relations including $\Vdash^c$.

Theorem 15. *Let S be a finite set of normal basic sequents. Then positive components of bimodels of any $\{\vee, \neg\}$-coherent biconsequence relation including $\Vdash^c_S$ form a stable class and any stable class of S is determined in this way by some $\{\vee, \neg\}$-coherent biconsequence relation extending $\Vdash^c_S$.*

Thus, our construction can serve as a natural generalization of the stable class semantics to more general programs. Moreover, since the nonmonotonic completion of $\Vdash_S$ is also the least coherent extension of $\Vdash_S^c$, we obtain that SEM_S in this case contains exactly those propositions that hold in all stable classes.

Remark. Baral and Subrahmanian considered some 'preferred' stable classes as determining the meaning of a logic program. In fact, it is possible to describe the corresponding preference ordering in terms of the corresponding ordering on maximal coherent extensions of $\Vdash_S^c$. This indicates a possible direction in which our basic construction could be extended. As it seems, both this and similar 'preference-based' approaches can be accounted for in terms of some further *maximization principles* imposed on the nonmonotonic completion.

In many respects, the $\{\vee, \neg\}$-semantics is the largest semantics in our classification having all the good properties a reasonable semantics could have. For example, the $\{\vee, \neg\}$-completion still enjoys the confluence property (see above), and hence the coherence rules can be applied before and in the course of circumscription. In addition, such a semantics always exists for disjunctive logic programs. Unfortunately, this semantics still does not capture some plausible desiderata suggested for logic programs. For example, in the case of stratified disjunctive programs, it is weaker than the perfect semantics. However, stronger semantics that we are going to consider below will already lack the virtue of existence for any disjunctive logic program.

8 Invariant Completion and Partial Stable Semantics

An interesting additional requirement that can be imposed on possible connectives is that they should behave similarly with respect to truth and non-falsity (after all, both have the same meaning for us in the classical case). Making precise this requirement would lead us to the class of connectives we call *invariant* (see [7]). It turns out that invariant connectives are precisely connectives that are expressible via $\{\vee, \neg, \sim\}$.

The coherence rules in the the language $\{\vee, \neg, \sim\}$ amount to the following structural rule:

(Invariance)
$$\frac{a : b \Vdash c : d}{d : c \Vdash b : a}$$

The rule corresponds to a semantic requirement that if (u, v) is a bimodel, then (v, u) is also a bimodel. The following result shows that the corresponding nonmonotonic completion (that we will call *invariant*) gives us a generalization of the partial stable semantics for normal programs from [19].

Theorem 16. *If P is a normal program, then consistent bimodels of the invariant completion of $\Vdash_P$ are exactly partial stable models of P.*

Przymusinski has also suggested a generalization of partial stable semantics for disjunctive programs in [19]. The resulting *disjunctive partial stable semantics* turns out to be very similar to ours. Thus, the following result shows that consistent bimodels of the invariant completion are disjunctive partial stable models.

Theorem 17. *If P is a disjunctive program, then any consistent bimodel of the invariant completion of $\Vdash_P$ is a disjunctive partial stable model of P.*

However, the following simple example demonstrates that the two semantics do not coincide:
$$\Vdash A, B: \qquad : A \Vdash A:$$

The invariant completion of this program contains a single consistent bimodel $(\{A\}, \{A\})$ (that corresponds to a stable model $\{A, \sim B\}$), while Przymusinski's semantics accepts also $\{B\}$ (without negative literals) as another disjunctive partial stable model. Thus, the disjunctive partial stable semantics is somewhat weaker than ours.

Using the results of Przymusinski stated in [19], it can be shown that in the case of disjunctive programs both the above semantics subsume the perfect semantics for stratified disjunctive programs. Unfortunately, the following example given in [19] shows that they are not always consistent even for disjunctive programs:

$$Work \lor Tired \lor Sleep$$
$$Work \leftarrow \textbf{not}\, Tired$$
$$Sleep \leftarrow \textbf{not}\, Work$$
$$Tired \leftarrow \textbf{not}\, Sleep$$

The static, and even stable class semantics for this program contains $Work \lor Tired \lor Sleep$, and $\neg Work \lor \neg Tired \lor \neg Sleep$. However, the corresponding circumscribed biconsequence relation contains no invariant bimodels and hence it does not have a consistent $\{\lor, \neg, \sim\}$-completion. It also does not have disjunctive partial stable models.

9 Classical Completion and Stable Semantics

It can be shown that coherence with respect to the full language of classical connectives reduces a biconsequence relation to an ordinary classical sequent calculus: any bisequent $a : b \Vdash c : d$ in this case will be equivalent to $a, d : \Vdash b.c : $, while all our connectives will be reduced to their classical counterparts. As a result, the bimodels of the classical completion of a biconsequence relation $\Vdash$ are precisely positively minimal classical bimodels of $\Vdash$. As was shown in [5], such objects coincide with stable models, or answer sets, of logic programs of a most general kind (see, e.g., [15, 16]). As an immediate consequence of this fact we have

Theorem 18. *Stable models of any program S coincide with bimodels of the nonmonotonic completion of* $\Vdash_S$ *in the full classical language.*

Thus, SEM in the classical language is precisely the stable semantics of logic programs, since it contains all the propositions that are, respectively, true and false in all stable models. Thus, both brave and skeptical reasoning with respect to stable models amount, in fact, to a classical reasoning in the nonmonotonic completion. In other words, after performing circumscription of the source biconsequence relation, we can simply identify $\sim$ with $\neg$, delete **L** and treat the resulting biconsequence relation as an ordinary classical sequent calculus. Propositions provable in this sequent calculus will be exactly ones that belong to the stable semantics, while propositions that are consistent with respect to it will coincide with that holding in at least one stable model.

Finally, note that the stable semantics constitutes a limit case – no nontrivial extension of it is possible in the framework of our general construction.

10 Conclusions and Further Issues

This paper is a part of a broader study that aims to build a general formalism for nonmonotonic reasoning. What we see as the main advantage of this formalism is that it allows us to provide *a clear separation of logical and nonmonotonic aspects of nonmonotonic reasoning.* As a result of this separation, we have 'discerned' a logic appropriate for logic programs, and thereby restored the connection between Logic and Logic Programming. Moreover, it has turned out that common kinds of nonmonotonic reasoning are reducible, in effect, to different kinds of logical reasoning in a certain well-defined (nonmonotonic) extension of the source theory. In a sense, in this paper we have described only *one* general nonmonotonic semantics, more specific semantics being merely partial cases obtained by restricting the underlying language.

Among other things, this representation of various nonmonotonic semantics as species of one general semantics suggests an entirely different, more tolerant, view of these semantics. Instead of the question what is the best semantics in all cases, we can consider the question what expressive means are most appropriate for a particular reasoning task. On this view, the main question is an acceptable trade-off between expressive means and computational costs for a particular context of reasoning. On any choice, we are dealing, in effect, with the same semantics.

As to the computational costs, our construction shows that the computation of nonmonotonic semantics involves only one nontrivial step, namely circumscription. All the rest is a rule-based monotonic reasoning. It should be clear, however, that this issue deserves further study.

Among the vast number of issues and problems that still need to be studied about our formalism, we want to mention only two.

One major issue is what logical rules are admissible or appropriate to use *before* circumscription. If a logical rule is admissible in this sense, it may greatly facilitate the computation of the nonmonotonic completion. Thus, the correspondence between our construction and stationary semantics can be used to show that $\{\vee, \neg\}$-coherence rules can also be used before (as well as in the course of) circumscription. The confluence property of D-WFS (see [11]) is a special case of this fact. Moreover, some of the suggested semantics for logic programs can be obtained by imposing certain logical rules on the source biconsequence relation, e.g., Schlipf's stable-by-case semantics [24] (see [4] for details). In addition, the issue is intimately connected with some current approaches to *nonmonotonic revision* of nonmonotonic theories (see, e.g., [27]), according to which in cases when the resulting nonmonotonic semantics is inconsistent, we can extend the source program by new rules (e.g., contrapositions of some of the existing rules) that would restore consistency.

Another issue is that the nonmonotonic semantics can be strengthened in many cases by considering only some 'preferred' bimodels of the nonmonotonic completion. This approach has been intensively studied, mainly in the context of normal programs, but see, e.g., [26], where it is applied to disjunctive programs. As we already mentioned in discussing the stable class semantics, many such constructions can be accounted for in our framework by applying some general *maximization principles* to the nonmonotonic completion.

Finally, there is a fairly general way of 'lifting' our formalism to a formalism that subsumes classical inference. In this way we will obtain a representation of extended logic programs containing a second, 'classical' negation, as well as of such nonmonotonic formalisms as default logic and various modal nonmonotonic logics. In addition, the approach allows to capture some recent attempts to 'transfer' various semantics for logic program to broader contexts. This is the main subject of the second part of this study [6].

References

1. C. Baral and V.S. Subrahmanian (1992) Stable and extension class theory for logic programs and default logics. *J. of Automated Reasoning*, **8**: 345–366.

2. N.D. Belnap, Jr. (1977) A useful four-valued logic. In M. Dunn and G. Epstein (eds.) *Modern Uses of Multiple-Valued Logic*, D. Reidel, Dordrecht, pp. 8–41.

3. H.A. Blair and V.S. Subrahmanian (1989) Paraconsistent logic programming. *Theoretical Computer Science*, **68**: 135–154.

4. A. Bochman (1995) Default consequence relations as a logical framework for logic programs. *Proc. Third International Conference on Logic Programming and Nonmonotonic Reasoning, LPNMR'95*, Lecture Notes in Artificial Intelligence, 928, pp. 245–258.

5. A. Bochman (1995) On bimodal nonmonotonic logics and their unimodal and nonmodal equivalents. *Proc. IJCAI'95*, pp. 1518–1524.

6. A. Bochman (1996) Biconsequence relations for nonmonotonic reasoning. In L.C. Aiello, J. Doyle, and S.C. Shapiro (eds.) *Principles of Knowledge Representation and Reasoning: Proc. Fifth Int. Conference (KR'96)*, Morgan Kaufmann, San Francisco, CA.

7. A. Bochman (1995) What is a four-valued reasoning and how it can be nonmonotonic. (submitted)

8. A. Bochman (1996) A logical foundation for logic programming. (in preparation)

9. A. Bochman (1996) A study of Przymusinski's static semantics. (in preparation)

10. S. Brass and J. Dix (1995) Disjunctive semantics based upon partial and bottom-up evaluation. In L. Sterling (ed.) *Proc. 12th Int. Conf. on Logic Programming*, Tokyo, MIT Press, pp. 199–213.

11. S. Brass and J. Dix (1996) Characterizing D-WFS: confluence and iterated GCWA. In J.J. Alferes, L.M. Pereira, and E. Orlowska (eds.) *Logics in Artificial Intelligence (JELIA'96)*, LNCS 1126, Springer, pp. 268–283.

12. S. Brass, J. Dix and T. Przymusinski (1996) A comparison of static semantics and d-wfs. Technical report TR 2/96, University of Koblenz, Department of Computer Science.

13. J. Dix (1995) A classification theory of semantics of normal logic programs: II. Weak properties. *Fundamenta Informaticae*, **22**: 257–288.

14. M.C. Fitting (1989) Bilattices and the theory of truth. *J. of Philosophical Logic*, **18**: 225–256.

15. K. Inoue and C. Sakama (1994) On positive occurrences of negation as failure. In *Proc. 4th Int. Conf. on Principles of Knowledge Representation and Reasoning, KR'94*, Morgan Kauffman, San Francisco, CA., 1994, pages 293–304.

16. V. Lifschitz (1994) Minimal belief and negation as failure. *Artificial Intelligence*, 70:53–72, 1994.

17. J. Lobo, J. Minker and A. Rajasekar (1992) *Foundations of Disjunctive Logic Programming*, The MIT Press, 1992.

18. M. Müller and J. Dix (1993) Implementing semantics of disjunctive logic programs using fringes and abstract properties. In *Proc. Second Int. Workshop on Logic Programming and Nonmonotonic Reasoning*, L.M. Pereira and A. Nerode (eds.), MIT Press, Cambridge, MA, 1993, pages 43–59.

19. T.C. Przymusinski (1991) Stable semantics for disjunctive programs *New Generation Computing*, **9**: 401–424.

20. T.C. Przymusinski (1991) Semantics of disjunctive logic programs and deductive databases. In *Proc. Second Int. Conf. on Deductive and Object-Oriented Databases, DOOD'91*, Springer Verlag, pp. 85–107.

21. T.C. Przymusinski (1995) Static semantics for normal and disjunctive logic programs. *Annals of Mathematics and Artificial Intelligence*

22. C. Sakama and K. Inoue (1995) Paraconsistent stable semantics for disjunctive logic programs. *J. of Logic and Computation*, **5**: 265–285.

23. C. Sakama and H. Seki (1994) Partial deduction of disjunctive logic programs: A declarative approach. In L. Fribourg, F. Turini (eds.) *Logic Program Synthesis and Transformation - Meta-Programming in Logic*, LNCS 883, pp. 170–181.

24. J. S. Schlipf (1992). Formalizing a logic for logic programming. *Annals of Mathematics and Artificial Intelligence* 5:279–302.

25. L. Y. Yuan and J.-H. You (1993) Autoepistemic circumscription and logic programming *J. of Automated Reasoning* 10: 143–160.

26. J.-H. You and L. Y. Yuan (1994) A three-valued semantics for deductive databases and logic programs. *J. of Computer and System Sciences*, **49**: 334–361.

27. C. Witteveen and W. van der Hoek (1995) Revision by communication. *Proc. Third International Conference on Logic Programming and Nonmonotonic Reasoning, LPNMR'95*, Lecture Notes in Artificial Intelligence, 928, pp. 189–202.

A New Logical Characterisation
of Stable Models and Answer Sets

David Pearce

German Research Centre for Artificial Intelligence (DFKI),
Stuhlsatzenhausweg 3, 66123 Saarbrücken, Germany,
E-mail: pearce@dfki.uni-sb.de

Abstract. This paper relates inference in extended logic programming with nonclassical, nonmonotonic logics. We define a nonmonotonic logic, called *equilibrium logic*, based on the least constructive extension, $N2$, of the intermediate logic of "here-and-there". We show that on logic programs equilibrium logic coincides with the inference operation associated with the stable model and answer set semantics of Gelfond and Lifschitz. We thereby obtain a very simple characterisation of answer set semantics as a form of minimal model reasoning in $N2$, while equilibrium logic itself provides a natural generalisation of this semantics to arbitrary theories. We discuss briefly some consequences and applications of this result.

1 Introduction

By contrast with the minimal model style of reasoning characteristic of several approaches to the semantics of logic programs, the stable model semantics of Gelfond and Lifschitz [8] was, from the outset, much closer in spirit to the styles of reasoning found in other well-known nonmonotonic logics, such as default and autoepistemic logic. Whilst every stable model of a normal logic program is also a minimal Herbrand model, and hence a classical model of the program, the converse relation does not hold, meaning that stable model inference is not a classical form of minimal model reasoning. But it does correspond, via a suitable translation, to default and autoepistemic reasoning.

Despite its solid reputation, stable model semantics has been criticised on a number of counts: it is not defined for all logic programs, it is computationally less tractable than some other rival semantics, it fails to satisfy some general properties of nonmonotonic inference that are sometimes thought to be desirable, and so forth. From a logical point of view, its main drawback seems to be that the stable models of a program are defined by a fixpoint equation that involves a transformation or reduction of the original program. Although this definition is easily generalised to cover disjunctive programs, as well as programs containing an additional form of negation, it is not obvious how it should be extended to deal with arbitrary theories and more general forms of queries. Consequently, there is no known counterpart to stable models for, say, conditional logic programs involving nested implications.

The aim of this paper is to provide a new logical characterisation of stable models and their generalisations, so-called answer sets. This characterisation is equivalent to the original one of Gelfond and Lifschitz, but in my view it is much easier to work with. It has the advantage of being fully declarative, or 'logical', and does not involve any fixpoint construction, but uses instead a simple definition in the style of preferential models. This definition is also not restricted to logic progams. In fact it yields a nonmonotonic form of inference, which I call equilibrium logic, that applies to arbitrary first-order theories.

In my view, the new characterisation can be used to rebut several of the criticisms leveled against the stable model semantics. In addition, it has a number of practical uses and applications, some of which will be discussed briefly at the end of the paper. Before introducing equilibrium logic I shall review some standard logical notions, and mention some recent results in the area of intermediate and constructive logic.

2 Stable Models and Answer Sets

First let me recall the definition of stable models and answer sets. I use standard logical notation, rather than the special notation often employed in logic programming. In the general setting of extended disjunctive logic programs, program formulas are built-up from atomic formulas using the logical constants: $\wedge, \vee, \rightarrow, \sim, \neg$, standing respectively for conjunction, disjunction, implication, strong negation and weak negation. Strong negation is sometimes called 'explicit' negation or even 'classical' negation; weak negation corresponds to negation-as failure, often denoted by the symbol 'not'. The nonlogical vocabulary comprises a fixed set of predicate symbols (no function symbols) and a nonempty set of names. This language will be left implicit throughout.

Program formulas with free variables are treated as shorthand for the set of their ground instances, so that a logic program can be represented as a collection Π of closed program formulas having the following form:

$$L_1 \wedge \ldots \wedge L_m \wedge \neg\, L_{m+1} \wedge \ldots \wedge \neg\, L_n \rightarrow K_1 \vee \ldots \vee K_k \qquad (1)$$

where the L_i and K_j are ground *literals*, ie. atoms or strongly negated atoms. These formulas are often called *rules* and written in a different notation, actually back-to-front; but the form is always the same. There is a single arrow, preceded by conjunctions of literals and literals prefixed by a negation-as-failure, '$\neg$', and followed by a disjunction of literals. We may have m or n zero, or $m = n$; but we always have $k \geq 1$.

Stable models were actually defined for the case where $k = 1$ and all literals are (positive) atoms; so-called *normal* programs. But the definition was quickly generalised to cover programs with formulas of type (1) in [10]; the new models being called *answer sets*. The main difference is that stable models are sets of atoms, while answer sets are sets of ground literals. The collection of all ground literals in the language of a program is denoted by *Lit*.

Take any set S of ground literals in the language of Π and imagine that S is to act as a potential interpetation of the program. First, following [7] we consider what it means for boolean formulas to be true or false wrt S; ie. we define truth ($\models$) or falsity ($=\!\!\mid$) of formulas in $\mathcal{L} = \mathcal{L}(\wedge, \vee, \sim)$ wrt a set S of ground literals, inductively by:

$$\text{For atomic } A, \quad S \models A \text{ if } A \in S; \quad S =\!\!\mid A \text{ if } \sim A \in S$$

$$S \models \sim A \text{ if } S =\!\!\mid A; \quad S =\!\!\mid \sim A \text{ if } S \models A$$

$$S \models \varphi \wedge \psi \text{ if } S \models \varphi \text{ and } S \models \psi$$

$$S =\!\!\mid \varphi \wedge \psi \text{ if } S =\!\!\mid \varphi \text{ or } S =\!\!\mid \psi$$

And $(\varphi \vee \psi)$ is regarded as an abbreviation for $\sim(\sim\varphi \wedge \sim\psi)$.

Secondly, suppose that φ is a program formula of form (1) not containing weak negation '$\neg$', ie. a formula of form

$$L_1 \wedge \ldots \wedge L_m \to K_1 \vee \ldots \vee K_k \tag{2}$$

We say that $S \subseteq Lit$ satisfies φ, in symbols $S \models \varphi$, if and only if

$$S \models L_1 \wedge \ldots \wedge L_m \;\Rightarrow\; S \models K_1 \vee \ldots \vee K_k. \tag{3}$$

Now answer sets can be defined by a two-stage process. First, let Π be a program without weak negation. An *answer set* of Π is a minimal set S of literals satisfying

(A1) for each formula $\varphi \in \Pi$, $S \models \varphi$.

(A2) if S contains a pair of complementary literals of the form $A, \sim A$ (where A is an atom), then $S = Lit$.

Secondly, for a program Π containing weak negation one considers the following reduction of Π. Given a set $S \subseteq Lit$ and a formula $\varphi \in \Pi$ of the form (1), let φ^S be the formula

$$L_1 \wedge \ldots \wedge L_m \to K_1 \vee \ldots \vee K_k \tag{4}$$

if for each $i = m+1, \ldots, n$, $L_i \notin S$. Otherwise, if for some $i = m+1, \ldots, n$, $L_i \in S$, let φ^S be the empty formula. Set $\Pi^S = \{\varphi^S : \varphi \in \Pi\}$. Then, for the 'reduced' program Π^S, from which all occurrences of '$\neg$' have been eliminated, one can apply the earlier definition of answer sets as follows: a set S of ground literals is said to be an *answer set* of Π if and only if S is an answer set of Π^S. An answer set S of Π is said to be *consistent* if it does not contain a complementary pair of literals. A program Π is said to be *noncontradictory* if it does not possess an inconsistent answer set.

For programs without strong negation, answer sets are simply sets of atoms (and clause (A2) is not required, since no inconsistencies can arise). In that case answer sets are called stable models.

It is easily seen that stable models are also minimal Herbrand models, and thus classical models of the program viewed as a set of first-order sentences. But not every minimal Herbrand model is stable. So whilst stable models, and answer sets, are defined by a fixpoint that involves minimality conditions, the semantics does not correspond to minimal model reasoning in classical logic.

2.1 Constructive Logic

I shall assume the reader has some familiarity with Heyting's intuitionistic logic, denoted by H, and with the standard Kripke semantics for H. An alternative approach to constructive reasoning was developed by Nelson [22] in 1949. Nelson's logic N is known as *constructive logic with strong negation*. It adds to Heyting's logic the insight that primitive propositions may not only be constructively *verified* but also constructively *falsified*. The language of intuitionistic logic is accordingly extended by adding a new, strong negation symbol, '$\sim$', with the intepretation that $\sim A$ is true if A is constructively false. Actually, Nelson presented strong negation as an alternative to intuitionistic negation, '$\neg$', but it is convenient to work with the calculus of Vorob'ev [29,30], where N is treated as an extension of intuitionistic logic, H. So terms and formulas are built-up in the usual manner, using the logical constants of H: $\wedge, \vee, \neg, \rightarrow$ and the additional negation '$\sim$'. Intuitionistic negation is actually definable in N by

$$\neg\varphi := \varphi \rightarrow \sim\varphi.$$

The axioms and rules of N are those of H (see eg. [5]) together with the following axiom schemata involving strong negation (where '$\alpha \leftrightarrow \beta$' abbreviates $(\alpha \rightarrow \beta) \wedge (\beta \rightarrow \alpha)$:[1]

N1. $\sim(\alpha\rightarrow\beta)\leftrightarrow\alpha \wedge \sim\beta$
N2. $\sim(\alpha\wedge\beta)\leftrightarrow\sim\alpha\vee \sim\beta$
N3. $\sim(\alpha\vee\beta)\leftrightarrow\sim\alpha \wedge \sim\beta$
N4. $\alpha\leftrightarrow \sim\sim\alpha.$
N5. $\sim \neg\alpha\leftrightarrow\alpha$
N6. (for atomic α) $\quad \sim\alpha \rightarrow \neg\alpha$

N is a conservative extension of H in the sense that any formula without strong negation is a theorem of N if and only if it is a theorem of H. Notice that Nelson's negation '$\sim$' is termed 'strong', since in N, $\sim\varphi \rightarrow \neg\varphi$ is a theorem, for all φ (not only atomic φ). (See eg. [12,5]). The derivability relation for N is denoted by $\vdash_N$, that for H by $\vdash_H$. Gentzen-style sequent systems for N can be found in [3,12] (cf. also [29,30]). A tableau proof system for N is discussed in [27].

2.2 Kripke-Models for Constructive Logic

A Kripke-style semantics (and completeness proof) for N is given in [12,1], and for a slight variant of N in [28]. We start by defining a suitable collection of models for N. In general, one may take Kripke-frames for intuitionistic logic, but require valuations V to be partial rather than total, extending the truth-conditions to include the strongly negated formulas (see eg. [12,5]). Since an intuitionistic frame can be regarded as a partially-ordered collection of classical

---

[1] For present purposes we can restrict attention to propositional logic

structures, the appropriate counterpart for N will be a partially-ordered collection of *partial* structures. Since we shall deal with fully instantiated or ground logic programs we shall omit here the semantics of quantification. Accordingly, for our present purposes we consider Kripke frames $\mathcal{F}$, where

$$\mathcal{F} = \langle W, \leq \rangle$$

such that W is a set of stages or possible worlds and $\leq$ is a partial-ordering on W. A Nelson-model $\mathcal{M}$ is then defined to be a frame $\mathcal{F}$ together with an N-valuation V assigning 1, 0 or -1 to each sentence φ and world $w \in W$. Moreover, V satisfies the following. If A is an atom, then if $V(w, A) \neq 0$ then $V(w', A) = V(w, A)$ for all w' such that $w \leq w'$. In addition,

$$V(w, \sim\varphi) = -V(w, \varphi)$$

$$V(w, \varphi \vee \psi) = max\{V(w, \varphi), V(w, \psi)\}$$

$$V(w, \varphi \wedge \psi) = min\{V(w, \varphi), V(w, \psi)\}$$

$$V(w, \varphi \to \psi) = \begin{cases} 1 & \text{iff for all } w' \geq w, \ V(w', \varphi) = 1 \text{ implies } V(w', \psi) = 1 \\ -1 & \text{iff } V(w, \varphi) = 1 \text{ and } V(w, \psi) = -1 \end{cases}$$

$$V(w, \neg\varphi) = 1 \quad \text{iff} \quad V(w', \varphi) < 1 \quad \text{for all } w' \geq w$$

$$V(w, \neg\varphi) = -1 \quad \text{iff} \quad V(w, \varphi) = 1$$

A sentence φ is said to be true in a Nelson-model $\mathcal{M}$, written $\mathcal{M} \models_N \varphi$, if for all $w \in W$, $V(w, \varphi) = 1$. Similarly, $\mathcal{M}$ is said to be an N-model of a set Π of N-sentences, if $\mathcal{M} \models_N \varphi$, for all $\varphi \in \Pi$. The notion of N-consequence is defined as follows: A sentence ψ is said to be an *N-consequence* of Π, written $\Pi \models_N \psi$, if and only if for every N-model $\langle W, \leq, V \rangle$ and each $w \in W$, if $V(w, \varphi) = 1$ for all $\varphi \in \Pi$, then $V(w, \psi) = 1$. By the completeness theorem for N ([12]), we have for all Π and φ

$$\Pi \vdash_N \varphi \quad \text{iff} \quad \Pi \models_N \varphi.$$

Kripke models for intuitionistic logic are obtained by replacing V with a suitable 2-valued interpretation.

2.3 Constructive Extensions of Intermediate Logics

We shall also consider *intermediate* logics, obtained by adding additional axioms to H. An intermediate logic is called *proper* if it is contained in classical logic. Whilst intermediate propositional logics have been extensively investigated, constructive or strong negation variants have not been systematically studied in the literature. However, for any intermediate logic *Int*, we can define a least constructive (strong negation) extension of *Int*, obtained simply by adding to *Int* the above Vorob'ev axioms, N1- N6. Some general results on constructive extensions of intermediate logics were very recently obtained by Marcus Kracht [14], who has characterised the top elements of the lattice of least constructive extensions of intermediate logics. Two general results mentioned in [14] are:

Lemma 1. *For each intermediate logic, Int, the least constructive extension of Int is a conservative extension.*

Lemma 2. *Let Int be an intermediate logic complete for a class $\mathcal{K}$ of Kripke-frames under the usual (2-valued) valuations. The least constructive extension of Int is complete for the same class $\mathcal{K}$ of frames under the above (3-valued) Nelson valuations.*

In the lattice of intermediate logics, classical logic has a unique lower cover which is the supremum of all proper intermediate logics. This greatest proper intermediate logic I shall denote by I. It is often referred to as the logic of "here-and-there", since it is characterised by linear Kripke frames having precisely two elements or worlds: 'here' and 'there'. I is also characterised by the three element Heyting algebra, and is known by a variety of other names, including the Smetanich logic, and the logic of 'present and future'. I was first presented by Heyting in his [13] and later appeared in a paper by Gödel [11]. However, it was apparently first axiomatised by Lukasiewicz [19] on the basis of Heyting's three-valued truth tables.[2] Lukasiewicz characterised I by adding to H the axiom schema

$$(\alpha \to \neg\beta) \to (((\beta \to \alpha) \to \beta) \to \beta).$$

He also showed that disjunction is definable in I.

Let us denote by $N2$ the least constructive extension of I, which, by Lemma 2, is complete for the above class of 2-element, here-and-there frames under 3-valued, Nelson valuations. An algebraic characterisation of $N2$ is straightforward; for details the reader is referred to [14] where $N2$ is presented as a many-valued logic with 5 truth-values. For present purposes, however, it is more practical to use the Kripke-model characterisation. This logic forms the basis for equilibrium reasoning, to which I now turn.

3 Equilibrium Logic

Equilibrium logic can be described as a special kind of minimal model reasoning in $N2$. As we saw, $N2$ is the the logic determined by Nelson models based on the 2-element, 'here-and-there' frame. Therefore an $N2$-model $\mathcal{N}$ can be represented as a structure $\langle \{h,t\}, \leq, V \rangle$, where the worlds h and t are reflexive, and $h \leq t$. For any world h_i the corresponding upper-case letter H_i denotes the set of all literals true at h_i; ie. we set $H_i = \{L \in Lit : V(h_i, L) = 1\}$. Given a world h_i of $\mathcal{N}$ we shall usually write '$h_i \models \varphi$', instead of '$V(h_i, \varphi) = 1$'. Note that for any such model $\langle \{h,t\}, \leq, V \rangle$ we always have $H \subseteq T$.

Definition 3. *An $N2$-model $\langle \{h,t\}, \leq, V \rangle$ of Π is said to be h-minimal over t iff for every model $\langle \{h',t'\}, \leq, V \rangle$ of Π, if $T' = T$ then $H \subseteq H'$.*

---

[2] Heyting regarded the 'third' truth value as representing a correct proposition that cannot be false, yet whose truth cannot be proved.

Definition 4. An N2-model $\langle\{h,t\},\leq,V\rangle$ of Π is said to be an *equilibrium* model of Π iff it is h-minimal over t and $H = T$.

Thus an equilibrium model is a model $\langle\{h,t\},\leq,V\rangle$ in which $H = T$ and no other model verifying the same literals at its t-world verifies fewer literals at its h-world. Clearly this model is equivalent to a one-element model.

Definition 5. A sentence φ is said to be an *equilibrium* consequence of a theory Π, in symbols $\Pi \hspace{0.15em}\vdash_e \varphi$, iff $\mathcal{N} \models \varphi$, for every equilibrium model $\mathcal{N}$ of Π.

Equilibrium logic is the logic determined by the equilibrium consequences of a theory.

It is readily seen that not all consistent theories in N2 can have equilibrium models. A simple example is the theory comprising a single sentence, $\neg\neg A$, for some atom A. Its models must have A true at t, but need not have A true at h, so models that are h-minimal over t will not be in equilibrium.

4   Logic Programs

On logic programs, the truth-conditions for program formulas of form (1) in N2-models become rather simple. Let us consider them. Let $\mathcal{N} = \langle\{h,t\},\leq,V\rangle$ be any N2-model and let φ be a program formula of form

$$L_1 \wedge \ldots \wedge L_m \wedge \neg\, L_{m+1} \wedge \ldots \wedge \neg\, L_n \rightarrow K_1 \vee \ldots \vee K_k \qquad (5)$$

Since t is a final world, we have

$$t \models \varphi \quad \text{iff}$$

$$(L_i \in T, \forall i \leq m\ \&\ L_j \notin T, \forall j = m+1, n\ \Rightarrow\ K_l \in T \text{ for some } l = 1, k). \quad (6)$$

In the world h, φ is evaluated by considering each world reachable from h, ie. t and h itself, and an intuitionistically negated literal $\neg L$ is true at h if and only if L is not true at t. So we obtain

$$h \models \varphi \quad \text{iff} \quad t \models \varphi \text{ and}$$

$$(L_i \in H, \forall i \leq m\ \&\ L_j \notin T, \forall j = m+1, n\ \Rightarrow\ K_l \in H \text{ for some } l = 1, k). \quad (7)$$

The following lemmas will be useful.

Lemma 6. *Let Π be a logic program and let $\mathcal{N} = \langle\{h,t\},\leq,V\rangle$ be an N2-model of Π, where $T = \{L \in Lit : V(t,L) = 1\}$. Then $\mathcal{N} \models \Pi^T$.*

Proof. Consider any N2-model $\mathcal{N} = \langle\{h,t\},\leq,V\rangle$ of Π. That

$$t \models \psi, \quad \forall\psi \in \Pi^T.$$

follows immediately from the fact that each formula φ of form (5) is true at t and its reduced form (8) φ^T, viz.

$$L_1 \wedge \ldots \wedge L_m \rightarrow K_1 \vee \ldots \vee K_k \qquad (8)$$

is in Π^T iff for each L_j in (5) with $j = m+1, n$, $L_j \notin T$. Likewise, for each $\varphi \in \Pi$, $h \models \varphi$ and hence (7) holds; and if the reduced form (8) φ^T of φ belongs to Π^T, then $L_j \notin T$, for all $j = m+1, n$. Hence $h \models \varphi^T$, for all $\varphi^T \in \Pi^T$; and so $\mathcal{N} \models \Pi^T$. $\square$

Lemma 7. *Let Π be a logic program and $\mathcal{N} = \langle \{h, t\}, \leq, V \rangle$ be a model of Π. $\mathcal{N}$ is h-minimal over t iff H is a minimal set of literals satisfying Π^T.*

Proof. Let $\mathcal{N} = \langle \{h, t\}, \leq, V \rangle$ be a model of Π. Then, by Lemma 3, $\mathcal{N} \models \Pi^T$ and so H satisfies Π^T. Suppose H' satisfies Π^T, where $H' \subseteq H$, and consider the model $\mathcal{N}' = \langle \{h', t\}, \leq, V \rangle$ verifying exactly H' at h'. Then for each formula (2) of Π^T, h' satisfies

$$h' \models L_1 \wedge \ldots \wedge L_m \Rightarrow h' \models K_1 \vee \ldots \vee K_k.$$

Therefore h' satisfies

$$h' \models L_1 \wedge \ldots \wedge L_m \ \& L_{m+1}, \ldots, L_n \notin T \ \Rightarrow h' \models K_1 \vee \ldots \vee K_k.$$

It follows that, for each $\varphi^T \in \Pi^T$, $h' \models \varphi$. For any $\varphi \in \Pi$ such that φ^T is empty, for some L_i, $(m+1 \leq i \leq n)$, $L_i \in T$. Hence $h' \not\models \neg L_i$ implying that $h' \models \varphi$. Thus $\mathcal{N}' \models \varphi$ for all $\varphi \in \Pi$. Consequently, if $\mathcal{N}$ is h-minimal over t, then $H' = H$ and H is a minimal set satisfying Π^T. Conversely, if H is a minimal set satisfying Π^T, then $H' = H$, and so $\mathcal{N}$ is h-minimal over t. $\square$

Let Π be any theory and $\mathcal{N} = \langle \{h, t\}, \leq, V \rangle$ an $N2$ model.

Definition 8. $\mathcal{N}$ is said to be a *t-minimal* model of Π iff $\mathcal{N} \models \Pi$ and for every $N2$-model $\langle \{h', t'\}, \leq, V \rangle$ of Π, $T' \subseteq T \Rightarrow T' = T$.

We can now show that, where logic programs are concerned, equilibrium models are always t-minimal.

Proposition 9. *Let Π be a logic program. If $\mathcal{N}$ is an equilibrium model of Π then $\mathcal{N}$ is a t-minimal model of Π.*

Proof. Let $\langle \{h, t\}, \leq, V \rangle$ be an equilibrium model of Π; we verify that it is a t-minimal model of Π. Consider any model $\langle \{h', t'\}, \leq, V \rangle$ of Π, with $T' \subseteq T$, hence $H' \subseteq H$. By Lemma 3, $\langle \{h', t'\}, \leq, V \rangle \models \Pi^{T'}$. Since $T' \subseteq T$, $\Pi^T \subseteq \Pi^{T'}$, therefore $\langle \{h', t'\}, \leq, V \rangle \models \Pi^T$. Hence H' satisfies Π^T. Since $\langle \{h, t\}, \leq, V \rangle$ is an equilibrium model it is h-minimal over t, and by Lemma 4 H is a minimal set satisfying Π^T, and so $H' = H$ and therefore, by equilibrium again, $T' = T$. $\square$

We now show that equilibrium models generalise the notion of answer set.

Proposition 10. *Let Π be a logic program. A consistent set H of literals is an answer set of Π if and only if H is the set of literals true in some equilibrium model of Π.*

Proof. Let Π be a logic program and $\mathcal{N} = \langle\{h,t\}, \leq, V\rangle$ be an equilibrium model of Π. Since $\mathcal{N}$ is h-minimal over t, by Lemma 4 H is a minimal set of literals satisfying Π^T; and since $H = T$ it is also minimal set satisfying Π^H and therefore an answer set of Π. Conversely, suppose that T is any answer set of Π; then it is a minimal set satisfying Π^T. Form a corresponding $N2$-model $\mathcal{N} = \langle\{h,t\}, \leq, V\rangle$, where $H = T$. We show that $\mathcal{N}$ is an equilibrium model of Π. First, note that $\mathcal{N}$ is a model of Π: since T satisfies the condition (3) for each reduced formula φ^T in Π^T, t also satisfies the corresponding formula φ of Π in the sense of (6). For any other formula φ of Π of form (5), $L_j \in T$, for some $j = m+1, n$, implying that also φ is true in $\mathcal{N}$ at t. Lastly we verify that $\mathcal{N}$ is an equilibrium model. Suppose not, then there is a model $\mathcal{N}' = \langle\{h',t'\}, \leq, V\rangle$ of Π with $T' = T$ and $H' \subset T$. By Lemma 3, $\mathcal{N}' \models \Pi^T$, and consequently H' satisfies each $\varphi^T \in \Pi^T$ in the sense of condition (3) of answer sets. This contradicts the fact that T is a minimal set with this property and establishes that $\mathcal{N}$ is an equilibrium model. $\square$

By Lemmas 1 and 2, $N2$ is a conservative extension of the intermediate logic of 'here-and-there', I, and is characterised by the same class of frames. So for theories without strong negation we obtain a corresponding equilibrium logic, based on I, whose models are 2-element Kripke models under the usual 2-valued intuitionistic valuations. Worlds can thus be represented as sets of atoms instead of sets of literals, and all of the above results continue to hold with the obvious adjustments. In this restricted setting therefore equilibrium models characterise the stable models of normal and disjunctive logic programs without strong negation.

5 Some Applications

5.1 Extending the Language

The natural sceptical inference relation $\vdash\!\sim$ for answer set semantics is defined between programs and boolean sentences $\varphi \in \mathcal{L}$ by stipulating that $\Pi \vdash\!\sim \varphi$ if and only if $S \models \varphi$ for each answer set S of Π. Then clearly on logic programs and boolean queries $\vdash\!\sim$ coincides with $\vdash\!\sim_e$. However, equilibrium logic provides a proper extension of answer set inference, since it is defined for arbitrary theories and queries in $N2$. Even if one restricts attention to theories having the form of logic programs, one can use the semantics of $N2$ to interpret an extended query language for any program Π, involving all the logical connectives. Notice that on the most general kinds of logic programs Π, a query, $?\varphi$, may receive four kinds of answers, according to whether φ, $\neg\varphi$, $\sim\varphi$, or none of these, is an equilibrium consequence of Π.

5.2 Existence of Answer Sets

The new characterisation of answer sets can also be applied to yield model-theoretic conditions on a program Π that are necessary and sufficient to ensure the existence of answer sets. These conditions are quite different from the standard ones given in the literature, involving syntactic criteria like stratification or signings. The latter are nonlogical (being based only on syntactic structure) and provide only sufficient conditions for the existence of stable models and answer sets.

First, for any logic program Π let $Neg(\Pi)$ denote the set of literals $L \in Lit$ such that $\neg L$ appears in some formula of Π. Then we have:

Proposition 11. *Let Π be a consistent logic program. Π has an equilibrium model if and only if there exists a t-minimal N2-model $\mathcal{N}$ of Π such for each $L \in Neg(\Pi)$, $\mathcal{N} \models \neg\neg L \to L$.*

Proof. Clearly, if Π has an equilibrium model $\mathcal{N}$, then by Proposition 1 $\mathcal{N}$ is a t-minimal model of Π, and for every literal L, $\mathcal{N} \models \neg\neg L \to L$. Suppose therefore that Π is consistent but has no equilibrium models. Then for any t-minimal model $\mathcal{N}' = \langle\{h', t'\}, \leq, V\rangle$ of Π there is a model $\mathcal{N} = \langle\{h, t\}, \leq, V\rangle$ of Π with $T = T'$ and $H \subset T$. Since $\mathcal{N} \models \Pi$, for each $\varphi \in \Pi$, (7) holds. Now suppose that for each $L \in Neg(\Pi)$, $L \in H$ iff $L \in T$. Then (7) holds where T is replaced by H. However, we could then form a model $\langle\{h, h\}, \leq, V\rangle$ of Π, having exactly the literals in H true at each world; but this is impossible by the t-minimality of $\mathcal{N}'$. Consequently, for some $L \in Neg(\Pi)$, we have $L \in T$ and $L \notin H$. This means that in $\mathcal{N}$, $h \models \Pi$, $h \models \neg\neg L$, but $h \not\models L$. It follows that for every t-minimal model $\mathcal{N}$ of Π there is some $L \in Neg(\Pi)$ such that $\mathcal{N} \not\models \neg\neg L \to L$. $\square$

Propositions 1 and 2 offer a simple way to describe, in logical terms, how to isolate the answer sets (or stable models) of a logic program Π. First, select the t-minimal N2 (resp. I) models of Π. Then discard from this collection any models that are not h-minimal over t. Choose from the remaining models those whose 'h'-worlds verify the same literals (resp. atoms) as their 't'-worlds. The selected models define the answer sets (resp. stable models) of Π. Where logic programs are concerned, therefore, equilibrium reasoning can be characterised as a form of preferential model reasoning, of the following kind. In the first step one maximizes in models $\mathcal{N}$ the set of literals L that are false in the sense that $\mathcal{N} \models \neg L$ (t-minimality of $\mathcal{N}$). In the second step one additionally minimizes the set of literals that are true in $\mathcal{N}$ (h-minimality over t). And from the models thus chosen one then picks out only those with the property that if a formula is not true then its weak negation *is* true. Therefore equilibrium logic supports the law of double negation, in the sense that $\neg\neg\varphi \to \varphi$ is true in all equilibrium models; though its underlying base logic, N2 validates only weaker laws, like the weak excluded middle, $\neg\varphi \lor \neg\neg\varphi$. Equilibrium logic remains however nonclassical, in virtue of the presence of strong negation, '$\sim$'. In particular, where the double negation law is concerned, the equivalence of φ and $\neg\neg\varphi$ holds only with respect to truth, not with respect to (strong) falsity, ie. $\sim\neg\neg\varphi \leftrightarrow\sim\varphi$ is not a theorem.

5.3 Deductive Bases

A corollary of Proposition 2 is that N2 is a deductive basis (in the sense of [6]) of equilibrium logic, hence of the inference operation associated with answer set semantics. This means that, in addition to $N2$ being a monotonic sublogic of answer set inference, the answer set consequences of a program are closed under $N2$-derivability, and moreover $N2$-equivalent programs have the same answer sets. This also has the consequence that the inference relation of $N2$ can be used to preprocess a logic program Π; in fact to reduce it to a program in which the only occurrences of weak negation are those that precede those literals L such that neither L nor $\neg L$ is $N2$-derivable from Π. One may infer from the results of [14] that $N2$ is actually the greatest deductive basis of answer set inference. The above observations apply equally to stable model inference, replacing $N2$ by I. The fact that both types of nonmonotonic inference possess nonclassical monotonic bases helps to explain why they fail to satisfy some of the standard conditions on inference relations that have been studied in the literature (see [24]). This helps to answer at least some of the criticism that has been leveled against the inference relation associated with answer sets. For instance, the property of *relevance* (see eg.[4]), often thought desirable in the context of logic programming, fails not only in answer set inference but already in the underlying logic $N2$; indeed it seems to fail in any 'reasonable' logic extended by strong negation.

6 Related Work

Most of the logical characterisations of inference based on stable models and answer sets, eg. [23,17,21,16], involve a translation of the language of logic programs into a modal or epistemic logical framework. Although our main result can be used to obtain, and in some sense explain, modal embeddings of stable model inference (this will be the topic of a future paper), as it stands our result is independent of any modal or epistemic considerations. Moreover, of the works just cited, only [23] is based on a recursive modal translation of all formulas, and therefore suggests a modal counterpart to stable model inference for arbitrary theories. In [20] (Theorem 12.16), there is a characterisation of stable model inference (in the non-disjunctive case) using structures called simply *program models*. There is no indication, however, whether these structures can be considered *models*, in the usual sense, for some (non-modal) logic (though they *are* clearly related to certain modal logical structures).

In [18] Lin and Shoham provide a characterisation of stable models (without strong negation) for normal and disjunctive programs in terms of circumscription. Mathematically, there is an analogy between their main result (Theorem 5.2) and ours.[3] However, in *logical* terms our approaches are very different in origin, style, content and proof methods. Lin and Shoham work entirely within the framework of *classical* logic and relate answer sets to certain *classical* models (of a circumscripted version of a translation of the original program into an extended language). Whilst they can relate every answer set to such a model, it would not be appropriate to *identify* an answer set with its corresponding classical model.

---

[3] I am grateful to an anonymous referee of an earlier version of the paper for pointing this out to me.

In our case, identifying an answer set with the corresponding $N2$-model, is very natural, and immediately suggests an extended query language based on the $N2$-semantics. In addition, the characterisation given in [18] is restricted to programs without strong negation, and the translation of program formulas is not defined recursively on arbitrary formulas; so it is unclear how their method should be extended to full, first-order theories. Lastly, our approach leads to several immediate and fruitful consequences that would not be easily obtainable in other ways. These include the fact that $N2$ is the greatest deductive basis of stable model inference (and various consequences associated with that), and therefore that negation-as-failure can be regarded in this semantics as a nonmonotonic strengthening of intuitionistic negation.[4]

7 Concluding Remarks and Further Topics

I have shown that stable models semantics for normal and disjunctive logic programs can be presented as a form of minimal model reasoning in the logic I of here-and-there, the greatest intermediate logic properly contained in classical logic. Similarly, answer set semantics for extended and extended disjunctive programs is a form of minimal model reasoning in $N2$, the least constructive extension of I. Equilibrium logic, which characterises the style of reasoning involved in each case, provides a natural extension of answer set and stable model reasoning to arbitrary theories. Equilibrium logic can also be syntactically characterised via a simple fixpoint equation, a topic that will be explored in forthcoming papers, see in particular [25,26].

The new characterisation of stable models and their generalisations helps to place this semantics in the tradition of preferential model approaches to nonmonotonic reasoning that are also commonplace within the foundations of logic programming. By varying the preference relation on models, one can show how other semantics, notably the well-founded semantics for normal logic programs, can also be characterised as minimal model reasoning on 2-element, linear Kripke frames. The latter has a natural, strong negation extension, which, though weaker than answer set inference, is defined on a larger class of logic programs. This topic is also under investigation at present. A further area of future study concerns implementation aspects. In particular, the question arises whether automated deduction in the logics I and $N2$, as monotonic approximations of stable model and answer set inference, can be usefully employed to provide more efficient ways of implementing these logic programming semantics.

---

[4] As the final corrections were being made to this paper I became aware of an interesting contribution of Leone, Rullo and Scarcello [15] who also provide a declarative style of characterisation of stable models (without strong negation). Although their notions of *model* and *minimal model* are somewhat different to those used here, it seems that their concept of an *interpretation satisfying* a program Π is basically equivalent to that of a here-and-there *model* of Π, though it is expressed somewhat differently. In place of h-minimal models, as here, they talk of maximal *unfounded* sets, but the results are quite analogous.

Acknowledgements

Numerous discussions with Marcus Kracht helped to clarify my ideas. Moreover, the results he established in [14] proved decisive for this paper. I am also grateful to Michael Zakharyashev and José Julio Alferes for many valuable discussions on the topics of here-and-there and logic programming.

References

1. Akama, S, Constructive Predicate Logic with Strong Negation and Model Theory, *Notre Dame J Formal Logic* 29 (1988), 18–27.
2. Akama, S, On the Proof Method for Constructive Falsity, *Zeitschr. f. math. Logik und Grundlagen d. Math.* 34 (1988), 385–392.
3. Almukdad, A & Nelson, D, Constructible Falsity and Inexact Predicates, *JSL* 49 (1984), 231–233.
4. Alferes, J J & Pereira, L M, *Reasoning with Logic Programming* LNAI 1111, Springer, 1996.
5. van Dalen, D, Intuitionistic Logic, in D Gabbay, & F Guenthner (eds), *Handbook of Philosophical Logic, Vol. III*, Kluwer, Dordrecht, 1986.
6. Dietrich, J & Herre, H, Outline of Nonmonotonic Model Theory, NTZ Report, Universität Leipzig, 1994.
7. Gelfond, M, Logic Programming and Reasoning with Incomplete Information, *Annals of Mathematics and Artificial Intelligence* 12 (1994), 89-116.
8. Gelfond, M, & Lifschitz, V, The Stable Model Semantics for Logic Programs, in K Bowen & R Kowalski (eds), *Proc 5th Int Conf on Logic Programming 2*, MIT Press, 1070-1080.
9. Gelfond, M & Lifschitz, V, Logic Programs with Classical Negation, in D Warren & P Szeredi (eds), *Proc ICLP-90*, MIT Press, 1990, 579–597.
10. Gelfond, M, & Lifschitz, V, Classical Negation in Logic Programs and Disjunctive Databases, *New Generation Computing* (1991), 365-387.
11. Gödel, K, Zum intuitionistischen Aussagenkalkül, *Anzeiger der Akademie der Wissenschaften in Wien 69* 65-66; reprinted in em Kurt Gödel, Collected Works, Volume 1, OUP, 1986.
12. Gurevich, Y, Intuitionistic Logic with Strong Negation, *Studia Logica* 36 (1977), 49-59.
13. Heyting, A, Die formalen Regeln der intuitionistischen Logik, *Sitz. Berlin* 1930, 42-56.
14. Kracht, M, On Extensions of Intermediate Logics by Strong Negation, *Journal of Philosophical Logic*, 1997, forthcoming.
15. Leone, N, Rullo, P, & Scarcello, F, Declarative and Fixpoint Characterizations of Disjunctive Stable Models, in J Lloyd (ed), *Proc ILPS '95*, MIT Press, 1995.
16. Lifschitz, V, Minimal Belief and Negation as Failure *Artificial Intelligence.*70 (1994), 53-72.
17. Lifschitz, V & Schwarz, G, Extended Logic Programs as Autoepistemic Theories, in L M Pereira & A Nerode (eds), *Logic Programming and Non-Monotonic Reasoning*, MIT Press, 1993.
18. Lin, F & Shoham, Y, A Logic of Knowledge and Justified Assumption, *Artificial Intelligence* 57 (1992), 271-290.

19. Lukasiewicz, J, Die Logik und das Grundlagenproblem, in *Les Entretiens de Zurich sur les Fondaments et la Methode des Sciences Mathematiques 1938*, Zurich, 1941.
20. Marek, V & Truszczynski, M, *Nonmonotonic Logic*, Springer Verlag, 1993.
21. Marek, V & Truszczynski, M, Reflexive Autoepistemic Logic and Logic Programming, in L M Pereira & A Nerode (eds), *Logic Programming and Non-Monotonic Reasoning*, MIT Press, 1993.
22. Nelson, D, Constructible Falsity, *JSL* 14 (1949), 16–26.
23. Pearce, D, Answer Sets and Nonmonotonic S4, in R Dyckhoff (ed), *Extensions of Logic Programming*, LNAI 798, Springer Verlag, 1994.
24. Pearce, D, Nonmonotonicity and Answer Set Inference, to appear in A. Nerode (ed), *Logic Programming and Nonmonotonic Reasoning. Proceedings LPNMR 95* LNAI, Springer-Verlag, 1995.
25. Pearce, D, From Here to There: Stable Negation in Logic Programming, in D Gabbay & H Wansing (eds), *What is Negation?*, Kluwer, 1997, forthcoming.
26. Pearce, D, Stable Inference Made Simple, in Proc DGNMR97, Third Dutch/German Workshop on Nonmonotonic Reasoning Techniques and their Applications, MPI Saabrücken, 1997.
27. Rautenberg, W, *Klassische und Nichtklassische Aussagenlogik*, Vieweg, Wiesbaden, 1979.
28. Thomason, R H, A Semantical Study of Constructible Falsity, *Zeit. f. math. Logik und Grundlagen der Mathematik* 15 (1969), 247–257.
29. Vorob'ev, N N, A Constructive Propositional Calculus with Strong Negation (in Russian), *Doklady Akademii Nauk SSR* 85 (1952), 465–468.
30. Vorob'ev, N N, The Problem of Deducibility in Constructive Propositional Calculus with Strong Negation (in Russian), *Doklady Akademii Nauk SSR* 85 (1952), 689–692.
31. Wójcicki, R, *Theory of Logical Calculi*, Kluwer, Dordrecht, 1988.

Aggregation and Well-Founded Semantics[+]

Mauricio Osorio[1] and Bharat Jayaraman[2]

[1] Universidad de las Americas,
Departamento de Ingenieria en Sistemas Computacionales,
Sta. Catarina Martir, Cholula, Puebla,
72820 Mexico
email: `osorio@cs.buffalo.edu`
[2] Department of Computer Science
State University of New York at Buffalo,
Buffalo, NY 14260, USA,
email: `bharat@cs.buffalo.edu`

Abstract. Set-grouping and aggregation are powerful non-monotonic operations of practical interest in database query languages. We consider the problem of expressing aggregation via negation as failure (NF). We study this problem in the framework of partial-order clauses introduced in [JOM95]. We show a translation of partial-order programs to normal programs that is very natural: Any *cost-monotonic* partial-order program P becomes a *stratified* normal program *transl*(P) such that the declarative semantics of P is equivalent to the *stratified* semantics of *transl*(P). The ability to effect such a translation is significant because the resulting normal programs do not make any explicit use of the *aggregation* capability, yet they are concise and intuitive. The success of this translation is due to the fact that the translated program is a *stratified* normal program. That would not be the case for other more general classes of programs than *cost-monotonic* partial-order programs. We therefore investigate a second (and more natural) translation that does not require the translated programs to be *stratified*, but requires the use of a suitable NF strategy. The class of normal programs originating from this translation is itself interesting. Every program in this class has a clear intended total model, although these programs are in general not stratified and not even call-consistent and do not have a stable model. The partial model given by the well-founded semantics is consistent with the intended total model and the extended well founded semantics WFS^+ indeed defines the intended model. Since there is a well-defined and efficient operational semantics for partial-order programs [JOM95, JM95] we conclude that the gap between expression of a problem and computing its solution can be reduced with the right level of notation.

Keywords: Partial Order Clauses, Aggregation, Negation as Failure, Well-Founded Semantics, Database Query Languages, Declarative Programming, Deductive Databases

1 Introduction

This work is part of an ongoing effort on the logical foundations, design, implementation, and application of a purely declarative language whose principal building blocks are partial-order clauses and lattice data types. Our focus here is on aggregate operations, which are of considerable interest in deductive database systems [RS92, Van92]. An aggregate operation is a function that maps a set to some value, e.g., the maximum or minimum in the set, the cardinality of this set, the summation of all its members, etc. Aggregate operations are typically non-monotonic in nature: for example, the maximum or minimum value of a set can change if an additional fact is added to the underlying database. Hence recursive programs making use of aggregate operations must be suitably restricted in order that they have a well-defined meaning.

In a recent paper [JOM95] we showed that partial-order clauses help render clear and concise formulations to problems involving aggregate operations and recursion in database querying. In this paper, we consider the problem of expressing partial-order programs via negation as failure. In this way, we can consider a partial-order program as a macro for a normal program. Such an approach has been used in the literature, since it has the advantage that normal programs are well accepted and relatively well-known. LDL1's *choice* construct [SZ90] provides an example of this nature. We examine this approach, expecting to contribute to the understanding of the nature of aggregation, set-grouping, negation-as-failure, and their relationship. We show in this paper a translation of partial-order programs to normal programs that is very natural. Any *cost-monotonic* partial order program P becomes a *stratified* normal program such that the declarative semantics of P is equivalent to the *stratified* semantics of the translated program.

We present a second (and more natural) translation that does not require the translated programs to be *stratified*, but requires the use of a suitable NF strategy. The class of normal programs generated from this translation is interesting in its own right. Any program in this class has a clear intended supported total model. A large subclass of these programs are not locally stratified and not even call-consistent [Kun88] and moreover they do not even have a two-valued stable model. The good news is that the partial model given by the well founded semantics is consistent with the intended total model. Moreover, a cumulative extension of the well founded semantics, i.e., the WFS$^+$ due to Dix [Dix92], defines this intended model. Since there is an operational semantics for partial-order programs [JOM95] we conclude that the gap between expression of a problem and computing its solution can be reduced with the right level of notation.

The rest of this paper is organized as follows: section 2 gives the general background on well-founded semantics, and section 3 gives the background for partial-order programs [JOM95]. Section 4 defines stratified partial-order programs, presents a translation of stratified programs to normal stratified programs, and defines the declarative semantics of stratified partial-order programs in terms of the stratified model of the generated normal program. Section 5 considers a more direct translation and studies the behaviour of the stable and well-founded semantics under this translation. Section 6 presents conclusions and comparisons with other related work. We illustrate in an appendix the operational semantics of partial-order programs as defined in [JOM95]. We assume familiarity with basic concepts in the semantics of declarative programs.

2 Background

We give here only a brief description of the relevant background for this paper. A standard introduction to logic programming is [Llo87]. Definite clause programs are programs formed from Horn clauses of the form $A \leftarrow A_1, \ldots, A_n$ with $A, A_1, \ldots, A_n$ being positive atoms. Normal programs extend definite programs by allowing negation. Each clause now is of the form $A \leftarrow A_1, \ldots, A_n$ with A a positive atom and $A_1, \ldots, A_n$ being literals. Instead of classic negation, logic programming adopts *negation as failure*, i.e., we infer $\neg A$ to be true if we fail to find a proof for A. Negation-as-failure is pragmatically motivated, as it provides the right meaning of negation for most logic programs and database queries.

The first proposal for a declarative semantics for negation-as-failure is the Clark's completion, denoted here by *comp(P)*. The details are given in [Llo87]. However, it is now well-accepted that the Clark's completion does not always capture the intended meaning of logic programs. In view of the limitations of the completion semantics for negation-as-failure, a key property of logic programs investigated was that of *stratification*. Informally, a program is said to be *stratified* if no predicate depends upon itself negatively (through recursion). And, a program is said to be *call-consistent* if no predicate depends both positively and negatively on itself. Since not every program is stratified, this idea had to be extended in a number of ways, such as *local stratification* [Prz88], and *weak stratification* [PP90]. The *stable* semantics [GL88] and *well-founded* semantics [VRS91] are general approaches to assigning semantics to a logic program that generalize the approaches based on stratification. But these semantics do not always coincide.

Let *Lit* be the set of literals of a program P. Following [Dix95b], a *well-behaved* semantics is a mapping

$$\{P : P \ a \ program\} \rightarrow 2^{Lit}$$

such that the following conditions are satisfied: *cut, closure, isomorphy, M_P-extension, modularity, relevance, reduction, partial evaluation, transformation,* and the *weak-model* property. We refer the reader to [Dix95b] for a discussion and formal definitions of this properties. We review some of these properties below. The property *cut* states that, for every program P, every finite set of ground atoms A, and every set of finite literals L, if $A \subseteq SEM(P)$ and $L \subseteq SEM(P \cup A)$ then $L \subseteq SEM(P)$. The principle of *isomorphy* states that, if P and Q are isomorphic, i.e., there is an isomorphism I from $B_{\mathcal{L}_P}$ onto $B_{\mathcal{L}_Q}$ such that $I(P) = Q$, then $I(SEM(P)) = SEM(Q)$. The property of *relevance* states that the truth value of a literal L with respect to $SEM(P)$ only depends on the subprogram formed from the "relevant rules" of P respect to L. The *reduction* property states that if M is a consistent set of literals, then $SEM(P \cup M) = SEM(P^M) \cup M$, where P^M is the reduction of P by M. The principle of partial evaluation (PPE) allows to replace any positive occurrence of an atom A by the associated defining rules. The principle of *cautious monotony* states that, for every program P and every finite set of ground atoms A and every set of finite literals R, if $A \subseteq SEM(P)$ and $R \subseteq SEM(P)$ then $R \subseteq SEM(P \cup A)$ [Dix95b]. This principle is not considered part of the definion of a well-behaved semantics in [Dix95a, Dix95b], but is a candidate for a stronger definition of a well-behaved semantics.

We now discuss the *well-founded semantics* (WFS) of a program P, as it will be needed for our subsequent work. A *partial interpretation* I is a consistent set of literals (i.e., both a and $\neg a$ do not belong to I) whose atoms are in the Herbrand base of P. We say a ground literal is *true in* I if it is in I, and we say it is *false in* I if its complement is in I. Let the Herbrand base H of P and its partial interpretation I be given. We say $A \subseteq H$ is an *unfounded set of P with respect to I* if each atom $p \in A$ satisfies the following condition: For each instantiated rule R of P whose head is p, at least one of the following holds: (i) some (positive or negative) subgoal q of the body is false in I, and (ii) some positive subgoal of the body occurs in A. Now, the *greatest unfounded set* of P with respect to I, denoted by $U_P(I)$, is the union of all sets that are unfounded with respect to I.

The well-founded semantics is defined in terms of three transformations T_P, U_P and W_P, as follows: (i) $p \in T_P(I)$ iff there is some instantiated rule R of P such that R has head p, and each subgoal literal in the body of R is true in I; (ii) $U_P(I)$ is the greatest unfounded set of P with respect to I; and (iii) $W_P(I) = T_P(I) \cup \neg U_P(I)$. Let α range over all countable ordinals. The sets I_α and I^∞, whose elements are literals in the Herbrand base of a program P, are defined recursively as follows: For limit ordinal α, $I_\alpha = \bigcup_{\beta < \alpha} I_\beta$. Note that $I_0 = \emptyset$. For a successor ordinal $\alpha = \beta + 1$, $I_{\beta+1} = W_P(I_\beta)$. Finally, define $I^\infty = \bigcup_\alpha I_\alpha$. The *well founded semantics* of a program P is the "meaning" represented by the limit I^∞.

The WFS$^+$ is defined as follows: For a three-valued interpretation J, let $J - MIN\text{-}MOD(P)$ denote the class of all minimal two-valued Herbrand models of P that are consistent with J. For a set S of Herbrand models, let $True(S)$ stand for the set of all ground atoms A, which are true. Furthermore, let $\mathbf{T}(J) := True(J - MIN\text{-}MOD(P))$. Let $M_0 := \emptyset$ and $M_{i+1} := \mathbf{T}(WFS(P \cup M_i))$. Let γ such that $M_\gamma = M_{\gamma+1}$. Then the WFS$^+$ for the program P is defined as WFS$(P \cup M_\gamma)$. A characterization of WFS$^+$ is given in [Dix95a] as the weakest extension of WFS that satisfies Cut and Superclassicality, which is defined as: if $P \models a$ then $a \in$ WFS$^+$ (for atoms a). Moreover, lemma 5.30 of [Dix95b] states that WFS$^+$ is well-behaved.

Schlipf recently proposed the semantics WFS$_C$ which is related to our work [Sch92b]. Dix subsequently showed that WFS$_C$=WFS$^+$, and gave a simpler construction of WFS$^+$ using *rationality* of WFS [Dix95b]—a result that shows the importance of WFS$^+$. One of the contributions of this paper is that it further shows that WFS$^+$ can be used to describe aggregation.

3 Partial Order Programs

We give an informal introduction of the paradigm of partial-order clauses. There are two kinds of partial-order clauses: unconditional and conditional. Unconditional partial-order clauses have the form

> $f(terms) \geq expression$
> $f(terms) \leq expression$

where each variable in *expression* also occurs in *terms*. For simplicity of presentation in this paper, we assume that every function f is defined either with $\geq$ or $\leq$ clauses, but not both—this restriction has been easy to meet and it covers a large class of practical programs. The syntax of *terms* and *expression* is as follows:

> *term* ::= *variable* | *constant* | *c(terms)*
> *terms* ::= *term* | *term , terms*
> *expression* ::= *term* | *c(exprs)* | *f(exprs)*
> *exprs* ::= *expression* | *expression , exprs*

Conditional partial-order clauses are of the form:

> $f(terms) \geq expression$:- *condition*
> $f(terms) \leq expression$:- *condition*

where each variable in *expression* occurs either in *terms* or in *condition*, and *condition* is in general a conjunction of relational or equational goals defined as follows.

> *condition* ::= *goal* | *goal, condition*
> *goal* ::= *p(terms)* | ¬ *p(terms)* | *f(terms)* = *term*

Declaratively speaking, the meaning of a clause is that, for all its ground instantiations, the partial-order at the head is taken to be true if the *condition* is true. In general, multiple clauses may be used in defining some function f. For a function defined by $\geq$ clauses, we define the meaning of a ground expression $f(terms)$ to be equal to the *least-upper bound* (respectively, *greatest-lower bound* for $\leq$ clauses) of the resulting terms defined by the different partial-order clauses for f. Procedurally, *condition* is processed first before *expression* is evaluated. When new variables appear in *condition* (i.e., those that are not on the left-hand side), the goals in *condition* are processed in such an order so that all functional goals ($f(terms)$) and all negated goals (¬ $p(terms)$) are invoked with ground arguments—note that negation-as-failure may be unsound for nonground negated goals. The predicates appearing in *p(terms)* are referred to as *extensional database predicates* because they are defined by ground unconditional (or unit) clauses.

Our lexical convention in this paper is to begin constants with lowercase letters and variables with uppercase letters. The symbol c stands for a constructor symbol whereas f stands for a non-constructor function symbol (also called user-defined function symbol). Terms are built up from constructors and stand for data objects of the language. The constructors in this language framework may be constrained by an *equational theory*; we only require that matching a ground term against a pattern (i.e., non-ground term) produces a finite number of matches. In the general case, when multiple partial-order clauses define a function f, all matches of a ground goal $f(terms)$ against the left-hand sides of all clauses defining f will be used in instantiating the corresponding right-hand side expressions; and, depending upon whether the partial-order clauses are $\geq$ or $\leq$, the *lub* or the *glb* respectively of all the resulting terms is taken as the result. In case none of the clauses match the goal, the result will respectively be $\perp$ or $\top$ of the lattice.

We only consider complete semilattices of *finite* terms in our language framework. Of special interest to us is the complete lattice of *finite* sets under the partial orderings subset and superset: union and intersection stand for the *lub* and *glb* respectively, and the empty set (ϕ) is the least element. In order to meet the requirements of a complete lattice, a special element $\top$ is introduced as the greatest element. We use the notation $\{X \backslash T\}$ to match a set S such that $X \in S$ and $T = S - \{X\}$, i.e., the set S with X removed. For example, matching $\{a,b,c\}$ against the pattern $\{X \backslash T\}$ yields three different substitutions: $\{X \leftarrow a, T \leftarrow \{b,c\}\}$, $\{X \leftarrow b, T \leftarrow \{a,c\}\}$, and $\{X \leftarrow c, T \leftarrow \{a,b\}\}$. When used on the left-hand sides of program clauses, $\{X \backslash T\}$ allows one to decompose a set into *strictly smaller* sets.

A *partial-order program* is a collection of partial-order clauses, normal cluases, and an extensional database. When the resulting domain of all functions being defined are totally ordered, we say that the program is a *total-order program*. The significance of such programs is that they are amenable to a more efficient implementation than general partial-order programs.

We now present a few examples to explain the use of conditional partial-order clauses. The following table summarizes the various forms of clauses to be used in these examples.

Type of Partial Order	Least/Greatest Element	LUB/GLB
$\geq$	ϕ ($\perp$)	$\cup$ (*lub*)
$\leq$	max_int ($\top$)	min2 (*glb*)
$\geq$	false ($\perp$)	or (*lub*)

Our implemented language is flexible in that a programmer can declare, for any given function definition, what should be the least/greatest element [JM95]. Thus max_int in the above table is chosen by the programmer to suit the problem at hand. It is also possible in principle to let the user specify the definitions of the *lub/glb* operations. It may be seen that specifying the least/greatest element is similar to the notion of *defaults* in the terminology of Sudarshan *et al* [SSRB93], while specifying the *lub/glb* corresponds to the notion of *first-order* aggregate operations in the sense of Van Gelder [Van92]. Furthermore, the inductive aggregates are user-definable; that is, we are not restricted to a fixed set of built-in aggregate operations.

Example 2.1 The definition of set-intersection shows how set patterns can finesse iteration over sets (the result is ϕ if any of the input sets is ϕ, as desired):

```
intersect({X\_}, {X\_}) ≥ {X}
```

This function works as follows: For a function call intersect($\{1, 2, 3\}, \{2, 3, 4\}$), we have the following two clauses: intersect($\{1, 2, 3\}, \{2, 3, 4\}$) $\geq \{2\}$, and intersect($\{1, 2, 3\}, \{2, 3, 4\}$) $\geq \{3\}$. Since the *lub* of $\{2\}$ and $\{3\}$ is $\{2, 3\}$, we obtain intersect($\{1, 2, 3\}, \{2, 3, 4\}$) $= \{2, 3\}$.

Example 2.2 (Reach). The definition of a transitive-closure operation using partial-order clauses illustrates a basic use of the paradigm. The function reach below takes a node (in a directed graph) as input and finds the set of reachable nodes from this node.

```
reach(X) ≥ {X}
reach(X) ≥ reach(Y) :- edge(X,Y)
```

As the graph may be cyclic, our intended operational semantics employs memoization in order to detect cyclic function calls that may arise.

Example 2.3 (Nullables): For a more substantial example of transitive-closures and one which combines set-terms, predicates and partial-order clauses, we define below the set of its nullable nonterminals of a context-free grammar.

```
grammar({[p,q], [q], [r,a]})
belongKleene([ ], _)
belongKleene([X], {X\_})
belongKleene([X,Y|Z], S) :- belongKleene([X],S), belongKleene([Y|Z],S)
null({[H|R]\_}) ≥ {H} :- grammar(G), null(G) = S, belongKleene(R,S)
```

For convenience, we represent the production rules of the grammar as a set of lists, where each list represents a rule: the first element of the list is the left-hand side of the rule and the rest of the list is right-hand side of the rule. The predicate belongKleene(X,S) is true if $X \in S^*$, where the string X is represented by a list, and S is a set. The function null computes the set of *nullables* of grammar.

Example 2.4 (Shortest Distance): The formulation of the shortest-distance problem is one of the most elegant and succinct illustrations of partial-order clauses:

```
short(X,Y) ≤ C :- edge(X,Y,C)
short(X,Y) ≤ C+short(Z,Y) :- edge(X,Z,C)
```

This definition for short is very similar to that for reach, except that the aggregate operation here min2 (instead of $\cup$). The relation edge(X,Y,C) means that there is a directed edge from X to Y with distance C which is non-negative. The default distance between any two nodes is max_int. The + operator is monotonic with respect to the numeric ordering, and hence the program is well-defined. The *logic* of the shortest-distance problem is very clearly specified in the above program. (Note that the result domain of the short function is totally-ordered. This knowledge can be used to tailor a very efficient implementation for this program, resembling Dijkstra's algorithm.)

Example 2.5 (Company Controls [RS92]): The company-controls problem has become a standard example for monotonic aggregation.

controls(X,Y) ≥ gt(sum(holdings(X,Y)), 50)
holdings(X,Y) ≥ {N} :- shares(X,Y,N)
holdings(X,Y) ≥ {N} :- shares(Z,Y,N), controls(X,Z) = true

This example illustrates the use of an inductive aggregate operation, sum. The function controls(X,Y) returns true if company X controls Y, and false otherwise. The relation shares(X,Y,N) means that company X holds N % of the shares of company Y. Cyclic holdings are possible, i.e., company X may have directly holdings in company Y, and *vice versa*. Here we see recursion over aggregation: a company X controls Y if the sum of X's ownership in Y together with the ownership in Y of all companies Z controlled by X exceeds 50%.[3]

4 Stratification

In this section we present stratified partial-order programs and their declarative semantics. For simplicity of presentation, we consider only $\geq$ clauses in this section; the treatment of $\leq$ is symmetric. We also disallow interaction of inequalities, i.e., we assume that every program has only one type of inequality. As noted earlier, not all syntactically well-formed programs have a well-defined meaning. In particular, circularity in function definitions is allowable as long as this occurs through *monotonic* functions. Thus, non-monotonic functions are permissible as long as there are no circular definitions through such functions. This motivates our interest in stratified partial-order programs.

The notation used to introduce partial-order clauses will be referred as the *nested* form. But, formally, we will see each clause as a short hand of a normal clause. This is done by flattening all expressions so that the arguments of all function calls are terms. Since all variables range over the universe of terms, this flattened form makes more explicit that the result of an expression must be a term. For example, a clause

f(X, {Y \ S}) ≥ g(h(X), k(Y, S)) :- r(X).

will be flattened as follows, where g, h, and k are assumed to be non-constructor functions:

f(X, {Y \ S}) ≥ S2 :- r(X), h(X) = T1, k(Y, S) = S1, g(T1, S1) = S2

The associated normal clause will be :

f≥(X, {Y \ S}, S2) :- r(X), h=(X, T1), k=(Y, S, S1),
            g=(T1,S1,S2).

where each atom with predicate symbol f≥ is called an *atom*≥; each atom with predicate symbol f= is called an *atom*=; and f is called a functional symbol.

---

[3] It would be more appropriate in this example to build a multiset (instead of a set) as the argument to sum. However, one can re-program this problem retaining the use of sets, by tagging each percentage value with the corresponding company-name.

We assume that the new predicate symbols $f_\geq$ and $f_=$ were not present in the original language. We will sometimes call these predicates *cost-predicates* because the last argument always evaluates to an element of the corresponding cost-domain. In this paper we also assume that every translated clause has the property that every occurrence of the set constructor has ground arguments. Therefore our example clause should be rewritten as:

$$f_\geq(\texttt{X, S3, S2}) \quad \texttt{:- scons(Y, S, S3), r(X), h}_=(\texttt{X, T1}),$$
$$\texttt{k}_=(\texttt{Y, S, S1}), \texttt{g}_=(\texttt{T1, S1, S2}).$$

where the intended meaning of scons is that scons(X,S,S1) is true if $\{X\} \cup S = S1, X \notin S$. We assume that scons belongs to the extensional database. The *flattened form* of a partial-order program clause is in general

Head :- *Body*,

where *Head* is $f(t) \geq u$, where t and u are terms, and *Body* is of the form *condition*, $E_1, \ldots, E_n$, where *condition* is as in the original conditional clause (but perhaps including also scons atoms as shown in our example) , each E_i is $f_i(t_i) = x_i$, where f_i is a user-defined function, t_i is a term, and x_i is a new variable not present on the l.h.s. Notes: (i) The order of equalities on the right-hand side of a flattened partial-order clause reflects the *innermost reduction order* for expressions. (ii) According to our convenience we will select our desired notation: *nested* form, *flattened* form, or *normal* form.

We will work with Herbrand Interpretations, where the Herbrand Universe of a program P consists only of ground terms, and is referred to as U_P. A subset of it is the cost-domain which has the structure of a complete lattice. The Herbrand Base B_P of a program P consists of ground atoms as usual[4].

We will now introduce several classes of programs based on a stratification notion. The following definition is adapted from [Llo87] to our framework.

Definition 4.1 *A level mapping of a partial-order program in its normal form is a mapping from its set of predicate symbols to the non-negative integers. We refer to the value of a predicate symbol under this mapping as the $level^P$ of that predicate symbol. Furthermore, we require that for every functional symbol $f_=$, $level^P(f_=) = level^P(f_\geq)$. The $level^P$ of every predicate symbol of the extensional database is 0, and the $level^P$ of every other predicate symbol is positive.*

Definition 4.2 *A program is hierarchical if it has a $level^P$ mapping such that, in every program clause A :- Body, the $level^P$ of any predicate symbol that occurs in Body is less than that in A.*

Definition 4.3 *A program is simple stratified if it has a $level^P$ mapping such that, in every program clause, A :- condition, $E_1, \ldots E_n$, the $level^P$ of any predicate symbol that occurs in condition is less than that in A, the $level^P$ of the*

---

[4] Strictly speaking, we should work with equivalence classes of terms and atoms, due to the equality theory of the constructors. However, we will talk of terms, instead of equivalence classes of terms, for simplicity of presentation; the results for terms carry over to the equivalence classes of terms.

predicate symbol of E_n is less than or equal the level^P of A, the level^P of the predicate symbol of every literal in $E_1, \ldots, E_{n-1}$ is less than the level^P of A.

Note that every *hierarchical* program is *simple stratified*. An example of a *simple stratified* (but not *hierarchical*) program is the **Reach** program.

Definition 4.4 *A function f is monotonic in its ith argument if $t_1 \leq t_2 \Rightarrow f(\ldots, t_1, \ldots) \leq f(\ldots, t_2, \ldots)$, where the ith argument is the one shown and all other argument positions remain unchanged in $f(\ldots, t_1, \ldots)$ and $f(\ldots, t_2, \ldots)$. A function f is increasing in its ith argument if $t_1 \leq f(\ldots, t_1, \ldots)$, where the ith argument is the one shown regardless of the values of the rest of the arguments. The symmetric case corresponds to decreasing functions.*

Definition 4.5 *A clause is called cost-monotonic if it is of the form:*

   $f(terms) \geq p(lexprs, g(lexprs), lexprs) :- condition$

In the above cases, f and g are both of level^P j and are not necessarily different, lexpr is an expression composed of functions from levels^P $1, \ldots, j-1$, and lexprs is a sequence of zero or more lexpr. Any goal in condition is of level^P 0. The function p is cost-monotonic in the argument where g appears. We define cost-decreasing clauses as monotonic clauses but p should be decreasing instead of monotonic. The symmetric case defines cost-increasing clauses.

Definition 4.6 *A program is cost-monotonic if it includes clauses as for the simple stratified as well as cost-monotonic clauses. A program is cost-increasing if it includes only $\leq$ clauses and they are as for the simple stratified as well as cost-increasing clauses. Moreover, the cost-domain must include a $\perp$ element. The symmetric definition corresponds to cost-decreasing programs.*

Note that, to check whether a clause is cost-monotonic, we do not have to know the semantics of the entire program; we only need to know the semantics of the "intended" monotonic function, which will be from the lower database. Moreover, many times this function corresponds to a predefined function and we therefore will know its properties. So, checking if a program is cost-monotonic in some cases reduces to verifying a simple syntactic condition. An example of a *cost-monotonic* program is program **Shortest Distance**, since + is monotonic where the recursion occurs. Observe also that if the cost-domain is the natural numbers then this program is also *cost-increasing*. Also, it is clear (from the definitions) that a *simple stratified* program is *cost-monotonic*. In a similar way we can define *locally hierarchical, locally simple stratified*, and *locally cost-monotonic* programs. But we do not consider these classes in this paper.

Definition 4.7 *A program is total-order cost-increasing if it is total-order and cost-increasing. A program is total-order cost-monotonic if it is total-order and cost-monotonic.*

4.1 Declarative Semantics

We assume that the reader is familiar with the definition of the Stratified Semantics [Llo87]. We also assume that programs are cost-monotonic and are given in its normal form, when this not the case we will say it explicitly. For simplicity of notation we assume functions with only one argument.

Definition 4.8 *Given a program P, we define Ax_P to be the universal closure of every formula in following set of formulas, one set for each $f_\geq \in P$. Symmetrical set of formulas are given for each $f_\leq \in P$.*

1) $(f_\geq(x, y) \wedge \exists z \ f_=(x, z)) \rightarrow z \geq y$,
2) $f_=(x, y) \rightarrow f_\geq(x, y)$,
3) $(f_\geq(x, y) \wedge y \geq z) \rightarrow f_\geq(x, z)$,
4) $\exists! z \ f_=(x, z)$

Our position is that in the intended model of any cost-stratified program P, Ax_P holds. We will develop a declarative semantics with this idea in mind.

Definition 4.9 *Given a program P, we define P' to be as follows: Replace each clause of the form*
   $E_0 \ :- \ condition, E_1, \ldots, E_k, \ldots, E_n$
by the clause
   $E_0 \ :- \ condition, E_1, \ldots, E_k^*, \ldots, E_n$
where E_0 is of the form $f_\geq(t_1, X_1)$, E_k is of the form $g_=(t_k, X_k)$, E_k^* is of the form $g_\geq(t_k, X_k)$ and f and g are (not necessarily different) functions at the same $level^P$. Note that when P is simple-stratified we have $k = n$.

Definition 4.10 *Given a program P, we define head(P) to be the set of head symbols of P, i.e., the head symbols on the literals on the left-hand sides of partial-order clauses.*

Definition 4.11 *Given a program P, a predicate symbol $f_\geq$ which does not occur at all in P, we define $ext_1(f)$ as the following set of clauses:*

```
f=(Z, S)  :- f≥ (Z, S), ¬ f >(Z, S)
f>(Z, S)  :- f≥(Z,S1),  S1 > S
f≥(Z, S)  :- f≥(Z,S1),  S1 > S
f≥ (Z, ⊥)
f≥(Z,C)  :- f ≥(Z,C1), f≥(Z,C2),  lub(C1,C2,C).
```

We call the last clause, the *lub* clause, and it is ommited when the partial order is total. And $lub(C_1, C_2, C)$ interprets that C is the least upper bound of C_1 and C_2. Symmetric definitions have to be provided for $f_\leq$ symbols.

Definition 4.12 *Given a program P, we define*
   $ext_1(P) := \bigcup_{f \in \ head(P)} ext_1(f), \ and$
   $transl_1'(P) := P' \cup ext_1(P).$

Proposition 4.1 *For any cost-monotonic program P, $transl_1'(P)$ is stratified.*

Proof: Let $a_=$ be a predicate symbol in P, such that $level^P(a_=) = n$. Then define a mapping in $transl_1'(P)$ such that [5], $level(a_=) = (n-1)*2+2$ and $level(a_\geq) = level(a_>) = (n-1)*2+1$. Clearly, for every atom a of the extensional database $level(a) = 0$. This is a level mapping that shows that $transl_1'(P)$ is stratified.

As an example of the translation we use program **Reach** given in example 2.2. The relevant clauses of the translated program are:

```
reach≥(X,Y) :- scons(X, ∅, Y)⁶
reach≥(X,Z) :- edge(X,Y), reach≥(Y,Z)
reach≥(X,∅)
reach≥(Z, S) :- reach≥(Z,S1), S1 > S
reach≥(Z,S) :- reach≥(Z,S1), f≥(Z,S2), union(S1,S2,S)
reach=(Z, S) :- reach≥(Z, S), ¬ reach>(Z,S)
reach>(Z, S) :- reach≥(Z,S1), S1 > S
```

Definition 4.13 *For any cost-monotonic program P, we define its declarative semantics of P, denoted as $D(P)$, as the stratified model for $transl_1'(P)$.*

In the approach given in [JOM95] functions are total and some programs are considered inconsistent, as for instance the following programs, over the domain of finite set-terms:

$$p(1) \geq \{p(1)\}$$

and

$$f(X) \geq \{X\}$$
$$f(X) \geq f(\{X\}).$$

The first program violated the regularity axiom of set theory and for the second program, we note that the total function f must evalualute to an infinite set but we only allow finite sets. Note that on the other hand $transl_1'(P)$ is consistent in both cases; and moreover they possesse stratified models where f, and p are interpreted as a partial function. In accordance with [JOM95] we state:

Definition 4.14 *A cost-monotonic program is consistent if every function is total in $D(P)$.*

Proposition 4.2 *For any consistent cost-monotonic program P, Ax_P is true in $transl_1'(P)$.*

5 Well Founded Semantics

We now consider an alternative translation to $transl_1'$, that we will call $transl_1$. Both translations are very similar and closed variants of them have been studied in [GGZ91] and [Van92]. We desire to find a general strategy of negation as

---

[5] Here *level* is precisely the definition in [Llo87].

[6] To get rid of the set-constructor that has a variable as an argument in reach≥(X, {X})

failure that captures *aggregation*. We will see now that some programs, based on this translation, have a well-defined semantics captured by the stable and well founded semantics. But we will also see that this translation has a shortcoming which motivate us to define our proposed translation that will be defined in subsection 5.1.

Definition 5.1 *Given P, we define $transl_1(P) := P \cup ext_1(P)$.*

Proposition 5.1 *For any hierarchical program P, the $WFS(transl_1(P))$ agrees with $D(P)$.*

Proof: It suffices to note that $transl_1(P)$ is also stratified since it accepts the same stratification as $transl'_1(P)$ (see proposition 4.1).
We now turn to cost-increasing programs. The next result is due to [GGZ91], nevertheless their proof holds in this more general framework.

Proposition 5.2 *Every total-order cost-increasing program is weakly stratified, and so has a total WFS. Moreover, $D(P)=WFS(transl_1(P))$.*

As an example consider the program $transl_1(\textbf{Short})$:

```
short<(X,Y,0).
short<(X,Y,C) :- edge(X,Y,C).
short<(X,Y,C) :- edge(X,Z,C1), short=(Z,Y,C2), C = C1 + C2.
short<(W,W1,X) :- short<(W,W1,X1), X1 < X.
short<(W,W1,X) :- short<(W,W1,X1), X1 < X.
short=(W,W1,X) :- short<(W,W1,X), ¬short<(W,W1,X).
```

In this case, although the program is not locally stratified, the program is cost-increasing over the domain of the natural numbers. Note that the WFS gives the intended interpretation as pointed out by [Van92]. The proof of theorem 4.1 in [Van92] can be applied here to prove that the following proposition is true.

Proposition 5.3 *Every total-order cost-monotonic program P has a total well founded model. Moreover, $D(P)=WFS(transl_1(P))$.*

We now show that this proposition does not hold for partial-order cost-monotonic programs. The apparently simple program given in section 3 of this paper, program **Reach**, becomes a difficult one to have a well defined semantics after the translation. The need to perform a set-grouping operation by our *lub* clause complicates the situation, as we will next see. Observe that when **edge** induces an acyclic graph then the well founded semantics of $transl_1$ defines its intended model. This will be also true if edge has loops [7]. So, the problem arises when **edge** induces a graph with cycles as for instance: $\textbf{Edge}_2 := \{\textbf{edge}(1,2),\ \textbf{edge}(2,3),\ \textbf{edge}(3,2)\}$. The stable semantics fails with **Reach** $\cup$ **Edge**$_2$ because it gives no stable models at all. The well-founded semantics therefore has no total model for **Reach** $\cup$ **Edge**$_2$. The problem is not as serious as with the stable semantics

---

[7] that is if have for instance **edge(1,1)** as part of the definition of the extensional database.

since it has a partial model consistent with the intended interpretation. Now note that the WFS agrees in its true/false assignments with the intended model. The undefined values for reach(2) are:

$$\text{reach}(2) \geq \{3\}, \quad \text{reach}(2) \geq \{2,3\}, \quad \text{reach}(2) = \{2\},$$
$$\text{reach}(2) = \{2,3\}, \quad \text{reach}(2) \not\leq \{2\}, \quad \text{reach}(2) \not\leq \{1,2\}.$$

An interesting point is that the well-founded model agrees with the intended model in the assignments of many false values. For instance, $\text{reach}_{\geq}(2,\{1\})$ is false in the partial model. This "decision" pruned all the unaceptable "large" models of the program. Unfortunately, any possible semantics for $transl_1(P)$, where P is a partial-order cost-monotonic program, extending the well founded semantics to define $D(P)$ does not satisfies Cut and therefore is not well-behaved. To see this, suppose that WFS^{ext} is an extension of the well founded semantics that defines the declarative semantics $D(P)$ for every partial-order cost-monotonic program P. Let **Reach-Edge** be our current example **Reach** $\cup$ **Edge$_2$**. By definition of the declarative semantics

$$\{ \text{reach}_{>}(2,\{2\}), \text{reach}_{>}(3,\{3\}) \} \subseteq D(\textbf{Reach-Edge}) \text{ and so}$$
$$\{ \text{reach}_{>}(2,\{2\}), \text{reach}_{>}(3,\{3\}) \} \subseteq WFS^{ext}(transl_1(\textbf{Reach-Edge})).$$

Note that $WFS(transl_1(\textbf{Reach-Edge}) \cup \{ \text{reach}_{>}(2,\{2\}), \text{reach}_{>}(3,\{3\}) \})$ defines a total model where $\text{reach}_{=}(2,\{2,3\})$ is false. Since WFS^{ext} is an extension of the well-founded semantics then $\text{reach}_{=}(2,\{2,3\})$ is false in

$$WFS^{ext}(transl_1(\textbf{Reach-Edge}) \cup \{ \text{reach}_{>}(2,\{2\}), \text{reach}_{>}(3,\{3\}) \})$$

which contradicts Cut that requires that $\text{reach}_{=}(2,\{2,3\})$ is true in

$$WFS^{ext}(transl_1(\textbf{Reach-Edge}) \cup \{ \text{reach}_{>}(2,\{2\}), \text{reach}_{>}(3,\{3\}) \}).$$

We therefore consider convenient to adopt an improved translation.

5.1 WFS$^+$

We assume that the subset of the Herbrand base that is used to interpret the cost-domain is finite and has the structure of a complete lattice. By adding type restrictions in our language (as in Relationlog [Liu95]) this assumption is not inconsistent with the fact that we allow constructors in our language. For instance, we could write the type specification of the program **Reach** as:

```
TYPE 1,2,3,4,5,6,7,8,9:digit
PREDICATE edge(digit,digit)
FUNCTION reach(digit) --> { digit }
```

In this case the cost-domain is the power set of $\{1,2,3,4,5,6,7,8,9\}$ and is the codomain of the function reach. We can model this kind of typing (formally speaking the one based on many sorted logic) with an untyped program that include special unary predicate symbols with an attached intended meaning. For instance, for the **Reach** program we could add two predicate symbols d and s. Then intended meaning of them could be, for instance, that d(X) is true if $X \in \{1,\ldots,9\}$ and s(X) is true if X is a subset of $\{1,\ldots,9\}$. Then we could add this constraints in the right hand side of every clause. This paper does not address this issue, but only claims that the restriction of a finite cost-domain is legitimate. We are ready to present our final translation.

Definition 5.2 *Given a predicate symbol* $f_\geq$, *we define* $ext_2(f)$ *to be the following set of clauses:*

$f_=(Z, S)$:- $f_\geq$ (Z, S), $\bigwedge_{S<S1\leq T} \neg f_\geq(Z, S1)$ *for every cost-value S.*
$f_\geq(Z, S)$:- $f_\geq$ $(Z, S1)$, $f_\geq$ $(\bar{Z}, S2)$, $lub(S1,S2,S)$
$f_\geq(Z,\bot)$
$f_\geq(Z, S)$:- $f_\geq(Z,S1)$, $S < S1$

Note that $\bigwedge_{S<S1\leq T} \neg f_\geq(Z, S1)$ represents a formula of a conjunction of literals. In this way the first clause represents a set of normal clauses for the given symbol f. We also define $transl_2$ as $transl_1$, by using ext_2 instead of ext_1. Considering again example 2.2, we could take as the cost-domain set, the power set of $\{1,2,3\}$. For the cost-vaue $\{1,2\}$ we have to write the clause:

$reach_=(Z, \{1,2\})$:- $reach_\geq(Z,\{1,2\})$, $\neg$ $reach_>(Z,\{1,2,3\})$

and although $\{2,1,3\} > \{1,2\}$ is true, it is enough to consider only the representative $\{1,2,3\}$ of the equivalent class $[\{1,2,3\}]$. Also note that for the cost-value $\{1,2,3\}$, i.e. the top element of our complete lattice, the associated clause is just:

$reach_=(Z,\{1,2,3\})$:- $reach_\geq(Z,\{1,2,3\})$

since $\bigwedge_{\{1,2,3\}<S1\leq T} \neg f_\geq(Z, S1)$ is empty. The colollary of the following proposition says that our proposed translation $transl_2$ performs as well as $transl_1$ respect to expressing the declarative semantics of a program. Then we will see that it works even better.

Proposition 5.4 *For any program P, where the cost-domain set is finite, if the WFS of* $transl_1(P)$ *is total then* $WFS(transl_1(P))=WFS(transl_2(P))$, *respect to the language of* $transl_2(P)$.

Proof: If the cost-domain set is finite then we can assume that the extensional database for $<$ is finite. We can reduce $transl_1(P)$ by the semantics of $<$ preserving the semantics of the original program. Therefore, every clause of the form:

$f_>(Z, S)$:- $f_\geq(Z,S1)$, $S1 > S$

reduces to a finite set of clauses of the form:

$f_>(Z, S)$:- $f_\geq(Z,S1)$, where S1 and S are ground, and $S1 > S$.

We now unfold the negative literal $\neg$ $f_>(Z,S)$ in

$f_=(Z,S)$:- $f_\geq$ (Z,S), $\neg f_>(Z,S)$

as explained in [AD94] to obtain:

$f_=(Z,S)$:- $f_\geq(Z,S)$, $not_{f_>}(Z,S)$,

and the set of clauses:

$not_{f_>}(Z, S)$:- $\bigwedge_{S<S1\leq T} \neg f_\geq(Z, S1)$ *for every cost-value S.*

(Note that $not_{f_>}$ is a new predicate symbol in the above definitions.) Since the original program has a total WFS then according to [AD94], the resulting program preserves the WFS respect to the common language. We now apply a PPE step respect to $not_{f>}$ and the WFS still preserves. Since we do not care about $not_>$ and $f_>$, by relevance we can drop their definitions without affecting the WFS of the rest of the program. Our program corresponds now to $transl_2(P)$, and our proof is finished.

Corollary 5.1 *For any program P where the cost-domain set is finite and that is hierarchical, total-order cost increasing or total-order cost monotonic,*

$WFS^+(transl_2(P)) = WFS(transl_2(P)) = D(P)$ *respect to the language of $transl_2(P)$.*

The class of cost-monotonic programs that are generated with this extended translation are itself interesting. They are in general not call-consistent, the well-founded semantics for $transl_2(\textbf{Reach})$ still does not define $D(P)$. Do they deserve to have a total model? if that is the case, should the declarative semantics for $transl_2(\textbf{Reach})$ agree with $D(\textbf{Reach})$? We found a positive answer for both questions. We found that WFS$^+$ is strong enough to define the declarative semantics for $transl_2(\textbf{Reach})$. We first note, in the following proposition, that for our cost-monotonic programs, the definition of the declarative semantics could be given using $transl'_2$ instead of $transl'_1$.

Proposition 5.5 *For every cost-monotonic program P where the cost-domain is finite, $transl'_2(P)$ is stratified and $WFS^+(transl'_2(P)) = WFS^+transl'_1(P))$ respect to the language in $transl'_2(P)$*

Proof: We can show that $transl'_2(P)$ is stratified in the same form as we showed in proposition 4.1 that $transl'_1(P)$ is stratified. Since $transl'_1(P)$ is stratified $WFS(transl'_1(P))$ has a total model an then we can apply the same transformations to $transl'_1(P)$ as in the proof of the last proposition to obtain $transl'_2(P)$ such that the WFS is preserved. Then $WFS^+(transl'_2(P)) = WFS^+transl'_1(P))$ respect to the language in $transl'_2(P)$ as desired.

Proposition 5.6 *For every cost-monotonic program P where the cost-domain is finite, $WFS^+(transl'_2(P)) = WFS^+(transl_2(P))$.*

Proof: Use induction on the level^P of P.

Base case: The program P is of level^P 0. Then $transl'_2(P)$ and $transl_2(P)$ are both the same program which is just an extensional data base. The statement is trivially true.

Induction step: Suppose that the level^P of P is $n+1$. By relevance, reduction, and the induction hypothesis we only have to show that $WFS^+(transl_2(P)^Q) = STRAT(transl'_2(P)^Q)$ where Q is the semantics of the predicates of levels^P 0 to n. Let R be the ground instance program of $transl_2(P)^Q$ and R' be the ground instance program of $transl'_2(P)^Q$. Note that both programs share the same language $(\mathcal{L})$. We first show that $R' \models \alpha$ then $R \models \alpha$. This is equivalent to prove that if M is a model of R then M is a model of R'. So, assume that M is a model of R. Consider a clause in R' and not in R. This clause is of the form $f_>(e,c) :- g_>(e1,d)$. We also know that there is a monotonic function such that $m(d) = c$ [8]. Suppose $M \models g_\geq(e1, d)$. From $ext_2(f)$ is easy to check that exists $d1$ such that $M \models g_=(e1, d1)$ and $M \models d1 \geq d$. Let $m(d1) = c1$. Note that there is clause in R' of the form: $f_\geq(e, c1)$:- $g_\geq(e1, d1)$ and therefore $f_\geq(e, c1)$:- $g_=(e1, d1)$ is in R and by hypothesis true in M. Therefore $M \models f_\geq(e, c1)$. Since m is monotonic $M \models c1 \geq c$, hence by $ext_2(f)$ it follows that $M \models f_\geq(e, c)$ concluding that (L) $R' \models \alpha$ then $R \models \alpha$.

To prove that $\text{STRAT}(R') = \text{WFS}^+(R)$ we need four steps.

1. We show that for every ground atom $f_\geq(e, c) \in \text{STRAT}(R')$ then $f_\geq(e, c) \in \text{WFS}^+(R')$. Note that R' is a stratified normal program of two levels. The definition of every $f_\geq$ occurs at the first level and so (A) $f_\geq(e, c) \in \text{STRAT}(R')$ implies that $R' \models f_\geq(e, c)$. By taking α as the ground atom $f_\geq(e, c)$ we obtain (B) $R' \models f_\geq(e, c)$ implies $R \models f_\geq(e, c)$. By Superclassicality (C) $R \models f_\geq(e, c)$ implies that $f_\geq(e, c) \in \text{WFS}^+(R)$. Finally, by (A),(B) and (C) we get that $f_\geq(e, c) \in \text{STRAT}(R')$ then $f_\geq(e, c) \in \text{WFS}^+(R)$.

2. We show that if a ground atom a is false in $\text{STRAT}(R')$ then a is false in $\text{WFS}^+(R)$. This follows by noting that the set $\{\neg p | p \in \text{STRAT}(R)\}$ is an unfounded set or R respect to the partial interpretation $\{f_\geq(e, c) | f_\geq(e, c) \in \text{STRAT}(R')\}$.

3. For every ground atom $f_=(e, c)$, $f_=(e, c) \in \text{STRAT}(R)$ implies that $f_=(e, c) \in \text{WFS}^+(R')$ since the definition of $f_=$ in both programs depends on the same literals that by steps one and two have the same semantics.

4. Note that every literal in $(\mathcal{L})$ was considered in the first three steps finishing the proof.

Our main result is a corollary of the last two propositions.

Corollary 5.2 *For every cost-monotonic program P where the cost-domain is finite, $\text{WFS}^+(\text{transl}_2(P)) = D(P)$ respect to the language in $\text{transl}'_2(P)$.*

As we become independent from the stratified semantics used with transl'_1, we can use this more general approach to check other examples as for instance:
Example min-max, from [Van92]: A minimax game defined on a bipartite graph.

```
v(X,C) :- f(X,C).
v(X,C) :- p=(X,C).
v(X,C) :- q=(X,C).
p<(X,C) :- edgea(X,Y), v(Y,C).
q>(X,C) :- edgeb(X,Y). v(Y,C).

f(e,3).     f(f,2).     f(k,2).     f(m,1).
edgea(g,f). edgea(g,e). edgea(h,e). edgea(h,i). edgea(h,j).
edgeb(i,g). edgeb(i,h). edgeb(i,m). edgeb(j,m). edgeb(j,k).
```

The above example illustrates an interaction of $\geq$ and $\leq$, so the program is not cost-monotonic (respect to our definitions). We therefore can't use transl'_1

---

[8] For simple stratified programs d and c is the same term and so m is the identity function

to define the declarative semantics, but the well-founded semantics considering $transl_1$ or $transl_2$ defines a total model where v(h)=2, and v(i)=2. We think that this is the intended model of the program. Van Gelder pointed out (personal communication) that the conclusion can be established by simple negation-as-failure semantics, without getting involved in WFS at all. Our operational semantics as defined in [JOM95, M97] computes also the intended model of this program with a procedure that does not involve negation as failure.

6 Conclusions and Related Work

We considered the problem of expressing aggregation in terms of negation as failure (NF), by showing how aggregate operations expressed in terms of partial-order clauses [JOM95] can be given a succinct translations in terms of normal programs. The resulting normal programs do not make any explicit use of *aggregation* capability, yet they are concise and intuitive. The translated programs do not have to be *stratified* and are they more general than cost-monotonic programs. Every program in this class has a clear intended total model, but not necessarily a unique stable model. The partial model given by the well-founded semantics is consistent with the intended total model and the extended well-founded semantics, WFS$^+$, indeed defines the intended model. Since there is a well-defined and efficient operational semantics for partial-order programs [JOM95, JM95] we conclude that the gap between expression of a problem and computing its solution can be reduced with the right level of notation.

There has been continued interest in the topic of aggregation and set-grouping. LDL [BN87], COL [AG91], Relationlog [Liu95] are logic-languages that are concerned with set-grouping. All of them have used the approach of defining *ad hoc* semantics to set-grouping, and the their relation with negation-as-failure has not been examined. Moreover, according to [Liu95], neither COL or LDL can give a semantics to a program like:

ancestors(X,<Y>) :- parents(X,<Z>), ancestors(Z,<Y>).

A direct translation to an atom like ancestors(X,<Y>) is ancestors$\geq$(X,{Y}) and in this way we just have to use $transl_1$ and the stratified semantics. Moreover Relationlog only allows atoms with complete set terms in the right hand side of a clause if they belong to a lower level. Atoms with complete set terms correspond to $atoms_=$ in our approach, therefore in general any stratified Relationlog program can be translated via $transl_1$ to a stratified normal program. These languages only consider partial-orders based on sets.

Along the same lines as [Van92], we showed that the framework of the well-founded semantics is adequate to express the meaning of what we call total-order programs. Van Gelder also shows *ad hoc* translations for some "non-monotonic" programs. We adopt a uniform approach, that is, by considering always the same translation scheme. We noticed that WFS$^+$ defines the intended model for a large class of programs. Since partial-order programs have a well-defined and efficient operational semantics, we feel that use of an appropriate notation does help bridge the gap between a declarative expression of a problem and its efficient implementation. Our current research suggests that there is a well-behaved semantics that is stronger than WFS but weaker than WFS$^+$ that defines the intended model of every cost-momotonic partial-order program. This will be the topic of a future paper.

References

[AG91] S. Abiteboul and S. Grumbach, "A Rule-Based Language with Functions and Sets," *ACM Trans. on Database Systems*, 16(1):1-30,1991.

[AD94] C. Aranvindam and P.M. Dung, "Partial deduction of Logic Programs wrt Well-Founded Semantics," *New Generation Computing, 13 pp. 45-74, 1994*

[BN87] C. Beeri, S. Naqvi, et al, "Sets and Negation in a Logic Database Language (LDL1)," *Proc. 6th ACM Symp. on Principles of Database Systems*, pp. 21-37, 1987.

[Dix92] J.Dix, "A framework for representing and characterizing semantics of Logic Programs," *Proc. 3rd Intl. Conf. on Principles of Knowledge Representation and Reasoning* pp. 591-602, 1992.

[Dix95a] J.Dix, "A Classification-Theory of Semantics of Normal Logic Programs: I. Strong Properties," *Fundamenta Informaticae XXII(3)* pp. 227-255, 1995.

[Dix95b] J.Dix, "A Classification-Theory of Semantics of Normal Logic Programs: II. Weak Properties," *Fundamenta Informaticae XXII(3)* pp. 257-288, 1995.

[GGZ91] G. Ganguly, S. Greco, and C. Zaniolo, "Minimum and maximum predicates in logic programs", *Proc. 10th ACM Symp. on Principles of Database Systems*, pp 154-163, 1991.

[GL88] Gelfond and V. Lifschitz, "The Stable Model Semantics for Logic Programming," *Proc. 5th Intl. Conf. of Logic Programming*, pp. 1070-1080, Seattle, August 1988.

[JM95] B. Jayaraman, and K. Moon, "Implementation of Subset-Logic Programs," Submitted for publication.

[JOM95] B. Jayaraman, M. Osorio and K. Moon, "Partial Order Programming (revisited)", *Proc. Algebraic Methodology and Software Technology*, Springer-Verlag, July 1995.

[Liu95] M. Liu, "Relationlog: A typed Extension to Datalog with Sets and Tuples," *Proc. Intl. Symp. of Logic Programming*, pp 83-97, 1995.

[Llo87] J. Lloyd, "Foundations of Logic Programming," (2 ed.) Springer-Verlag, 1987.

[Moo97] K. Moon, "Implementation of Subset Logic Languages," Ph.D. dissertation, Department of Computer Science, SUNY-Buffalo, 1997.

[Prz88] T.C. Przymusinski, "On the Declarative Semantics of Stratified Deductive Databases" in J. Minker (ed.), *Foundations of Deducive Databases and Logic Programming*, 1988, pp. 193-216.

[PP90] T.C. Przymusinski and H. Przymusinska, "Semantic Issues in Deductive Databases and Logic Programs" in R.B. Banerji (ed.), *Formal Techniques in Artificial Intelligence*, 1990, pp. 321-367.

[RS92] K.A. Ross and Y. Sagiv, "Monotonic Aggregation in Deductive Databases," *Proc. 11th ACM Symp. on Principles of Database Systems*, pp. 114-126, San Diego, 1992.

[Sch92b] J. Schlipf, "Formalizing a Logic for Logic Programming", *Annals of Mathematics and Artificial Intelligence*, 5:279–302, 1992.

[SZ90] D. Sacca and C. Zaniolo, "Stable models and non-determinism in logic programs with negation", *Proc. 9th ACM Symp. on Principles of Database Systems,* 1990, pp. 205-217.

[Van92] A. Van Gelder, "The Well-Founded Semantics of Aggregation," *Proc. ACM 11th Principles of Database Systems,* pp. 127-138, San Diego, 1992.

[VRS91] A. Van Gelder, K.A. Ross, and J.S. Schlipf, "The Well-Founded Semantics for General Logic Programs," *JACM,* 38(3):620-650.

Nonmonotonic Reasoning by Monotonic Inferences with Priority Constraints

Xianchang Wang, Jia-Huai You, Li Yan Yuan

Department of Computing Science, University of Alberta
Edmonton, Alberta, Canada T6G 2H1
{xcwang, you, yuan}@cs.ualberta.ca

Abstract. The purpose of this paper is to argue that nonmonotonic reasoning in general can be viewed as monotonic inferences constrained by a simple notion of priority constraint. More important, these type of constrained inferences can be specified in a knowledge representation language where a theory consists of a collection of logic programming-like rules and a priority constraint among them: that the application of one rule blocks that of the lower ranked rules. We thus present a formal system for representing common sense knowledge, and call it *priority logic*. As applications, we recast default reasoning by priority reasoning, and show that Horty's defeasible inheritance networks can be represented by priority logic. This latter result is a partial answer to Horty's challenge that it is impossible to relate path-based reasoning to general nonmonotonic formalisms.

1 Introduction

In the past nonmonotonic reasoning has mainly been studied in formalisms where default assumptions constitute a necessary component, e.g. defaults in default logic [26], negation-as-failure in logic programming [7], disbeliefs in various nonmonotonic modal logics [24], and assumptions in Theorist and some abductive and argumentation frameworks [10].

In classic logic, reasoning is based on monotonic inferences. Such a sequence of inferences can be viewed as an *argument* that supports one's assertion. The notion of constrained monotonic inferences is about selecting some of these monotonic inferences according to a specified constraint. As an example, consider the bird-fly example: *Birds normally fly unless it can be shown otherwise.* Suppose we know that dead birds don't fly, neither do hungry birds. The problem can be represented as a program (for simplicity, we remove the condition *bird*):

$$1.\ fly \leftarrow$$
$$2.\ \neg fly \leftarrow dead\_bird$$
$$3.\ \neg fly \leftarrow hungry\_bird$$

with priority $1 \prec 2$ and $1 \prec 3$, meaning when either 2 or 3 is applied, the application of 1 should be blocked.

Now, assume we know that the bird is dead:

$$4.\ dead\_bird \leftarrow$$

Consider the two monotonic derivations, $I_1 = \{1\}$ which concludes fly, and $I_2 = \{4, 2\}$ which concludes $\neg fly$. The specified priority selects I_2, because rule 2 being applicable blocks the application of rule 1.

Schematically, one can use a general rule to express "unless it can be shown otherwise":

$$5.\ \neg fly \leftarrow \neg fly$$

and priority relation $1 \prec 5$. Now specific reasons for not flying need not be related to 1, i.e. the priorities like $1 \prec 2$ and $1 \prec 3$ are no longer needed.

The idea of constrained inferences suggests a general formalism for knowledge representation and reasoning, which we call *priority logic*, where a theory consists of a collection of inference rules and a priority constraint among rules. In priority logic, reasoning is based on derivations using these inference rules. Priority constraint plays the role of selecting those derivations that satisfy it. A rule is applicable if its premises are already derived. A sequence of applicable rules then forms what we call an *argument*, such as I_1 and I_2 above. The fully extended arguments that satisfy the specified priority are then regarded as the "semantics" of a theory, since they describe what follows from the theory.

Priority logic offers a number of advantages over the conventional formalisms relying on default assumptions. First, a specification in this language is free from potential complications arising from the use of default constructs; e.g. the need of (sometimes a large number of) abnormality predicates as done in using circumscription; whether to use normal or semi-normal defaults in knowledge representation using default logic; and in logic programming, the confusion between default and explicit negation.

Second, in this formalism one can specify some evidence is stronger than others directly. For example, the transformer is far more likely to fail than is the power supply; the evidence that Quakers are pacifists is stronger than the evidence that Republicans are not. This feature seems to be particularly important in legal reasoning, since it is generally assumed that legal norms are generally incoherent and conflicting because legal norms can be issued by different authorities at different times to reach incompatible socio-political objectives. The coordination of conflicting profiles of legal relevance is often accomplished by establishing preference relations among assertions: one norm prevails over others, some arguments are stronger than others. We note that problems of this kind traditionally fall into the area of belief revision.

Furthermore, knowledge representation with a priority constraint in many cases can resolve the multiple extension problem in default reasoning. This line of research was first carried out by Reiter and Cirscuolo [27], where they embed a defeasibility relation into defaults by modifying their justifications. The formalism proposed in this paper allows one to specify such defeasibility relation directly.

The purpose of this paper is to argue for the following thesis:

Nonmonotonic reasoning = monotonic inferences + priority constraint

In other words, nonmonotonic reasoning is just a process of constructing monotonic derivations that satisfy a priority constraint.

To support this claim, we show how some of the nonmonotonic reasoning formalisms can be recast in priority logic. Specifically, we show that default reasoning in the sense of Reiter [26] and defeasible inheritance networks of Horty [15] can be represented by priority logic. In each case, we show a transformation from a default theory or an inheritance network to a priority logic program.

There are at least three important reasons for choosing these two formalisms to demonstrate the generality of priority logic. First, default logic is perhaps the most prominent nonmonotonic reasoning formalism, and its relationship with other nonmonotonic formalisms has been studied extensively [13, 16, 21]. Secondly, default logic and logic programming with negation are often related at the level of literals (e.g. [20]). The fact that default logic is syntactically richer often makes it unclear whether an idea in logic programming can be successfully applied to default reasoning. Thirdly, in view of Horty's claim that it is impossible to relate the path-based reasoning to general nonmonotonic formalisms [15], it is important to consider the former as a candidate for testing of generality.[1]

We should comment that the proposed framework not only can capture existing nonmonotonic reasoning formalisms, it can also help study possible semantic variations of these formalisms. We will illustrate this point later in this paper through an example.

The paper is organized as follows. Before formally introducing priority logic, we discuss various notions of priority, including the one used in this paper. This summaries some of the key differences between this work and those in the literature. In section 3, we introduce priority logic-its syntax and semantics. In Sections 4 and 5 we show how default logic and defeasible inheritance networks can be captured in priority logic. This is followed by further remarks on related work and comments on proof theory of priority logic.

2   Priority: A Clarification

A number of authors investigated adding a priority into a nonmonotonic reasoning formalism (e.g. [3, 4, 5]). For example, Baader and Hollunder introduce priorities among defaults and define a notion of extension so that the extensions of the theory with priority are a subset of those under Reiter's original default logic [3]. Our work aims at characterizing nonmonotonic reasoning in terms of constrained inferences, i.e., it is a proposal of a general framework for knowledge representation without using defaults.

Although priority seems to be a simple concept, its technical treatment often causes controversy. Conceptually, a priority is a relation that characterizes

---

[1] Recently, we have also shown in [32] that McCarthy's circumscription [23] can be captured by priority logic.

precedence in position or preference in rating. Such a preference may be further classified as *inclusive* or *exclusive*.

An inclusive priority is one by which objects are admitted according to their preference until the condition for admitting is no longer satisfied. Usually, such a condition is based on a form of conflict, e.g., logic contradiction. A conceptual example of inclusive priority is that of admitting students into a graduate program with financial assistance, which is constrained by a budget. Awards are given according to the ranking of the applicants until the budget runs out.

The technical treatment of inclusive priority in a nonmonotonic reasoning formalism is not so simple. One problem is that it is not clear whether or not the application of lower ranked objects can affect the applicability of the higher ranked ones. For example, the priority in both Brewka's approach [4] and Baader and Hollunder's [3] may be characterized as inclusive, but the former commits the applicability, or non-applicability, of a default in the construction of an extension, while the latter allows the change of the applicability of a default when lower ranked defaults have been applied.

In comparison, an exclusive priority involves a simple concept: the admission of an object automatically blocks the admission of lower ranked objects without exception. For a conceptual example, and for comparison, let us consider again admitting students into a graduate program but this time with only one (perhaps distinguished) scholarship. One first ranks applicants, and then tries to have the highest ranked applicant accept the award. If this applicant decides to go to another university, then the next highest ranked applicant should be considered. This process continues until the award is accepted by some applicant. Once the award is accepted, no lower ranked applicants can get it.

In priority logic, we place no restriction on a priority constraint. Properties like transitivity may be specified by the user, depending on the intended applications. When such a constraint relation is transitive, it is an exclusive priority relation as described above and thus its intended behavior is clear and easy to understand. When it is not transitive, it is simply a defeasibility relation: that r_1 defeats r_2 means the application of r_1 blocks that of r_2, and this effect need not propagate. For a slight abuse of terminology, we still call such a relation a "priority" relation (or priority constraint).

In this paper we are only concerned with *static priority constraint*, i.e., the kind of constraint that does not change during reasoning, since it is sufficient for the purpose of this paper of recasting nonmonotonic reasoning by constrained monotonic inferences. Brewka recently proposes *dynamic priority* where a priority predicate is used in program rules just like any other predicate, and preferences are determined dynamically [5]. Extension of priority logic with dynamic priority constraint presents an interesting but challenging future research topic.

3 Priority Logic

3.1 Language

Suppose $\mathcal{L}$ is a *first order* language with equality $=$ and connectives $\neg, \vee, \wedge, \supset$, $\equiv, \exists, \forall$. The *formulas* of $\mathcal{L}$ are defined as usual. They are denoted by α, β, γ, possibly with a subscript. We consider a fixed domain, such as the Herbrand domain of the language $\mathcal{L}$, We denote it by $\mathcal{H}_{\mathcal{L}}$, or simply $\mathcal{H}$.

An *inference scheme* is of the form $\beta \leftarrow \alpha_1, ..., \alpha_m$ where $m \geq 0$, α_i's and β are formulas of $\mathcal{L}$. When $m = 0$, we may simply write β.

Each inference scheme represents a set of *inference rules*, where the free variables in the scheme have been instantiated by terms from the underlying domain, in this case, $\mathcal{H}$. Generally we use a label with variables to name a rule scheme. The variables in a label are the free variables appearing in the scheme. For example, we use $l(x, y)$ to label the rule scheme $q(x) \leftarrow p(x, y)$. Like a scheme, a label with variables represents all the instantiated labels.

A *priority theory* (or, called a *priority logic program*) is a couple $\langle R, \prec \rangle$ where R is a set of inference schemes and $\prec$ is a relation on R.

In the sequel, we assume rule schemes and priorities are already instantiated so we only deal with inference rules and ground priorities.

For an inference rule $r = \beta \leftarrow \alpha_1, ..., \alpha_m$, $Pre(r)$ refers to $\{\alpha_1, ..., \alpha_m\}$ and $Cons(r)$ to β. Intuitively, a priority constrains whether a rule can be applied or not: if $l \prec l'$ and l' is applied, then the inference rule l should be suspended.

Given the standard entailment relation $\models$, we define the *closure* of a set S of formulas as: $Th(S) = \{C : S \models C\}$. Suppose P is a set of inference rules and S a set of formulas. The familiar consequence operator $\mathcal{T}_P$ is defined as:

$$\mathcal{T}_P(S) = \{Cons(r) : r \in P, S \models Pre(r)\}$$

Since $\mathcal{T}_P$ is monotonic, it has a unique least fixpoint. As usual, this least fixpoint is denoted by $\mathcal{T}_P^{\uparrow \omega}$. S is *contradictory* if $\mathcal{T}_S^{\uparrow \omega} \models \mathcal{L}$; otherwise it is said to be *consistent*. The *applicable* rules in a rule set R, denoted $App(R)$, is defined as: $App(R) = \{r \in S : \mathcal{T}_R^{\uparrow \omega} \models Pre(r)\}$.

3.2 Arguments as semantics

A primary interest in a priority logic program lies in what can be derived by using which inference rules. A derivation is just a chain of reasoning using inference rules. At a level of conceptualization, this can be understood as a notion of argument which serve as an important building block in reasoning with priority.

Definition 1. (Argument on $\langle P, \prec \rangle$)

Let $\langle P, \prec \rangle$ be a priority logic program. An *argument* is a (finite or infinite) set of inference rules in P such that I's rules can be arranged into a sequence, say $I = \{w_1, ..., w_n, ...\}$, such that for every $w_i \in I$, where $i \geq 0$, we have $\mathcal{T}_{\{w_1, ..., w_{i-1}\}}^{\uparrow \omega} \models Pre(w_i)$.

That is, an argument is just a sequence of rules, each of which is applicable by the rules prior to it. The set notation used in the definition is for convenience.

Given a priority logic program $\langle R, \prec \rangle$, we are interested in those arguments that agree with the specified constraint $\prec$. The construction of such an argument involves how to extend an argument I by possibly admitting more rules into it.

Since when we specify $r \prec r'$, we mean the applicability of r' blocks that of r, a natural notion of extending an argument I is: I admits a rule r (i.e. r *extends I*) if there is no other rule r' in I that blocks r.

For example, consider the example *bird_fly_ostrich_don't*:

$$1 : fly \leftarrow bird$$
$$2 : \neg fly \leftarrow ostrich$$
$$3 : bird \wedge ostrich \leftarrow$$

where $1 \prec 2$. Let $I = \{3, 2\}$. Thus, 1 cannot extend I.

Since the notion of priority may have different interpretations, in general one can take the approach that the semantics of a priority logic program depends on a parameter $\mathcal{R}$, which is a mapping over arguments. We call such a mapping an *extensibility function*. We now define the most intuitive extensibility function discussed above.

Definition 2. Let $\langle R, \prec \rangle$ be a priority logic program, I be an argument, r be a rule in R. We define an extensibility function $\mathcal{R}_1$ as follows:

$$\mathcal{R}_1(I) = App(\{r : \forall r' \in I, r \not\prec r'\}).$$

Note that, since each rule in an argument must be applicable in the argument itself, the employment of *App* is technical and ensures that the resulting set of rules is an argument.

Definition 3. Given an extensibility function $\mathcal{R}$, an argument I is said to be *self-extensible* under $\mathcal{R}$ if $I \subseteq \mathcal{R}(I)$.

Not all arguments are self-extensible. For example, consider

$$P = \langle \{1 : a \leftarrow\}, \{1 \prec 1\} \rangle$$

under $\mathcal{R}_1$. Clearly, the argument $\{1\}$ is not self-extensible, since $\mathcal{R}_1(\{1\}) = \emptyset$.

The approach based on extensibility function is sufficiently flexible to allow various application-dependent extensions and modifications. For example, one can strengthen the notion of extensibility by insisting on consistent extension: given an argument I and rule r, r extends I if there is no $r' \in I$ such that $r \prec r'$ *and if I implies the precondition of r then r's conclusion must not contradict I.* More formally,

Definition 4. Let $\langle P, \prec \rangle$ be a priority logic program and I be an argument. The extensibility function $\mathcal{R}_2$ is defined as:

$$\mathcal{R}_2(I) = App(\{r \in P : T_I^{\uparrow \omega} \not\models \neg Con(r) \text{ and } \forall r' \in I, r \not\prec r'\}).$$

The purpose of presenting this extensibility function is two-fold. First, later in this paper, we will illustrate how different behavior of default logic may be studied by constrained monotonic inferences under different extensibility functions. Further, we will show that this extensibility function can be used to express defeasible inheritance networks by priority logic.

From now on, we will say "a priority logic program $\langle P, \prec \rangle$ with $\mathcal{R}$ (or under $\mathcal{R}$)", to reflect the fact that the first step in choosing a semantics is to specify how to extend an argument.

Definition 5. (Stable argument)

Let $\langle P, \prec \rangle$ be a priority logic program with extensibility function $\mathcal{R}$. An argument I is said to be a *stable argument* if $\mathcal{R}(I) = I$.

A stable argument I is just a fixpoint of extending I. That is, the rules in I are precisely those applicable rules that are not blocked by rules in it, no more, no less.

Example 1. (Closed world assumption)

Suppose there are n cities. Consider a database of flight connections between pairs of these cities. This can be represented by a priority logic program, under $\mathcal{R}_1$, as follows:

$$1 : \{flight(A, B) \leftarrow : \text{if } A, B \text{ are directly connected}\}$$
$$2(x, y) : \neg flight(x, y) \leftarrow$$
$$3(x, y) : flight(x, y) \leftarrow flight(x, y)$$
$$2(x, y) \prec 3(x, y)$$

This priority logic program has one and only one consistent stable argument I such that any two cities A and B are connected if and only if it is known they are connected.

Obviously, this is a simple application of the *closed world assumption* of Reiter [25].

Example 2. Consider the frequently cited *bird-fly* example, represented by a priority logic program consisting of the following rules:

$$1(x) : fly(x) \leftarrow bird(x)$$
$$2(x) : \neg fly(x) \leftarrow ostrich(x)$$
$$3(x) : bird(x) \leftarrow ostrich(x)$$
$$4(x) : fly(x) \leftarrow super\_ostrich(x)$$
$$5(x) : ostrich(x) \leftarrow super\_ostrich(x)$$
$$6 : bird(a) \wedge ostrich(b) \wedge super\_ostrich(c)$$

and a priority relation: $1(x) \prec 2(x) \prec 4(x)$. Suppose $\mathcal{H} = \{a, b, c\}$. Then, there is only one stable argument under $\mathcal{R}_1$, which is $\{6, 1(a), 3(b), 2(b), 5(c), 4(c), 3(c)\}$. It concludes $fly(a)$, $\neg fly(b)$ and $fly(c)$.

A stable argument is a kind of *total argument*. For example, suppose I is a stable argument under $\mathcal{R}_1$. Then by definition, any rule r in I extends I (self-extensible) and for any rule r not in I, if r's precondition can be concluded from I, then there is some rule r in I such that $r' \prec r$. Because of this totality, a priority logic program may not have a stable argument. For example,

$$P = \langle \{1 : a \leftarrow; \ 2 : b \leftarrow \}, \{1 \prec 1\} \rangle$$

has no stable argument under $\mathcal{R}_1$: for any argument I, if $1 \notin I$ then $1 \in \mathcal{R}_1(I)$, and if $1 \in I$ then $1 \notin \mathcal{R}_1(I)$. This problem is analogous to the one where a default theory may not have an extension, and a logic program with default negation may not have a stable model. One can use the logic programming techniques to define well-founded semantics and other partial semantics (see [32]).

4 From Default to Constrained Monotonic Inferences

In this section we show default reasoning is just a special case of priority reasoning. This is accomplished through a simple transformation from a default theory to a priority logic program. We will see that the priority embedded in default logic is very intuitive and uniform.

Recall that a *default theory* is a pair (W, D) where W is a set of propositional formulas and D a set of *defaults*. A default is of the form

$$d = \frac{A : B_1, ..., B_m}{C}$$

where A, B_i's, and C are propositional formulas, and A is called the *prerequisite*, B_i's the *justifications* and C the *consequent*. For the purpose of reference, we define $Pre(d) = A$, $Cons(d) = C$ and $Just(d) = \{B_1, ..., B_m\}$. When we write $Just(D)$ we mean the set of the justifications in all the defaults in D.

We say two defaults d_1, d_2 are *similar* if $Pre(d_1) = Pre(d_2)$ and $Cons(d_1) = Cons(d_2)$. Obviously, if two defaults are similar, we can tactically change them into defaults which are not similar without changing the semantics of the default theory. For example, we can add a new fact p_{d_1} into W, and change the default d_1 into

$$\frac{pre(d_1) \wedge p_{d_1} : Just(d_1)}{Cons(d_1)}$$

without changing the default theory's semantics. Hence, to simply our discussion, in the rest of this section we assume that no defaults in an default theory are similar.

Definition 6. (Extension [26]) E is an R-*extension* of default theory $T = (W, D)$ if $E = Th(\bigcup_{i=0}^{\infty} E_i)$, where $E_0 = W$, and for every $i \geq 0$, $E_{i+1} = E_i \cup \{Cons(d) : d \in D, Pre(d) \in Th(E_i) \ \& \ \neg Just(d) \cap E = \emptyset\}$.

We now give a translation from a default theory to a priority logic program.

Definition 7. Let $T = (W, D)$ be a default theory. The translation of T, denoted $\Pi(T)$, is defined as yielding a priority logic program $\langle R, \prec \rangle$, where

$$R = W \cup \{Cons(r) \leftarrow Pre(r) \ : \ r \in D\} \cup \{\neg B \leftarrow \neg B \ : \ B \in Just(d), d \in D\}$$
$$\prec = \{Cons(d) \leftarrow Pre(d) \prec \neg B \leftarrow \neg B \ : \ B \in Just(d), d \in D\}$$

A priority logic program $\langle P, \prec \rangle$ translated from a default theory is of a particular kind of format: for any rule $r \in P$ and $r' \in P$, if $r \prec r'$ then r' is the rule of the form $\neg B \leftarrow \neg B$ and there is no rule more prior than r'. Due to this structural property, such a program is called a *flat* program.

Example 3. Suppose

$$T = (\{sunday\}, \{ \frac{sunday : \neg raining}{go\_fishing}, \frac{sunday : \neg go\_fishing}{stay\_home} \})$$

The translated priority logic program is :

1. *sunday $\leftarrow$*
2. *go_fishing $\leftarrow$ sunday*
3. *stay_home $\leftarrow$ sunday*
4. *raining $\leftarrow$ raining*
5. *go_fishing $\leftarrow$ go_fishing*

with the priority relation: $\{2 \prec 4, 3 \prec 5\}$ under $\mathcal{R}_1$.

The following theorem shows a one-one correspondence between a default theory and its translated priority logic program.

Theorem 8. *Let $T = (W, D)$ be a default theory. T has an R-extension E iff the priority logic program $\Pi(T)$ has a stable argument under $\mathcal{R}_1$, such that $Th(T_I^{\uparrow\omega}) = E$.*
PROOF:
$(\Longrightarrow)$ Since E is an extension of default theory $T = (W, D)$. So we can define $E_0 = W$ and for every $i \geq 0$

$$E_{i+1} = Th(E_i) \cup \{C : \frac{A : B_1, ..., B_n}{C} \in D, E_i \models A, \text{ for } 1 \leq k \leq n \ E \not\models \neg B_k\}$$

such that $E = \bigcup_{i=0}^{\infty} E_i$. We now construct a stable argument I under $\mathcal{R}_1$ as the concatenation of the sequence of arguments $I_0, I_1, ...,$ as follows: $I_0 = W$, and

$$I_{i+1} = \{\neg B \leftarrow \neg B \notin \bigcup_{j=1}^{j=i} I_j : B \in Just(D), E_i \models \neg B\} \cup$$
$$\{C \leftarrow A \notin \bigcup_{j=1}^{j=i} I_j : \frac{A:B_1,...,B_n}{C} \in D, E_i \models A, \text{ for } 1 \leq k \leq n \ E \not\models \neg B_k\}$$

It is easy to check that (a) I is an argument; (b) $Th(\mathcal{T}_I^{\uparrow\omega}) = E$; (c) for any $r \in I$, there is no $\neg B \in Th(\mathcal{T}_I^{\uparrow\omega})$ such that $r \prec \neg B \leftarrow \neg B$; (d) for any $r \in P - I$, if $\mathcal{T}_I^{\uparrow\omega} \models Pre(r)$ then $\exists B \in Just(r)$ such that $E = Th(\mathcal{T}_I^{\uparrow\omega}) \models \neg B$.

From (a) (b) (c) and (d), we conclude that I is a stable argument under $\mathcal{R}_1$.

($\Longleftarrow$) Let $I = \{w_0, w_1, ..., w_n, ...\}$ be a stable argument of priority logic program $\Pi(T)$ under $\mathcal{R}_1$ and $E = Th(\mathcal{T}_I^{\uparrow\omega})$. We define a sequence as follows: $E_0 =_{df} W$ and for every $i \geq 0$,

$$E_{i+1} =_{df} Th(E_i) \cup \{C : \frac{A : B_1, ..., B_n}{C} \in D, E_i \models A, \text{ for } 1 \leq k \leq n \; E \not\models \neg B_k\}$$

We need to prove $E = \bigcup_{i=0}^{\infty} E_i$. That is E is an extension of default theory T.

First, we can prove that for every $i \geq 0$, $E_i \subseteq E$ by induction on i. Hence we get that $\bigcup_{i=0}^{i=\infty} E_i \subseteq E$.

Conversely, we prove that for every $i : i \geq 0$, $\exists j : j \geq 0$, such that $Cons(w_i) \in E_j$.

If $w_0 \in W$, then we can see that $w_0 \in E_0$. Else, since $w_0 \not\prec I$, $Pre(w_0) \in Th(\{\})$, hence $Cons(w_0) \in E_1$. Suppose for every i, where $n \geq i \geq 0$, $\exists j$ such that $Cons(w_i) \in E_j$. Then we can see that $Pre(w_{n+1}) \in Th(E_j)$, and $\forall B \in Just(r)$, $\mathcal{T}_I^{\uparrow\omega} \not\models \neg B$, else $\neg B \leftarrow \neg B \in I$ and I is not self-extensible. Since $r \in \mathcal{R}_1(I)$, we get $Cons(w_{n+1}) \in Th(E_{j+1})$.

Thus we conclude $E = Th(\mathcal{T}_I^{\uparrow\omega}) = \bigcup_{i=0}^{\infty} E_i$. That is E is an extension of default theory T. This concludes the proof. $\square$

4.1 Variations of default logic by constrained monotonic inferences

In this subsection, we demonstrate that behavior of default logic may be studied through the use of different extensibility functions in constructing constrained monotonic inferences.

As an example, we will be using the extensibility function $\mathcal{R}_2$. Since it insists on consistent extension of an argument, its behavior is clearly related to Delgrande et al.'s constrained semantics [8]. On the other hand, if we define a semantics still based on the notion of a stable argument, its behavior is also related to R-extension. As a result, we get a semantics that lies in between.[2]

First, let's look at an example. The following default theory

$$\{\frac{: a}{c}, \frac{: b}{\neg c}, \frac{: p}{q}\}$$

has no R-extension. The reason is that the first two defaults give a contradiction, the global effect of which nullifies the applicability of any default.

---

[2] Note that our interest in this subsection is not in proposing yet another semantics for default logic.

The translated priority logic program is:

1. $c \leftarrow$
2. $\neg a \leftarrow \neg a$
3. $\neg c \leftarrow$
4. $\neg b \leftarrow \neg b$
5. $q \leftarrow$
6. $\neg p \leftarrow \neg p$

with the priority relation:

$$\{1 \prec 2, 3 \prec 4, 5 \prec 6\}.$$

This program has two stable arguments under $\mathcal{R}_2$, one of which is $\{1, 5\}$, and the other is $\{3, 5\}$. Under this semantics, we conclude q.

The correspondence between default theories and their translated priority logic programs suggests that the same behavior can be captured directly for default theories: we only need to modify the definition of R-extension (Definition 4) by replacing

$$E_{i+1} = E_i \cup \{Cons(d) : d \in D, Pre(d) \in Th(E_i) \ \& \ \neg Just(d) \cap E = \emptyset\}$$

with

$$E_{i+1} = E_i \cup \{Cons(d) : d \in D, Pre(d) \in Th(E_i) \ \& \\ \neg Just(d) \cap E = \emptyset \ \& \ \neg Cons(d) \notin E\}$$

The resulting semantics of default logic behaves precisely like the stable semantics of the corresponding priority logic programs under the extensibility function $\mathcal{R}_2$. Let's call such an extension an *S-extension*. Then it is not difficult to show that every R-extension is an S-extension and every S-extension is a constrained extension of Delgrande *et al.*, but the reverse is not true.

5 Nonmonotonic Inheritance Networks

In this section we show that Horty's defeasible inheritance networks [15] can be expressed as priority logic programs.

A defeasible inheritance network Γ is defined as a finite collection of positive and negative direct links between nodes. If x, y are nodes then $y \leftarrow x$ (resp. $y \not\leftarrow x$) represents a positive (resp. negative) *direct link* from x to y where x is called root and y is called head. Nodes of a network are divided into two disjoint node sets, object node set and predicate node set and object node can only appear in the root. A direct link with object root node is called *root direct link*.

A network Γ is *consistent* if there exists no two nodes x, y such that both $y \leftarrow x$ and $y \not\leftarrow x$ belong to Γ. A path of Γ is either a direct link or a sequence of Γ's direct links $x_1 \rightarrow x_2, ..., x_n \rightarrow x_{n+1}$ (called positive path), $n \geq 1$ (resp. $x_1 \rightarrow x_2, ..., x_{n-1} \rightarrow x_n, x_n \not\rightarrow x_{n+1}$, called negative path). When $n \geq 2$, we

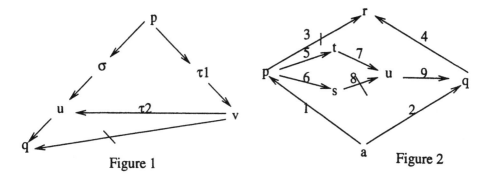

Figure 1   Figure 2

also simply denote it by $x_1 \sigma x_n \to x_{n+1}$ (resp. $x_1 \sigma x_n \not\to x_{n+1}$). The credulous semantics of a consistent defeasible inheritance network Γ is regarded as a path set of Γ, Φ, in which every path is regarded as a defeasible inheritance path. In the sequel we only consider consistent networks.

All the following definitions are adopted from Horty [15].

Definition 9. (Path constructibility and conflict in a path set)

A path σ is *constructible* in a path set Φ if $\sigma = x \sigma_1 y \overset{l}{\to} z$ (resp. $\sigma = x \sigma_1 y \overset{l}{\not\to} z$) and $x \sigma_1 y \in \Phi$ or σ is a root direct link. A path σ is *conflicting* in Φ if $\sigma = x \sigma_1 y \overset{l}{\to} z$ (resp. $\sigma = x \sigma_1 y \overset{l}{\not\to} z$) and $\sigma' = x \sigma_1' y' \overset{l'}{\not\to} z \in \Phi$ (resp. $\sigma' = x \sigma_1' y' \overset{l'}{\not\to} z \in \Phi$).

Definition 10. (Preemption)

A positive path $\pi(x, \sigma, u) \to y$ is *preempted* (see Figure 1) in Φ iff there is a node v such that (i) $v \to y \notin \Gamma$ and (ii) either $v = x$ or there is a path of the form $\pi(x, \tau 1, v, \tau 2, u) \in \Phi$.

A negative path $\pi(x, \sigma, u) \not\to y$ is preempted in Φ iff there is a node v such that (i) $v \to y \notin \Gamma$ and (ii) either $v = x$ or there is a path of the form $\pi(x, \tau 1, v, \tau 2, u) \in \Phi$

The credulous semantics of an inheritance network is given in the following definition.

Definition 11. (Defeasible inheritance path)

Path σ is *defeasible inheritable* in Φ, written as $\Phi \vdash_d \sigma$, iff either σ is a root direct link or σ is a compound path, $\sigma = \pi(x, \tau, y)$ (likewise for negative path) such that (i) σ is constructible in Φ, (ii) σ is not conflicted in Φ, and (iii) σ is not preempted in Φ.

Definition 12. (Credulous extension, consequence of a path set)

A set Φ of paths is a *credulous extension* of the net Γ iff $\Phi = \{\sigma : \Phi \vdash_d \sigma\}$.

We denote by $Cons(\Phi)$ the union of the following two node sets:

$\{u(a)$: if there is a positive path from object node a to u in $\Phi\}$
$\{\neg u(a)$: if there is a negative path from object node a to u in $\Phi\}$.

Example 4. Consider the defeasible inheritance network Γ of Figure 2, as given in [30]. This inheritance theory has three credulous extensions:

$$\Phi_1 = \{1, 2, 13, 15, 16, 157, 1579\}$$
$$\Phi_2 = \{1, 2, 13, 15, 16, 168\}$$
$$\Phi_3 = \{1, 2, 24, 15, 16, 168\}$$

Given an inheritance network Γ, a path $\pi(u, \sigma, x)$ is said to be *simple* if there is no path $\pi(u, \sigma', x)$ such that the set of links in $\pi(u, \sigma', x)$ is a proper subset of the links in $\pi(u, \sigma, x)$.

We now relate the semantics of nonmonotonic inheritance network with the stable arguments of its translated priority logic program under $\mathcal{R}_2$. First, we transform a consistent network to a priority logic program.

Definition 13. Given an inheritance network Γ, we transform it into a priority logic program, $\Pi(\Gamma) = \langle R_\Gamma, \prec_\Gamma, \mathcal{R}_2 \rangle$ as follows:

1. R_Γ contains only the following rules:
   $\{r_l(x) : (p_l(x) \wedge q(x)) \leftarrow p(x) \mid l = q \leftarrow p \in \Gamma\}$;
   $\{r_l(x) : (p_l(x) \wedge \neg q(x)) \leftarrow p(x) \mid l = q \not\leftarrow p \in \Gamma\}^3$;
   $\{r_{\pi(u,\sigma,q)}(x) : q(x) \leftarrow u(x) \wedge \bigwedge_{l \in \pi(u,\sigma,q)} p_l(x) \mid \pi(u, \sigma, q)$ is a positive simple
   path such that there is a node p such that $p \leftarrow q$ and $p \not\leftarrow u$ are in Γ or $p \not\leftarrow q$ and $p \leftarrow u$ are in $\Gamma\}$;
   Notice that $p_l, p_{\pi(u,\sigma,q)}$ are newly introduced predicate symbols.
2. $\prec_\Gamma$ is defined as following:
   $r_l(x) \prec_\Gamma r_{\pi(u,\sigma,q)}(x)$: For every $l = p \leftarrow q \in R_\Gamma$, every $p \not\leftarrow u \in \Gamma$ and every simple positive path $\pi(u, \sigma, q)$;
   $r_l(x) \prec_\Gamma r_{\pi(u,\sigma,q)}(x)$: For every $l = \neg p \leftarrow q \in R_\Gamma$, every $p \leftarrow u \in \Gamma$ and every simple positive path $\pi(u, \sigma, q)$ of Γ.

Note that in the transformed program, R_Γ is not simply the collection of all the links.

The following example illustrates the semantic relationship between a defeasible inheritance network and its translated priority logic program.

---

[3] When l is a positive root direct link, the translated rule is $r_l : p_l(p) \wedge q(p) \leftarrow$; when l is a negative root direct link, the translated rule is $r_l : p_l(p) \wedge \neg q(p) \leftarrow$

Example 5. Continue with the network Γ in Example 4. The translated priority logic program $\Pi(\Gamma)$ is:

$$r_1 : (p_1(a) \wedge p(a)) \leftarrow$$
$$r_2 : (p_2(a) \wedge q(a)) \leftarrow$$
$$r_3(x) : (p_3(x) \wedge \neg r(x)) \leftarrow p(x)$$
$$r_4(x) : (p_4(x) \wedge r(x)) \leftarrow q(x)$$
$$r_5(x) : (p_5(x) \wedge t(x)) \leftarrow p(x)$$
$$r_6(x) : (p_6(x) \wedge s(x)) \leftarrow p(x)$$
$$r_7(x) : (p_7(x) \wedge u(x)) \leftarrow t(x)$$
$$r_8(x) : (p_8(x) \wedge \neg u(x)) \leftarrow s(x)$$
$$r_9(x) : (p_9(x) \wedge q(x)) \leftarrow u(x)$$
$$r_{579}(x) : q(x) \leftarrow p(x), p_5(x), p_7(x), p_9(x)$$

The priority relation is: $\prec_\Gamma = \{r_4(x) \prec r_{579}(x)\}$. The reason for $r_4(x) \prec r_{579}(x)$ is that when both rules are applicable, there are two conflicting inheritance paths from node r to node p; one is through negative rule r_3, and the other is through r_4 and the corresponding path 579. Clearly, the latter path is more distant than the former, and hence rule r_4 should be blocked.

This priority logic program has exactly three stable arguments under the extensibility function $\mathcal{R}_2$ (Suppose $\mathcal{H} = \{a\}$):

$$I_1 = \{r_1, r_2, r_3(a), r_5(a), r_6(a), r_7(a), r_9(a), r_{579}(a)\}$$
$$I_2 = \{r_1, r_2, r_3(a), r_5(a), r_6(a), r_8(a)\}$$
$$I_3 = \{r_1, r_2, r_4(a), r_5(a), r_6(a), r_8(a)\}$$

These stable arguments correspond to the three extensions given in Example 4.

Let us verify that, for example, I_1 is a stable argument under $\mathcal{R}_2$. Clearly, for every rule $r \in I_1$ and rule r', if $r \prec r'$ then $r' \notin I_1$ and $T_{I_1}^{\uparrow \omega} \not\models \neg Cons(r)$. Hence, I_1 is self-extensible under the extensibility function $\mathcal{R}_2$.

Now, for every $r \in R_\Gamma - I_1 = \{r_4, r_8\}^4$, we can prove that $r \notin \mathcal{R}_2(I_1)$. It is easy to check that $T_{I_1}^{\uparrow \omega} \models \neg r$ and $T_{I_1}^{\uparrow \omega} \models u$. It then follows from the constraint $r_4 \prec r_{579}$ that for any rule $r \in \{r_4, r_8\}$, we have $r \notin \mathcal{R}_2(I_1)$.

The following theorem shows that the relationship demonstrated above holds true for all (consistent) networks.

Theorem 14. *Suppose Γ is a defeasible inheritance network. Then Φ is a credulous extension of Γ iff there is a stable argument I of $\Pi(\Gamma)$ such that $T_I^{\uparrow \omega}/\Gamma = Cons(\Phi)$, where S/Γ is the maximal subset of S such that every formula of that subset must be formula of Γ.*
PROOF:

($\Longrightarrow$) Suppose Φ is a credulous extension of Γ. Now we define that: $inf(\Phi)$ is the set $\{r_l(a) : l \in \Gamma$ appears in a path with object root node a of $\Phi\} \cup \{r_{\pi(u,\sigma,x)}(a) : r_{\pi(u,\sigma,x)} \in R_\Gamma$ and $\pi(u, \sigma, x)$ is a partial simple path of a path

---

^{4} In case of no confusion, we also denote $r_l(a)$ simply by r_l.

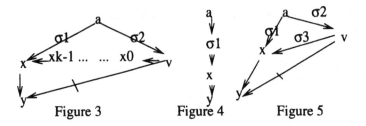

Figure 3   Figure 4   Figure 5

with object root node a of Φ}. Then $inf(\Phi)$ is a stable argument of $\Pi(\Gamma) = (R_\Gamma, \prec_\Gamma, \mathcal{R}_2)$.

For simplicity, we denote R_Γ by R and $\prec_\Gamma$ by $\prec$. We prove that $inf(\Phi)$ satisfies the following properties:

1. $inf(\Phi)$ is self-extensible.

Suppose $inf(\Phi)$ is not self-extensible, then we can see that there is a rule $r(a)$ of $inf(\Phi)$, such that $r(a) \notin \mathcal{R}_2(inf(\Phi))$. In the first case, $r(a)$ must be a rule corresponding to direct link. Suppose $r(a) = r_l(a)$ and $l = x \to y$, $r_{\pi(v,\sigma,x)}(a) \in inf(\Phi)$ such that $r_l(a) \prec r_{\pi(v,\sigma,x)}(a)$ and $v \not\to y \in \Gamma$ (see figure 3) (we let $\pi(v, \sigma, x)$ be $v \to x_0 \to ... \to x_{k-1} \to x$).

We know that there are σ_1 and σ_2 such that $a \to \sigma_1 \to x \to y \in \Phi, a \to \sigma_2 \to v\sigma x \in \Phi$. Since $a \to \sigma_1 \to x \to y$ is preempted in Φ, Φ cannot be a credulous extension.

In the second case, we can see that there exists $l = x \to y \in \Phi$ and $r_l(a) = (y(a) \wedge p_l(a)) \leftarrow x(a) \in inf(\Phi)$, such that $\mathcal{T}^{\uparrow\omega}_{inf(\Phi)} \models \neg y(a) \vee \neg p_l(a)$. Since $\mathcal{T}^{\uparrow\omega}_{inf(\Phi)} \models p_l(a)$, we have $\mathcal{T}^{\uparrow\omega}_{inf(\Phi)} \models \neg y(a)$. Clearly, Φ must contain two conflicting paths. Hence this is contradictory to the assumption that Φ is a credulous extension. Thus $inf(\Phi)$ is self-extensible under extensibility function $\mathcal{R}_2$.

2. For every rule $r \in R_\Gamma - inf(\Phi)$, if $Pre(r) \in \mathcal{T}^{\uparrow\omega}_{Inf(\Phi)}$ then $r \notin \mathcal{R}_2(inf(\Phi))$.

First let $r(a) \notin Inf(\Phi)$ be the rule translated from a direct link $l = x \to y$. From the premise of 2, i.e., $Pre(r) \in \mathcal{T}^{\uparrow\omega}_{Inf(\Phi)}$, we get $x(a) \in \mathcal{T}^{\uparrow\omega}_{Inf(\Phi)}$. Now we prove $r(a) \notin \mathcal{R}_2(inf(\Phi))$.

Since $x(a) \in \mathcal{T}^{\uparrow\omega}_{Inf(\Phi)}$, there is σ_1 such that $a \to \sigma_1 \to x \in \Phi$. Notice that σ_1 can be empty (see Figure 4). Suppose $\sigma = a \to \sigma_1 \to x \to y$, $\sigma \notin \Phi$. Since σ is constructible in Φ, σ must satisfy one of the following two conditions.

Condition 1. σ is conflicting in Φ. In this case, Φ has a path $a \to \sigma_2 \to x \not\to y$. Hence $x(a) \not\to y(a) \in inf(\Phi)$, $\mathcal{T}^{\uparrow\omega}_{inf(\Phi)} \models \neg y(a)$ and $\mathcal{T}^{\uparrow\omega}_{inf(\Phi)} \models \neg(y(a) \wedge p_l(a))$. Hence $r(a) \notin \mathcal{R}_2(inf(\Phi))$.

Condition 2. σ is preempted in Φ. In this case, Φ must have a path (and hence a simple path) $a \to \sigma_2 \to v \to \sigma_3 \to x \in \Phi$ such that $v \not\to y \in \Gamma$ (see Figure 5). Obviously, $r_{v \to \sigma_3 \to x}(a) \in inf(\Phi)$ and $r(a) \prec r_{v \to \sigma_3 \to x}(a)$. Hence, $r(a) \notin \mathcal{R}_1(inf(\Phi))$.

Second, if $r(a) \notin Inf(\Phi)$ be the rule translated from the path link $r_{\pi(u,\sigma,x)}$, then it is impossible that $Pre(r) \in \mathcal{T}^{\uparrow\omega}_{Inf(\Phi)}$. Else, $r(a)$ must be in Φ.

($\Longleftarrow$) Suppose Γ is a consistent defeasible network. If I is a stable argument of $\Pi(\Gamma) = (R_\Gamma, \prec_\Gamma, \mathcal{R}_2)$, then we define $Arg(I)$ is the set {σ : σ is a path from the object root node a such that for every link l of σ, $r_l(a)$ appears in I}. It is easy to check that $Arg(I) = \{\sigma : Arg(I) \vdash_d \sigma\}$, and hence $Arg(I)$ is a credulous extension of Γ. $\square$

Recently, Dung and Son [11] show a relationship between argumentation and *acyclic* defeasible inheritance networks. Given an acyclic network Γ with node size being n, they transform it into an argument theory $AF_\Gamma = \langle AR_\Gamma, attack_\Gamma \rangle$ where AR_Γ is the set of *all the paths* on Γ and $attack_\Gamma$ is a relation among paths. Apparently, AR_Γ can be huge even for a small network. Our transformation results in $\langle R_\Gamma, \prec_\Gamma \rangle$ where R_Γ is a set of rules corresponding to *direct links* and a subset of *simple path*, and $\prec_\Gamma$ a priority relation among rules formed out of these links and paths. Although in the worst case both AF_Γ's size and R_Γ's are exponential to the size of the network, the latter is much smaller than the former in almost all practical situations. In addition, the condition *acyclic* in their case is too strong as it even prevents expressing *if and only if*. In our case, the transformation works for all consistent networks.

We note that Horty was correct when he claimed that it was impossible to relate path-based reasoning to general nonmonotonic reasoning formalisms, as we can see that such a relationship has to rely on the use of (relevant) paths, and thus arguably involves partial computation.

6 Remarks on Proof Theory

On the one hand, since priority logic is based on monotonic inferences guided by priorities, there is always a naive, ineffective procedure for propositional priority programs, based on exhaustive search and comparison using the underlying extensibility function. On the other hand, since priority logic is such a powerful knowledge representation language, as it subsumes default logic of various semantics and nonmonotonic inheritance networks, the fact that these knowledge representation languages do not have general, effective proof procedures implies that the same holds true for priority logic.

On the other hand, it is possible to develop realistic proof procedures for special classes of priority theories. In fact, many such procedures exist. Since normal logic programs can be considered as a special class of priority logic programs, the elegant proof procedure by Eshghi and Kowalski for abductive reasoning [12] (also see [31]), and the various efficient proof procedures for the well-founded semantics, can be adopted for the corresponding class of priority logic programs (under the corresponding semantics). Since default theories are a class of priority logic programs, Reiter's backward chaining procedure to prove theorems of default theories with normal defaults can be adopted for the corresponding class of priority logic programs. How to extend these proof procedures to accommodate some larger classes of priority theories is an important topic of future research. In fact, viewing nonmonotonic reasoning as constrained monotonic inferences points to a new direction for investigating proof theoretic properties of nonmonotonic reasoning.

7 More on Related Work

In some traditional nonmonotonic reasoning formalisms, such as default reasoning and logic programming, preference relations can be specified implicitly and indirectly through the structure of defaults or program clauses. Shoham [29] shows that preference among models of a theory can provide the semantic bases of nonmonotonic reasoning. However the preference relation in his work is also implicit and it cannot directly reflect user's intention in explicitly describing which knowledge is more important than others.

Marek and Truszczynski (cf. [22], Chapter 3) show that Reiter's extension can be captured by a well-ordering over defaults. A well-ordering of this kind specifies which defaults should be performed before which others. This is a useful priority constraint, but it is different from ours where the notion of priority constraint means that a rule's application automatically blocks another.

Allen Brown *et al.* [1, 2] (also see [14, 19]) propose a family of modal logics of preference where preference is used in selecting models. By introducing the preference, they argue that the resulting theory turns out to be surprisingly general and powerful. In general, the preference logic there is based on two modal operators, P_f and P_b where $P_f F$ means that F suffices for preference and $P_b F$ means that F precludes such a preference relation [1]. To our knowledge, this is the first framework allowing preference operator to appear in a logic framework.

The concept of logic programming without default negation was first suggested in [18] and further developed in [9]. The authors argue that a knowledge representation language without using default negation can avoid the possible confusions arising from the use of default and explicit negation. Priority in this framework however relies on the existence of contradiction. That is, if there is no contradiction, the specified priority is ineffective. The effect of its interaction with contradiction is usually hard to predicate. As a result, the semantics of a program under this notion of priority may not be intuitive to what is intended. For example, the natural representation of the bird-fly example presented in the introduction of this paper is not applicable.[5] This treatment of priority also complicates the relation between programs with default negation (normal programs) and those without. This is because the transformation from the former to the latter has to resort to contradiction in order to have a one-one correspondence (cf. [33] for more details). Furthermore, their work is restricted to logic programs (i.e. rules of literals), and thus it is impossible to answer the question that whether nonmonotonic reasoning in general can be viewed as monotonic inferences with priority.

Recently, Sakama and Inoue proposed *prioritized logic programming*, where priorities can be explicitly specified in a program [28]. Priority here is among literals and inclusive and the purpose is to reduce the number of answer sets in disjunctive logic programming.

---

[5] For the program with the rule set $\{1, 2, 3, 4, 5\}$ and priority $1 \prec 5$, since $\{1, 2, 3, 5\}$ is consistent, it forms an *admissible extension*, from which one concludes *fly*.

Order logic program proposed by F. Buccafurri *et al.* [6] provides a mechanism for constructing a set of components organized into an inheritance hierarchy. Each component consists of a set of rules which may have logical negative heads. Like in the object-oriented approach, properties defined for the higher components in the hierarchy flow down to the lower ones. When a contradiction arises, a conclusion from the lower rules is considered a refinement of the conclusion from the higher rules. Thus in this framework priority is achieved automatically by program structure.

As for the notion of priority, we believe that different priorities may be needed for different purposes and a real system may need several kinds of priorities together to work. Recently, Jagadish *et al.* [17] analyze various types of interactions between rules in active databases and find that exclusive priority is one of the basic interactions between rules of active databases.

References

1. Jr. Allen L. Brown, Surya Mantha, and Toshiro Wakayama. Constraint optimization using preference logics: A new role for modal logic. In Isabel F. Cruz, editor, *Using a Visual Constraint Language for Data Display Specification*, pages 22–23, 1993.
2. Jr. Allen L. Brown, Surya Mantha, and Toshiro Wakayama. Preference logics: Towards a unified approach to non-monotonicity in deductive reasoning. *Annals of Mathematics and Artificial Intelligence*, pages 10: 233–280, 1994.
3. F. Baader and B. Hollunder. Priorities on default with prerequisite and their application in treating specificity in terminological default logic. *Journal of Automata Reasoning*, 15:41–68, 1995.
4. G. Brewka. *Nonmonotonic reasoning: Logical Foundations of Commonsense.* Cambridge University Press, 1991.
5. G. Brewka. Well-founded semantics for extended logic programming with dynamic preference. *Journal of Artificial Intelligence Research*, 4:19–36, 1996.
6. F. Buccafurri, N. Leone, and P. Rullo. Stable models and their computation for logic programming with inheritance and true negation. *J. Logic Programming*, pages 27: 5–44, 1995.
7. K.L. Clark. Negation as failure. In H. Gallaire and J. Minker, editors, *Logic and Data Bases*, pages 293–322. Plenum Press, 1978.
8. J. Delgrande, T. Schaub, and W. Jackson. Alternative approach to default logic. *Artificial Intelligence*, 70:167–237, 1994.
9. V. Dimopoulos and A. Kakas. Logic programming without negation as failure. In *Proc. ILPS '95*. MIT Press, 1995.
10. P. Dung. An argumentation theoretic foundation for logic programming. *J. Logic Programming*, 22:151–177, 1995.
11. P. Dung and T. Son. Nonmonotonic inheritance, argumentation and logic programming. In *Proc. 3rd International conference on LPNMR*, pages 316–329. MIT Press, 1995.
12. K. Eshghi and R.A. Kowalski. Abduction compared with negation by failure. In *Proc. 6th ICLP*, pages 234–254. MIT Press, 1989.
13. D. Etherington and R. Reiter. On inheritance hierarchies with exceptions. In *AAAI-83*, pages 104–108. Morgan Kaufmann, 1983.

14. K. Govindarajan, B. Jayaraman, and S. Mantha. Preference logic programming. In *Proc. 12th ICLP*, pages 731–746. MIT Press, 1995.
15. J.F. Horty. Some direct theories of nonmonotonic inheritance. In M. Cabbay and C. Hogger, editors, *Handbook of Logic and Artificial Intelligence*, pages 111–187. Oxford University, 1991.
16. T. Imielinski. Results on translating defaults to circumscription. *Artificial Intelligence*, 32:131–146, 1987.
17. H. Jagadish, A. Mendelzon, and I. Mumick. Managing conflicts between rules. In *Proc. ACM PODS*. Montreal Quebec, Canada, 1996.
18. A. Kakas, P. Mancarella, and P.M. Dung. The acceptability semantics for logic programs. In *Proc. 11th ICLP*, pages 504–519, 1994.
19. S. Mantha. *first-Order Preference Theories and their Applications*. PhD thesis, University of Utah, 1991.
20. V. Marek and V.S. Subrahmanian. The relationship between logic program semantics and non-monotonic reasoning. In *Proc. 6th International Conference on Logic Programming*, 1989.
21. V. Marek and M. Truszcynski. Relating autoepistemic and default logic. In *Proc. Principles of Knowledge Representation and Reasoning*, pages 276–288. Morgan Kaufmann, 1989.
22. V. Marek and M. Truszczybski. *Nonmonotonic Logic, Context-Dependent Reasoning*. Springer-Verlag, 1993.
23. J. McCarthy. Circumscription – a form of non-monotonic reasoning. *Artificial Intelligence*, 13:27–39, 1980.
24. R. Moore. Semantical consideration on nonmonotonic logic. *Artificial Intelligence*, 25(1):234—252, 1985.
25. R. Reiter. On closed world data bases. In H. Gallaire and J. Minker, editors, *Logic and Data Bases*, pages 55—76. Plenum Press, 1978.
26. R. Reiter. A logic for default reasoning. *Artificial Intelligence*, 13:81–132, 1980.
27. R. Reiter and G. Cirscuolo. On interacting defaults. In *Proc. 7th IJCAI*, pages 270–276, 1981.
28. C. Sakama and K. Inous. Representing priorities in logic programs. In *Proc. Int'l Conference and Symposium on Logic Programming*, 1996.
29. Y. Shoham. A semantics approach to non-monotonic logics. In *Proc. IJCAI*, pages 388–392, 1987.
30. R.H. Thomason and J.F. Horty. Logics for inheritance theory. In *2nd International Workshop for Non-Monotonic Reasoning*, pages 220–237, 1988.
31. F. Toni and A.C. Kakas. Computing the acceptability semantics. In *Proc. 3rd International Conference on Logic Programming and Non-monotonic Reasoning*, pages 401–415, 1995.
32. X. Wang, J. You, and L. Yuan. Circumscription by inference rules with priority. In *Proc. 12th European Conf. on Artificial Intelligence*, pages 110–115, 1996.
33. X. Wang, J. You, and L. Yuan. Logic programming without default negation revised. TR96-25, Department of Computing Science, University of Alberta, 1996.

Update-Programms Can Update Programs

José Júlio Alferes[1] and Luís Moniz Pereira[2]

[1] DM, U. Évora and CITIA, U. Nova de Lisboa 2825 Monte da Caparica, Portugal
[2] DCS and CITIA, U.Nova de Lisboa 2825 Monte da Caparica, Portugal

Abstract. In the recent literature the issue of program change via updating rules (also known as revision rules) has been reduced to the issue of obtaining a new set of models, by means of the update rules, from each of the models of an initial program. Any program whose models are exactly the new set of models will count as an update of the original program. Following the classical approaches to theory updating, it is of course essential to start by specifying precisely how a program's models are to change, before even attempting to specify program change. But to stop there is to go only halfway.

Another limitation of existing approaches to logic program updating concerns their not dealing with 3-valuedness, i.e. with partial models. The limitation is twofold: on the one hand, only programs under 2-valued semantics are approachable; on the other, when there are contradictory update rules, in lieu of leaving undefined the effects of the contradictory rules and keeping those of the others, no update is possible at all.

In this paper, we generalize the notion of justified update to partial (or 3-valued) interpretations and expound a correct transformation on normal programs which, from an initial program, produces another program whose models enact the required change in the initial program's models, as specified by the update rules. Forthwith, we generalize our approach to logic programs as well as update programs extended with explicit negation.

1   Introduction

Logic program evolution by specifying update rules has hardly been studied. As the world changes so must programs that represent knowledge about it. Whereas simple fact by fact updates have long been addressed [9, 10, 6], providing transitional rules to govern the change of one program into another is still a blind spot in the research literature. The overall purpose of this paper is to show how transition rules for updating a logic program can be specified by some other logic program.

Program updating is distinct from program revision, where a program accommodates, perhaps non-monotonically by revising assumptions, additional information about a *static* world state. Work on program revision (or contradiction removal) has received more attention (e.g. in [1, 8, 2, 19, 18]) then transitional updating. The following realistic situation chisels the differences between program update and revision crisply.

Example 1. My secretary has just booked me on a flight from here to London on wednesday but can't remember to which airport, Gatwick or Heathrow. Clearly, this statement can be represented by:

$$booked\_for\_gatwick \lor booked\_for\_heathrow$$

Now someone tells me there never are flights from here to Gatwick on wednesday, i.e. I'm told ¬*booked_for_gatwick*. I conclude that I'll be flying to Heathrow, i.e. *booked_for_heathrow*. This is knowledge revision. The state of the world hasn't changed with respect to the flight information, but on obtaining more information I have thereby revised accordingly my knowledge about that same state of the world.

Alternatively, I hear on the radio that all flights to Gatwick on wednesday have been canceled, i.e. the world changed such that now ¬*booked_for_gatwick* holds. I'm at a loss regarding whether I still have a flight to London on wednesday. This is knowledge update. The world of flights has changed, and refining my knowledge about its previous state is inadequate: I cannot conclude that I'm booked to fly to Heathrow (*booked_for_heathrow*). I have obtained knowledge about the new world state but it doesn't help me to disambiguate the knowledge I had about its previous state. What I can do is pick up the phone and book me a flight to Heathrow on wedsnesday, on any airline. That will change my flight world and at the same time update my knowledge about that change. However, I'm now unsure whether I might not have two flights booked to Heathrow. But if my secretary suddenly remembers he had definitely booked me to Gatwick, then I will no longer believe I have two flights to Heathrow on wednesday.

Notice how updating may produce models that are further refinable by revision. Another example of revision is when assumptions are revised in the light of new information about the same world state. For example, the reader may have presupposed that the secretary in this example is a woman till we used the giveaway pronoun "he".

Knowledge or theory update is usually performed "model by model" [17, 11], where a set of formulae T_U is a *theory update* of T, following an update request U, iff the models of T_U result from updating each of the models of T by U. Thus a theory update is determined by the update of its models.

The same idea can be applied to logic programming: a program P_U is a *program update* of P, following an update request U, iff the models of P_U (according to some logic program semantics S) are the result of updating each of the models of P (given by semantics S) by U. So, to obtain P_U, first compute all models of P according to a given semantics S; to each of these models apply the update request U to obtain a new set of models $\mathcal{M}$; P_U is then any logic program whose models are exactly $\mathcal{M}$. This process can be depicted as in Figure 1.

In the recent literature [12, 13, 3, 16], the issue of program change via updating rules (also known as revision rules) has been reduced, rather simply, to the issue of obtaining a new set of models by means of the update rules, from each of the models of the given program (i.e. only the part of the above picture which is inside the box). Any program whose models are exactly the new set of

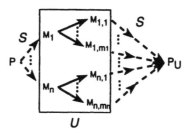

Fig. 1. Model by model theory update

models will count as an update of the original program. However, no procedure is set forth by the cited authors for obtaining one. (Except in the trivial case where the original and final programs are just sets of facts [3, 16].) Following [17, 11], it is of course essential to start by specifying precisely how a program's models are to change, before even attempting to specify program change. But to stop there is to go only halfway.

Another limitation of these first inroads into the problems of logic program change concerns their not dealing with 3-valuedness, i.e. with partial models. The limitation is twofold: on the one hand, only programs under 2-valued semantics are approachable; on the other, when there are contradictory update rules, in lieu of leaving undefined the effects of the contradictory rules and keeping those of the others, no update is possible at all. Furthermore, these authors have not considered models comprising explicit negation.

In the sequel, we begin with a short overview of previous work on interpretation updating in what concerns its basic definitions, and move on to generalize the latter to partial interpretations. Next we expound a correct transformation on normal programs which, from an initial program, produces another program whose models enact the required change in the initial program's models, as specified by the update rules. Forthwith, we generalize our approach to logic programs as well as update programs extended with explicit negation. In the end we draw some conclusions.

2 Overview of Interpretation Updates

For more detailed motivation and background to this section of the present paper the reader is referred to [12, 16]. For the purpose of our generalization we prefer the basic definitions as deployed in [12], which we will adapt: on account of the required distinction between revison and update, we will speak instead of update rule, update program, and justified update, rather than use those authors' vocabulary of revision rule, revision program, and justified revision. Otherwise the definitions are the same.

The language used is similar to that of logic programming: *update programs* are collections of *update rules*, which in turn are built of atoms by means of the special operators: ←, *in*, *out*, and ",".

Definition 1 (Update rules for atoms). Let U be a countable set of atoms. An *update in-rule* or, simply, an *in-rule*, is any expression of the form:

$$in(p) \leftarrow in(q_1), \ldots, in(q_m), out(s_1), \ldots, out(s_n) \qquad (1)$$

where p, q_i, $1 \leq i \leq m$, and s_j, $1 \leq j \leq n$, are all in U, and $m, n \geq 0$.

An *update out-rule* or, simply, an *out-rule*, is any expression of the form:

$$out(p) \leftarrow in(q_1), \ldots, in(q_m), out(s_1), \ldots, out(s_n) \qquad (2)$$

where p_i, q_i, $1 \leq i \leq m$, and s_j, $1 \leq j \leq n$, are all in U, and $m, n \geq 0$.

Intuitively, update programs can be regarded as operators which, given some initial interpretation I_i, produce its updated version I_u.

Example 2. Let P be the update program:

$$in(a) \leftarrow out(b)$$
$$in(b) \leftarrow out(a)$$

Assume the initial 2-valued interpretation $I_i = \langle \{\}; \{a, b\} \rangle^3$. There are two viable 2-valued updated interpretations: $I_u = \langle \{a\}; \{b\} \rangle$ and $I_u = \langle \{b\}; \{a\} \rangle$.

Example 3. Let $P = \{out(a) \leftarrow in(a)\}$ and let $I_i = \langle \{a\}; \{\} \rangle$ be the initial interpretation. No interpretation can be regarded as the update of I_i by P. For example, imagine $I_u = \langle \{\}; \{a\} \rangle$ were such an update. Making a false could only be justified on the basis of the single update rule. But the body of that rule requires a to be true *in the final interpretation* for the rule to take effect. Similarly, $I_u = I_i$ cannot be an update as well.

Definition 2 (Necessary change). Let P be an update program with least (2-valued) model $M = \langle T_M; F_M \rangle$. The *necessary change* determined by P is the pair (I_P, O_P), where:

$$I_P = \{a : in(a) \in T_M\}$$
$$O_P = \{a : out(a) \in T_M\}$$

If $I_P \cap O_P = \{\}$ then P is said *coherent*.

Intuitively, the necessary change determined by a program P specifies those atoms that must be added and those atoms that must be deleted, whatever the initial interpretation.

Example 4. Take the update program $P = \{out(b) \leftarrow out(a); \ in(b); \ out(a)\}$. The necessary changes are irreconcilable and P is incoherent.

---

[3] In the sequel, an interpretation I will be represented as a pair $I = \langle T; F \rangle$, where T and F are disjoint sets of atoms. Atoms in T are true in I; atoms in F are false in I; all other atoms are undefined in I. An interpretation I is dubbed 2-valued (or total) iff there are no undefined atoms.

Definition 3 (Justified update[4]). Let P be an update program and $I_i = \langle T_i; F_i \rangle$ and $I_u = \langle T_u; F_u \rangle$ two (total) interpretations, whose true and false atoms are made explicit. The *reduct* $P_{I_u|I_i}$ with respect to I_i and I_u is obtained by the following operations:

- Removing from P all rules whose body contains some $in(a)$ and $a \in F_u$;
- Removing from P all rules whose body contains some $out(a)$ and $a \in T_u$;
- Removing from the body of remaining rules of P all $in(a)$ such that $a \in T_i$;
- Removing from the body of remaining rules of P all $out(a)$ such that $a \in F_i$.

Whenever P is coherent, I_u is a P-justified update of I_i if the two update stability conditions hold:

$$T_u = (T_i - O_{P_{I_u|I_i}}) \cup I_{P_{I_u|I_i}}$$
$$F_u = (F_i - I_{P_{I_u|I_i}}) \cup O_{P_{I_u|I_i}}$$

The first two operations delete rules which are useless given $I_u = \langle T_u; F_u \rangle$. Because of stability, the initial interpretation is preserved as much as possible in the final one. The last two rules achieve this because any exceptions to preservation are explicitly dealt with by the union and difference operations in the two stability conditions.

With its insistance on total interpretations, the above definition runs into problems:

Example 5. Let $I_i = \langle \{a, b\}; \{c\} \rangle$. Let $P = \{in(c) \leftarrow; \ out(b) \leftarrow \}$. Clearly, the meaning of this program is that c must be made true and b must be made false. Hence $I_u = \langle \{a, c\}; \{b\} \rangle$. Now add to P the rule $out(a) \leftarrow in(a)$. There is no longer any justified update, even though we might want to retain the results concerning b and c while remaining undecided about a, i.e. obtain the partial interpretation $\langle \{c\}; \{b\} \rangle$.

Example 6. Consider again the update program P of Example 2 and the same initial interpretation, $I_i = \langle \{\}; \{a, b\} \rangle$. There is no P-justified update of I_i corresponding to the final empty interpretation $I_u = \langle \{\}; \{\} \rangle$, even though it would be desirable to have an update result that remained undecided between the alternatives of making a or making b true.

Furthermore, the insistance on total interpretations allows less freedom in the modelling of knowledge about the world since, often, our knowledge about it is incomplete to start with.

3 Updates of Partial Interpretations

To remedy the above shortcomings we have generalized the definitions of necessary update and justified update to cope with partial interpretations, whilst preserving their results in the case of total ones.

---

[4] This slightly different formulation is clearly equivalent to the original one.

Example 7. Consider the following logic program P:

$$gatwick \quad \leftarrow not\ heathrow$$
$$heathrow \leftarrow not\ gatwick$$

representing two conflicting defaults about a flight being booked for Gatwick or Heathrow, and consider also the update request $\{out(gatwick)\}$.

The stable models of P are:

$$\langle\{gatwick\}; \{heathrow\}\rangle \quad \text{and} \quad \langle\{heathrow\}; \{gatwick\}\rangle$$

the latter stating that the flight is booked for Heathrow and not for Gatwick, and the former that the flight is booked for Gatwick and not for Heathrow. The P-justified updates of these models by $\{out(gatwick)\}$ are, respectively, $\langle\{\}; \{heathrow, gatwick\}\rangle$ and $\langle\{heathrow\}; \{gatwick\}\rangle$, the former stating that the flight is booked for neither Heathrow nor Gatwick, and the latter as before.

If the well-founded semantics is used instead, another model of P exists, viz. $\langle\{\}; \{\}\rangle$, stating that one remains undecided about the flight being booked either for Gatwick or for Heathrow. Intuitively, one expects that the above update request should not modify this model of P in what regards *heathrow*, but should falsify *gatwick*. However, the definitions presented before cannot come to this conclusion, since they do not apply to partial models.

Example 8. Consider the initial interpretation $\langle\{\}; \{heathrow, gatwick\}\rangle$, and the update program:

$$in(gatwick) \quad \leftarrow out(heathrow)$$
$$in(heathrow) \leftarrow out(gatwick)$$

stating that, in the final interpretations, if the flight is not booked for Heathrow then it must be booked for Gatwick, and if the flight is not booked for Gatwick, then it must be booked for Heathrow.

The previous definition yields two updated interpretations:

$$\langle\{gatwick\}; \{heathrow\}\rangle \quad \text{and} \quad \langle\{heathrow\}; \{gatwick\}\rangle$$

whose readings can be found in Example 7. Intuitively, the partial interpretation $\langle\{\}; \{\}\rangle$, stating that one is undecided about both the flight being booked for Gatwick or for Heathrow, is also expectable as a result of the update. In fact, before the update one is sure that the flight is booked for neither airport. After the update, because of the conflict between the update rules, one expectable situation is to be undecided whether the flight is booked for Heathrow or for Gatwick.

This example shows that update programs should desirably be able to undefine atoms, i.e. it might then happen that a P-justified update of a model I has more undefined atoms than I: an update may cause additional undefinedness. To cater for this possible behaviour, the definition of necessary change must be modified. Before, necessary change was simply determined by a set of atoms that must become true (I_P), and a set of atoms that must become false (O_P). In the generalization below, necessary change is also defined by a set of atoms, NI_P, that cannot remain true (even if they do not become false), and a set of atoms, NO_P, that cannot remain false (even if they do not become true).

Definition 4 (3-valued necessary change). Let P be an update program with least 3-valued model $M = \langle T_M; F_M \rangle$.
The *necessary change* determined by P is the tuple (I_P, O_P, NI_P, NO_P), where

$$I_P = \{a : in(a) \in T_M\}$$
$$O_P = \{a : out(a) \in T_M\}$$
$$NI_P = \{a : out(a) \notin F_M\}$$
$$NO_P = \{a : in(a) \notin F_M\}$$

Atoms in I_P (resp. O_P) are those that must become true (resp. false). Atoms in NI_P (resp. NO_P) are those that cannot remain true (resp. false). If $I \cap O = \{\}$ then P is said *coherent*.

In the sequel, we omit the index P whenever the update program is clear from the context. Note that, by definition of 3-valued interpretation, $I = \langle T; F \rangle$, and T and F are disjoint, and so $I_P \subseteq NO_P$ and $O_P \subseteq NI_P$; i.e., as expected, atoms that must become true cannot remain false, and atoms that must become false cannot remain true.

Intuitively, $out(a) \notin F_M$ means that $out(a)$ is either true or undefined in M, but definitely not false. Thus, a should not remain true. If, additionally, $out(a) \in T_M$ then the a should also become false. Similar arguments justify the definition of NO_P.

3-valued justified updates rely on this new definition of necessary change, which falls back on the previous one for 2-valued interpretations. Only the third and fourth operations below are new, forged to deal with the effect on update rules of undefined literals in I_u.

Definition 5 (3-valued justified update). Let P be an update program and $I_i = \langle T_i; F_i \rangle$ and $I_u = \langle T_u; F_u \rangle$ two partial (or 3-valued) interpretations. The *reduct* $P_{I_u|I_i}$ with respect to I_i and I_u is obtained by the following operations, where u is a reserved atom undefined in every interpretation:

- Removing from P all rules whose body contains some $in(a)$ and $a \in F_u$;
- Removing from P all rules whose body contains some $out(a)$ and $a \in T_u$;
- Substituting in the body of remaining rules of P the reserved atom u for every $in(a)$, such that a is undefined in I_u[5] and $a \in T_i$;
- Substituting in the body of remaining rules of P the reserved atom u for every $out(a)$ such that a is undefined in I_u and $a \in F_i$;
- Removing from the body of remaining rules of P all $in(a)$ such that $a \in T_i$;
- Removing from the body of remaining rules of P all $out(a)$ such that $a \in F_i$.

---

[5] I.e. $a \notin T_u$ and $a \notin F_u$.

Let (I, O, NI, NO) be the 3-valued necessary change determined by $P_{I_u|I_i}$. Whenever P is coherent, I_u is a P-justified update of I_i if the two stability conditions hold:

$$T_u = (T_i - NI) \cup I$$
$$F_u = (F_i - NO) \cup O.$$

The two new operations are justified as follows. In a rule with $in(a)$ in its body, where a is undefined in I_u and $a \notin T_i$, $in(a)$ cannot be true, and also it cannot be substituted by undefined for, otherwise, the irrelevant rule $in(a) \leftarrow in(a)$, which must be possible to add to any update program inconsequently, would become $in(a) \leftarrow u$, with the paradoxical effect of including a in NO for subtraction from F_i. More generally, in such a case $in(a)$ cannot become undefined in the reduct of P by virtue of undefining it in the body of a rule. Not so if $a \in T_i$. In that case, $in(a)$ in a rule body can and should be replaced by u to test stability. Finally, because of the inertial character of the stability conditions, any literal undefined in I_i will remain so in I_u, unless explicitly added as true or as false by the reduct of P. So no inertia operations are called for regarding undefined literals in I_i.

A similar, symmetric, reasoning applies in the case of occurences of $out(a)$ in the rule bodies.

Example 9. Consider the update program $P = \{out(gatwick)\}$ and an initial interpretation where both *gatwick* and *heathrow* are undefined, i.e. $\langle\{\}; \{\}\rangle$.

Trivially, the reduct of P is equal to P, independently of the final interpretation: in the reduct all modifications to the original program are conditional on literals in the body of update rules, and P has none. The least model of P is:

$$\langle\{out(gatwick)\}; \{in(gatwick), in(heathrow), out(heathrow)\}\rangle$$

Thus, the necessary change is $I = \{\}$, $O = \{gatwick\}$, $NI = \{gatwick\}$, $NO = \{\}$. Accordingly, the only P-justified update of $\langle\{\}; \{\}\rangle$ is $\langle\{\}; \{gatwick\}\rangle$.

Example 10. Consider the update program P of Example 8, and the initial model

$$I_i = \langle\{\}; \{heathrow, gatwick\}\rangle.$$

It is easy to check that the two P-justified updates

$$\langle\{gatwick\}; \{heathrow\}\rangle \quad \text{and} \quad \langle\{heathrow\}; \{gatwick\}\rangle,$$

obtained as per Definition 3, are also 3-valued justified updates. Moreover, $I_u = \langle\{\}; \{\}\rangle$ is also a 3-valued justified update.

In fact, the reduct with respect to this final model is:

$$in(gatwick) \leftarrow u$$
$$in(heathrow) \leftarrow u$$

Note that *heathrow* is undefined in I_u and false in I_i. So $out(heathrow)$ was replaced by u. Similarly for $out(gatwick)$.

The reduct's least model is $\langle\{\};\{out(gatwick),out(heathrow)\}\rangle$. Thus the necessary change is $I = O = NI = \{\}$, $NO = \{gatwick, heathrow\}$. Given that $\{\} = (\{\} - NI) \cup I$, and $\{\} = (\{\} - NO) \cup O$, $\langle\{\};\{\}\rangle$ is indeed a 3-valued justified update.

Example 11. Consider again the same update program, but now the initial model

$$I_i = \langle\{gatwick, heathrow\};\{\}\rangle.$$

In this case the only justified update is I_i itself. Note that $I_u = \langle\{\};\{\}\rangle$ is not a justified update.

In this case the reduct of P with respect to I_i and I_u is:

$$in(gatwick) \leftarrow out(heathrow)$$
$$in(heathrow) \leftarrow out(gatwick)$$

where $out(heathrow)$ was not replaced by u because, even though $heathrow$ is undefined in I_u, it is not false in I_i.

The least model of the reduct is:

$$\langle\{\};\{in(gatwick),in(heathrow),out(gatwick),out(heathrow)\}\rangle$$

and so $I = O = NI = NO = \{\}$. $\langle\{\};\{\}\rangle$ is not in fact a (3-valued) justified update because: $\{\} \neq (\{gatwick, heathrow\} - \{\}) \cup \{\}$.

Example 12. Consider again Example 5. Now the partial interpretation $\langle\{c\};\{b\}\rangle$ is a (3-valued) justified update of augmented P.

Example 13. Consider once again Example 6. The empty interpretation $I_u = \langle\{\};\{\}\rangle$ is indeed a (3-valued) P-justified update of $I_i = \langle\{\};\{a,b\}\rangle$ as desired. The other two updates are preserved.

Theorem 6 (Generalization of updates). *The 3-valued versions of necessary change and justified update both reduce to their 2-valued versions whenever the initial and final interpretations are total.*

Proof. If the final and initial interpretations are total then the new rules introduced in the definition of reduct are useless, and thus the definition of reduct for three-valued justified update exactly coincides with the one for a two-valued justified update. Moreover, no symbol u occurs in the reduct. Thus the least model of the reduct is total, and so $NI = O$ and $NO = I$. Clearly, under these conditions the stability equalities also coincide.

An update is to be performed only if necessary. In other words, if an update program does not contradict the initial model, the only justified update should equal the initial model. This is indeed the case for 3-valued justified updates[6].

---

[6] In [12], its authors prove that this is also the case for their (2-valued) justified updates.

Definition 7. An interpretation $M = \langle T; F \rangle$ satisfies $in(a)$ (resp. $out(a)$) iff $a \in T$ (resp. $a \in F$). It satisfies the body of a rule iff it satisfies each literal of the body, and it satisfies a rule iff whenever it satisfies the body it also satisfies the head of the rule. An interpretation M satisfies an update program P iff it satisfies all its rules.

Theorem 8. *Let M be an interpretation satisfying an update program P. Then the only 3-valued justified update of M by P is M.*

Proof. If an interpretation $M = \langle T_i; F_i \rangle$ satisfies an update program P then:

1. *It is a justified update.* I_P adds nothing to T_i, and O_P adds nothing to F_i, because any conclusion of a rule with satisfied body in the reduct of P is necessarily satisfied as well. Furthermore, NI_P can subtract nothing from T_i: first, because for any true conclusion $out(a)$, since O_P adds nothing to F_i, a cannot belong to T_i; second, because any undefined literal in M cannot introduce u in the rules of the reduct of P, since that requires the literal being in F_i. Similarly, NO can subtract nothing from F_i. Consequently $F_u = F_i$ and $T_u = T_i$.

2. *There is no other justified update $R = \langle T_u; F_u \rangle$.* Indeed, first note that $T_u \subseteq T_i$ and $F_u \subseteq F_i$, since I_P can add nothing to T_i and O_P can add nothing to F_i, because of the form of the justified update operations and because I_i satisfies P. Second, neither NI nor NO can subtract from I_i and F_i. Consider NI. Again, there can be no new *out* conclusion from the reduct of P. Also there cannot be any undefined $out(a)$ arising from the reduct of P. Such an undefined $out(a)$ would require some $in(b)$ (resp. $out(b)$) to be undefined in the body of some rule and that $b \in T_i$ (resp. $b \in F_i$). But for $in(b)$ (resp. $out(b)$) to be undefined, since $b \in T_i$ (resp. $b \in F_i$) there must be some rule with conclusion $out(b)$ (resp. $in(b)$) undefined so that b, which does not belong to R, is subtracted from T_i (resp. F_i). Applying this reasoning systematically, eventually either $out(b)$ (resp. $in(b)$) depends on $in(b)$ or on $out(b)$. If it depends on $in(b)$ then, because $b \in T_i$ and M satisfies P, $b \in F_i$ (contradiction). If it depends on $out(b)$ then $b_i \in F_i$ too (contradiction). The same reasoning applies to NO, showing that neither NI nor NO subtract from T_i and F_i, respectively, and consequently $R = M$.

Example 14. Consider the update program P of Example 8, and the initial model

$$I = \langle \{heathrow, gatwick\}; \{\} \rangle.$$

Since neither $out(gatwick)$ nor $out(heathrow)$ are satisfied by I, both rules of P are trivially satisfied by I. As shown in Example 11, I is in fact the only justified update of itself.

An obvious consequence of the above theorem is that tautological update rules (i.e. update rules satisfied by every interpretation, e.g. $in(L) \leftarrow in(L)$) do not modify the initial interpretation.

4 Normal Program Updates

We've seen in the introduction that, till now, program updating has been only implicitly achieved, by recourse to the updating of each of a program's models to obtain a new set of updated models, via the update rules. Following [11], any program whose models are exactly the updated models counts as a program update. But how to obtain such a program?

Our stance, while consistent with the view depicted in Figure 1, is quite different. We aim at producing a program transformation path to updating that directly obtains, from the original program, an updated program with the required models, which is similar to the first. The update program's models will be exactly those derivable, one by one, from the original program's models through the update rules. Thus we are able to sidetrack the model generation path. Furthermore, due to the similarity between both programs, any revisions targeted for the old program can be correctly performed on the new one. This new approach can be depicted as in Figure 2.

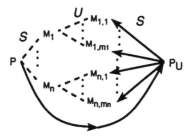

Fig. 2. Program update via program transformation

We shall see that any update program can be transformed into an extended logic program which, by the way, becomes part of the new updated program. This transformation is similar in character to the one in [16], which serves a different purpose though[7]. The normal program which is subjected to the update program, has to be transformed too. The final updated program is the union of the two transformations.

We will resort to a 3-valued well-founded semantics of extended logic programs, namely $WFSX$ [14], that introduces explicit negation in Well-Founded Semantics [7] by means of its *coherence principle*, stating that explicit negation $\neg L$ entails default negation *not* L, for every objective literal L^8. In the case of stratified (and locally stratified) programs $WFSX$ coincides with Answer-Sets

---

[7] In the next section, we shall have to consider a more complex transformation, in the case where the program to be updated is also an extended logic program.

[8] An objective literal is, as usual, an atom A or its explicit negation $\neg A$.

Semantics. However, its 3-valued character is essential for dealing with partial interpretations, and its skeptical character for allowing (otherwise impossible) skeptical updates (viz. Example 13).

Definition 9 (Translation of update programs into extended LPs).
Given an update program UP, its translation into the update logic program ULP is defined as follows.

- Each update in-rule of the form (1) translates into:

$$p \leftarrow q_1, \ldots, q_m, \neg s_1, \ldots, \neg s_n$$

- Each update out-rule of the form (2) translates into:

$$\neg p \leftarrow q_1, \ldots, q_m, \neg s_1, \ldots, \neg s_n$$

The rationale for this translation can best be understood in conjunction with the next definition, for they go together. Suffice it to say that we can simply equate explicit negation $\neg$ with *out*, since the programs to be updated are normal ones, and thus devoid of explicit negation (so no confusion can arise).

Definition 10 (Update transformation of a normal program). Given an update program UP, consider its corresponding update logic program ULP. For any normal logic program P, its updated program U with respect to ULP (or to UP) is obtained through the operations:

- The rules of ULP belong to U;
- The rules of P belong to U, subject to the changes below;
- For each atom A figuring in a head of a rule of ULP:
      Replace in every rule of U originated in P all occurences of A by A', where A' is a new atom;
      Include in U the rules $A \leftarrow A', not \neg A$ and $\neg A \leftarrow not A', not A$.

The purpose of the first operation is to ensure change according to the update program. The second operation guarantees that, for inertia, rules in P remain unchanged unless they can be affected by some update rule. The third operation changes all atoms in rules originating in P which are possibly affected by some update rule, by renaming such atoms. The new name stands for the atom as defined by the P program. The fourth operation introduces inertia rules, stating that any possibly affected atom contributes to the definition of its new version, unless actually affected through being overriden by the contrary conclusion of an update rule; the $not \neg A$ and $not A$ conditions cater for this test.

Example 15. Consider again the update program of Example 8, and the initial empty program with respect to the vocabulary $\{g, h\}$, where g stands for *gatwick* and h for *heathrow*. The updated logic program is U:

$$
\begin{array}{lll}
g \leftarrow \neg h & h \leftarrow h', not \neg h & g \leftarrow g', not \neg g \\
h \leftarrow \neg g & \neg h \leftarrow not h', not h & \neg g \leftarrow not g', not g
\end{array}
$$

The WFSX model of the initial (empty) program is $\langle\{\};\{g,h\}\rangle$. The WFSX models of U are $\langle\{\};\{h',g'\}\rangle$, $\langle\{g,\neg h\};\{\neg g,h,g',h'\}\rangle$, and $\langle\{\neg g,h\};\{g,\neg h,g',h'\}\rangle$. Modulo the primed and explicitly negated atoms we have:

$$M_1 = \langle\{\};\{\}\rangle \qquad M_2 = \langle\{g\};\{h\}\rangle \qquad M_3 = \langle\{h\};\{g\}\rangle$$

These models exactly correspond to the justified updates obtained in Example 10.

Example 16. Consider once more the update program of Example 8, and the initial program $P = \{g \leftarrow; \quad h \leftarrow\}$. In this case, the updated logic program is again U, of the previous example, plus the facts $\{g' \leftarrow; \quad h' \leftarrow\}$, and its only WFSX model is:

$$\langle\{g,h,g',h'\};\{\neg g,\neg h\}\rangle$$

Modulo the primed and explicitly negated atoms, this model exactly corresponds to the result of Example 11.

Example 17. Let $UP = \{in(p) \leftarrow in(q)\}$. Then $ULP = \{p \leftarrow q\}$. Take the normal program P:

$$p \leftarrow not\ q$$
$$q \leftarrow not\ p$$

The updated logic program U of P with respect to ULP (or to UP) is U:

$$p \leftarrow q \qquad p' \leftarrow not\ q \qquad p \leftarrow p', not\ \neg p$$
$$q \leftarrow not\ p' \qquad \neg p \leftarrow not\ p', not\ p$$

The *WFSX* models of P are:

$$M_0 = \langle\{\};\{\}\rangle \qquad M_1 = \langle\{p\};\{q\}\rangle, \qquad M_2 = \langle\{q\};\{p\}\rangle$$

The *WFSX* models of U are:

$$M_3' = \langle\{\};\{\}\rangle \qquad M_4' = \langle\{p,q\};\{p',\neg p\}\rangle \qquad M_5' = \langle\{p,p'\};\{q,\neg p\}\rangle$$

Modulo the primed and explicitly negated atoms we have:

$$M_3 = \langle\{\};\{\}\rangle \qquad M_4 = \langle\{p,q\};\{\}\rangle \qquad M_5 = \langle\{p\};\{q\}\rangle$$

which happen to be the UP−justified updates of the models of P.

Example 18. Let UP be:

$$out(q) \leftarrow out(p)$$
$$out(p) \leftarrow$$

Then ULP is:

$$\neg q \leftarrow \neg p$$
$$\neg p \leftarrow$$

Take again the normal program P of Example 17. The updated logic program U of P with respect to ULP (or UP) is U:

$$
\begin{array}{lll}
\neg q \leftarrow \neg p & p' \leftarrow not\ q' & p \leftarrow p', not\ \neg p \\
\neg p \leftarrow & q' \leftarrow not\ p' & \neg p \leftarrow not\ p', not\ p \\
& & q \leftarrow q', not\ \neg q \\
& & \neg q \leftarrow not\ q', not\ q
\end{array}
$$

The $WFSX$ models of U are:

$$\langle\{\neg p, \neg q\}; \{p, q\}\rangle\ \langle\{\neg p, \neg q, p'\}; \{p, q, q'\}\rangle\ \langle\{\neg p, \neg q, q'\}; \{p, q, p'\}\rangle$$

Modulo the primed and explicitly negated atoms all these models coincide with $\langle\{\}; \{p, q\}\rangle$, corresponding to the single UP-justified update of the models of P.

Theorem 11 (Correctness of the update transformation). *Let P be a normal logic program and UP a coherent update program. Modulo any primed and explicitly negated elements, the $WFSX$ models of the updated program U of P with respect to UP, are exactly the (3-valued) UP-justified updates of the $WFSX$ models of P.*

Proof. In this proof with assume that every atom A of the original program has been replaced by a new atom A', and that "inertia" rules have been added for all atom. While the transformation only does so for atoms that actually occur in the head of some update rule, this is clearly a simplification, and adding them for all atoms does not change the results.

Let I be a $WFSX$ model of ULP. Then I_i represents the restriction of I to primed atoms, and I_u the remainder of I.

Given the properties of $WFSX$ (namely those of relevance and modularity), it is easy to prove that:

- If I is a $WFSX$ model of ULP then I_i is a $WFSX$ model of P.
- If I' is a $WFSX$ model of P then there exists at least one $WFSX$ model I of ULP such that $I' = I_i$.

Given this, it suffices to prove that:

1. If I is a $WFSX$ model of ULP then I_u is a justified update of I_i.
2. If I_i is a $WFSX$ model of P and I_u a justified update of I_i then $I = I_i \cup I_u$ is a $WFSX$ model of ULP.

(1) To prove this point, we begin by removing all primed atoms of ULP, by taking I_i into account, thus constructing a program $T(ULP)$, as follows:

- remove all rules whose head is primed;
- for all primed atoms A' true in I_i, add to ULP a rule $A \leftarrow not\ \neg A$;
- for all primed atoms A' false in I_i, add to ULP a rule $\neg A \leftarrow not\ A$;
- for all primed atoms A' undefined in I_i, add to ULP the rules:
  $A \leftarrow\mathbf{u}, not\ \neg A$ and $\neg A \leftarrow\mathbf{u}, not\ A$.

$T(ULP)$ corresponds to ULP after a partial evaluation with respect to I_i. Given that partial evaluation does not change the $WFSX$ semantics of programs, and that I is a $WFSX$ model of ULP, clearly I_u is a $WFSX$ model of ULP_u.

The proof proceeds by showing that[9], one by one, the modifications on $T(ULP)$ corresponding to the modifications made to construct the reduct $P_{I_u|I_i}$ do not change the semantics of $T(ULP)$. In the end, we conclude that I_u is a $WFSX$ model of the translation of the reduct $P_{I_u|I_i}$, as per Definition 9, plus the rules added when constructing $T(ULP)$. Let R denote the resulting program.

It remains to be proven that such an I_u satisfies the two stability conditions on the reduct $P_{I_u|I_i}$. Below we prove that I_u satisfies the first stability condition. Proving that it also satisfies the second stability condition is quite similar, and is omitted for brevity.

By definition, $A \in I_{P_{I_u|I_i}}$ iff $in(A) \in least(P_{I_u|I_i})$. Since the translation of $P_{I_u|I_i}$ does not introduce any default negated literals, $in(A) \in least(P_{I_u|I_i})$ iff A belongs to the least model of the translation of the reduct. Given that I_u is a $WFSX$ model of R, and R contains the translation of the reduct, clearly $A \in T_u$.

Again by definition of justified update, $A \in T_i$ and $A \notin NI_{P_{I_u|I_i}}$ iff $A \in T_i$ and $not\ out(A) \in least(P_{I_u|I_i})$. Again, since the translation of $P_{I_u|I_i}$ does not introduce any default negated literals, $not\ out(A) \in least(P_{I_u|I_i})$ iff $not\ \neg A$ belongs to the least model of the translation of the reduct. If $A \in T_i$, then $A \leftarrow not\ \neg A \in T(ULP)$, and $T(ULP)$ has no rules for $\neg A$. Thus, given that I_u is a $WFSX$ model of R, $A \in T_u$.

Consequently, if $A \in (T_i - NI) \cup I$ then $A \in T_u$. If $A \in T_u$ then either there is a rule in the translation of the reduct proving A, in which case $A \in I$, or $not\ \neg A \in I_u$ and $A \in T_i$ (otherwise no enertia rule capable of proving A would exist in $T(ULP)$). Thus $A \in T_i - NI$. This proves that I_u satisfies the first stability condition.

(2) The proof of this point is similar to the reverse of the previous point's proof. First note that if I_u is a justified update of I_i by the update program UP, it is also one by the reduct of the update program. The proof proceeds by showing that I_u is a $WFSX$ model of R, the translation of the reduct plus the rules in $T(ULP)$. This is done similarly to the last part of the previous point's proof. The proof proceeds by showing that, one by one, the modifications on R corresponding to the reverse of the modifications made to construct the reduct $P_{I_u|I_i}$ do not change the semantics of R. After all the modifications, the resulting program clearly corresponds to ULP. Since the semantics is not changed, I_u is also a $WFSX$ model of ULP.

5 Updating models and programs with explicit negation

Since the updated programs of normal programs are, in general, extended programs, to update them in turn we need to address the issue of updating extended

---

[9] This part of the proof is quite long and is not presented here.

programs. This is one motivation for defining updates for models and programs with explicit negation. Another motivation is to be able to update knowledge bases represented by extended logic programs. In fact, much work has been done in representing knowledge with extended logic programs (see e.g. [4, 15]). For this knowledge to be updated one needs a definition of updates of models and of programs with explicit negation. To do so, we first generalize the language of update rules:

Definition 12 (Update rules for objective literals). Let U be a countable set of objective literals. Update in-rules or, simply, in-rules, and update out-rules or, simply, out-rules, are as per Definition 1, but with respect to this new set U.

Intuitively, an objective literal is quite similar to an atom. For example, $in(\neg a)$, simply means that $\neg a$ must become true, and this can be achieved as for atoms. The same applies to $out(\neg a)$, which means that $\neg a$ must become false. Thus, it is not surprising that the definitions of necessary change and justified update for models with explicit negation are quite similar to those for models without explicit negation.

Despite the similarities, there is a subtle but important additional condition that justified updates of models with explicit negation must obey.

Example 19. Consider the initial model (with explicit negation):

$$\langle \{gatwick, \neg heathrow\}; \{\neg gatwick, heathrow\} \rangle$$

meaning that one knows that a flight is booked for Gatwick, and no flight is booked for Heathrow.

Consider now the update program $\{in(\neg gatwick)\}$. This update means that $\neg gatwick$ must become true, i.e. $gatwick$ must become (explicitly) false. Performing this update on the initial model requires more than simply adding $\neg gatwick$: it also requires the removal of $gatwick$ from the positive part of the model. In fact, if the world changed so that $gatwick$ became explicitly false, certainly the truth of $gatwick$ will have to be removed. Intuitively, the result of this update on the initial model is $\langle \{\neg gatwick, \neg heathrow\}; \{gatwick, heathrow\} \rangle$.

If later we are told $in(heathrow)$, the result should then be:

$$\langle \{\neg gatwick, heathrow\}; \{gatwick, \neg heathrow\} \rangle.$$

What this example shows is that $in(\neg a)$ additionally requires $out(a)$, and $in(a)$ additionally requires $out(\neg a)$. This can be seen as a consistency requirement on updated models. If $\neg a$ (resp. a) must become true, then a (resp. $\neg a$) must be guaranteed absent from the truth part of the model. Instead of changing the definitions of necessary change and justified update to cope with these impositions, for simplicity we add instead, to every update program, the two update rules:

$$out(A) \leftarrow in(\neg A) \qquad \text{and} \qquad out(\neg A) \leftarrow in(A)$$

for every atom A in the language, and then determine the justified updates as before:

Definition 13 (Extended Justified Update). Let P be an update program with explicit negation, and $I_i = \langle T_i; F_i \rangle$ and $I_u = \langle T_u; F_u \rangle$ two partial interpretations with explicit negation[10].

Let $P' = P \cup \{out(L) \leftarrow in(\neg L) : L \in U\}$, where U is the set of all objective literals. I_u is a P-justified update of I_i iff it is a P'-justified update of I_i according to Definition 5, where all explicitly negated atoms are simply viewed as new atoms.

Mark that, when the initial program does include explicit negation, the update transformation for normal programs of Definition 10 does not yield an updated extended program whose models are the updates of the initial program's models. This is so because the transformation does not distinguish between making $\neg a$ true $(in(\neg a))$ and making a false $(out(a))$: both are transformed into $\neg a$. However, the definition of justified update of models with explicit negation views the two updates differently:

Example 20. Consider the initial model $\langle \{a\}; \{\neg a, b, \neg b\} \rangle$, and the update $out(a)$. It is easy to check that the only justified update is $\langle \{\}; \{a, \neg a, b, \neg b\} \rangle$, resulting from removing the truth of a.

If the update $in(\neg a)$ is considered instead, then the only justified update is $\langle \{\neg a\}; \{a, b, \neg b\} \rangle$.

In the transformation for normal programs, explicit negation $\neg A$ is used to falsify A. Since in $WFSX$ $\neg A$ entails $not\ A$, and the original programs have no objective literals of the form $\neg A$, the only outcome of having $\neg A$ is, in fact, that of imposing $not\ A$, as desired. However, if the program being updated differentiates $\neg A$ from $not\ A$, the former can no longer be used as a means to impose the latter.

Intuitively, an update out-rule $out(A) \leftarrow Body$ means that whenever $Body$ is true in the updated interpretation $not\ A$ must be true. If extended programs allowed default negated literals in the head of rules, this could be solved by transforming $out(A)$ in the head of an update rule by $not\ A$. The intended meaning of a rule $not\ L \leftarrow Body$ would then be "If the body is true then $not\ L$ must be true".

In [5] is shown that $WFSX$ is expressive enough to capture the semantics of extended logic programs with default literals in the heads of rules. This is accomplished via a program transformation, such that the partial stable models of the transformed extended program exactly correspond to those models of the program with default literals at the head, given the above intended reading for such rules. The transformed extended program P^{not} of a program P with default literals in the head is simply constructed as follows:

- For each objective literal A (resp. $\neg A$) in the language of P, program P^{not} contains the rule $A \leftarrow A^p$ (resp. $\neg A \leftarrow A^n$), where A^p (resp. A^n) is a new atom;

---

[10] Recall that in such interpretations, if $\neg L \in T$ then $L \in F$, for every objective literal L. See [14] for a formal definition.

– For each rule of the form $A \leftarrow Body$ (resp. $\neg A \leftarrow Body$) in P, program P^{not} contains the rule $A^p \leftarrow Body$ (resp. $A^n \leftarrow Body$);
– For each rule of the form $not\ A \leftarrow Body$ (resp. $not\ \neg A \leftarrow Body$) in P, program P^{not} contains the rule $\neg A^p \leftarrow Body$ (resp. $\neg A^n \leftarrow Body$).

The whole idea of the transformation is to allow $not\ A$ and $not\ \neg A$ conclusions, once transmuted into $\neg A^p$ and $\neg A^n$, to falsify the single rules for A and for $\neg A$.

The translation of update programs with explicit negation into extended logic programs mirrors this transformation, where atoms $out(A)$ (resp. $out(\neg A)$) are first translated into $not\ A$ (resp. $not\ \neg A$), both in the bodies and heads of rules.

Definition 14 (Translation of extended update programs into LPs).
Given an update program with explicit negation UP, its translation into the update logic program ULP is defined as follows:

1. Each in-rule $in(L_0) \leftarrow in(L_1), \ldots, in(L_m), out(L_{m+1}), \ldots, out(L_n)$ where $n \geq 0$, and the L_i are objective literals, translates into:

$$L_0^* \leftarrow L_1, \ldots, L_m, not\ L_{m+1}, \ldots, not\ L_n$$

where $L_0^* = A^p$ if $L_0 = A$, and $L_0^* = A^n$ if $L_0 = \neg A$;
2. Each out-rule $out(L_0) \leftarrow in(L_1), \ldots, in(L_m), out(L_{m+1}), \ldots, out(L_n)$ where $n \geq 0$, and the L_i are objective literals, translates into:

$$\neg L_0^* \leftarrow L_1, \ldots, L_m, not\ L_{m+1}, \ldots, not\ L_n$$

where $L_0^* = A^p$ if $L_0 = A$, and $L_0^* = A^n$ if $L_0 = \neg A$;
3. For every objective literal L such that $in(L)$ belongs to the head of some in-rule of UP, ULP contains $\quad \neg L^* \leftarrow L \quad$ where $L^* = A^n$ if $L = A$, and $L^* = A^p$ if $L = \neg A$;
4. For every atom A occuring in the head of some update rule of UP, ULP contains $\quad A \leftarrow A^p \quad$ and $\quad \neg A \leftarrow A^n$.

Items (1) and (2) directly reflect the transformation P^{not} on the rules that result from translating $in(L)$ by L, and $out(L)$ by $not\ L$. Item (3) reflects the transformation on the update rules $out(L) \leftarrow in(\neg L)$ for each objective literal L (implicitly added to all update programs). Note that if there are no rules in the update program for $in(\neg L)$ then there is no need to add the corresponding rule, as it would be useless. Item (4) simply adds the rules required by P^{not} for establishing a link between objective literals L and the corresponding L^p and L^n ones. Again, if the atom A never occurs in the heads of update rules, then there is no need for adding such rules for it.

Definition 15 (Update transformation of an extended program).
Given an update program with explicit negation UP, consider its corresponding ULP. For any extended program P, its updated program U with respect to ULP (or to UP) is obtained by the operations:

- The rules of ULP belong to U;
- The rules of P belong to U, subject to the changes below;
- For each atom A occuring in the head of some update rule of UP:

  Replace in every rule of U originated in P all occurences of A by A', where A' is a new atom;

  Include in U the rules:

$$A^p \leftarrow A', not \ \neg A^p \qquad A^n \leftarrow \neg A', not \ \neg A^n$$
$$\neg A^p \leftarrow not \ A', not \ A^p \qquad \neg A^n \leftarrow not \ \neg A', not \ A^n$$

As before, atoms A of the initial program that may change their truth value are replaced by new atoms A'. The added rules implement inertia for those atoms. The first rule on the left states that "if A was true in the initial program, and it is not the case that $out(A)$, then A should be in" (note that, in heads, $out(A)$ is transformed into $\neg A^p$). The second rule on the left states that "if A was false in the initial program, and it is not the case that $in(A)$, then A should be out". The rules on the right express correspondingly the same, but for explicitly negated atoms.

Example 21. [11] Consider a university that periodically updates its evaluation of faculty members based on their research and teaching record. Faculty members who are known to be strong researchers and good teachers receive positive evaluation. Those who are not known to be strong researchers are not positively evaluated, and those that are poor teachers receive a negative evaluation. This leads us to the following update program, with the obvious abbreviations, and where non-ground rules stand for the set of their ground instances:

$$in(g\_eval(X)) \leftarrow in(g\_res(X)), in(g\_teach(X))$$
$$out(g\_eval(X)) \leftarrow out(g\_res(X))$$
$$in(\neg g\_eval(X)) \leftarrow in(\neg g\_teach(X))$$

At this university, it is common knowledge that anyone who receives a teaching award is considered a good teacher, and anyone who has published many papers is considered a good researcher. It is part of the records that Scott is a good teacher, Jack has received a teaching award, Lisa and Scott have already published many papers but not Jack, and that, in the previous evaluation period, Lisa and Jack obtained good evaluations. This leads to the knowledge representation program P:

$$g\_teach(X) \leftarrow award(X) \qquad award(jack) \leftarrow$$
$$g\_res(X) \leftarrow many(X) \qquad \neg many(jack) \leftarrow$$
$$g\_eval(jack) \leftarrow$$
$$g\_teach(scott) \leftarrow \qquad many(lisa) \leftarrow$$
$$many(scott) \leftarrow \qquad g\_eval(lisa) \leftarrow$$

---

[11] This example is inspired on a similar one due to Teodor Przymusinski.

whose only $WFSX$ model $M = \langle T; F \rangle$ contains the following evaluation record:

$$\{g\_eval(jack), g\_eval(lisa)\} \subset T$$
$$\{g\_eval(scott), \neg g\_eval(jack), \neg g\_eval(lisa)\} \subseteq F$$

The update logic program U obtained by the transformation above is as follows:

$$g\_eval^p(X) \leftarrow g\_res(X), g\_teach(X)$$
$$\neg g\_eval^p(X)) \leftarrow not\ g\_res(X)$$
$$g\_eval^n(X)) \leftarrow \neg g\_teach(X)$$

$$g\_teach(X) \leftarrow award(X) \qquad\qquad award(jack) \leftarrow$$
$$g\_res(X) \leftarrow many(X) \qquad\qquad \neg many(jack) \leftarrow$$
$$\qquad\qquad\qquad\qquad\qquad\qquad g\_eval'(jack) \leftarrow$$
$$g\_teach(scott) \leftarrow \qquad\qquad\qquad many(lisa) \leftarrow$$
$$many(scott) \leftarrow \qquad\qquad\qquad g\_eval'(lisa)) \leftarrow$$

$$g\_eval(X) \leftarrow g\_eval^p(X) \qquad\qquad \neg g\_eval(X) \leftarrow g\_eval^n(X)$$

$$g\_eval^p(X) \leftarrow g\_eval'(X), not\neg g\_eval^p(X)$$
$$\neg g\_eval^p(X) \leftarrow not\ g\_eval'(X), not\ \neg g\_eval^p(X)$$
$$g\_eval^n(X) \leftarrow \neg g\_eval'(X), not\ \neg g\_eval^n(X)$$
$$\neg g\_eval^n(X) \leftarrow not\ \neg g\_eval'(X), not\ \neg g\_eval^n(X)$$

The single justified update of the only $WFSX$ model of P is the single $WFSX$ model of $U = \langle T_u; F_u \rangle$, modulo primed, p-ed and n-ed literals, containing the evaluation record:

$$\{g\_eval(scott), g\_eval(lisa)\} \subset T_u$$
$$\{g\_eval(jack), \neg g\_eval(jack), \neg g\_eval(lisa)\} \subseteq F_u$$

Scott now has a good evaluation because he has many papers (which makes him a good researcher) and he was already know to be a good teacher. Jack has no longer a good evaluation because it is known that he does not have many papers (and so he cannot be considered a good researcher). Though Lisa is not explicitly known to be a good teacher, she keeps her good evaluation record because it is neither the case that she cannot be considered a good researcher nor is it the case that she does not have many papers.

Theorem 16 (Correctness of the transformation). *Let P be an extended logic program and UP a coherent update program. Modulo any primed and A^p and A^n elements, the $WFSX$ models of the updated program U of P with respect to UP are exactly the UP-justified updates of the $WFSX$ models of P.*

The structure of this theorem's proof is similar to that of Theorem 11. The details of the proof are slightly more complex, mainly because the translation T of update rules can now contain default negated literals in the the body of rules of T. To solve this additional complexity the proof appeals to most of the arguments used in [5] to prove that, with the construction above, $WFSX$ is expressive enough to capture the semantics of extended logic programs with default literals in the heads.

6 Conclusion

In this paper we have motivated, demonstrated, and illustrated how to make more general use of update programs. Firstly, their application was extended to encompases partial interpretations. Secondly, we showed how to apply update programs directly to normal and extended logic programs, rather than to their models. For doing so, we generate an updated program whose models are exactly those that would be obtained by individually updating each model of the original program. The updated programs result from transformations, proven correct, which apply jointly to update programs and the given logic programs they operate on. Whereas uptading models may be an exponential process, due to a possible exponential number of models, our updating transformation of programs is clearly a polynomial process. The additional complexity in obtaining the models of the updated program is only exacted on demand. Furthermore successive update transformation may take place before any models are desired.

Acknowlegments

This work was partially supported by JNICT-Portugal project ACROPOLE no. 2519/TIT/95. Thanks are due to Teodor Przymusinski and Mirek Truszczyński for their comments.

References

1. J. J. Alferes, C. V. Damásio, and L. M. Pereira. A logic programming system for non-monotonic reasoning. *Journal of Automated Reasoning*, 14:93–147, 1995.
2. J. J. Alferes and L. M. Pereira. Contradiction: when avoidance equal removal. In R. Dyckhoff, editor, *4th ELP*, volume 798 of *LNAI*. Springer–Verlag, 1994.
3. C. Baral. Rule-based updates on simple knowledge bases. In *AAAI'94*, pages 136–141, 1994.
4. C. Baral and M. Gelfond. Logic programming and knowledge representation. *J. Logic Programming*, 19/20:73–148, 1994.
5. C. V. Damásio and L. M. Pereira. Default negated conclusions: why not? In R. Dyckhoff, H. Herre, and P. Schroeder-Heister, editors, *ELP'96*. Springer-Verlag, 1996.
6. H. Decker. Drawing updates from derivations. In *Int. Conf on Database Theory*, volume 460 of *LNCS*, 1990.
7. A. Van Gelder, K. A. Ross, and J. S. Schlipf. The well-founded semantics for general logic programs. *Journal of the ACM*, 38(3):620–650, 1991.

8. L. Giordano and A. Martelli. Generalized stable models, truth maintenance and conflit resolution. In D. Warren and P. Szeredi, editors, *7th ICLP*, pages 427–441. MIT Press, 1990.

9. A. Guessoum and J. W. Lloyd. Updating knowledge bases. *New Generation Computing*, 8(1):71–89, 1990.

10. A. Guessoum and J. W. Lloyd. Updating knowledge bases II. *New Generation Computing*, 10(1):73–100, 1991.

11. H. Katsuno and A. Mendelzon. On the difference between updating a knowledge base and revising it. In J. Allen, R. Fikes, and E. Sandewall, editors, *KR'91*, pages 387–394. Morgan-Kaufmann, 1991.

12. V. Marek and M. Truszczyński. Revision specifications by means of programs. In C. MacNish, D. Pearce, and L. M. Pereira, editors, *JELIA'94*, volume 838 of *LNAI*, pages 122–136. Springer-Verlag, 1994.

13. V. Marek and M. Truszczyński. Revision programming, database updates and integrity constraints. In *ICDT'95*, pages 368–382. Springer-Verlag, 1995.

14. L. M. Pereira and J. J. Alferes. Well founded semantics for logic programs with explicit negation. In B. Neumann, editor, *European Conf. on AI*, pages 102–106. John Wiley & Sons, 1992.

15. L. M. Pereira, J. N. Aparício, and J. J. Alferes. Non–monotonic reasoning with logic programming. *Journal of Logic Programming*, 17(2, 3 & 4):227–263, 1993.

16. T. Przymusinski and H. Turner. Update by means of inference rules. In V. Marek, A. Nerode, and M. Truszczyński, editors, *LPNMR'95*, volume 928 of *LNAI*, pages 156–174. Springer-Verlag, 1995.

17. M. Winslett. Reasoning about action using a possible models approach. In *AAAI'88*, pages 89–93, 1988.

18. C. Witteveen and W. Hoek. Revision by communication. In V. Marek, A. Nerode, and M. Truszczyński, editors, *LPNMR'95*, volume 928 of *LNAI*, pages 189–202. Springer-Verlag, 1995.

19. C. Witteveen, W. Hoek, and H. Nivelle. Revision of non-monotonic theories: some postulates and an application to logic programming. In C. MacNish, D. Pearce, and L. M. Pereira, editors, *JELIA'94*, volume 838 of *LNAI*, pages 137–151. Springer-Verlag, 1994.

An Abductive Proof Procedure for Reasoning About Actions in Modal Logic Programming

Matteo Baldoni, Laura Giordano, Alberto Martelli and Viviana Patti

Dipartimento di Informatica - Università di Torino
C.so Svizzera 185 - 10149 Torino, ITALY
Tel. +39 11 7429111, Fax +39 11 751603
E-mail: {baldoni,laura, mrt}@di.unito.it

Abstract. In this paper we propose a modal approach for reasoning about actions in a logic programming framework. We introduce a modal language which makes use of abductive assumptions to deal with persistency, and provides a solution to the ramification problem, by allowing one-way "causal rules" to be defined among fluents.
We define the abductive semantics of the language and a goal directed abductive proof procedure to compute abductive solutions for a goal from a given domain description. Both the semantics and the procedure are defined within the argumentation framework. In particular, we focus on a specific semantics, which is essentially an extension of Dung's admissibility semantics to a modal setting. The proof procedure is proved to be sound with respect to this semantics.

1 Introduction

Reasoning about a world dynamically changing under effects of actions is one of the central problems of knowledge representation. In this context, starting from Gelfond and Lifschitz' work [17], several proposals have been put forward for representing actions in logic programming, which provides simple and well studied nonmonotonic mechanisms. Gelfond and Lifschitz have defined a high-level action language A and they have given its translation into logic programming with negation as failure. [7] and [10] have proposed translation of (extensions of) the language A into abductive logic programming. Among other approaches to reasoning about action in logic programming, we mention the one in [25] which uses logic programs extended with explicit negation and a contradiction removal semantics. Extensions of the language A have been proposed in the literature, for instance to deal with the ramification problem, as the AR_0 language of Kartha and Lifschitz [19], for which a translation is given into a formalism based on circumscription, rather than into logic programming.

In this paper we introduce a modal logic programming language, called $\mathcal{L}^A$, for reasoning about actions: rather than following the path of defining a language with an 'ad hoc' (and high level) semantics and then translating it into a logic programming language with negation as failure, we introduce a modal language in which actions are represented by modalities, and whose semantics is a standard Kripke semantics.

The adoption of a modal language is common with other proposals for modeling actions [5,12,28], which are based on Dynamic Logic [18]. In fact, modal logic allows very naturally to represent actions as state transition, through the accessibility relation of Kripke structures.

As a difference with [5,12] and similarly to [28], we adopt a non-monotonic solution for the frame problem by making use of *abduction*. We show that our language can naturally deal with (forward and backward) persistency (by making use of persistency assumptions), and with the ramification problem (by allowing the definition of "causal rules" among fluents). In particular, to capture ramifications, "causal rules" are allowed among fluent expressions, following the approach advocated in [4,24,23,29].

Both an abductive semantics and a goal directed abductive proof procedure for the language $\mathcal{L}^A$ are defined within the argumentation framework [9,3]. The argumentation framework provides a general setting in which an abductive semantics and a proof procedure for computing it can be defined. Moreover, the framework is modular with respect to the monotonic logic adopted, and it can be applied, for instance, to a modal language. In this way, the aspects concerning modalities, which are non-standard in logic programming, can be factored out and dealt with separately both in the semantics and in the proof procedure.

Within the argumentation framework, we develop a three-valued semantics which can be regarded as a generalization of Dung's admissibility semantics [8] to our modal setting. With respect to this semantics, we can prove a soundness result for the abductive proof procedure.

When a totality requirement is added to the semantics a stronger semantics is obtained, that is essentially a generalization of stable models semantics [15]. This specific case has been analized in [14]. In particular, when no ramification is allowed, the language can be proved to be equivalent to Gelfond and Lifschitz' $\mathcal{A}$ language. Indeed, the semantics of the language $\mathcal{A}$ is defined in terms of a transition function among states, and it appears to be quite near to Kripke structures.

2   The language $\mathcal{L}^A$

The action language $\mathcal{L}^A$ contains two kinds of modalities: a finite number of modalities $[a_1], \ldots, [a_k]$, where each a_i is a constant denoting an action, and a modal operator $\Box$, which represents an arbitrary sequence of actions. The intended meaning of a formula $[a_1] \ldots [a_k]\alpha$ is that α holds after performing the sequence of actions $[a_1] \ldots [a_k]$. The intended meaning of a formula $\Box\alpha$ is that α holds after any sequence of actions.

The modal logic we use is rather standard, and we will describe it in detail in the following section. For the moment, we just want to mention the fact that $[a_1], \ldots, [a_k]$ are modalities of type K, while $\Box$ is a modality of type $S4$.

In the following examples a *domain description* is given as a pair (Π, Obs), where Π is a set of clauses representing action laws and causal rules, and Obs is a set of observations (on the initial or later states).

Example 1. (*The shooting problem*)

$$\Pi: \qquad \Box(true \rightarrow [load]loaded)$$
$$\Box(loaded \rightarrow [shoot]\neg alive)$$
$$\Box(true \rightarrow [shoot]\neg loaded)$$

$$Obs: \quad alive$$
$$\neg loaded$$

Given this domain description, if we want to know whether $\neg alive$ holds after the sequence of actions *load, wait, shoot*, we may ask the goal

$$G_1 = [load][wait][shoot]\neg alive.$$

G_1 is expected to succeed, while the goal

$$G_2 = [load][wait][shoot]alive$$

is, instead, expected to fail. $\qquad\qquad\qquad\qquad\qquad\qquad\qquad\qquad\qquad\Box$

Note that the negation symbol $\neg$ which may occur within rules and observations must be regarded as "explicit negation" [16]. We will come back to this later on.

In example above, the observations are on the initial situation only. However, there are cases when the initial state is incompletely specified, while there are observations on later states. Consider the Murder Mistery.

Example 2. We only know that the turkey initially is alive; there is a shooting and waiting event; then the turkey is dead.

The domain description is obtained from the previous one by changing the set of observations as follows:

$$Obs: \quad alive$$
$$[shoot][wait]\neg alive$$

To deal with this problem, we follow an abductive approach as in [7], by determining which are the assumptions on the initial state that are needed to explain observations on later states. Here, to explain the observation that the turkey is dead after shooting and waiting, i.e., to prove the goal $G = [shoot][wait]\neg alive$, we have to assume that the gun is loaded in the initial situation.

$$\qquad\qquad\qquad\qquad\qquad\qquad\qquad\qquad\qquad\qquad\qquad\qquad\Box$$

The following example involves the well known ramification problem, which is concerned with the additional effects produced by an action besides its immediate effects.

Example 3. Consider the case when there are two switches. When both of them are on, the light is on. The action of toggling a switch changes the state of the switch from on to off (i.e., ¬*on*) and vice-versa.

$$\Pi: \quad \begin{aligned} &\Box(\neg on_1 \rightarrow [toggle_1]on_1) \\ &\Box(on_1 \rightarrow [toggle_1]\neg on_1) \\ &\Box(\neg on_2 \rightarrow [toggle_2]on_2) \\ &\Box(on_2 \rightarrow [toggle_2]\neg on_2) \\ &\Box(\neg on_1 \rightarrow \neg light\_on) \\ &\Box(\neg on_2 \rightarrow \neg light\_on) \\ &\Box(on_1 \wedge on_2 \rightarrow light\_on) \end{aligned}$$

$$Obs: \quad \begin{aligned} &\neg on_1 \\ &\neg on_2 \\ &\neg light\_on. \end{aligned}$$

The first four rules in Π describe the immediate effects of the action of toggling a switch. The last three rules describe the effects of the switches on the light. They must be regarded as being directional implications. Following [24,23], we consider rules such as $\Box(on_1 \wedge on_2 \rightarrow light\_on)$ as causal rules, meaning that there is a causal relationship between the two switches being on, and the light being on. In particular, we do not want to allow contraposition (cf. below).

In the initial situation, both the switches and the light are off. After the actions $toggle_1$, and $toggle_2$ are performed, we expect that the light is on, i.e., that the goal $G = [toggle_1][toggle_2]light\_on$ succeeds. □

The matter of representing causal relationships has been widely discussed in [24,23]. In particular, their use is essential in the previous example, in order to avoid the unexpected solution in which, after execution of action $toggle_1$ that makes switch_1 on, performing the action $toggle_2$ has the undesirable effect of changing the state of switch_1 from on to off. To exclude this solution contrapositives of causal rules must be avoided. As we will show, in a logic programming setting it is quite natural to represent causal rules by making use of "explicit" negation.

Before describing the semantics underlying our language, let us define more carefully the language itself. For simplicity, we consider the propositional case.

In our language we will use atomic propositions for *fluent names*, and we will denote by F a *fluent expression*, consisting of a fluent name p or its negation $\neg p$. Let *true* be a distinguished proposition. The syntax of the language $\mathcal{L}^A$ is the following:

$$\begin{aligned} D &::= \Box(G \rightarrow H) \\ G &::= true \mid F \mid G_1 \wedge G_2 \mid [A]G \\ H &::= F \mid [A]H \end{aligned}$$

where A stands for an action name, D stands for a clause, G stands for a goal, and H for a clause head. Note that in general clauses may have the form $\Box(G \rightarrow \Gamma_h F)$, where Γ_h is a possibly empty sequence of modal operators $[a_i]$ and G

may contain modalities. When Γ_h is empty, clauses represent *causal rules*, which allow to define causal relationships among fluents.

A *domain description* is a pair (Π, Obs), where Π is a set of clauses representing action laws and causal rules, and Obs is a set of observations, of the form $[a_1] \ldots [a_n]F$ (with $n \geq 0$), about the value of fluents in different states, including the initial one (when $n = 0$). Note that observations are syntactically goals.

3 The Logical Semantics

In this section we propose an abductive semantics for this modal language for reasoning about actions, in which "persistency assumptions" are taken as being abducibles. Such a semantics is defined within the argumentation framework [9,3]. The argumentation framework is a very general framework, which has been shown to capture many non-monotonic reasoning formalisms, including logic programming, abductive logic programming, logic programs extended with explicit negation, default logic, and other non-monotonic logics. In particular, many of the semantics proposed for logic programming with negation as failure, e.g. stable models, partial stable models, preferred extensions, well-founded models, can be captured within acceptability semantics, which is a particular argumentation semantics [20,30].

In this paper we will focus on a specific acceptability semantics namely on *admissibility* semantics [8], whose definition we adapt to our modal setting. With respect to this semantics, we will be able to prove a soundness result for the abductive proof procedure that we'll present in the next section.

The argumentation framework has the nice property of being modular with respect to the chosen logic and set of hypotheses. This will allow us to define the logical semantics of our language in two steps: first by describing the monotonic modal logic on which the language is based; and then by introducing the non-monotonic abductive construction.

Let us call $\mathcal{L}$ the modal logic on which the language is based. In such logic, the modalities $[a_i]$, associated with each action, are ruled by the axioms of the logic K, while the modality $\Box$ is ruled by the axioms of S4. Moreover, the axiom system for $\mathcal{L}$ contains the following *interaction axiom* schema: $\Box\alpha \to [A]\alpha$, where $\to$ is material implication, α stands for an arbitrary formula, and A for an action. The modality $\Box$ is used to denote information which holds in any state, since from $\Box\alpha$ it follows that $[a_1]\ldots[a_j]\alpha$, for any sequence of actions $a_1,\ldots,a_j$. Note that , in Examples 1 and 3, $\Box$ occurs in front of action laws and of causal rules.

The language $\mathcal{L}^A$, we have introduced in the previous section, is a clausal fragment of $\mathcal{L}$. In such a language we express the directionality of implications by making use of "explicit negation", as in Gelfond and Lifschitz' *answer set semantics* [16] for extended logic programs, i.e. programs which allows for "explicit", or "classical", negation to occur in clause heads and in clause bodies. In the answer set semantics, clause contrapositives are not allowed, that is, clauses are regarded as inference rules (as in the case of positive programs). Gelfond and Lifschitz also show that an extended logic program can be transformed into an essentially equivalent program that does not contain explicit negation, by replacing the negation of each atom p by a new predicate p'. Along this line, in the following, we will regard $\neg p$ as a new proposition, different from all other propositions, so as to reduce to a "positive fragment" of the modal logic $\mathcal{L}$.

While the modalities in the language are used to describe how the state changes under effects of actions, abduction is used to deal with the *frame problem*: abductive assumptions are used to model persistency from one state to the following one, when an action is performed. In particular, we will assume that a fluent expression F persists through an action unless it is inconsistent to assume so, i.e. unless $\neg F$ holds after the action.

We define a new set of atomic propositions, of the form $\mathbf{M}[a_1]\ldots[a_n]F$, and we take them as being *abducibles* [1]. Their meaning is that the fluent expression F can be assumed to hold in the state obtained by executing actions $a_1,\ldots,a_n$, in the order. Each abducible can be assumed to hold, provided it is consistent with Π and with other assumed abducibles. More precisely, in order to deal with the frame problem, we add to $\mathcal{L}$ the *persistency axiom schema*

$$[a_1]\ldots[a_{n-1}]F \,\wedge\, \mathbf{M}[a_1]\ldots[a_n]F \,\to\, [a_1]\ldots[a_n]F, \tag{1}$$

where $a_1,\ldots,a_n$ $(n>0)$ are actions, and F is a fluent. Its meaning is that, if F holds after action sequence $a_1,\ldots,a_{n-1}$, and F can be assumed to persist after action a_n (i.e., it is consistent to assume $\mathbf{M}[a_1]\ldots[a_n]F$), then we can conclude that F holds after performing the sequence of actions $a_1,\ldots,a_n$.

Besides these persistency assumptions, we also allow assumptions on initial situation. For each fluent expression F, we introduce an abducible $\mathbf{M}F$ and an *axiom schema*

$$\mathbf{M}F \to F \tag{2}$$

in order to allow F to be assumed in the initial state. As we will see, these assumptions are needed to deal with incompletely specified initial states. Note that assumptions on the initial state are just a special case of persistency assumptions, "$\mathbf{M}[a_1]\ldots[a_n]F$", in which the sequence of actions is empty (i.e., $n=0$). In the following, we denote by $\mathcal{H}$ the set containing all possible abducibles (both persistency assumptions and assumptions about the initial state).

Let $\vdash_{\mathcal{L}}$ be the consequence relation in the monotonic modal logic defined above (including axiom schema 1 and 2), and Π a set of action laws and causal rules. In the following, $\neg\neg p$ is regarded as being equal to p.

Definition 4. Given two disjoint sets of *abducibles* Δ_T and Δ_F, we say that (Δ_T, Δ_F) is an *abductive solution* for Π if,

(a) $\forall \mathbf{M}[a_1]\ldots[a_n]F \in \Delta_F$, $\Pi \cup \Delta_T \vdash_{\mathcal{L}} [a_1]\ldots[a_n]\neg F$;

---

[1] Notice that $\mathbf{M}$ has not to be regarded as a modality. Rather, $\mathbf{M}\alpha$ is the notation used to denote a new atomic proposition associated with α. This notation has been adopted in analogy to default logic, where a justification $\mathbf{M}\alpha$ intuitively means "α is consistent"

(b) $\forall M[a_1]\ldots[a_n]F \in \Delta_T$, $\Pi \cup (\mathcal{H} - \Delta_F) \not\vdash_{\mathcal{L}} [a_1]\ldots[a_n]\neg F$.

The assumptions in Δ_T cannot be contradicted without assuming abducibles in Δ_F. On the other hand, the assumptions in Δ_F are blocked by those in Δ_T.

The notion of abductive solution defined above corresponds to that of admissible solution [8], in the case of normal logic programs (in particular, Δ_T corresponds to an admissible solution). Our formulation is very similar to the formulation of admissible solutions given in [20] within the argumentation framework. In that context, a set of abducibles Δ is defined to be admissible if, for any set of abducibles A which attacks Δ, there is a subset of the assumptions in Δ (a defence) which in turn attacks A. In our formulation, the additional set of assumptions Δ_F within an admissible solution represents the set of culprits, i.e., those assumptions whose failure guarantees a defence to the solution. More precisely, Δ_F must contain at least one assumption from each attack A to Δ_T, and this assumption, in turn, must be counterattacked by Δ_T. In the following section we define an abductive proof procedure for computing admissible solutions.

Admissible semantics is a rather weak semantics, with respect, for instance to the stable model semantics. In particular, preferred extensions [8] and three-valued stable models [26] correspond to maximal admissible solutions. If the *totality* requirement, $\Delta_T \cup \Delta_F = \mathcal{H}$, is added in the above definition, we obtain the notion of abductive solution as it has been presented in [14], which is, essentially, a generalization of the stable model semantics [15] (we will call these solutions *total* abductive solutions).

Since p and $\neg p$ are two different propositions, it might occur that both of them hold in the same state, in an abductive solution. To avoid this, we introduce a consistency condition to accept only those solutions without inconsistent states. We say that an abductive solution (Δ_T, Δ_F) is *consistent* for Π if for every sequence of actions $a_1,\ldots,a_n$, $(n \geq 0)$, and fluent name p:

$$\Pi \cup \Delta_T \not\vdash_{\mathcal{L}} [a_1]\ldots[a_n]p \wedge [a_1]\ldots[a_n]\neg p.$$

Definition 5. We say that (Δ_T, Δ_F) is a *consistent abductive solution for* (Π, Obs) if it is a consistent abductive solution for Π, and $\Pi \cup \Delta_T \vdash_{\mathcal{L}} Obs$.

Given a domain description (Π, Obs) and a goal G, a *consistent abductive solution for G in* (Π, Obs) is defined to be a consistent abductive solution for (Π, Obs) such that $\Pi \cup \Delta_T \vdash_{\mathcal{L}} G$.

There are cases when there is no consistent solution for (Π, Obs). This happens, for instance, when the initial state is itself inconsistent, or when there are actions with complementary effects.

In the following we give some examples of consistent abductive solutions (shortly, consistent solution).

Example 6. Let us consider the domain description in Example 1. The goal $G_1 = [load][wait][shoot]\neg alive$ has a consistent solution (Δ_T, Δ_F), with $\Delta_T = \{M\ alive,\ M\neg loaded,\ M[load][wait]loaded\}$, and $\Delta_F = \{M\neg alive,\ M\ loaded,$

M[*load*] ¬*loaded*}. We have that ¬*alive* holds after the shooting, if the gun remains loaded after wait (see the assumption M [*load*][*wait*]*loaded* in Δ_T). On the other hand, there is no consistent solution for the goal $G_2 = [load][wait][shoot]alive$.

□

It is worth pointing out that the abductive construction we have introduced enforces *chronological minimization* of changes. In this regard, it is essential that implications can be seen as inferences rule and that inconsistencies which may block assumptions (see point (b) in Definition 1) are defined as being local, rather than global. Hence, the state obtained after execution of the sequence of actions $a_1, \ldots, a_n$, is solely determined by the assumptions on the initial state and by the persistency assumptions made up to that state (i.e., those assumptions $M[a_1] \ldots [a_i]F$ such that $i \leq n$).

As in [7], in our language backward persistence, that is, reasoning from the future to the past, is modelled by making use of abductive reasoning, i.e. by taking those abductive solutions which explain (entail) the observations on the states different from the initial one. This also corresponds to what in [27] is called "filtering".

Example 7. Let us come back to the Murder Mistery (Example 2). The domain description has a consistent abductive solution (Δ_T, Δ_F) with $\Delta_T = \{M\ alive,\ M\ loaded,\ M[shoot][wait]\neg alive\}$, and $\Delta_F = \{M\neg alive,\ M\neg loaded,\ M[shoot]alive\}$, which explains the observation that the turkey is dead after shooting and waiting (while being initially alive), by assuming that the gun is initially loaded.

□

Example 8. In Examples 3 the goal $G = [toggle_1][toggle_2]light\_on$ has a consistent solution (Δ_T, Δ_F), with $\Delta_T = \{M\ \neg on_1,\ M\neg on_2,\ M\ [toggle_1]\neg on_2,\ M\ [toggle_1][toggle_2]on_1\}$ and $\Delta_F = \{M\ on_1,\ M\ on_2,\ M[toggle_1]\neg on_1\}$. In particular, the assumption M $[toggle_1]\neg on_2$ in Δ_T says that $\neg on_2$ persists after the action $toggle_1$, while the assumption M $[toggle_1][toggle_2]on_1$ in Δ_T says that on_1, which is made true by action $toggle_1$, persists after action $toggle_2$. On the other hand, the goal $G = [toggle_1][toggle_2]\neg light\_on$ has no consistent solution. In particular, it cannot be assumed that $\neg light\_on$ (which is true after action $toggle_1$) persists after performing the action $toggle_2$, since the assumption M $[toggle_1][toggle_2]\neg light\_on$ is not acceptable.

□

It is clear that a domain description may have more than a consistent solution when the initial situation is incompletely determined. However, there are cases when there is more than one solution even if the initial state is completely determined.

Example 9. There are three blocks, and only two of them can stay on the table. There is an action *put_i* of putting block i on the table. Consider the following domain description and observations:

$$\Pi : \quad \Box(on_1 \wedge on_2 \rightarrow \neg on_3)$$
$$\Box(on_2 \wedge on_3 \rightarrow \neg on_1)$$
$$\Box(on_3 \wedge on_1 \rightarrow \neg on_2)$$
$$\Box[put_1]on_1$$
$$\Box[put_2]on_2$$
$$\Box[put_3]on_3$$

$$Obs : \quad on_1$$
$$on_2$$
$$\neg on_3.$$

We expect that executing the action put_3 in the state when both block 1 and block 2 are on the table makes either block 1 or block 2 to fall down [2]. After action put_3 either on_1 or on_2 holds, but not both of them. In fact, $[put_3]on_1$ has a consistent solution (Δ_T, Δ_F), in which Δ_T contains the assumption $\mathbf{M}\ [put_3]on_1$, while Δ_F contains the assumption $\mathbf{M}\ [put_3]on_2$. Moreover, the goal $[put_3]on_2$ has also a consistent solution, which is complementary to the one above. □

For the case when consistent solutions are total, in [14] we have proved that our language is equivalent to Gelfond and Lifschitz language $\mathcal{A}$ [17], when, as in $\mathcal{A}$, no state constraints are allowed. In particular, we can naturally express by modal formulas the *value propositions* and *effect propositions* of the language $\mathcal{A}$.

Given a domain description D in the language $\mathcal{A}$, we may denote by (Π_D, Obs_D) the corresponding domain description in our modal language. Π_D is the set of action laws (of the form $\Box(P_1 \wedge \ldots \wedge P_n \rightarrow [A]F)$) corresponding to the effect-propositions (A **causes** F *if* $P_1, \ldots, P_n$), while Obs_D are the observations (of the form $[A_1] \ldots [A_n]F$) on the initial and later states, corresponding to the value-propositions (F **after** $A_1; \ldots; A_n$).

Under the assumption that the domain description is *e-consistent* [7] (i.e. D has a model in the $\mathcal{A}$ language), we have proved that there is a one to one correspondence between the models (according to [17]) of D and the total consistent solutions of (Π_D, Obs_D). In particular, each $\mathcal{A}$-model can be regarded as the "canonical" Kripke model determined by some total consistent solution, each world of the Kripke model corresponding to some possible "state".

In presence of ramification constraints (i.e. causal rules), we have established a one to one correspondence between our formalization and the one in [24], for the case when actions have deterministic immediate effects.

4　Proof Procedure

In this section we define a goal directed proof procedure for our action language. It is an abductive proof procedure that, given a set of clauses (action laws and

---

[2] However, since we assume minimization of change, we do not expect both block 1 and block 2 to fall down

causal rules) Π and a goal G, returns an abductive solution (Δ_T, Δ_F) to the goal w.r.t. Π, if there is one.

The procedure is defined in the style of Eshghi and Kowalski's abductive procedure for logic programs with negation as failure [11], and is similar to the procedures proposed in [30] to compute the acceptability semantics. As a difference with respect to these procedures, the one we present carries out the computation by making use of two auxiliary sets, Δ_T and Δ_F, of abductive hypotheses. These sets are initially empty, and are augmented during the computation. The procedure interleaves two different phases of computation; the first phase collects in Δ_T a set of hypotheses which support the success of the goal to be proved, while the second one assures the failure of all the attacks to such a set of hypotheses (and, in particular, for each attack, it collects in Δ_F one culprit whose failure may block the attack). At the end, if the computation terminates successfully, the computed (global) set of hypotheses represents an abductive solution in which the query holds.

The abductive proof procedure is defined in terms of an auxiliary nondeterministic procedure *support*, which carries out the computation for the monotonic part of the language. Given a goal G and a program Π, *support(G,Π)* returns an abductive support for the goal G in Π, that is, a set Δ of abducibles such that $\Pi \cup \Delta \vdash_{\mathcal{L}} G$).

In this way, all the details concerning the implementation of the monotonic modal language $\mathcal{L}$ are hidden in the definition of the procedure *support*, and they can be ignored by the abductive procedure.

Since the aim of the auxiliary procedure *support* is to compute supports for a goal, here we define a goal directed proof procedure which, given a goal G and a program Π, non-deterministically computes a support for G in Π.

Since the language $\mathcal{L}$ allows modal operators, and in particular free occurrence of modalities in front of a goal, we define the operational derivability of a goal G from a program Π in a certain *modal context*, on the line of [1,2]. A modal context Γ is a sequence of modal operators $[a_1]\ldots[a_k]$, and it keeps track of the sequence of actions performed during the computation. Intuitively a modal context is a name for a possible world. We will write $\Pi, \Gamma \vdash_o G$ *with* Δ, to mean that the goal G can be operationally proved from the program Π in the modal context Γ, making the assumptions Δ.

In the following, we denote with ε the empty context and by $\Gamma|\Gamma'$ the *concatenation* of two modal contexts Γ and Γ'. Operational derivability of a goal G from a program Π is defined, by induction on the structure of G, by introducing the following proof rules.

Definition 10. Let Π be a domain description, Γ a modal context and G a goal.

1. $\Pi, \Gamma \vdash_o true$ with $\emptyset$;
2. $\Pi, \Gamma \vdash_o F$ with Δ if
    (a) there exists a clause $\Box(G \to \Gamma_h F) \in \Pi$ such that, for some Γ', $\Gamma = \Gamma'|\Gamma_h$, and $\Pi, \Gamma' \vdash_o G$ with Δ, or

(b) if $\Gamma = \Gamma'|[a]$ (for some modality $[a]$) and $\Pi, \Gamma' \vdash_o F$ with Δ', and $\Delta = \Delta' \cup \{\mathbf{M} \; \Gamma F\}$, or

(c) $\Gamma = \varepsilon$ and $\Delta = \{\mathbf{M} \; F\}$;

3. $\Pi, \Gamma \vdash_o G_1 \wedge G_2$ with Δ if $\Pi, \Gamma \vdash_o G_1$ with Δ_1 and $\Pi, \Gamma \vdash_o G_2$ with Δ_2 and $\Delta = \Delta_1 \cup \Delta_2$;

4. $\Pi, \Gamma \vdash_o [a]G$ with Δ if $\Pi, \Gamma|[a] \vdash_o G$ with Δ.

In the definition above, to prove a modalized goal $[a]G$, rule 4), the modal operator $[a]$ is added to the current context and G is proved in the resulting context. To prove a fluent F, we can either select a clause in the initial program Π, rule 2a), or add a new assumption from $\mathcal{H}$ to the assumption set Δ, rules 2b) and 2c). In rule 2a), to verify that a clause is applicable in the current context, it must be checked whether the sequence of modal operators in front of the head of the clause is a suffix of the current context. Notice that rules 2b) and 2c) are mutually exclusive: 2b) is only applicable when the context is nonempty, while 2c) is only applicable when the context is empty.

A goal G can be operationally derived from a program Π with assumptions Δ if, using the rules above, we can derive $\Pi, \varepsilon \vdash_o G$ *with* Δ.

In the monotonic procedure above, rules 2(b) and 2(c) are needed to collect abductive assumptions to compute a support for a goal. If we omit them, such a procedure happens to be a special case of the one introduced in [2] to deal with several modal logic programming languages. From the soundness and completeness results proved in [2], we can easily prove soundness and completeness of the monotonic procedure above. In particular, we can show that: if $\Pi, \varepsilon \vdash_o G$ with Δ can be operationally derived, then $\Pi \cup \Delta \vdash_{\mathcal{L}} G$. Moreover, if $\Pi \cup \Delta \vdash_{\mathcal{L}} G$, than $\Pi, \varepsilon \vdash_o G$ with Δ' can be operationally derived, for some $\Delta' \subseteq \Delta$.

Furthermore, we will use a procedure $all\_supports(G, \Pi)$ which collects a set of abductive supports to G non-deterministically computed by proof procedure of Definition 10, containing at least all the minimal supports.

Example 11. Let us consider again Example 2. We want to find an abductive support for the observations:

$$Obs: \quad alive$$
$$[shoot][wait]\neg alive.$$

We show that

$$\Delta = \{\mathbf{M}alive, \mathbf{M}[shoot][wait]\neg alive, \mathbf{M}loaded\}$$

is such an abductive support. Let us give a sequence of steps to compute it, using the proof rules in Definition 10. We will use a instead of $alive$, s instead of $shoot$, w instead of $wait$ and ld for $loaded$. To prove that

$$\Pi, \varepsilon \vdash_o a \wedge [s][w]\neg a \text{ with } \Delta, \tag{3}$$

by rule 3, we have to prove that:

1. $\Pi, \varepsilon \vdash_o a$ with Δ_1
2. $\Pi, \varepsilon \vdash_o [s][w]\neg a$ with Δ_2,

where $\Delta = \Delta_1 \cup \Delta_2$.

First notice that 1 holds by rule 2(c), with $\Delta_1 = \{\mathbf{M}a\}$. Moreover,

$\Pi, \varepsilon \vdash_o [s][w]\neg a$ with Δ_2, if
$\Pi, [s][w] \vdash_o \neg a$ with Δ_2, by rule 4, if
$\Pi, [s] \vdash_o \neg a$ with Δ' and $\Delta_2 = \Delta' \cup \{\mathbf{M}[s][w]\neg a\}$, by rule 2(b), if
$\Pi, \varepsilon \vdash_o ld$ with Δ', by rule 2(a), using action law $\Box(ld \rightarrow [s]\neg a)$.

The last step holds, by rule 2(c), by taking $\Delta' = \{\mathbf{M}ld\}$. Hence, $\Delta_2 = \{\mathbf{M}[s][w]\neg a,$ $\mathbf{M}ld\}$, and, thus, (3) holds with $\Delta = \{\mathbf{M}a, \mathbf{M}[s][w]\neg a, \mathbf{M}ld\}$.

Now we can define our abductive proof procedure for $\mathcal{L}^A$. It is worth noting that the abductive procedure does not need any modal context because the aspects concerning the dynamic evolution of the program are specifically dealt with by procedure *support*.

Before defining the goal-directed abductive proof procedure, we give a more general iterative abductive procedure for computing an abductive solution (Δ_T, Δ_F) for a given goal G. In the following, given an abductive assumption $\mathbf{M}[A_1]$ $\ldots[A_n]F$, we define $\overline{\mathbf{M}[A_1]\ldots[A_n]F} = [A_1]\ldots[A_n]\neg F$.

The procedure computes iteratively Δ_T and Δ_F using two auxiliary sets: a set of assumptions S_T and a set of sets of assumptions S_F. At each step of the computation, S_T contains the assumptions which must be true, i.e. which we want to put in Δ_T. On the other hand, S_F contains the sets of assumptions which must fail, i.e. at least one assumption for each set of assumptions in S_F must be put in Δ_F.

Iterative procedure

$S_T \leftarrow support(G, \Pi)$
$S_F \leftarrow \emptyset$
$\Delta_T \leftarrow \emptyset$
$\Delta_F \leftarrow \emptyset$

Repeat nondeterministically the following steps

(1) select an assumption $h \in S_T$ such that $h \notin \Delta_F$
$\qquad S_T \leftarrow S_T - \{h\}$
$\qquad$ if $h \notin \Delta_T$ then
$\qquad \Delta_T \leftarrow \Delta_T \cup \{h\}$
$\qquad S_F \leftarrow S_F \cup all\_supports(\overline{h}, \Pi)$
(2) select a set of assumptions $\Delta \in S_F$
$\qquad$ select an assumption $h \in \Delta$ such that $h \notin \Delta_T$
$\qquad S_F \leftarrow S_F - \{\Delta\}$
$\qquad$ if $h \notin \Delta_F$ then
$\qquad \Delta_F \leftarrow \Delta_F \cup \{h\}$
$\qquad S_T \leftarrow S_T \cup support(\overline{h}, \Pi)$

until $S_T = \emptyset$ and $S_F = \emptyset$

This procedure is quite abstract and contains many nondeterministic choices. Different more concrete procedures can be obtained by fixing a search strategy, and by doing some optimizations. In the following, we give a goal directed formulation of proof procedure above, which proves a given goal by interleaving steps (1) and (2), i.e the phase looking for success and the phase looking for failure. To this purpose, we introduce a set of proof rules which involve statements of the form $(\Delta_T, \Delta_F) \vdash_t G$ *with* (Δ'_T, Δ'_F), (and similarly for $\vdash_f$). Their intuitive meaning is that, given the initial set of assumptions (Δ_T, Δ_F), the goal G *succeeds* (*fails*) from the program with an abductive solution (Δ'_T, Δ'_F) such that $\Delta'_T \supseteq \Delta_T$ and $\Delta'_F \supseteq \Delta_F$ [3]. The abductive procedure allows to enlarge a set of hypotheses to obtain an abductive solution. Initially, we assume that $\Delta_T = \Delta_F = \emptyset$.

In the following, given an abductive assumption $\mathbf{M}[A_1] \ldots [A_n]F$, we define $\overline{\mathbf{M}[A_1] \ldots [A_n]F} = [A_1] \ldots [A_n]\neg F$. Moreover, we denote by Δ both a set of abducibles and their conjunction. The atom *true* represents the empty conjunction of hypotheses.

Definition 12. Given a pair (Δ_T, Δ_F) of disjoint sets of abducibles, and a domain description Π, we define success (failure) of a goal G with (Δ'_T, Δ'_F) through the following proof rules (where h is an abducible in $\mathcal{H}$):

(S-T) $(\Delta_T, \Delta_F) \vdash_t$ *true* with (Δ_T, Δ_F)

(S-G) $(\Delta_T, \Delta_F) \vdash_t G$ with (Δ'_T, Δ'_F) if
         there exists $\Delta_i \in all\_supports(G, \Pi)$ such that
         $(\Delta_T, \Delta_F) \vdash_t \Delta_i$ with (Δ'_T, Δ'_F)

(S-$\wedge$) $(\Delta_T, \Delta_F) \vdash_t \Delta_1 \wedge \Delta_2$ with (Δ''_T, Δ''_F) if
         $(\Delta_T, \Delta_F) \vdash_t \Delta_1$ with (Δ'_T, Δ'_F) and
         $(\Delta'_T, \Delta'_F) \vdash_t \Delta_2$ with (Δ''_T, Δ''_F)

(S-h(i)) $(\Delta_T, \Delta_F) \vdash_t h$ with (Δ_T, Δ_F) if $h \in \Delta_T$

(S-h(ii)) $(\Delta_T, \Delta_F) \vdash_t h$ with (Δ'_T, Δ'_F) if
         $h \notin \Delta_T$ and $h \notin \Delta_F$ and $(\Delta_T \cup \{h\}, \Delta_F) \vdash_f \overline{h}$ with (Δ'_T, Δ'_F)

(F-G) $(\Delta_T, \Delta_F) \vdash_f G$ with (Δ'_T, Δ'_F) if
         $all\_supports(G, \Pi) = \{\Delta_1, \ldots, \Delta_m\}$ and
         $(\Delta_T, \Delta_F) \vdash_f \Delta_1$ with $(\Delta'_{T1}, \Delta'_{F1})$ and $\ldots$
         $\ldots$ and $(\Delta'_{Tm-1}, \Delta'_{Fm-1}) \vdash_f \Delta_m$ with (Δ'_T, Δ'_F)

(F-$\wedge$) $(\Delta_T, \Delta_F) \vdash_f \Delta_1 \wedge \Delta_2$ with (Δ'_T, Δ'_F) if
         $(\Delta_T, \Delta_F) \vdash_f \Delta_1$ with (Δ'_T, Δ'_F) or
         $(\Delta_T, \Delta_F) \vdash_f \Delta_2$ with (Δ'_T, Δ'_F)

(F-h(i)) $(\Delta_T, \Delta_F) \vdash_f h$ with (Δ_T, Δ_F) if $h \in \Delta_F$

(F-h(ii)) $(\Delta_T, \Delta_F) \vdash_f h$ with (Δ'_T, Δ'_F) if
         $h \notin \Delta_F$ and $h \notin \Delta_T$ and $(\Delta_T, \Delta_F \cup \{h\}) \vdash_t \overline{h}$ with (Δ'_T, Δ'_F)

---

[3] The meaning of these statements will be defined more precisely by Lemma 15.

Given a set of assumptions (Δ_T, Δ_F) and a goal G, in order to prove that there is an abductive solution (Δ'_T, Δ'_F) in which G holds (i.e., $G \in \Delta_T$), we have to find a set of assumptions Δ_i supporting the goal, and show that these assumptions can be consistently added to our current set of assumptions Δ_T (rule (S-G)). In essence, we have to show that all the assumptions in Δ_i can be made true. Then, for each assumption h in the support set Δ_i, we try to add h to Δ_T. If h is already in Δ_T, we have nothing to check (rule (S-h(i))). Otherwise, we add h to Δ_T and we check that its complementary formula $\overline{h}$ fails from the new set of assumptions (rule (S-h(ii))). If, on the other hand, we want to show that there is an abductive solution in which a given goal G is false (i.e., $G \in \Delta_F$), we make use of rules that are perfectly symmetrical with respect to the previous ones.

We say that a goal G succeeds from Π with solution (Δ_T, Δ_F) if $(\emptyset, \emptyset) \vdash_t G$ with (Δ'_T, Δ'_F) can be derived from Π by the rules above.

Example 13. Let us show the computation of the consistent abductive solution

$$\Delta_T = \{\mathbf{M}alive, \mathbf{M}[shoot][wait]\neg alive, \mathbf{M}loaded\}$$
$$\Delta_F = \{\mathbf{M}\neg alive, \mathbf{M}\neg loaded, \mathbf{M}[shoot]alive\}$$

for the Murder Mistery given in the Example 2 which explains the observations $alive \wedge [shoot][wait]\neg alive$. The following derivation is obtained by applying the proof rules in Definition 12. We have that

$$(\emptyset, \emptyset) \vdash_t a \wedge [s][w]\neg a \text{ with } (\Delta_T, \Delta_F)$$

holds (by rule (S-G)) if there is a set of assumptions supporting the observations, and such that all of the assumptions in the set are true in some abductive solution. Let us take $\Delta_1 = \{\mathbf{M}a, \mathbf{M}[s][w]\neg a, \mathbf{M}ld\} \in all\_supports((a \wedge [s][w]\neg a), \Pi)$, as computed in the Example 11. We have to prove that:

(i) $(\emptyset, \emptyset) \vdash_t \mathbf{M}a$ with (Δ'_T, Δ'_F),

(ii) $(\Delta'_T, \Delta'_F) \vdash_t \mathbf{M}[s][w]\neg a$ with (Δ''_T, Δ''_F), and

(iii) $(\Delta''_T, \Delta''_F) \vdash_t \mathbf{M}ld$ with (Δ_T, Δ_F).

Let us consider each of the three cases separately. We start from case **(i)**.

> $(\emptyset, \emptyset) \vdash_t \mathbf{M}a$;
> $(\{\mathbf{M}a\}, \emptyset) \vdash_f \neg a$ by rule (S-h(ii));
> $(\{\mathbf{M}a\}, \emptyset) \vdash_f \mathbf{M}\neg a$ by rule (F-G),
>   since $all\_supports(\neg a, \Pi) = \{\Delta_3\}$, and $\Delta_3 = \{\mathbf{M}\neg a\}$;
> $(\{\mathbf{M}a\}, \{\mathbf{M}\neg a\}) \vdash_t a$ by rule (F-h(ii));
> $(\{\mathbf{M}a\}, \{\mathbf{M}\neg a\}) \vdash_t \mathbf{M}a$ by rule (S-G),
>   since $all\_supports(a, \Pi) = \{\Delta_4\}$, where $\Delta_4 = \{\mathbf{M}a\}$,

which succeeds by rule (S-h(i)). Therefore,

$$(\emptyset, \emptyset) \vdash_t \mathbf{M}a \text{ with } (\Delta'_T = \{\mathbf{M}a\}, \Delta'_F = \{\mathbf{M}\neg a\}).$$

Let us now consider case **(ii)**.

$(\Delta'_T, \Delta'_F) \vdash_t \mathbf{M}[s][w]\neg a;$
$(\Delta'_T \cup \{\mathbf{M}[s][w]\neg a\}, \Delta'_F) \vdash_f [s][w]a$ by rule (S-$h(ii)$);
$(\Delta'_T \cup \{[s][w]\neg a\}, \Delta'_F) \vdash_f \Delta_5$ by rule (F-G),
  since $all\_supports([s][w]a, \Pi) = \{\Delta_5\}$, and $\Delta_5 = \{\mathbf{M}[s]a, \mathbf{M}[s][w]a, \mathbf{M}a\}$.

We can show failure of Δ_5 from the current set of the assumptions by showing that one of the assumptions in Δ_5, namely $\mathbf{M}[s]a$, fails (see rule (F-$\wedge$)).

$(\Delta'_T \cup \{\mathbf{M}[s][w]\neg a\}, \Delta'_F) \vdash_f \mathbf{M}[s]a;$
$(\Delta'_T \cup \{\mathbf{M}[s][w]\neg a\}, \Delta'_F \cup \{\mathbf{M}[s]a\}) \vdash_t [s]\neg a$ by rule (F-$h(ii)$);
$(\Delta'_T \cup \{\mathbf{M}[s][w]\neg a\}, \Delta'_F \cup \{\mathbf{M}[s]a\}) \vdash_t \mathbf{M}ld$ by rule (S-G),
  since $\Delta_6 \in all\_supports([s]\neg a, \Pi)$, where $\Delta_6 = \{\mathbf{M}ld\}$;
$(\Delta'_T \cup \{\mathbf{M}[s][w]\neg a, \mathbf{M}ld\}, \Delta'_F \cup \{\mathbf{M}[s]a\}) \vdash_f \neg ld$ by rule (S-$h(ii)$);
$(\Delta'_T \cup \{\mathbf{M}[s][w]\neg a, \mathbf{M}ld\}, \Delta'_F \cup \{\mathbf{M}[s]a\}) \vdash_f \mathbf{M}\neg ld$ by rule (F-G),
  since $all\_supports(\neg ld, \Pi) = \{\Delta_8\}$, and $\Delta_8 = \{\mathbf{M}\neg ld\}$;
$(\Delta'_T \cup \{\mathbf{M}[s][w]\neg a, \mathbf{M}ld\}, \Delta'_F \cup \{\mathbf{M}[s]a, \mathbf{M}\neg ld\}) \vdash_t ld$ by rule (F-$h(ii)$);
$(\Delta'_T \cup \{\mathbf{M}[s][w]\neg a, \mathbf{M}ld\}, \Delta'_F \cup \{\mathbf{M}[s]a, \mathbf{M}\neg ld\}) \vdash_t \mathbf{M}ld$ by rule (S-G),
  since $all\_supports(ld, \Pi) = \{\Delta_9\}$, where $\Delta_9 = \{\mathbf{M}ld\}$,

which succeeds by rule (S-$h(i)$). Then,

$$(\Delta'_T, \Delta'_F) \vdash_t \mathbf{M}[s][w]\neg a \text{ with } (\Delta''_T, \Delta''_F),$$

where

$\Delta''_T = \Delta'_T \cup \{\mathbf{M}[s][w]\neg a, \mathbf{M}ld\}$ and
$\Delta''_F = \Delta'_F \cup \{\mathbf{M}[s]a, \mathbf{M}\neg ld\}.$

Finally, we have to prove (iii). We have that

$$(\Delta''_T, \Delta''_F) \vdash_t \mathbf{M}ld$$

succeeds, by the rule (S-$h(i)$), with the desired explanation ($\Delta_T = \Delta''_T, \Delta_F = \Delta''_F$). □

To prove the soundness of the abductive procedure we need the following definitions.

Definition 14. Given a program Π and a set of assumptions Δ, we say that:

- Δ *supports success* of a goal G if $\Pi \cup \Delta \vdash_{\mathcal{L}} G$
- Δ *supports failure* of a goal G if $\Pi \cup (\mathcal{H} - \Delta) \nvdash_{\mathcal{L}} G$

We can now prove the following lemma.

Lemma 15. *Assume that the statement* $(\Delta_T, \Delta_F) \vdash_t G$ *with* (Δ'_T, Δ'_F) *has been derived from* Π *by the rules above. Then the following conditions hold:*

a) $\forall h \in (\Delta'_T - \Delta_T), \Delta'_F$ *supports failure of* $\overline{h}$

b) $\forall h \in (\Delta'_F - \Delta_F), \Delta'_T$ supports success of $\overline{h}$
c) Δ'_T supports success of G

Similarly, if the statement $(\Delta_T, \Delta_F) \vdash_f G$ with (Δ'_T, Δ'_F) has been derived, then the following conditions hold:

a) $\forall h \in (\Delta'_T - \Delta_T), \Delta'_F$ supports failure of $\overline{h}$
b) $\forall h \in (\Delta'_F - \Delta_F), \Delta'_T$ supports success of $\overline{h}$
c') Δ'_F supports failure of G

Proof. The proof can be easily carried out by induction on the proof rules.

(S-T) Obvious.
(S-G) a) and b) are immediate by induction. By induction we also have that Δ'_T supports success of Δ_i. Since, in turn, Δ_i supports success of G, we have c).
(S-∧) By induction on the derivation of Δ_1 we have that
$\forall h \in (\Delta'_T - \Delta_T), \Delta'_F$ supports failure of $\overline{h}$.
Since $\Delta'_F \subseteq \Delta''_F$, and the property of supporting failure is monotonic, we also have
$\forall h \in (\Delta'_T - \Delta_T), \Delta''_F$ supports failure of $\overline{h}$
From this and the inductive hypothesis for Δ_2, a) can be proved.
Analogously for b) and c).
(S-h(i)) Obvious.
(S-h(ii)) a) holds by induction for all members of $(\Delta'_T - \Delta_T)$ except h. But by property c') of the inductive hypothesis we know that Δ'_F supports failure of $\overline{h}$. Thus a) holds for h as well. b) is immediate from the inductive hypothesis, and c) holds because $h \in \Delta'_T$.

The proofs for the cases of failure derivation are similar. □

From this lemma it is immediate to prove the following theorem.

Theorem 16. *Assume that the statement $(\emptyset, \emptyset) \vdash_t G$ with (Δ_T, Δ_F) has been derived from Π by the rules above. Then (Δ_T, Δ_F) is an abductive solution for G.*

It is worth noting that *all_supports* could be non terminating, and thus the abductive procedure is not complete in general. Moreover, the procedure does not check whether the abductive solution it computes is consistent. However, in some cases the computed solutions are guaranteed to be consistent solutions. For instance, when we restrict to a language corresponding to the language $\mathcal{A}$, and we impose the conditions that the domain description is *e-consistent* [7] and it contains a set of consistent initial facts. We argue that, under such a restriction, our proof procedure is also complete.

5 Conclusions and related work

In this paper we have presented a modal logic programming language $\mathcal{L}^A$ for reasoning about actions, in which actions are represented by modalities. The adoption of a modal language is common to other proposals for modelling actions [5,12,28], which are based on dynamic logic, and relies on the fact that modal logic allows very naturally to represent state transitions, through the accessibility relation of Kripke structures.

The language $\mathcal{L}^A$ can be regarded as an extension of Gelfond and Lifschitz' A language, in which the ramification problem is tackled by making use of "causal rules", following the approach proposed in [4,24,23,29]. In particular, in $\mathcal{L}^A$ causal rules are represented in a natural way by making use of "explicit negation" [16], as it is natural in a logic programming setting. When no causal rules are present in a domain description, our language is equivalent to the language A.

We have defined an abductive semantics for the language, together with a sound goal directed proof procedure. Since we have followed an abductive approach, our work has strong connections with [7,10,21,22]. In [7], a translation of the language A to abductive logic programming with integrity constraints is presented, and it is shown to be sound and complete with respect to a completion semantics. In [6], the abductive event calculus has been applied to solve a number of benchmark problems in temporal reasoning. In [21] the language A is extended to deal with concurrent actions, and a sound and complete translation to abductive normal logic program is defined. As a difference with these proposals and the one in [10], rather than providing a translations to logic programs by employing either situation or event calculus, here we directly use a modal logic programming language, with a rather simple and standard semantics, by introducing a goal directed proof procedure for it.

A further difference with respect to [7,21] is that they consider as abducibles only the fluents in the initial state, whereas persistence through actions is dealt with by means of negation as failure. In this paper instead we use abduction as the unique mechanism to describe all nonmonotonic aspects of the language, including persistency. This allows to deal in a uniform way with multiple solutions, which, as we have shown in Example 9, may arise in any state, and not only in the initial state as in language A. Note that, this uniform abductive framework would allow the language to be easily extended so as to represent actions with nondeterministic immediate effects, and not only nondeterministic indirect effects as in Example 9.

As a difference with [21] our language does not deal with concurrent actions. On the other hand, it deals with ramifications. The adoption of a three-valued semantics is an aspect which our language has in common with [21]: the value of a fluent may be undefined, i.e. neither true nor false, in a given state.

From the methodological point of view, an advantage of the abductive approach we have adopted is its modularity, which allows to apply it to different languages and nonmonotonic formalisms. In particular, the abductive procedure is divided in two parts: Procedure *support* deals with the monotonic part of the language, whereas the second procedure which builds the sets of assumptions deals with the nonmonotonic aspects, and is independent of the particular language. Therefore the abductive procedure can be easily adapted to other languages by modifying procedure *support*. In particular, the same approach was followed in [13] to define an abductive semantics and procedure for the logic programming language *Cond LP+* in which hypothetical updates make the database dynamically change.

The abductive proof procedure for the action language presented in this paper has been implemented in Prolog by defining a simple metainterpreter, which mimics the procedure as described in section 4. The prover has, for instance, been used to compute the solutions for the examples discussed in the paper. Currently, we only deal with the propositional case. Extension to the first order case will be subject of further work, as well as other extensions to deal with nondeterministic and concurrent actions.

References

1. M. Baldoni, L.Giordano, and A.Martelli. A multimodal logic to define modules in logic programming. In *Proc. ILPS'93* , pages 473–487, Vancouver, 1993.
2. M. Baldoni, L.Giordano, and A.Martelli. A framework for modal logic programming. to appear in *Proc. JICSLP'96*, 1996.
3. A. Bondarenko, F. Toni, R. A. Kowalski. An assumption based framework for non-monotonic reasoning. in *Proc. 2nd Int. Workshop on Logic Programming and Non-monotonic Reasoning*, 1993.
4. G. Brewka and J. Hertzberg. How to do things with worlds: on formalizing action and plans. In *J. Logic and Computation*, vol.3, no.5, pages 517–532, 1993.
5. G. De Giacomo, M. Lenzerini. PDL-based framework for reasoning about actions. In *LNAI 992*, pages 103–114, 1995.
6. M. Denecker, L. Missiaen, M. Bruynooghe. Temporal Reasoning with Abductive Event Calculus. In *Proc. ECAI-92* , pages 384–388, Vienna, 1992.
7. M. Denecker, D. De Schreye. Representing Incomplete Knowledge in Abductive Logic Programming. In *Proc. ILPS'93* , pages 147–163, Vancouver, 1993.
8. P. M. Dung. Negations as hypotheses: an abductive foundation for logic programming. In *Proc. ICLP'91* , pages 3–17, 1991.
9. P. M. Dung. On the acceptability of arguments and its fundamental role in non-monotonic reasoning and logic programming. In *Proc. IJCAI93*, pages 852–857, 1993.
10. P. M. Dung. Representing Actions in Logic Programming and its Applications to Database Updates. In *Proc. ICLP'93* , pages 222–238, Budapest, 1993.
11. K. Eshghi and R. Kowalski. Abduction compared with negation by failure. In *Proc. 6th ICLP'89* , pages 234–254, Lisbon, 1989.
12. L. Fariñas del Cerro and A. Herzig. Interference logic = conditional logic + frame axiom. In *Int. J. of Intelligent Systems*, 9(1):119–130, 1994.
13. L. Giordano, A. Martelli and M.L. Sapino. An abductive proof procedure for Conditional Logic Programming. In Proc. FAPR'96, *LNAI 1085*, pages 231–245, 1996.
14. L. Giordano and A. Martelli. Reasoning about actions in modal logic programming. Technical Report, 1996.

15. M. Gelfond and V. Lifschitz. The Stable Model Semantics for Logic Programming. In *Fifth International Conference and Symposium on Logic Programming*, pages 1070–1080, Seattle, 1988.

16. M. Gelfond and V. Lifschitz. Logic programs with classical negation. In *Proc. ICLP'90*, pages 579–597, Jerusalem, 1990.

17. M. Gelfond and V. Lifschitz. Representing Action and Change by Logic Programs. In *J. Logic Programming*, pages 301–321, 1993.

18. D. Harel. First order dynamic logic in *Extensions of Classical Logic, Handbook of Philosophical Logic II*, pp. 497–604, 1984.

19. G.N. Kartha and V. Lifschitz. Actions with Indirect Effects (Preliminary Report). In *Proc. KR'94* , pages 341–350, 1995.

20. A.C. Kakas, P. Mancarella, P.M. Dung. The acceptability semantics for logic programs. In *Proc. 11th ICLP'94*, Santa Margherita Ligure, pages 504–519, 1994.

21. R. Li and L.M. Pereira. Temporal Reasoning with Abductive Logic Programming. In *Proc. ECAI'96*, pages 13–17, 1996.

22. R. Li and L.M. Pereira. Representing and Reasoning about Concurrent Actions with Abductive Logic Programs. To appear in *Annals of Mathematics and AI*, Special Issue for Gelfondfest, 1996.

23. F. Lin. Embracing Causality in Specifying the Indirect Effects of Actions. In *Proc. IJCAI'95*, pages 1985–1991, 1995.

24. N. McCain and H. Turner. A Causal Theory of Ramifications and Qualifications. In *Proc. IJCAI'95*, pages 1978–1984, 1995.

25. L. M. Pereira, J. N. Apariicio and J. J. Alferes. Non-Monotonic Reasoning with Logic Programming, In *J. of Logic Programming*, 17, pages 227–263, 1993.

26. T. C. Przymusinski. Extended stable semantics for normal and disjunctive programs. in *Proc. ICLP90 Conference*, pp. 459-477, 1990.

27. E. Sandewall. Feature and Fluents, Oxford University Press, 1994.

28. C. Schwind. A Logic Based Framework for Action Theories. In *Proc. TSLLC*, Jean-Jacques Levy and Zurab Khasidashvil (eds.), to appear in CSLI-series Stanford,USA, 1996.

29. M. Thielscher. Ramification and Causality. To appear in Artificial Intelligence, 1996.

30. F. Toni and A. Kakas. Computing the acceptability semantics. In *LNAI 928*, pages 401–415, 1995.

Update Programs Versus Revision Programs

N. Bidoit and S. Maabout*

LIPN. CNRS URA1507.
Université de Paris XIII. Avenue J.B. Clément.
93430 Villetaneuse, France.
{nicole.bidoit, sofian.maabout}@ura1507.univ-paris13.fr

Abstract. This paper presents an update rule language whose semantics is defined using a slight modification of the well founded semantics. This language is compared with revision programs proposed by Marek and Truszczynski in [MT95, MT94]. The relationships existing between revised databases and updated databases extend those previously established between stable and well founded models.

Keywords: update programs, revision programs, well founded semantics, stable semantics, partial databases.

1 Introduction

In this paper we introduce an update semantics of partial or incomplete databases in presence of *update rules*. Intuitively, an update rule specifies a set of events and conditions that when they are met, trigger an action. In fact, update rules can be seen as a special kind of ECA (Event, Condition, Action) rules widely studied in the context of active databases [WC96]. In our framework, the event as well as the action are elementary updates. The condition is a query. Thus, given a set of updates, an update rule serve to derive new updates, called derived updates. An update program (a set of update rules) is a special kind of logic programs and the well founded model semantics [vGRS91] is the tool that we propose in order to define update derivation.

Revision programs have been introduced in [MT94, MT95] in order to express and enforce integrity constraints. Roughly speaking, the approach of [MT94] works as follows: given a database instance and a revision program, one can check if a new database (a revision candidate) is a *revision* of the initial database with respect to the revision program. One feature of this approach is that a database may admit none, one or many revisions. The problem of deciding if a database admits a revision w.r.t. a program is NP_Complete and the algorithm which computes the revisions of a database is exponential in the size of the database. Thus, in order to be applicable, the approach needs to be restricted to some classes of revision programs. [MT95] exhibited two such classes: safe and stratifiable programs. These programs determine for every initial database a unique

---

* This work was partially supported by the GDR1140 of CNRS.

revision which is computable in polynomial time. However, as it will be showed in section 3, these properties (safety and stratifiability) still leave the existence of the revision dependent of the user update; each time the database is updated, i.e. updates are embedded into the revision program and these properties must be checked.

[PT95] shows that revision programs can be embedded into logic programs under the stable model semantics [GL88]. Thus, all known properties of stable semantics can be extended to revision programs.

First, the following examples introduce the classical problems encountered when considering update rules.

Example 1. Let $\Delta = \{p, q\}$ be a database and assume that we want to insert both s and t into Δ. So, the initial user update is $\delta = \{+s, +t\}$. Suppose that we have the following program

$$\mathcal{P}_1 = \left\{ \begin{array}{l} \rho_1 : +s, p \longrightarrow +r \\ \rho_2 : +t, q \longrightarrow -r \end{array} \right\}$$

The intuitive meaning of ρ_1 is: whenever s is being inserted, if p holds in the database then insert r.

Since the insertions of s and t are requested and since both p and q are in Δ, the update rules ρ_1 and ρ_2 can be "executed" simultaneously. This leads to a conflicting update because ρ_1 tries to insert r while ρ_2 tries to delete it. The problem is then: what should we do about r?

Consider now the case where ρ_1 is executed first. Its action will insert r. At this stage, we have to fire ρ_2 which deletes r. The condition of ρ_1 remains true, so it is executed once again. Thus, we enter a non terminating rule execution. The same would happen if we start by executing ρ_2 first. □

Example 2. Consider the same database $\Delta = \{p, q\}$ and the user update $\delta = \{+s, +t, +r\}$, but this time the rules are

$$\mathcal{P}_2 = \left\{ \begin{array}{l} \rho_1 : +s, p \longrightarrow -t \\ \rho_2 : +t, q \longrightarrow -s \end{array} \right\}$$

If we execute ρ_1 and ρ_2 simultaneously, we obtain $\Delta' = \{p, q, r\}$. t is deleted, by executing ρ_1 because s is inserted. However, in the updated database Δ', as s has been deleted by ρ_2, the deletion of t is no more "justified" (or explained) by the rules of $\mathcal{P}_2$. The same remark holds for the deletion of s.

Now suppose that at first ρ_1 is executed, so that the deletion of t id derived. After this, ρ_2 cannot be executed since the insertion of t is no more triggering ρ_2. The resulting updated database contains s but not t. If we execute ρ_2 before considering ρ_1, then the alternative resulting database contains t but not s. Thus, the final database depends on the order of rules execution. Notice also that in both cases, the justification of the updates remains valid in the new database. □

In the following section, we present the semantics of update rule programs and show some of its properties. Next, we compare our approach and that of

[MT95]. For doing so, we define a transformation which maps a revision program to an update program. It turns out that all revisions can be obtained by considering a class of stable models of the corresponding update program. Moreover, we show that the revised databases, when they exist, all extend the updated database. Hence, the semantics of updated databases can be considered as a well suited approximation of revisions. One of the most important contribution of our proposal is that update rules semantics is P_time computable. This is a crucial feature in the context of database management.

2 Update Rule Programming

In this paper we adopt the terminology of propositional logic programming. We distinguish between two sets of atoms; the set B_F of base atoms, hereafter denoted by $p, q, r, \ldots$ and the set U_F of update atoms which are of the form $+p, -p, \ldots$. The intuitive meaning of $+p$ is the insertion of p and $-p$ means the deletion of p. We also distinguish between base and update literals. If I is a set of literals, then $\neg.I$ denotes the set $\{\ell \mid \neg\ell \in I\}$. An update rule ρ is an expression of the form

$$U_1, \ldots, U_n, B_1, \ldots, B_m \longrightarrow U \tag{1}$$

where, U_i's are update-literals, B_j's are base literals, and U is an update atom. $Body(\rho) = \{U_1, \ldots, U_n, B_1, \ldots, B_m\}$ and $Head(\rho) = U$. An update program $\mathcal{P}$ is a finite set of update rules.

Example 3. The following is an update program:

$$\mathcal{P} = \left\{ \begin{array}{ll} \rho_1 : & -q, p, \neg-p \longrightarrow +t \\ \rho_2 : & \neg+p, +r \longrightarrow +t \\ \rho_3 : & +s \longrightarrow -t \\ \rho_4 : & p, s \longrightarrow -t \end{array} \right\}$$

The intuitive meaning of ρ_3 is: if s is being inserted then delete t. Notice that if we insert p into the database $\Delta = \{s\}$, ρ_4 is not "executed", because its condition is on p not on $+p$. This highlights the distinction we make between base and update literals when the conditions of the rules are evaluated.   □

A partial interpretation, or simply an interpretation, I is a set of literals such that, if $POS(I)$ and $NEG(I)$ denote respectively, positive and negative literals of I, then $POS(I) \cap \neg.NEG(I) = \emptyset$. An interpretation I satisfies a literal ℓ denoted by $I \models \ell$ iff $\ell \in I$ and I satisfies a rule ρ iff $Body(\rho) \subseteq I \Rightarrow Head(\rho) \in I$, in this case we note $I \models \rho$. If $\mathcal{P}$ is an update program, then I is a model of $\mathcal{P}$ iff I satisfies each rule of $\mathcal{P}$. If I and J are both partial interpretations, then $I \sqsubseteq J$ iff $POS(I) \subseteq POS(J)$ and $NEG(I) \subseteq NEG(J)$.

Well Founded Semantics - In this section we review the well founded semantics of propositional logic programs [vGRS91]. The semantics of $\mathcal{P}$ is defined by two fixpoint operators; $T^{\in}$ (the immediate consequence operator) and NF (the non founded operator). Let I be a partial interpretation and $\mathcal{P}$ a propositional Datalog¬ program. Then

- $T^{\in}_{\mathcal{P}}(I) = \{Head(\rho) |\, \rho \in \mathcal{P} \text{ and } \forall \ell \in Body(\rho) : \ell \in I\}$
- A set of facts F is called *unfounded set* with respect to I, iff:
  $\forall f \in F, \forall \rho \in \mathcal{P} : [Head(\rho) = f] \Longrightarrow \exists \ell \in Body(\rho) : [\neg \ell \in I \text{ or } \ell \in F]$.
  $NF_{\mathcal{P}}(I)$ is the greatest unfounded set with respect to I.

Now, consider the sequence $(I_i)_{(i \geq 0)}$ of partial interpretations defined by:

$$I_0 = \emptyset$$
$$I_{i+1} = WF_{\mathcal{P}}(I_i) = T^{\in}_{\mathcal{P}}(I_i) \cup \neg.NF_{\mathcal{P}}(I_i)$$

The sequence $(I_i)_{(i \geq 0)}$ is increasing (i.e. $I_j \sqsubseteq I_{j+1}$). Hence, because the domain is finite, there exists an integer k such that $I_k = I_i$ for all $i \geq k$. We denote this fixpoint by $WF(\mathcal{P})$.

The well founded model of $\mathcal{P}$ is, by definition, the partial interpretation $WF(\mathcal{P})$. Let $\mathcal{B}_{\mathcal{P}}$ denote the Herbrand base of $\mathcal{P}$. The well founded model $\mathcal{M}$ of $\mathcal{P}$ is bivalued (or total) if $POS(\mathcal{M}) \cup \neg.NEG(\mathcal{M}) = \mathcal{B}_{\mathcal{P}}$. □

In our approach, databases are incomplete in a very simple way. Their semantics relies on a three valued logic. Thus, a database is represented not only by the set of true facts, but also by the set of *unknown* facts. This representation of incomplete databases is the trivial alternative to the classical representation based on true and false facts.

Definition 1 - Database. A database instance Δ is a pair of disjoint sets of base facts: $< T(\Delta); U(\Delta) >$. Facts in $T(\Delta)$ (resp. in $U(\Delta)$) are *true* (resp. *unknown*) facts. The facts in B_F which are neither in $T(\Delta)$ nor in $U(\Delta)$ are *false*. This set is denoted by $F(\Delta)$. Δ is bivalued (or total) iff $U(\Delta) = \emptyset$. □

2.1 Update Semantics

An update represents a "partial specification" of a new database state [Che91]. If we request the insertion of the fact p, this means that we intend to move the database to a state where p is true. Nothing else is specified concerning the evolution of the other facts. For conventional databases (without update program), the update is performed simply by adding p to the old state. The contents of the initial database is kept in the new one "by default". This is how *the frame problem* is solved in the context of simple database update[2]. In presence of update rules, performing updates is more complicated. Indeed, an update program acts as an "inference mechanism" which derives updates

---

[2] "Commonsense law of inertia".

from those proposed by the user. For example, suppose we want to insert p into a database which contains the facts t and q. Assume that we have the rule $+p, t \longrightarrow -q$. Performing the update is achieved not only by adding p but also by deleting q. The deletion of q has been derived from the initial database state and the update request using the update rule.

Hence, in presence of update rules, we have to define a mechanism which derives a set of updates from a set of insertions and deletions requested by a user, a database instance and an update program. The derived updates are those which will actually be performed. Next, we formalize the process of update derivation.

Definition 2 - Updates. An update is a partial interpretation $\mathcal{I}$ which contains only update-literals. $\mathcal{I}$ is conflict free iff there is no fact p in B_F such that $\{+p, -p\} \subseteq \mathcal{I}$. A user (or, input) update is an update δ which contains only update-atoms[3]. □

Before defining the process of update derivation, the syntax of update rules is refined based on the following natural reading of these rules. Indeed, the update rule $\rho : Body(\rho) \longrightarrow +p$ is read as

- If the *prerequisite* $Body(\rho)$ is true, and
- if it is consistent to assume the *justification* $\neg -p$,
- then conclude *the consequence* $+p$.

One can recognize here that ρ is seen as a default rule [Rei80]. Our investigation of well founded models for defining the semantics of update programs is motivated by the fact that the well founded semantics provides a well suited formalism to approximate default reasoning [BF91].

In the remaining of the paper, we assume that for each update rule having $+p$ (resp. $-p$) in its head, there exists a negative literal $\neg -p$ (resp. $\neg +p$) in its body.

When specifying a query as a logic program $\mathcal{P}$, in order to define the answer of $\mathcal{P}$ on the input database Δ, Δ is embedded into $\mathcal{P}$. In our framework, updating is specified by a logic program $\mathcal{P}$ and in order to define the derived updates, we need to embed into $\mathcal{P}$ both the input database and the input update. This is done by adding the following rules to $\mathcal{P}$:

1. Each fact p in $T(\Delta)$ produces a rule $\longrightarrow p$.
2. Each $+p \in \delta$ produces a rule $\neg -p \longrightarrow +p$.
3. Each $-p \in \delta$ produces a rule $\neg +p \longrightarrow -p$.

Unknown Facts - Above, we do not take into account the unknown part of the input database. In fact, during the computation of the well founded model of $\mathcal{P}$, when applying the immediate consequence operator $T_{\mathcal{P}}^{\in}$, some rules body may contain an unknown database fact. The question arising here is: how should the rule be evaluated?

---

[3] We do not allow the user to request the "non insertion" or the "non deletion" of a fact p. We believe that this restriction is natural.

(i) Unknown database facts should be evaluated to unknown during the whole computation of the well founded model since "unknown" is their actual status. One solution is to achieve this is to add in the update program a rule $\neg p \longrightarrow p$ for each $p \in U(\Delta)$. Since this rule is the only one defining p, it guarantees that p will be unknown in the well founded model. The following example illustrates a problem arising from this solution.

Example 4. Let $\Delta =< \emptyset, \{p\} >$ be a database and $\delta = \{+q\}$ be a user update. Suppose that we have the update rule $\rho : +q, p, \neg\neg r \longrightarrow +r$. By embedding $U(\Delta)$ and δ, we obtain the final program:

$$\rho : \ +q, p, \neg\neg r \longrightarrow +r$$
$$\rho_1 : \qquad\quad \neg\neg q \longrightarrow +q$$
$$\rho_2 : \qquad\qquad\quad \neg p \longrightarrow p$$

In the well founded model of the above program, $+r$ is unknown because p is unknown. Notice however that by the definition of a model, an update rule is satisfied by an interpretation I as soon as its body is unknown (this is of course different from the definition of the well founded model). Thus, if we consider $+r$ as false in I instead of unknown, ρ is satisfied by I.

(ii) Now, suppose that we do not add special rules for unknown facts (i.e. the rule ρ_2 of example 4 is not added into the program). The well founded model $\mathcal{M}$ of $\{\rho, \rho_1\}$ makes p and $+r$ false. Although the status of p in $\mathcal{M}$ does not reflect its status in Δ, we could feel comfortable with the status of the insertion $+r$. Nevertheless, it suffices to examine another example to see that not doing anything to embed unknown facts of Δ leads to problems. Here follows such an example.

Example 5. Consider $\Delta =< \emptyset, \{p\} >$ and the update $\delta = \{+q\}$. Suppose now that we have the update rule $\rho : \ +q, \neg p, \neg\neg r \longrightarrow +r$. The update program obtained by integrating δ is

$$\rho : \ +q, \neg p, \neg\neg r \longrightarrow +r$$
$$\rho_1 : \qquad\qquad \neg\neg q \longrightarrow +q$$

Notice that $+r$ is true in the well founded model of this program. Notice that the derivation of the insertion $+r$ is wrong because it is based on the evaluation of p to false in the well founded model and this evaluation does not coincide with the status of p in the initial database. □

Finally, our solution in order to take into account unknown facts of the initial database consists in discarding the rules whose bodies contain an unknown literal.

Definition 3 - The program $\mathcal{P}_{\delta,\Delta}$. Let Δ be a database, δ a user update and $\mathcal{P}$ an update program. The program denoted by $\mathcal{P}_{\delta,\Delta}$ is the initial program $\mathcal{P}$ augmented by embedding $T(\Delta)$ and δ and then by removing each rule ρ such that $\exists \ell \in Body(\rho)$ and ℓ or $\neg\ell \in U(\Delta)$. □

Example 6. Let $\Delta = < \{p\}; \{q\} >$, $\delta = \{+r\}$ and $\mathcal{P}$ be the initial update program

$$\rho_1 : \quad +t, \neg\neg p \longrightarrow +p$$
$$\rho_2 : \neg p, \neg q, \neg+r \longrightarrow -r$$

The program $\mathcal{P}_{\delta,\Delta}$ is

$$\rho_1 : +t, \neg\neg p \longrightarrow +p$$
$$\rho_3 : \qquad\qquad \longrightarrow p$$
$$\rho_4 : \qquad \neg\neg r \longrightarrow +r$$

ρ_2 is removed because its body contains the literal $\neg q$ and $q \in U(\Delta)$. $\qquad\square$

Now, we emphasize the fact that in our framework, update and base atoms are treated independently. Hence, there is no semantic relationships between $+p$, $-p$ and p other than those specified by the program. Until now, the only link made between $+p$ and $-p$ follows from the rewriting of update rules into default rules by introducing $\neg-p$ (resp. $\neg+p$) in the body of the rules having head $+p$ (resp. $-p$).

The following definition extends the notion of the Herbrand base of a logic program $\mathcal{P}$. Usually, the Herbrand base is the set of all atoms which can be build up from the symbols appearing in $\mathcal{P}$.

In our framework, we consider all the atomic formulae, base and update, build up from the symbols of $\mathcal{P}$. For instance, this entails that if the base atom p appears in $\mathcal{P}$ but neither $+p$ nor $-p$ do, then the well founded model of $\mathcal{P}$ will give a truth value to p, and to $+p$ and $-p$, because all of them are in the extended Herbrand base.

Definition 4 - Extended Herbrand Base. The extended Herbrand base of $\mathcal{P}_{\delta,\Delta}$, denoted by $\mathcal{B}(\mathcal{P}_{\delta,\Delta})$, is the set

$$\{p, +p, -p \mid (\neg)p, (\neg)+p \text{ or } (\neg)-p \text{ appears in } \mathcal{P}, \delta \text{ or } \Delta\}.$$

$\qquad\square$

Example 6. **(Continued).**The extended Herbrand base of $\mathcal{P}_{\delta,\Delta}$ is the set

$$\mathcal{B}(\mathcal{P}_{\delta,\Delta}) = \{p, q, r, t, +p, +q, +r, +t, -p, -q, -r, -t\}$$

$\qquad\square$

The following definition of the *update model* is based on the definition of the well founded model and takes into account the notion of extended Herbrand base of a program and the unknown part of the initial database.

Definition 5 - Update Model. Let Δ be a database, δ a user update and $\mathcal{P}$ an update rule program. Let B be the Herbrand base of $\mathcal{P}_{\delta,\Delta}$ and $\mathcal{F}$ the set of facts defined as $\mathcal{B}(\mathcal{P}_{\delta,\Delta}) \setminus B$. Let $\mathcal{M}$ be the well founded model of $\mathcal{P}_{\delta,\Delta}$. The update model of $\mathcal{P}_{\delta,\Delta}$, denoted by $WFU(\mathcal{P}_{\delta,\Delta})$, is the interpretation $(\mathcal{M} \cup \neg.\mathcal{F}) \setminus \neg.U(\Delta)$.

$\qquad\square$

The set $\mathcal{F} = \mathcal{B}(\mathcal{P}_{\delta,\Delta}) \setminus B$ is, in fact, the set of atoms that appear in $\mathcal{B}(\mathcal{P}_{\delta,\Delta})$ but not in the program $\mathcal{P}_{\delta,\Delta}$. This means that they are considered as false when interpreting $\mathcal{P}_{\delta,\Delta}$. Notice also that since the facts in $U(\Delta)$ are not in $\mathcal{P}_{\delta,\Delta}$, they are necessarily in $\mathcal{F}$. These facts must be considered as unknown. This is why they (their negations) are removed from the update model.

Example 6. (**Continued**).The well founded model of $\mathcal{P}_{\delta,\Delta}$ is

$$WF(\mathcal{P}_{\delta,\Delta}) = \{p, \neg{+}p, \neg{-}p, \neg{-}r, {+}r, \neg{+}t\}$$

The set $\mathcal{F}$ is

$$\mathcal{F} = \mathcal{B}(\mathcal{P}_{\delta,\Delta}) \setminus B = \{q, {+}q, {-}q, r, t, {-}t\}$$

Finally, the update model $WFU(\mathcal{P}_{\delta,\Delta})$ is

$$(\{p, \neg{+}p, \neg{-}p, \neg{-}r, {+}r, \neg{+}t\} \cup \neg.\{q, {+}q, {-}q, r, t, {-}t\}) \setminus \neg.\{q\}$$

□

The update model satisfies the following property.

Proposition 6. *Let $\mathcal{I}$ be the greatest update included in $WFU(\mathcal{P}_{\delta,\Delta})$. $\mathcal{I}$ is conflict free.* □

Proof. From the definition of the well founded operator WF, we know that if a fact p is true in the well founded model $\mathcal{M}$ of a program $\mathcal{P}$, then there exists a rule $\rho \in \mathcal{P}$ such that $Body(\rho) \subseteq \mathcal{M}$. Thus, ${+}p$ (resp. ${-}p$) $\in WFU(\mathcal{P}_{\delta,\Delta}) \Rightarrow \neg{-}p$ (resp. $\neg{+}p$) $\in \mathcal{M}$, because $\forall \rho \in \mathcal{P}_{\delta,\Delta} : Head(\rho) = {+}p$ (resp. ${-}p) \Rightarrow Body(\rho) \ni \neg{-}p$ (resp. $\neg{+}p$). ∎

Now that we have defined how to derive updates from an update program given a database instance and a user update, it remains to explain what is the effect of the update (user + derived) on the initial database. This is the purpose of the application *Apply* defined below.

Definition 7 - Update Application. Let $\mathcal{M}$ be the update model $WFU(\mathcal{P}_{\delta,\Delta})$. $Apply(\mathcal{M}, \Delta) = \Delta'$, where:

- $T(\Delta') = \{p \mid {+}p \in \mathcal{M}$ or $\{p, \neg{-}p\} \subseteq \mathcal{M}\}$.
- $U(\Delta') = \{p \in \mathcal{B}(\mathcal{P}_{\delta,\Delta}) \mid p \notin T(\Delta')$ and $p \notin DEL(\mathcal{M})\}$, where $DEL(\mathcal{M}) = \{p \mid {-}p \in \mathcal{M}$ or $\{\neg p, \neg{+}p\} \subseteq \mathcal{M}\}$. □

Remark. Notice that $DEL(\mathcal{M}) \neq F(\Delta')$. Indeed, if p is an atom such that $p \notin \mathcal{B}(\mathcal{P}_{\delta,\Delta})$, then none of p, ${+}p$ and ${-}p$ is present in $\mathcal{M}$. This does not say that p is unknown in Δ'. It means that p was false in Δ and remains false in Δ'.

Notice also that since $\mathcal{M}$ is conflict free (Proposition 6), the mapping *Apply* is well defined.

Example 6. (**Continued**).The application of $WFU(\mathcal{P}_{\delta,\Delta})$ gives the new database $\Delta' = < \{p, r\}; \{q\} >$. □

The update model satisfies the following property.

Proposition 8. *Let $\mathcal{M} = WFU(\mathcal{P}_{\delta,\Delta})$, and $\Delta' = Apply(\mathcal{M}, \Delta)$. If $+p$ (resp. $-p$) $\in \delta$ then, either $p \in T(\Delta')$ (resp. $p \in F(\Delta')$) or $p \in U(\Delta')$.* □

Proof. It suffices to show that either $+p$ (resp. $-p$) $\in \mathcal{M}$ or both are unknown. Suppose that $+p \in \delta$ and $\neg+p \in \mathcal{M}$. This means that $\forall \rho \in \mathcal{P}_{\delta,\Delta}$, $Head(\rho) = +p \Rightarrow Body(\rho)$ is false in $\mathcal{M}$. Thus, the body of the particular $\hat{\rho} : \neg-p \longrightarrow +p$ is false. So, $-p \in \mathcal{M}$. This shows that we have the following situation

$$\hat{\rho}: \qquad \neg-p \longrightarrow +p$$
$$\rho: Cond(\rho), \neg+p \longrightarrow -p$$

with $\mathcal{M} \models Cond(\rho)$. Notice that ρ cannot be used to derive $-p$ since, during the computation of the fixpoint, we have to derive first $\neg+p$. Thus, $-p$ can be neither true nor false, and then $+p$ is neither true nor false. ■

Notice that, although in a loose manner, this proposition entails that user updates are never rejected. For instance, if p is subject to an insertion then the status of p in the new database is either true or unknown but never false. The update model satisfies the following property.

Example 7. Let $\mathcal{P} = \{+p, \neg+q \longrightarrow -q\}$, $\Delta = <\emptyset; \emptyset>$ and $\delta = \{+p, +q\}$. We have $WFU(\mathcal{P}_{\delta,\Delta}) = \mathcal{M} = \{\neg p, \neg q, \neg-p, +p\}$. So $Apply(\mathcal{M}, \Delta) = <\{p\}; \{q\}>$. □

In order to extend the semantics so that it will be possible to reject user updates, it suffices to consider the model obtained by the following definition.

Definition 9. Let

$$\beta = WFU(\mathcal{P}_{\delta,\Delta}) \cap \delta$$

We denote by $\mathcal{W}(\mathcal{P}_{\delta,\Delta})$ the interpretation $WFU(\mathcal{P}_{\beta,\Delta})$. □

Remark. In the above definition, β represents the set of user's updates that are confirmed in $WFU(\mathcal{P}_{\delta,\Delta})$.

Example 7. **(Continued).** $\beta = \{+p, +q\} \cap \mathcal{M} = \{+p\}$. Hence,

$$\mathcal{W}(\mathcal{P}_{\delta,\Delta}) = \mathcal{M} \cup \{-q, \neg+q\}$$

and $Apply(\mathcal{W}(\mathcal{P}_{\delta,\Delta}), \Delta) = <\{p\}; \emptyset>$. □

This extended semantics satisfies the following properties.

Proposition 10. $\quad - \mathcal{W}(\mathcal{P}_{\delta,\Delta})$ *is a model of $\mathcal{P}_{\delta,\Delta}$.*
$\quad - $ *If Δ is bivalued, then $\mathcal{W}(\mathcal{P}_{\delta,\Delta})$ is a partial stable model [Prz90] of $\mathcal{P}_{\delta,\Delta}$.*
$\quad - WFU(\mathcal{P}_{\delta,\Delta}) \sqsubseteq \mathcal{W}(\mathcal{P}_{\delta,\Delta})$. □

The last item of the above proposition entails that we can begin the computation of $WFU(\mathcal{P}_{\beta,\Delta})$ by considering $WFU(\mathcal{P}_{\delta,\Delta})$ as the first interpretation instead of beginning with the empty one. As another consequence of this result, we can see that databases obtained applying $\mathcal{W}(\mathcal{P}_{\delta,\Delta})$ instead of $WFU(\mathcal{P}_{\delta,\Delta})$ are more informative, that is they contain less unknown facts.

The next proposition gives a sufficient syntactic condition which ensures that the updated database is total.

Proposition 11. *Let $\mathcal{P}$ be an update program. If $\mathcal{P}$ is stratifiable then for all bivalued database Δ and all **user update** δ, we have $\mathcal{W}(\mathcal{P}_{\delta,\Delta})$ is bivalued. Thus, $Apply(\mathcal{W}(\mathcal{P}_{\delta,\Delta}),\Delta)$ is a total database.* □

Proof. (Sketch.) The only negative cycles that may exist in the program $\mathcal{P}_{\delta,\Delta}$ are those generated when embedding user updates. Since in the second step, we consider only updates which are not unknown, then each negative cycle generating unknown updates is removed. ∎

The graph below summarizes our update semantics. It illustrates state transition of a fact p. Vertices represent truth values of p and edges represent transitions. The edges are labeled by update-literals on p which appear in $\mathcal{W}(\mathcal{P}_{\delta,\Delta})$.

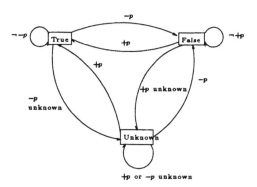

Fig. 1. State transition of fact p.

3 Relationship with Revision Programming

3.1 Revision Programming

Marek & Truszczynski [MT95] propose a language whose rules have the following syntax:

$$in(q_1),\ldots,in(q_m),out(s_1),\ldots,out(s_n) \longrightarrow in(p)$$
$$in(q_1),\ldots,in(q_m),out(s_1),\ldots,out(s_n) \longrightarrow out(p)$$

A revision program $\mathcal{P}^{\mathcal{R}}$ is a set of such rules. Expressions $in(p)$ and $out(p)$ are *literals*. They express, respectively, the *presence in* and the *absence from* the database of the fact p. Given an initial database D_I and a revision program $\mathcal{P}^{\mathcal{R}}$, [MT94] proposes an algorithm which checks if a database D_R is a "revision" of D_I according to $\mathcal{P}^{\mathcal{R}}$. The first step of the algorithm consists in simplifying the program: Let D_I and D_R be two databases. $\mathcal{P}^{\mathcal{R}}$ is transformed as:

1. Remove from $\mathcal{P}^{\mathcal{R}}$ all rules such that $q_i \notin D_R$ or $s_i \in D_R$. This simplification gives a new program $\mathcal{P}^{\mathcal{R}}_{D_R}$.
2. For each rule ρ in $\mathcal{P}^{\mathcal{R}}_{D_R}$, remove from $Body(\rho)$ every $in(q_i)$ if $q_i \in D_I$ and every $out(s_j)$ if $s_j \notin D_I$. The obtained program is $\mathcal{P}^{\mathcal{R}}_{D_R|D_I}$

Since $\mathcal{P}^{\mathcal{R}}_{D_R|D_I}$ is a positive program, it has a least model $\mathcal{M}$ that can be partitioned into $\mathcal{M}_{in} = \{p|\ in(p) \in \mathcal{M}\}$ and $\mathcal{M}_{out} = \{p|\ out(p) \in \mathcal{M}\}$. If $\mathcal{M}_{in} \cap \mathcal{M}_{out} = \emptyset$, and if $D_R = (D_I \cup \mathcal{M}_{in}) \setminus \mathcal{M}_{out}$, then D_R is a $\mathcal{P}^{\mathcal{R}}$-*justified revision* of D_I.

Example 8. Let $D_I = \{p,q\}$ and $\mathcal{P}^{\mathcal{R}} = \{in(p) \longrightarrow out(q);\ in(q) \longrightarrow out(p)\}$. Let $D_R = \{p\}$. $\mathcal{P}^{\mathcal{R}}_{D_R} = \{in(p) \longrightarrow out(q)\}$ and $\mathcal{P}^{\mathcal{R}}_{D_R|D_I} = \{\longrightarrow out(q)\}$. The least model of $\mathcal{P}^{\mathcal{R}}_{D_R|D_I}$ is $\mathcal{M} = \{out(q)\}$ and $(D_I \cup \mathcal{M}_{in}) \setminus \mathcal{M}_{out} = D_R$. So, D_R is a $\mathcal{P}^{\mathcal{R}}$-justified revision of D_I. One can see that $D' = \emptyset$ is not a revision of D_I.□

Following this semantics, a database may admit none, one, or several revisions.

Remark. In [MT95], input updates are embedded into the revision program by adding empty body rules: the insertion of p leads to the rule $\longrightarrow in(p)$ and the deletion of p is modeled by the rule $\longrightarrow out(p)$.

Notice also that [MT95] considers only total database. Thus in the rest of this section we consider initial databases as being total databases.

3.2 Comparison

Since update and revision programs have not the same syntax, we first define an application $\mathcal{U}$ which maps each revision program into an update program.

Definition 12. Let $\mathcal{P}^{\mathcal{R}}$ be a revision program. $\mathcal{U}(\mathcal{P}^{\mathcal{R}})$ is the update program obtained from $\mathcal{P}^{\mathcal{R}}$ by modifying each rule $\rho \in \mathcal{P}^{\mathcal{R}}$ as follows:

1. If $Head(\rho) = in(p)$ then replace it by $+p$ and add into $Body(\rho)$ the update literal $\neg-p$.
2. If $Head(\rho) = out(p)$ then replace it by $-p$ and add into $Body(\rho)$ the update literal $\neg+p$.
3. If $in(p) \in Body(\rho)$ then replace it by $(p \wedge \neg-p) \vee +p$.
4. If $out(p) \in Body(\rho)$ then replace it by $(\neg p \wedge \neg+p) \vee -p$. □

Example 8. (**Continued**). The update program corresponding to $\mathcal{P}^{\mathcal{R}}$ is

$$\mathcal{U}(\mathcal{P}^{\mathcal{R}}) = \left\{ \begin{array}{c} p, \neg\mathbf{-}p, \neg\mathbf{+}q \longrightarrow \neg q \\ \mathbf{+}p, \neg\mathbf{+}q \longrightarrow \neg q \\ q, \neg\mathbf{-}q, \neg\mathbf{+}p \longrightarrow \neg p \\ \mathbf{+}q, \neg\mathbf{+}p \longrightarrow \neg p \end{array} \right\}$$

□

The following proposition establishes a link between the two semantics. We introduce this result by the following example.

Example 8. (**Continued**). Clearly, D_I admits two revisions; $D_{R1} = \{p\}$ and $D_{R2} = \{q\}$. Now, let us consider $\mathcal{P} = \mathcal{U}(\mathcal{P}^{\mathcal{R}})$.

$$\mathcal{P}_{\emptyset, D_I} = \left\{ \begin{array}{ll} \rho_{11} : p, \neg\mathbf{-}p, \neg\mathbf{+}q \longrightarrow \neg q \\ \rho_{12} : \quad\;\; \mathbf{+}p, \neg\mathbf{+}q \longrightarrow \neg q \\ \rho_{21} : q, \neg\mathbf{-}q, \neg\mathbf{+}p \longrightarrow \neg p \\ \rho_{22} : \quad\;\; \mathbf{+}q, \neg\mathbf{+}p \longrightarrow \neg p \\ \rho_{31} : \qquad\qquad\qquad\; \longrightarrow p \\ \rho_{32} : \qquad\qquad\qquad\; \longrightarrow q \end{array} \right\}$$

$\mathcal{P}_{\emptyset, D_I}$ has two stable models, $\mathcal{M}_1 = \{p, q, -p\}$ and $\mathcal{M}_2 = \{p, q, -q\}$ (we do not represent the negative or the false part of the stable models since they are bivalued). Notice that $Apply(\mathcal{M}_1, D_I) = D_{R1}$ and $Apply(\mathcal{M}_2, D_I) = D_{R2}$. This gives the intuition behind the following proposition. □

Proposition 13. *Let Δ be a total database, $\mathcal{P}^{\mathcal{R}}$ a revision program and $\mathcal{P} = \mathcal{U}(\mathcal{P}^{\mathcal{R}})$. Let $\mathcal{D}_{\mathcal{R}}$ denote the set of the $\mathcal{P}^{\mathcal{R}}$-justified revisions of Δ. Then, for all $D \in \mathcal{D}_{\mathcal{R}}$, there exists an interpretation $\mathcal{M}$ such that*

- *$Apply(\mathcal{M}, \Delta) = D$ and*
- *$\mathcal{M}$ is a stable model of $\mathcal{P}_{\emptyset, \Delta}$.* □

In order to prove this proposition we need the following result of Fages [Fag91] which characterizes the stable models by means of well supported interpretations.

Definition 14. *Let I be an interpretation. I is well-supported by a program $\mathcal{P}$ iff there exists a well-founded ordering $<$ on the Herbrand base of $\mathcal{P}$ such that: $p \in I \Rightarrow \exists \rho \in \mathcal{P}$ such that $\rho = Body(\rho) \longrightarrow p$, $I \models Body(\rho)$ and for all positive literal p_i in $Body(\rho)$, we have $p_i < p$.* □

Theorem 15. [**Fag91**]. *An interpretation I is a stable model of a program $\mathcal{P}$ iff it is a well-supported model of $\mathcal{P}$.* □

Proof. (Proposition 13)

Let D be a $\mathcal{P}^{\mathcal{R}}$-justified revision of Δ and let $\mathcal{N}$ denote the least model of the program $\mathcal{P}^{\mathcal{R}}_{D|\Delta}$. Now consider $\mathcal{M}$ to be the interpretation defined as follows:

$$\mathcal{M} = \{p \,|\, p \in T(\Delta)\} \cup \{+p \,|\, in(p) \in \mathcal{N}\} \cup \{-p \,|\, out(p) \in \mathcal{N}\}.$$

It is clear that $Apply(\mathcal{M}, \Delta) = D$.

Now we show that $\mathcal{M}$ is a stable model for $\mathcal{P}_{\emptyset,\Delta}$. In order to do this, we show that $\mathcal{M}$ is a well-supported model of $\mathcal{P}_{\emptyset,\Delta}$.

Let us now define an ordering function $range$:

- $\forall p \in \mathcal{M}$, $range(p) = 0$, where p is a base fact.
- Let $+p \in \mathcal{M}$. Then by the definition of $\mathcal{M}$, $in(p) \in \mathcal{N}$. $\mathcal{N}$ is computed by the immediate consequence operator $\mathcal{T}_{\mathcal{P}_{D|\Delta}^{\mathcal{R}}}$. This defines a sequence of interpretations $(I_n)_{n \geq 1}$. If α is the integer such that $in(p) \in I_\alpha - I_{\alpha-1}$ then, $range(+p) = \alpha$ (the same definition is made for $-p$).

1. $\mathcal{M}$ is a model for $\mathcal{P}_{\emptyset,\Delta}$: First, notice that $\mathcal{P}_{\emptyset,\Delta}$ can be partitioned into two subprograms $\mathcal{P}^\Delta$ consisting in the empty body rules of the form $\longrightarrow p$, and $\mathcal{P}^c$ which is the set of the update rules.

   It is easy to see that $\mathcal{M}$ is a model of $\mathcal{P}^\Delta$.

   Now suppose that there exists $\rho \in \mathcal{P}^c$ such that $\mathcal{M} \not\models \rho$.

$$\rho = \bigwedge_{i=1}^{n} (p_i \wedge \neg{-}p_i) \vee +p_i, \bigwedge_{j=1}^{m} (\neg q_j \wedge \neg + q_j) \vee -q_j, \neg{-}p \longrightarrow +p.$$

There is a rule $\rho^{\mathcal{R}} \in \mathcal{P}^{\mathcal{R}}$ corresponding to ρ such that:

$$\rho^{\mathcal{R}} = \bigwedge_{i=1}^{n} in(p_i), \bigwedge_{j=1}^{m} out(q_j) \longrightarrow in(p)$$

$\mathcal{M} \not\models \rho \Rightarrow \mathcal{M} \models Body(\rho)$ and $\mathcal{M} \models \neg Head(\rho)$. Notice that:

- $\forall i = 1 \ldots n$, $\mathcal{M} \models (p_i \wedge \neg{-}p_i) \Rightarrow -p_i \notin \mathcal{M} \Rightarrow out(p_i) \notin \mathcal{N}$. On the other hand, $\mathcal{M} \models (p_i \wedge \neg{-}p_i) \Rightarrow p_i \in T(\Delta)$. Hence, $p_i \in T(\Delta) \wedge out(p_i) \notin \mathcal{N} \Rightarrow D \models in(p_i)$.
- $\forall i = 1 \ldots n$, $\mathcal{M} \models +p_i \Rightarrow in(p_i) \in \mathcal{N} \Rightarrow D \models in(p_i)$.
- In the same way, one can prove that $\mathcal{M} \models (\neg q_j \wedge \neg + q_j) \vee -q_j \Rightarrow D \models out(q_j)$.

Thus, we have proven that $\mathcal{M} \models Body(\rho) \Rightarrow D \models Body(\rho^{\mathcal{R}})$. Hence, $\rho^{\mathcal{R}} \in \mathcal{P}_D^{\mathcal{R}}$. From a theorem of [MT95], $\mathcal{N} = HEAD(\mathcal{P}_D^{\mathcal{R}})$ (the set of rules heads), thus $Head(\rho^{\mathcal{R}}) = in(p) \in \mathcal{N}$. So, $+p \in \mathcal{M}$, which contradicts the fact that $\mathcal{M} \models \neg{+}p$. Hence, $\mathcal{M}$ is a model of $\mathcal{P}_{\emptyset,\Delta}$.

2. $\mathcal{M}$ is a well-supported model of $\mathcal{P}_{\emptyset,\Delta}$:

   First, it is immediate to see for all base fact $p \in \mathcal{M}$, the conditions of definition 14 holds.

   Consider now $+p \in \mathcal{M}$ with $range(+p) = \alpha$. $+p \in \mathcal{M} \Leftrightarrow in(p) \in \mathcal{N}$. So, There exists $\rho^{\mathcal{R}} \in \mathcal{P}^{\mathcal{R}}$ such that $D \models Body(\rho^{\mathcal{R}})$ and $Head(\rho^{\mathcal{R}}) = in(p)$. If

$$\rho^{\mathcal{R}} = \bigwedge_{i=1}^{n} in(p_i), \bigwedge_{j=1}^{m} out(q_j) \longrightarrow in(p)$$

and if ρ is its corresponding rule in $\mathcal{P}_{\emptyset,\Delta}$, then it is immediate to see that $D \models Body(\rho^R) \Rightarrow M \models Body(\rho)$.

After the second step of simplification of [MT95], we get a rule ρ_1^R from which we have removed $in(p_i)$ if $p_i \in T(\Delta)$ and $out(q_j)$ if $q_j \notin T(\Delta)$. Since $I_{\alpha-1} \supseteq Body(\rho_1^R)$, then for every positive literal ℓ in $Body(\rho)$, $range(\ell) < range(+p)$. This demonstrates that M is a well supported model.

Hence M is a stable model of $\mathcal{P}_{\emptyset,\Delta}$. ∎

Notice however that the converse does not hold; *i.e.* not all stable models of $\mathcal{P}_{\emptyset,\Delta}$ define $\mathcal{P}^R$-justified revisions of Δ. This is illustrated by the following example.

Example 9. Let $D = \emptyset$ and $\mathcal{P}^R = \{\longrightarrow in(p); \longrightarrow out(p)\}$. D admits no revision. Now consider $\mathcal{P} = \mathcal{U}(\mathcal{P}^R)$.

$$\mathcal{P}_{\emptyset,D} = \left\{ \begin{array}{l} \rho_1 : \neg\!-p \longrightarrow +p \\ \rho_2 : \neg\!+p \longrightarrow -p \end{array} \right\}$$

Clearly, this program has two stable models, $\mathcal{M}_1 = \{+p\}$, and $\mathcal{M}_2 = \{-p\}$. Nevertheless, $Apply(\mathcal{M}_1, D) = \{p\}$ is not a $\mathcal{P}^R$-justified revision of Δ. The same holds for $\mathcal{M}_2$. □

The following proposition gives a sufficient and necessary condition on the stable model of $\mathcal{P}_{\emptyset,\Delta}$ for defining a revision.

Proposition 16. *Let Δ be a total database, $\mathcal{P}^R$ a revision program and $\mathcal{P} = \mathcal{U}(\mathcal{P}^R)$. Let M be a stable model of $\mathcal{P}_{\emptyset,\Delta}$. Let $\tilde{\mathcal{P}}$ be the program obtained from $\mathcal{P}$ by removing from the body of each rule ρ the literal $\neg\!+p$ (resp. $\neg\!-p$) whenever $Head(\rho) = -p$ (resp. $+p$). Then: M defines a $\mathcal{P}^R$-justified revision of Δ iff it is a stable model of $\tilde{\mathcal{P}}_{\emptyset,\Delta}$.* □

Example 9. **(Continued).**

$$\tilde{\mathcal{P}}_{\emptyset,D} = \left\{ \begin{array}{l} \rho_1' : \longrightarrow +p \\ \rho_2' : \longrightarrow -p \end{array} \right\}$$

One can see that neither $\mathcal{M}_1$ nor $\mathcal{M}_2$ is a stable model of $\tilde{\mathcal{P}}_{\emptyset,D}$. □

As a consequence of Propositions 13 and 16 , we prove the uniqueness of justified revisions when the well founded model is total.

Corollary 17. *Let M be the well founded model of $\mathcal{P}_{\emptyset,\Delta}$. If M is total, then $Apply(M, \Delta)$ is the unique $\mathcal{P}^R$-justified revision of Δ.* □

Proof. (Sketch .) It suffices to see that the total well founded model of $\mathcal{P}_{\emptyset,\Delta}$ is the unique stable model of $\tilde{\mathcal{P}}_{\emptyset,\Delta}$. ∎

The following theorem says that all revisions extend the updated databases we obtain with our semantics. Thus, it shows that our approach provides a well suited approximation of revision programs.

Theorem 18. *Let D_I be a database, $\mathcal{P}^{\mathcal{R}}$ a revision program and $\mathcal{P} = \mathcal{U}(\mathcal{P}^{\mathcal{R}})$. Let $\mathcal{D}_{\mathcal{R}}$ denote the set of the $\mathcal{P}^{\mathcal{R}}$-justified revisions of the database D_I. Let $\Delta = Apply(WFU(\mathcal{P}_{\emptyset, D_I}), D_I)$. If $\mathcal{D}_{\mathcal{R}} \neq \emptyset$, then $\forall D \in \mathcal{D}_{\mathcal{R}}: T(\Delta) \subseteq D$ and $F(\Delta) \cap D = \emptyset$* □

Proof. (Sketch) It suffices to note that each stable model of $\tilde{\mathcal{P}}_{\emptyset, \Delta}$ extends the well founded model of $\mathcal{P}_{\emptyset, \Delta}$. ■

[MT95] shows that the existence of justified revisions is NP-complete. This motivates the authors to propose restricted classes of revision programs whose semantics can be computed in polynomial time. [MT95] identifies two such classes, namely **safe** and **MT_stratifiable**[4]. Safe and MT_stratifiable revision programs have also the property that they define a unique revision for each initial database. In the following, we show that a revision program $\mathcal{P}^{\mathcal{R}}$ is MT_stratifiable iff $\mathcal{U}(\mathcal{P}^{\mathcal{R}})$ is stratifiable (in [ABW88] sense).

Definition 19 - Safety. A revision program $\mathcal{P}^{\mathcal{R}}$ is **safe** iff for all p,

- $\exists \rho \in \mathcal{P}^{\mathcal{R}}$ with $Head(\rho) = in(p) \Rightarrow \nexists \rho' \in \mathcal{P}^{\mathcal{R}}$ such that $Body(\rho') \ni out(p)$ or $Head(\rho') = out(p)$.
- $\exists \rho \in \mathcal{P}^{\mathcal{R}}$ with $Head(\rho) = out(p) \Rightarrow \nexists \rho' \in \mathcal{P}$ such that $Body(\rho') \ni in(p)$ or $Head(\rho') = in(p)$. □

It is worth noting that safety depends on user updates. Indeed, a program which is safe can become unsafe when user updates are taken into account. This is in contrast to our syntactic restriction of update programs (cf. Proposition 11) which is independent from user updates.

Example 10. Let $\mathcal{P}^{\mathcal{R}} = \{in(p) \longrightarrow out(q)\}$. $\mathcal{P}^{\mathcal{R}}$ is safe. Now, suppose that a user wants to insert q. By adding the rule $\longrightarrow in(q)$, the new revision program is unsafe. □

Now, we recall the definition of MT_stratifiable revision programs which is a larger class of revision programs.

Definition 20 - MT_Stratifiability. A revision program $\mathcal{P}^{\mathcal{R}}$ is MT_stratifiable iff there exists a partition $\{\mathcal{P}_i^{\mathcal{R}}\}_{0 < i < n}$ such that

- $\mathcal{P}_i$ is safe, and
- if $\rho \in \mathcal{P}_i^{\mathcal{R}}$ and $Head(\rho) = \alpha$, then there is no rule $\hat{\rho} \in \cup_{j < i} \mathcal{P}_j^{\mathcal{R}}$ such that α or $\alpha^D \in Var(\hat{\rho})$.

where $\alpha^D = in(p)$ (resp. $out(p)$) if $\alpha = out(p)$ (resp. $in(p)$) and $Var(\hat{\rho}) = \{\alpha | \alpha \in Body(\hat{\rho})$ or $\alpha = Head(\hat{\rho})\}$. □

The following gives an example of a revision program which is MT_stratifiable but not safe.

---

[4] [MT95] uses the term **stratifiable** whose meaning is different from the one introduced in the context of logic programs.

Example 11. Let $\mathcal{P}^{\mathcal{R}}$ be the following program.

$$\mathcal{P}^{\mathcal{R}} = \left\{ \begin{array}{l} \rho_1 : \ in(q) \longrightarrow in(p) \\ \rho_2 : out(p) \longrightarrow in(r) \end{array} \right\}$$

The partition $\mathcal{P}^{\mathcal{R}}_1 = \{\rho_1\}$ and $\mathcal{P}^{\mathcal{R}}_2 = \{\rho_2\}$ satisfies Definition 20 but not Definition 19. Notice that here again, if we consider the insertion of r, i.e. we add the revision rule $\longrightarrow in(r)$, the resulting program is no longer MT-stratifiable. $\square$

Proposition 21. *Let $\mathcal{P}^{\mathcal{R}}$ be a revision program and $\mathcal{P} = \mathcal{U}(\mathcal{P}^{\mathcal{R}})$. Then, $\mathcal{P}^{\mathcal{R}}$ is MT-stratifiable $\Leftrightarrow \mathcal{P}$ is* stratifiable *(in [ABW88] sense).* $\square$

It is well known that stratifiable programs admit total well founded models. If $\mathcal{M}$ denotes the well founded model of $\mathcal{P}_{\emptyset,\Delta}$ then, by Corollary 17, $Apply(\mathcal{M}, \Delta)$ is the unique justified revision of Δ. This gives an alternative proof of the uniqueness of revisions for this class of revision programs. Notice however that the class of logic programs which have bivalued well founded models is larger than that of (locally) stratifiable.

4 Discussion & Concluding Remarks

It is important to note that the semantics of [MT95] is intractable. We recall that well founded models are P-time computable [vGRS91].

Notice also that following the approach of [MT95], one cannot handle contradictory updates, thus even updates which are not involved in contradiction are discarded. Following our approach, all updates which are not involved in a contradiction are preserved and performed.

There is a slight difference between our treatment of update rules and that of revision rules. Indeed, [MT95] considers the rule $\rho : \ in(p) \longrightarrow out(q)$ as the constraint saying "if p is present, then q **should be absent**". Each revision D_R of a database D_I by a revision program $\mathcal{P}^{\mathcal{R}}$ that contains ρ will satisfies the constraint. Notice however, that updating D_I with the update program $\mathcal{U}(\mathcal{P}^{\mathcal{R}})$ gives a database which satisfies the constraint saying "if p is present, then q **should not be present**" (q could be unknown). For total databases, these two readings are equivalent. This is not the case when considering incomplete databases. Another difference between the two approaches is that [MT95] considers user updates as "constraints" which must hold in the new database (they are in the necessary change). We do not follow this approach since (part of) user updates can be "undone". In [BM97], we propose an approach to derive update rule programs from declarative specifications of integrity constraints. These derived programs enforce database consistency. Hence, we make a clear distinction between constraints which should be enforced and user updates which are not considered as constraints.

One of the postulates of the theories of change [KM91, AGM85, Win89] says that, when adding a formula ϕ to a knowledge base ψ, the resulting knowledge base ψ' must satisfy ϕ i.e. ϕ must be a logical consequence of ψ'. Concerning our update semantics, a request for adding an atomic formula (adding $p \equiv$ inserting p, and adding $\neg p \equiv$ deleting p) does not always lead to a database satisfying this atom. By contrast, under the approach of [MT95], when a revision exists, it satisfies the user request.

[Bar94] investigated a relationship between revision programs and the standard update operator o of [KM91]. Let us recall this result. Each revision rule is transformed into a propositional formula by: transforming $in(p)$ into p, $out(p)$ into $\neg p$, and $\longrightarrow$ into the logical implication $\Rightarrow$. Let $F_{\mathcal{P}^{\mathcal{R}}}$ denotes the conjunction of the logical formulae obtained from the rules of the revision program $\mathcal{P}^{\mathcal{R}}$. [Bar94] shows that the set of $\mathcal{P}^{\mathcal{R}}$-justified revisions of D_I is a subset of the models obtained by adding the formulae $F_{\mathcal{P}}$ to D_I (i.e. $D_I o F_{\mathcal{P}}$).

The non-determinism captured by the semantics of revision programs can be considered as a desirable property in some cases. For instance, consider the functional dependency "stated" by the following revision rule $\rho : in(P(x, y)), y \neq y' \longrightarrow out(P(x, y'))$ and the database $\Delta = \{P(a, b), P(a, b')\}$. If we revise Δ with ρ, we can obtain either $\Delta_1 = \{P(a, b)\}$ or $\Delta_2 = \{P(a, b')\}$. With our semantics, the database that we obtain is $\Delta'' = < \emptyset; \{P(a, b), P(a, b')\} >$.

As we have shown in the previous section, revision programs can be embedded in update programs under the stable semantics. Thus, database transformations that we can define by revision programs is a subset of the transformations that we can specify by using update programs under stable semantics. This is essentially due to the fact that update programs distinguish between update atoms and base atoms. One can notice that in definition 12 of the mapping $\mathcal{U}$, the literal $in(p)$ in the body is interpreted by: p is present in the initial database and not deleted or it is inserted. This means that p is present in the "next" database and shows that the condition of the revision rules are evaluated "a posteriori" [MT95]. Hence, revision rules cannot use conditions on the initial state[5]. Thus, we can say that update programs (under stable semantics) are more expressive that revision programs. This feature allowed us to consider transition integrity constraints enforcement by update programs (see [BM97]).

Studying the exact expressive power of update rules is one of our future research topic; *i.e.* the class of transformations definable in this language. Especially, the connection of this work with the deterministic semantics of Datalog$^{\neg *}$ of [AV91] where the negation allowed in the heads of rules is interpreted as deletion.

[MT94] extends revision programs by considering disjunctions in rules heads. [PT95] shows that the *minimal change* property is not preserved by disjunctive revision programs, e.g. if $\Delta = \{a\}$ and $\mathcal{P}^{\mathcal{R}} = \{\longrightarrow in(a) \vee in(b)\}$ then both $\Delta_1 = \{a\}$ and $\Delta_2 = \{a, b\}$ are justified revisions. Notice that Δ_2 in-

---

[5] [Bar94] proposes an extension of revision rules for this purpose.

volves more changes than Δ_1. We can translate $\mathcal{P}^{\mathcal{R}}$ into the update program $\mathcal{P} = \{\neg a, \neg b \longrightarrow +a \vee +b\}$. By adding $\longrightarrow a$ into $\mathcal{P}$, we obtain an update program whose unique minimal model is $\mathcal{M} = \{a, \neg b, \neg +a, \neg +b\}$ (plus $\neg -a, \neg -b$ which are in the extended Herbrand model). Notice that $Apply(\mathcal{M}, \Delta) = \Delta = \{a\}$. Adding disjunctions in update rule heads is one of our current interests.

Another interesting direction of future research would be to investigate if and how our approach relates to the theory of updating incomplete databases (e.g. [AG85]). In this context, null values generally represent disjunctive information.

One of the important properties of our semantics is that it associates to each input database, a resulting updated database which in turn may be incomplete. In this sense, we can say that our update semantics is always defined. This is by contrast to the translation of Przymusinski and Turner [PT95]. Indeed, [PT95] defines a translation of revision programs into logic programs whose "coherent" stable models correspond to justified revisions. In the conclusion, the authors say that the well founded semantics could be considered as an approximation of revisions, however we should point out that the well founded model of the obtained logic program may be conflictual in the sense that it may contain both $in(p)$ and $out(p)$. Let us illustrate this by the following example.

Example 12. Let $\mathcal{P}^{\mathcal{R}} = \{in(a) \longrightarrow out(b); \ in(c) \longrightarrow in(b); \ in(b) \longrightarrow out(d)\}$ and the database $\Delta = \{a, c\}$. Following [PT95], the corresponding logic program is

$$\begin{array}{ll} \longrightarrow in_I(a) & \longrightarrow in_I(c) \\ \longrightarrow out_I(b) & \longrightarrow out_I(d) \end{array}$$

$$\begin{array}{ll} in_I(a), \neg out(a) \longrightarrow in(a) & out_I(a), \neg in(a) \longrightarrow out(a) \\ in_I(b), \neg out(b) \longrightarrow in(b) & out_I(b), \neg in(b) \longrightarrow out(b) \\ in_I(c), \neg out(c) \longrightarrow in(c) & out_I(c), \neg in(c) \longrightarrow out(c) \\ in_I(d), \neg out(d) \longrightarrow in(d) & out_I(d), \neg in(d) \longrightarrow out(d) \end{array}$$

$$\begin{array}{ll} in(a) \longrightarrow out(b) & in(c) \longrightarrow in(b) \\ in(b) \longrightarrow out(d) \end{array}$$

The first group of rules serve to embed the initial database, the second one serve to model the "law of inertia" and the final group represents the initial rules of $\mathcal{P}^{\mathcal{R}}$.

The well founded model of this program is bivalued and its positive part is

$$\mathcal{M} = \{in_I(a), in_I(c), out_I(b), out_I(d), in(a), in(c), in(b), out(b), out(d)\}$$

$\mathcal{M}$ contains both $in(b)$ and $out(b)$. More generally, when the well founded model is not coherent, none of the stable models is and thus, the database admits no justified revision. Hence, in the framework of [PT95], using the well founded semantics does not solve the problem of undefined revisions, although it is expected that "partial" well founded models should take care of conflicts.

Following our semantics, the updated database is $\Delta' =< \{a, c\}, \{b\} >$. $\quad\square$

In this paper, we have considered user updates as a set of atomic updates. The case where user updates are programs themselves is an open topic of investigation. Indeed, database updates are generally conditioned. Thus, it would be more practical to allow users to express their update requests in a generic form. For instance suppose that a user wants to delete all $P(x)$ such that there exists an atom $Q(x, y)$ with $x > 20$. Instead of enumerating all the atoms $P(x)$ satisfying this condition, it would be easier to use the rule $Q(x, y), x > 20 \longrightarrow -P(x)$. The problem arising here is that some of the (to be) deleted $P(x)$ can be confirmed and others rejected, but there is no direct way to insure that the update $Q(x, y), x > 20 \longrightarrow -P(x)$ is globally confirmed or rejected.

References

[ABW88] K. Apt, H. Blair, and A. Walker. Towards a theory of declarative knowledge. In J. Minker, editor, *Foundations of Deductive Databases and Logic Programming*, pages 89–142. Morgan Kaufmann, 1988.

[AG85] S. Abiteboul and G. Grahne. Update semantics for incomplete databases. In *Proceedings of the 11th VLDB Conference*, 1985.

[AGM85] C.E. Alchourrón, P. Gärdenfors, and D. Makinson. On the logic of theory change: Partial meet contraction and revision functions. *Journal of Symbolic Logic*, 1985.

[AV91] S. Abiteboul and V. Vianu. Datalog extensions for database queries and updates. *Journal of Computer and System Sciences*, 43, 1991.

[Bar94] C. Baral. Rule based updates on simple knowledge bases. In *Proceedings of AAAI'94*, Seattle, USA, August 1994.

[BF91] N. Bidoit and C. Froidevaux. General logic databases and programs: Default logic semantics and stratification. *Information and Computation*, 91:15–54, 1991.

[BM97] N. Bidoit and S. Maabout. A model theoretic approach to update rule programs. In *Proceedings of ICDT Conference*, LNCS, Delphi, Greece, Jan. 1997. Springer-Verlag.

[Che91] W. Chen. Declarative specification of database updates. In *Proc. of DOOD'91*. Springer, 1991.

[Fag91] F. Fages. A new fixpoint semantics for general logic programs compared with the well-founded and the stable model semantics. *New Generation Computing*, 9(4), 1991.

[GL88] M. Gelfond and V. Lifschitz. The stable semantics for logic programs. In *Proceedings of the 5th international symposium on logic programming*. MIT Press, 1988.

[KM91] H. Katsuno and A. O. Mendelzon. On the difference between updating a knowledgebase and revisiting it. In *Proceedings of Intrl. Conf. on Knowledge Representation and Reasoning (KR'91)*, 1991.

[MT94]   V. Marek and M. Truszczynski. Revision specification by means of programs. In *Logics in AI. Proceedings of JELIA'94*, LNAI. Springer Verlag, 1994.

[MT95]   V. Marek and M. Truszczynski. Revision programming, database updates and integrity constraints. In *Proceedings of the 5th International Conference on Database Theory. ICDT'95*, Prague, Jan. 1995.

[PT95]   T. C. Przymusinski and H. Turner. Update by means of inference rules. In *Proceedings of the International Conf. on Logic Programming and Non Monotonic Reasoning, LPNMR'95*, LNAI, 1995.

[Rei80]   R. Reiter. A logic for default reasoning. *Artificial Intelligence*, 13:81–132, 1980.

[vGRS91] A. van Gelder, K.A. Ross, and J.S. Schlipf. The well-founded semantics for general logic programs. *journal of the ACM*, 38, 1991.

[WC96]   J. Widom and S. Ceri. *Active Database Systems: Triggers and Rules for Advanced Database Processing*. Morgan-Kaufman, 1996.

[Win89]   M.A. Winslett. Reasoning about action using possible model approach. In *Proceedings of the 7th national conference on AI*, 1989.

Transformation-Based Bottom-Up Computation of the Well-Founded Model

Stefan Brass[1] and Ulrich Zukowski[2] and Burkhard Freitag[2]

[1] Universität Hildesheim, Institut für Informatik
Marienburger Platz 22, D-31141 Hildesheim, Germany
brass@informatik.uni-hildesheim.de
[2] Universität Passau, Fakultät für Mathematik und Informatik
D-94030 Passau, Germany
{zukowski,freitag}@fmi.uni-passau.de

Abstract. We present a bottom-up algorithm for the computation of the well-founded model of non-disjunctive logic programs. Our method is based on the elementary program transformations studied by BRASS and DIX [6, 7]. However, their "residual program" can grow to exponential size, whereas for function-free programs our "program remainder" is always polynomial in the size, i.e. the number of tuples, of the extensional database (EDB). As in the SLG-resolution of CHEN and WARREN [11, 12, 13], we do not only delay negative but also positive literals if they depend on delayed negative literals. When disregarding goal-directedness, which needs additional concepts, our approach can be seen as a simplified bottom-up version of SLG-resolution applicable to range-restricted Datalog programs. Since our approach is also closely related to the alternating fixpoint procedure [27, 28], it can possibly serve as a basis for an integration of the resolution-based, fixpoint-based, and transformation-based evaluation methods.

1 Introduction

The next generation of deductive database systems will probably support the full class of normal programs. It seems also very likely that the well-founded semantics will be chosen by nearly all system designers, because it has a unique model. Furthermore, the time complexity of computing the well-founded model of a given intensional database (IDB), i.e. a set of rules, is polynomial in the size, i.e. the number of tuples, of the extensional database (EDB) [29]. In contrast, it has been shown by MAREK and TRUSZCZYNSKI [21] that even for a propositional logic program P, determining whether P has a stable model is NP-complete. Extensions of deductive database systems that can deal with the well-founded semantics are already realized in XSB [11, 13, 23] and announced for LOLA [18, 30, 31].

The SLG-resolution of CHEN and WARREN [11, 12, 13], as implemented in the XSB system, is the most prominent *top-down* method for the computation of the well-founded model of a normal program. In this paper we characterize "good" *bottom-up* methods in terms of elementary program transformations.

Essentially, the bottom-up algorithms that compute the well-founded model of a normal program are:

- The alternating fixpoint approach, introduced by VAN GELDER [27, 28] and further developed by KEMP, STUCKEY and SRIVASTAVA [20].
- The computation of the residual program, suggested by BRY [9, 10] and independently by DUNG/KANCHANASUT [16, 17], and extended by BRASS and DIX [6, 7].

The alternating fixpoint procedure is known to have efficiency problems, since in every iteration many facts have to be recomputed. The residual program approach avoids recomputations of this kind. But it is still possible that the residual program can grow to exponential size while for function-free programs the alternating fixpoint approach guarantees a number of derived facts that is polynomial in the size, i.e. the number of tuples, of the extensional database (EDB). However, the residual program contains important information which is not provided by the alternating fixpoint method.

It is natural to ask for an algorithm which combines the advantages of both bottom-up approaches. In this paper, we present a framework for the computation of the well-founded model that is based on the residual program method but guarantees polynomial complexity like the alternating fixpoint procedure. The residual program method is based on elementary program transformations and the concept of *conditional facts*. Conditional facts are ground rules having exactly those negative literals in their bodies that can not (yet) be resolved because their complement is not (yet) known to be true or false. This can be regarded as a non-procedural equivalent of the *delay* operation needed in SLG-resolution [11, 12, 13]. Like in SLG-Resolution, the key idea to avoid the exponential blow-up of the residual program is to delay not only negative literals but also positive literals which depend on delayed negative literals. The transformation-based *program remainder* method which we propose in this paper can be seen as a bottom-up equivalent of SLG-resolution for the case of range-restricted function-free programs. It should be mentioned, however, that we disregard goal-directedness for the moment because it needs additional concepts that are beyond the scope of this paper.

We feel that the simplicity of our method which is mainly due to its level of abstraction is one of its particularly appealing features. Another advantage is the fact that the causes for one or more atoms being undefined can be made visible. The "undefined" truth value is something unusual, often some kind of "localized error message". In a system based on the residual program, we can display the dependencies between the delayed facts directly. This information is not available in the alternating fixpoint method. Note also that the power of the transformation method lies in its generality: Although the main motivation of this paper is to compute the well-founded semantics, we will show that the program remainder, i.e., the "result" of our program transformations, is equivalent to the original program under a wide range of semantics. For instance, our transformation preserves stable models. So it can also be used as a preprocessing step for algorithms computing stable models, e.g. [2]. Interesting applications of stable models have recently been studied in [14, 26].

In the context of deductive databases it is customary to have a very simple ("naive") bottom-up procedure, which is later made goal-directed by means of a (suitable form of) magic set transformation. This separation of issues makes the approach easier to understand and simplifies the correctness proofs. In this paper, we concentrate on the first step. In [30], ZUKOWSKI and FREITAG propose a mixed top-down and bottom-up procedure for the evaluation of modularly stratified programs. The results we present in this paper give rise to hope that also for the class of normal programs a flexible mixed evaluation method is feasible.

The rest of the paper is organized as follows. After introducing preliminaries in Section 2, we recall the alternating fixpoint procedure in Section 3 and the residual program approach in Section 4. In Section 5, we introduce our concepts to delay positive and negative literals, and in Section 6 we present a variant of the immediate consequence operator that is appropriate in this context. Section 7 compares our approach to the alternating fixpoint procedure. In Section 8 we propose some optimizations. Section 9 concludes the paper with a summary.

2 Preliminaries

A rule is of the form $A \leftarrow L_1 \wedge \cdots \wedge L_n$, where the head A is an atom and each body literal L_i is a positive Literal, i.e. an atom, or a negative literal $L_i = \textbf{not } B$. We treat the rule body as a set of literals and write also $A \leftarrow B$ with $B = \{L_1, \ldots, L_n\}$. Consequently, a fact A is represented by the rule $A \leftarrow \emptyset$.

A program is a set of rules as introduced above. We consider normal, i.e., non-disjunctive, logic programs without function symbols. We assume that all rules are range-restricted, i.e. that each variable of the rule appears also in a positive body literal.

Let P be a program. $BASE(P)$ denotes the Herbrand base of P, i.e. the set of all ground atoms. It might happen that our transformations eliminate some constants and predicates from the program, but we often use the Herbrand base $BASE(P)$ of the original program. We write $ground(P)$ for the Herbrand instantiation of a program P. For a ground program P we define the following sets:

$$facts(P) := \{A \in BASE(P) \mid (A \leftarrow \emptyset) \in P\}$$
$$heads(P) := \{A \in BASE(P) \mid \text{there is a } B \text{ such that } (A \leftarrow B) \in P\}$$

The complement of a literal L is denoted by $\sim L$, i.e., $\sim(B) = \textbf{not } B$ and, conversely, $\sim(\textbf{not } B) = B$. For a set S of literals, $\sim S$ denotes the set of the complements of the literals in S. S is *consistent* if and only if $S \cap \sim S = \emptyset$. For a set S of literals we define the following sets:

$$pos(S) := \{A \in S \mid A \text{ is a positive literal }\}$$
$$neg(S) := \{A \mid \textbf{not } A \in S\}$$

Let P be a logic program. A *partial interpretation* for P is a consistent set I of ground literals such that

$$pos(I) \cup neg(I) \subseteq BASE(P)$$

i.e., its set of atoms is a subset of the Herbrand base of P. A *total interpretation* for P is a partial interpretation I such that

$$A \in BASE(P) \implies A \in I \text{ or } \mathbf{not}\, A \in I$$

i.e., for each atom A of the Herbrand base of P either A or its complement is contained in I. We rely on the definition of the *well-founded partial model* W_P^* of P as given in [29]. An operational characterization of W_P^* will be given in Section 3.

3 The Alternating Fixpoint Procedure

Let us recall the definition of the alternating fixpoint procedure. We introduce an extended version of the immediate consequence operator that uses two different sets of facts for positive and negative subgoals, respectively. Actually, this is an adaption of the stability transformation found in [27, 28] to our purposes.

Definition 1 Extended Immediate Consequence Operator.
Let P be a normal logic program. Let I and J be sets of ground atoms. The set $T_{P,J}(I)$ of *immediate consequences of I w.r.t. P and J* is defined as follows:

$$T_{P,J}(I) := \big\{ A\theta \mid \text{there is a rule } A \leftarrow L_1 \wedge \cdots \wedge L_n \text{ in } P$$
$$\text{and a ground substitution } \theta \text{ for this rule}$$
$$\text{such that for } i = 1, \ldots, n:$$
$$L_i \text{ is a positive literal and } L_i\theta \in I \text{ or}$$
$$L_i \text{ is a negative literal } \mathbf{not}\, B \text{ and } B\theta \notin J \big\}.$$

If P is definite, the set J is not needed and we obtain the standard immediate consequence operator T_P by $T_P(I) = T_{P,\emptyset}(I)$. □

$T_{P,J}$ checks negative subgoals against the set of possibly true atoms that is supplied as the argument J. This allows the following elegant formulation of the alternating fixpoint procedure.

Definition 2 Alternating Fixpoint Procedure.
Let P be a normal logic program. Let P^+ denote the subprogram consisting of the definite rules of P. Then the sequence $(K_i, U_i)_{i \geq 0}$ with sets K_i of true (known) facts and U_i of possible (unknown) facts is defined by:

$$
\begin{aligned}
K_0 &:= \mathrm{lfp}(T_{P^+}) \\
U_0 &:= \mathrm{lfp}(T_{P,K_0}) \\
K_i &:= \mathrm{lfp}(T_{P,U_{i-1}}), \, i > 0 \\
U_i &:= \mathrm{lfp}(T_{P,K_i}), \quad i > 0
\end{aligned}
$$

The computation halts when the sequence becomes stationary, i.e., when a fixpoint is reached in the sense that

$$(K_j, U_j) = (K_{j+1}, U_{j+1}).$$

This computation schema is called the *Alternating Fixpoint Procedure* (AFP).
□

Theorem 3 [28]. *Let the sequence $(K_i, U_i)_{i \geq 0}$ be defined as above and let j be the first index such that $(K_j, U_j) = (K_{j+1}, U_{j+1})$. The well-founded model W_P^* of P can be directly derived from the fixpoint (K_j, U_j), i.e.,*

$$W_P^* = \{L \mid L \text{ is a positive ground literal and } L \in K_j \text{ or}$$
$$L \text{ is a negative ground literal } \mathbf{not}\, A \text{ and } A \in BASE(P) - U_j\}.$$

□

Example 1 Even Numbers. Consider the following logic program *EvenNum*

> $even(0)$
> $even(1) \leftarrow \mathbf{not}\, even(0)$
> $even(2) \leftarrow \mathbf{not}\, even(1)$
> $even(3) \leftarrow \mathbf{not}\, even(2)$
> $\vdots$
> $even(n) \leftarrow \mathbf{not}\, even(n-1)$

which defines the even numbers between 0 and some fixed even number n. We would expect that it is possible to compute the well-founded model of this program in time $O(n)$. The alternating fixpoint procedure produces the following sequence:

$$K_0 = \{even(0)\}$$
$$U_0 = \{even(0), even(2), even(3), \ldots, even(n)\}$$
$$K_1 = \{even(0), even(2)\}$$
$$U_1 = \{even(0), even(2), even(4), even(5), \ldots, even(n)\}$$
$$K_2 = \{even(0), even(2), even(4)\}$$
$$U_2 = \{even(0), even(2), even(4), even(6), even(7), \ldots, even(n)\}$$
$$\vdots$$
$$K_{n/2} = U_{n/2} = \{even(0), even(2), even(4), \ldots, even(n)\}$$

Apparently, the alternating fixpoint approach needs n iterations, each costing $O(n)$ in terms of derived facts. So the total cost is $O(n^2)$.　□

The following example will serve as a running example to illustrate the transformation-based approach. It demonstrates the application of the alternating fixpoint procedure to non-ground programs.

Example 2 Odd Numbers. Consider the following logic program *OddNum*

$$odd(X) \leftarrow succ(Y, X) \land \textbf{not } odd(Y)$$
$$succ(0, 1) \ldots succ(n - 1, n)$$

which defines the odd numbers between 1 and some fixed even number n. Note, that in this example the odd numbers are computed to avoid confusion with Example 1. The alternating fixpoint procedure produces the following sequence:

$$K_0 = \{succ(0, 1), \ldots, succ(n - 1, n)\}$$
$$U_0 = K_0 \cup \{odd(1), \ldots, odd(n)\}$$
$$K_1 = K_0 \cup \{odd(1)\}$$
$$U_1 = K_0 \cup \{odd(1), odd(3), odd(4), \ldots, odd(n)\}$$
$$K_2 = K_0 \cup \{odd(1), odd(3)\}$$
$$U_2 = K_0 \cup \{odd(1), odd(3), odd(5), odd(6), \ldots, odd(n)\}$$
$$\vdots$$
$$K_{n/2} = U_{n/2} = K_0 \cup \{odd(1), odd(3), odd(5), \ldots, odd(n - 1)\}$$

As in Example 1, $O(n^2)$ derivations are needed to compute the well-founded model. $\square$

4 Elementary Program Transformations

BRASS and DIX [6, 7] have introduced a framework for studying and computing negation semantics by means of elementary program transformations.

Definition 4 Semantics. A *semantics* is a mapping $\mathcal{S}$, which assigns to every logic program P a set $\mathcal{S}(P)$ of (partial) models of P such that:

1. $\mathcal{S}$ is "instantiation invariant", i.e. $\mathcal{S}(P) = \mathcal{S}(ground(P))$.
2. If a ground atom A is not an instance of any rule head in P, then every $I \in \mathcal{S}(P)$ interprets A as false, i.e. $\textbf{not } A \in I$. $\square$

In this paper, we are mainly interested in the well-founded semantics:

$$\text{WFS}(P) := \{W_P^*\}.$$

However, the stable model semantics, which assigns to every program P the set of stable models, also has the properties required below.

Due to the instantiation invariance, a semantics $\mathcal{S}$ is completely determined by its values on ground programs. Therefore, we define program transformations only on ground programs:

Definition 5 Program Transformation. A *program transformation* is a relation $\mapsto$ between ground logic programs. A semantics $\mathcal{S}$ allows a transformation $\mapsto$ iff $\mathcal{S}(P_1) = \mathcal{S}(P_2)$ for all P_1 and P_2 with $P_1 \mapsto P_2$. $\square$

One such transformation is the deletion of tautological rules like $p \leftarrow p \wedge q$:

Definition 6 Deletion of Tautologies. Let P_1 and P_2 be ground programs. Program P_2 results from program P_1 by *deletion of tautologies* ($P_1 \mapsto_T P_2$) iff there is $A \leftarrow \mathcal{B} \in P_1$ such that $A \in \mathcal{B}$ and $P_2 = P_1 - \{A \leftarrow \mathcal{B}\}$. $\qquad\square$

Another very important program transformation is the "unfolding" of a body literal. For instance, consider the program

$p \leftarrow q \wedge \mathbf{not}\, r.$

Suppose that there are two rules about q, namely

$q \leftarrow s_1 \wedge \mathbf{not}\, t_1.$
$q \leftarrow s_2 \wedge \mathbf{not}\, t_2.$

Then, during bottom-up evaluation, q can only be derived by applying one of these two rules. So we can replace the body literal q by the bodies of the rules about q. This leads to the program

$p \leftarrow s_1 \wedge \mathbf{not}\, t_1 \wedge \mathbf{not}\, r.$
$p \leftarrow s_2 \wedge \mathbf{not}\, t_2 \wedge \mathbf{not}\, r.$

Definition 7 Unfolding. Let P_1 and P_2 be ground programs. Program P_2 results from program P_1 by *unfolding* ($P_1 \mapsto_U P_2$) iff there is a rule $A \leftarrow \mathcal{B}$ in P_1 and a positive literal $B \in \mathcal{B}$ such that

$$P_2 = P_1 - \{A \leftarrow \mathcal{B}\}$$
$$\cup \left\{A \leftarrow ((\mathcal{B} - \{B\}) \cup \mathcal{B}') \mid B \leftarrow \mathcal{B}' \in P_1\right\}.$$

$\qquad\square$

Unfolding is a very powerful transformation that has been studied by many researchers. For recent references see [1, 24, 25].

Let $\mapsto_{TU} := \mapsto_T \cup \mapsto_U$ be the rewriting system consisting of the two transformations introduced above. This system is interesting because already *unfolding* and *deletion of tautologies* allow to eliminate all positive body literals [5].

Next, if we have a rule like $p \leftarrow q$, it should be possible to delete a logically weaker rule like $p \leftarrow q \wedge r$:

Definition 8 Deletion of Nonminimal Rules. Let P_1 and P_2 be ground programs. Program P_2 results from the program P_1 by *deletion of non-minimal rules* ($P_1 \mapsto_M P_2$) iff there are rules $A \leftarrow \mathcal{B}$ and $A \leftarrow \mathcal{B}'$ in P_1 such that $\mathcal{B} \subset \mathcal{B}'$ and

$$P_2 = P_1 - \{A \leftarrow \mathcal{B}'\}.$$

$\qquad\square$

Let $\mapsto_{TUM}$ be the rewriting system consisting of these three transformations, i.e.

$$\mapsto_{TUM} := \mapsto_T \cup \mapsto_U \cup \mapsto_M.$$

As shown in [3], a semantics S allows $\mapsto_{TUM}$ iff it considers only the minimal models of the given program, i.e., $S(P_1) = S(P_2)$ for all programs P_1 and P_2 having the same minimal models with fixed interpretation of the negative literals.

The next two transformations describe the evaluation of negative body literals in trivial cases. For instance, if there is no rule with p in the head, there is obviously no way to derive p by bottom-up evaluation, so **not** p should be true. But then it should be possible to delete the condition **not** p from the body of a rule, since it is true anyway:

Definition 9 Positive Reduction. Let P_1 and P_2 be ground programs. P_2 results from P_1 by *positive reduction* $(P_1 \mapsto_P P_2)$ iff there is a rule $A \leftarrow B$ in P_1 and a negative literal **not** $B \in B$ such that $B \notin heads(P_1)$, i.e., there is no rule about B in P_1, and $P_2 = (P_1 - \{A \leftarrow B\}) \cup \{A \leftarrow (B - \{\textbf{not } B\})\}$. $\quad\square$

On the other hand, if p is given as a fact in the program, a condition of the form **not** p can never be true. So a rule with **not** p in its body is useless and it should be possible to delete it:

Definition 10 Negative Reduction. Let P_1 and P_2 be ground programs. P_2 results from P_1 by *negative reduction* $(P_1 \mapsto_N P_2)$ iff there is a rule $A \leftarrow B$ in P_1 and a negative literal **not** $B \in B$ such that $B \in facts(P_1)$, i.e., B appears as a fact in P_1, and $P_2 = P_1 - \{A \leftarrow B\}$. $\quad\square$

Definition 11. Let $\mapsto_R$ be the rewriting system consisting of the above five transformations, i.e.

$$\mapsto_R := \mapsto_T \cup \mapsto_U \cup \mapsto_M \cup \mapsto_P \cup \mapsto_N.$$

$\quad\square$

As shown in [8], $\mapsto_R$ has some nice properties (see also [3]) which we summarize in the following.

Definition 12 Normalform. A program P' is a *normalform* of a program P w.r.t. a transformation $\mapsto$ iff

1. $P \mapsto^* P'$, and
2. P' is irreducible, i.e. there is no program P'' with $P' \mapsto P''$. $\quad\square$

For $\mapsto_R$ we have the following strong normalform theorem.

Theorem 13 Residual Program [8]. *The rewriting system $\mapsto_R$ is*

1. *terminating, i.e. every program P has a normalform P', and*
2. *confluent, i.e. for all programs P, P_1, P_2 with $P \mapsto_R^* P_1$ and $P \mapsto_R^* P_2$, there is a program P_3 with $P_1 \mapsto_R^* P_3$ and $P_2 \mapsto_R^* P_3$.*

Thus, every program P has a unique normalform, which is called the residual program $res(P)$ of P. □

Obviously, rules in the residual program cannot contain positive body literals, since then *unfolding* would be applicable. So the residual program is a set of conditional facts [9, 10, 16, 17]:

Definition 14 Conditional Fact. A conditional fact is a ground rule with only negative body literals, i.e., a rule of the form $A \leftarrow \text{\textbf{not }} B_1 \wedge \cdots \wedge \text{\textbf{not }} B_n$. □

As shown in [6], the well-founded semantics is the weakest semantics which allows the above transformations. We can directly "read off" the well-founded model from the residual program:

Definition 15 Known Literals. Let P be a ground program and let S be a set of ground atoms. The set of positive and negative ground literals with atoms in S having an obvious truth value in P is denoted by $known_S(P)$:

$$
\begin{aligned}
known_S(P) := \{L \mid\ & L \in S \text{ is a positive ground literal} \\
& \text{and } L \in S \cap facts(P) \text{ or} \\
& L \text{ is a negative ground literal } \text{\textbf{not }} A \\
& \text{and } A \in S - heads(P)\}.
\end{aligned}
$$

□

Theorem 16 Computation of Well-Founded Semantics [6].
The well-founded model W_P^* of a program P consists of those positive and negative ground literals which have an obvious truth value in the residual program $res(P)$, i.e.,

$$W_P^* = known_{BASE(P)}(res(P))$$

□

Example 3 Even Numbers revisited. Consider the logic program *EvenNum* of Example 1. With the program transformations defined above, *EvenNum* can be transformed into the residual program $res(EvenNum)$ as follows:

$$
\begin{aligned}
EvenNum = \ & \{\ even(0), \\
& \quad even(1) \leftarrow \text{\textbf{not }} even(0), \ldots, even(n) \leftarrow \text{\textbf{not }} even(n-1)\ \} \\
\mapsto_N\ & \{\ even(0), \\
& \quad even(2) \leftarrow \text{\textbf{not }} even(1), \ldots, even(n) \leftarrow \text{\textbf{not }} even(n-1)\ \} \\
\mapsto_P\ & \{\ even(0), even(2),
\end{aligned}
$$

$$even(3) \leftarrow \text{not } even(2), \ldots, even(n) \leftarrow \text{not } even(n-1) \}$$
$$\mapsto_N \{ even(0), even(2)$$
$$even(4) \leftarrow \text{not } even(3), \ldots, even(n) \leftarrow \text{not } even(n-1) \}$$
$$\mapsto_P \{ even(0), even(2), even(4),$$
$$even(5) \leftarrow \text{not } even(4), \ldots, even(n) \leftarrow \text{not } even(n-1) \}$$

$$\vdots$$

$$\mapsto_R^* \{ even(0), even(2), even(4), \ldots, even(n) \}$$

Obviously, the residual program $res(EvenNum)$ can be derived in $O(n)$ transformation steps. In contrast, the alternating fixpoint procedure (cf. Example 1) needs $O(n^2)$ derivation steps. □

There are cases where the residual program can grow to exponential size. This problem with the delayed evaluation of negative literals was already noted in [13].

Example 4 Exponential Residual Program.
Consider the following program.

$$p(0).$$
$$p(X) \leftarrow p(Y) \wedge succ(Y, X) \wedge \text{not } q(Y).$$
$$p(X) \leftarrow p(Y) \wedge succ(Y, X) \wedge \text{not } r(Y).$$
$$q(X) \leftarrow succ(X, \_) \wedge \text{not } q(X).$$
$$r(X) \leftarrow succ(X, \_) \wedge \text{not } r(X).$$

$$succ(0, 1). \ldots succ(n-1, n).$$

The following diagram depicts all possible paths on which a p-fact can be derived:

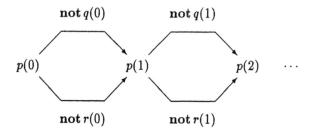

So the residual program contains the following conditional facts about p:

$$p(0).$$

$$p(1) \leftarrow \text{not } q(0).$$
$$p(1) \leftarrow \text{not } r(0).$$

$$p(2) \leftarrow \text{not } q(0) \wedge \text{not } q(1).$$
$$p(2) \leftarrow \text{not } q(0) \wedge \text{not } r(1).$$

$p(2) \leftarrow \textbf{not}\, r(0) \wedge \textbf{not}\, q(1).$

$p(2) \leftarrow \textbf{not}\, r(0) \wedge \textbf{not}\, r(1).$

$p(3) \leftarrow \textbf{not}\, q(0) \wedge \textbf{not}\, q(1) \wedge \textbf{not}\, q(2).$

$p(3) \leftarrow \textbf{not}\, q(0) \wedge \textbf{not}\, q(1) \wedge \textbf{not}\, r(2).$

$p(3) \leftarrow \textbf{not}\, q(0) \wedge \textbf{not}\, r(1) \wedge \textbf{not}\, q(2).$

$p(3) \leftarrow \textbf{not}\, q(0) \wedge \textbf{not}\, r(1) \wedge \textbf{not}\, r(2).$

$p(3) \leftarrow \textbf{not}\, r(0) \wedge \textbf{not}\, q(1) \wedge \textbf{not}\, q(2).$

$p(3) \leftarrow \textbf{not}\, r(0) \wedge \textbf{not}\, q(1) \wedge \textbf{not}\, r(2).$

$p(3) \leftarrow \textbf{not}\, r(0) \wedge \textbf{not}\, r(1) \wedge \textbf{not}\, q(2).$

$p(3) \leftarrow \textbf{not}\, r(0) \wedge \textbf{not}\, r(1) \wedge \textbf{not}\, r(2).$

$\vdots$

It is obvious that every possible path is encoded in the residual program. Each possible fact $p(n)$ is represented by 2^n conditional facts. $\qquad \Box$

5 Delaying Positive and Negative Literals

As we have seen in Example 4, the residual program can grow to exponential size. The main reason for this is the *unfolding* transformation which may replace a positive body literal by an exponential number of combinations of negative literals. In the rewriting system $\mapsto_R$ (Definition 11) only negative body literals are delayed, positive body literals are eliminated by *unfolding* and *deletion of tautologies*, even if their truth value is not yet known. In contrast to [6, 7], we propose not to replace a positive body literal A by the conditions C_i of conditional facts about A, but to *delay* the processing of positive body literals until their truth value is obvious. This simply means that we do not allow transformations on positive body literals except when they are given as facts (and thus known to be true) or do not occur in any rule head (and thus are known to be false). Facts containing both positive and negative conditions are called *extended conditional facts*.

Definition 17 Extended Conditional Fact.
An *extended conditional fact* $A \leftarrow C$ is a ground rule containing both positive and negative delayed literals in the body. $\qquad \Box$

To evaluate delayed negative literals when their truth value becomes known, we have the two transformations *positive reduction* $\mapsto_P$ and *negative reduction* $\mapsto_N$ (cf. Definitions 9 and 10). Let us now consider positive body literals. If there is a fact B, we obviously should be able to "simplify away" the condition B:

Definition 18 Success. A ground program P_2 results from a ground program P_1 by *success* ($P_1 \mapsto_S P_2$) iff there are a rule $A \leftarrow B$ and a fact B in P_1 such that $B \in \mathcal{B}$ and $P_2 = (P_1 - \{A \leftarrow B\}) \cup \{A \leftarrow (\mathcal{B} - \{B\})\}$. $\qquad \Box$

Lemma 19. *If a semantics S allows* unfolding *and the* deletion of nonminimal rules, *then it also allows* success.

Proof. *Success* corresponds to *unfolding*, when a program contains a fact $B \leftarrow \emptyset$ and B is replaced by $\emptyset$. However, there might be further rules about B besides this fact. But then the resulting rules are certainly non-minimal, so we can remove them with $\mapsto_M$. □

Next, when there is not (longer) any possibility to prove a literal B, we can remove rule instances depending on B:

Definition 20 Failure. Let $\mapsto_F$ (*failure*) be the program transformation defined by: $P_1 \mapsto_F P_2$ iff there is a rule $A \leftarrow \mathcal{B}$ in P_1 and a positive literal $B \in \mathcal{B}$ such that there is no rule about B in P_1, and $P_2 = P_1 - \{A \leftarrow \mathcal{B}\}$. □

Lemma 21. *If a semantics S allows* unfolding, *then it also allows* failure.

Proof. Obviously, the transformation $\mapsto_F$ is a very special case of *unfolding*, i.e., if there are no rules about the unfolded literal. □

Definition 22. Let $\mapsto_{PNSF}$ denote the rewriting system which evaluates negative literals by *positive* and *negative reduction* and positive literals by *success* and *failure*:

$$\mapsto_{PNSF} := \mapsto_P \cup \mapsto_N \cup \mapsto_S \cup \mapsto_F.$$

All sensible semantics allow these transformations:

Lemma 23. *Let S be a semantics which allows* unfolding, *deletion of nonminimal rules, and* positive *and* negative reduction. *Then also*

$$P_1 \mapsto_{PNSF} P_2 \implies S(P_1) = S(P_2)$$

for all ground programs P_1 and P_2.

Proof. The lemma follows immediately from the Lemmata 19 and 21. □

Example 5 Exponential Residual Program Revisited.
Starting from the program of Example 4, the rewriting system $\mapsto_{PNSF}$ yields the following irreducible rules about p:

$p(0).$

$p(1) \leftarrow p(0) \wedge \mathbf{not}\, q(0).$
$p(1) \leftarrow p(0) \wedge \mathbf{not}\, r(0).$

$p(2) \leftarrow p(1) \wedge \mathbf{not}\, q(1).$
$p(2) \leftarrow p(1) \wedge \mathbf{not}\, r(1).$

$p(3) \leftarrow p(2) \wedge \mathbf{not}\, q(2).$

$p(3) \leftarrow p(2) \wedge \mathbf{not}\, r(2).$

$p(4) \leftarrow p(3) \wedge \mathbf{not}\, q(3).$

$p(4) \leftarrow p(3) \wedge \mathbf{not}\, r(3).$

$\vdots$

Each possible fact $p(n)$ (for $n \geq 1$) is represented by exactly 2 rules. If we allow full *unfolding* of the positive body literals, we immediately get the exponential residual program of Example 4. □

In the approach of [6, 7], where only negative literals are delayed, the two reductions $\mapsto_P$ and $\mapsto_N$ are sufficient to compute the well-founded model. The transformations $\mapsto_S$ and $\mapsto_F$ seem to be the corresponding operations for positive literals. However, they are not strong enough, because delaying positive literals can introduce loops [13]. This does usually not happen in the context of bottom-up evaluation.

Example 6 Positive Loop. Consider the following program *Loop*:

$p.$

$q \leftarrow \mathbf{not}\, p.$

$q \leftarrow r.$

$r \leftarrow q.$

We can apply *negative reduction* to delete $q \leftarrow \mathbf{not}\, p$, since $\mathbf{not}\, p$ is obviously false. But $\mapsto_{PNSF}$ does not allow to delete $q \leftarrow r$ and $r \leftarrow q$. □

Apparently our reductions are still too weak. As for the residual program, we want to obtain the well-founded model of a program directly from its normal-form w.r.t. the rewriting system used. This is not possible in Example 6. In the rewriting system $\mapsto_R$ we could unfold one of the two last rules and delete the resulting tautology by the application of $\mapsto_T$. Since we do not want to allow full *unfolding*, we have to introduce a new transformation that detects this kind of tautology but does not imply the risk of an exponential blow-up.

Definition 24 Loop Detection. Let P_1 and P_2 be ground programs. P_2 results from P_1 by *loop detection* ($P_1 \mapsto_L P_2$) iff there is a set $\mathcal{A}$ of ground atoms such that

1. for each rule $A \leftarrow \mathcal{B}$ in P_1, if $A \in \mathcal{A}$, then $\mathcal{B} \cap \mathcal{A} \neq \emptyset$,
2. $P_2 := \{A \leftarrow \mathcal{B} \in P_1 \mid \mathcal{B} \cap \mathcal{A} = \emptyset\}$,
3. $P_1 \neq P_2$. □

Such a set $\mathcal{A}$ is nothing else than an unfounded set (cf. [29]). The greatest unfounded set consists of all positive ground atoms which are not possibly true, i.e., cannot be derived by assuming all negative literals to be true. According to Definition 1, the extended immediate consequence operator $T_{P_1, \emptyset}$ computes the possibly true atoms. Therefore, the greatest unfounded set is given by $BASE(P) - \mathrm{lfp}(T_{P_1, \emptyset})$. However, already the (smaller) set

$$\mathcal{A} := \{A \in BASE(P) \mid A \text{ occurs in } P_1\} - \mathrm{lfp}(T_{P_1, \emptyset})$$

of ground atoms $\mathcal{A}$ occurring in P_1, but not in $\mathrm{lfp}(T_{P_1, \emptyset})$, has the required properties (if non-empty). As a consequence we see that also the operation of *loop detection* can be performed in polynomial time w.r.t. the size of the EDB; it is not necessary to construct all possible sets $\mathcal{A}$ to check whether $\mapsto_L$ is applicable.

Lemma 25. *If $P_1 \mapsto_L P_2$, then also $P_1 \mapsto^*_{TU} P_2$. Thus any semantics $\mathcal{S}$, which allows unfolding and deletion of tautologies, also allows loop detection.*

Proof. Let $\mathcal{A}$ be a set of ground atoms such that for all rules $A \leftarrow \mathcal{B}$ in P_1, if $A \in \mathcal{A}$, then $\mathcal{B} \cap \mathcal{A} \neq \emptyset$. Let $P_2 := \{A \leftarrow \mathcal{B} \in P_1 \mid \mathcal{B} \cap \mathcal{A} = \emptyset\}$. We show by induction on the number n of atoms in $\mathcal{A}$, which actually appear in rule bodies of P_1, that $P_1 \mapsto^*_{TU} P_2$. In the case $n = 0$, we have $P_2 = P_1$. Let now $n > 0$ and $A \in \mathcal{A}$ an atom which appears in at least one rule body of P_1. Then we first eliminate all tautological rules containing A in head and body. After that, we unfold all remaining occurrences of A in rule bodies. Let the resulting program be called P_1'. Then we have the following:

- After these operations, A does not appear in any rule body. Furthermore, no new atoms appear in rule bodies, so the number n has decreased.
- The rules which were generated by the *unfolding* step still contain at least one atom from $\mathcal{A}$ in the body, since rules about A must contain another atom from $\mathcal{A}$ in the body. Thus, $P_2 = \{A \leftarrow \mathcal{B} \in P_1' \mid \mathcal{B} \cap \mathcal{A} = \emptyset\}$.

By the inductive hypothesis we get $P_1 \mapsto^*_{TU} P_1' \mapsto^*_{TU} P_2$. □

Example 7 Loop Detection. Consider again the program *Loop* of Example 6:

$$p.$$
$$q \leftarrow \mathbf{not}\, p.$$
$$q \leftarrow r.$$
$$r \leftarrow q.$$

After deleting the second rule by *negative reduction*, the resulting program *Loop'* is irreducible w.r.t. $\mapsto_{PNSF}$. Now *loop detection* has to be applied. First, the set $\{p\}$ of possible facts is computed by iterating the $T_{Loop', \emptyset}$ operator. We have $\mathcal{A} = \{p, q, r\} - \{p\}$. According to Definition 24 the last two rules are deleted because their positive body literals q and r are contained in $\mathcal{A}$. Note, that in operational terms it would have been sufficient to test whether q and r are elements of $\{p\} = \mathrm{lfp}(T_{Loop', \emptyset})$. □

Remark Loop Detection. To determine the program P_2 with $P_1 \longmapsto_L P_2$ it is sufficient to delete all rules $A \leftarrow B$ from P_1 having positive body literals not contained in $\mathrm{lfp}(T_{P_1,\emptyset})$, i.e.

$$P_2 = \{(A \leftarrow B) \in P_1 \mid pos(B) \subseteq \mathrm{lfp}(T_{P_1,\emptyset})\}$$

Since *loop detection* is performed w.r.t. the greatest unfounded set

$$\mathcal{A} = BASE(P) - \mathrm{lfp}(T_{P_1,\emptyset})$$

of P_1, the program P_2 is irreducible w.r.t. *loop detection.* □

Example 8 Repeated Loop Detection. Unfortunately, a single application of the (still) expensive *loop detection* is not always sufficient for computing the well-founded model:

$$p_1.$$
$$q_1 \leftarrow \textbf{not } p_1.$$
$$q_1 \leftarrow r_1.$$
$$r_1 \leftarrow q_1.$$

$$p_2 \leftarrow \textbf{not } q_1.$$
$$q_2 \leftarrow \textbf{not } p_2.$$
$$q_2 \leftarrow r_2.$$
$$r_2 \leftarrow q_2.$$

First, *negative reduction* eliminates the second rule because **not** p_1 is obviously false. In the next step, we need to apply *loop detection* in order to get rid of the rules $q_1 \leftarrow r_1$ and $r_1 \leftarrow q_1$. After that we can evaluate **not** q_1 to true and apply *positive reduction* and then **not** p_2 to false and apply *negative reduction*. Now *loop detection* is again necessary to delete the rules $q_2 \leftarrow r_2$ and $r_2 \leftarrow q_2$. □

Example 8 shows that we must iterate all five transformations.

Definition 26. Let $\longmapsto_X$ denote our final rewriting system:

$$\longmapsto_X := \longmapsto_P \cup \longmapsto_N \cup \longmapsto_S \cup \longmapsto_F \cup \longmapsto_L.$$

□

Failure might look like a special case of *loop detection*, but $\longmapsto_L$ forces us to remove all occurrences of a failed atom at once, while $\longmapsto_F$ is more liberal in this respect.

Example 9 Failure and Loop Detection. Consider the following program P:

$$p \leftarrow q \wedge r.$$
$$p \leftarrow q \wedge s.$$
$$r.$$
$$s.$$

Because there is no rule about q in P, *failure* $\mapsto_F$ may be applied to delete either of the first two rules separately. *loop detection* $\mapsto_L$ w.r.t. the greatest unfounded set

$$
\begin{aligned}
\mathcal{A} &= BASE(P) - \mathrm{lfp}(T_{P,\emptyset}) \\
&= \{p, q, r, s\} - \{r, s\} \\
&= \{p, q\}
\end{aligned}
$$

may also be applied to delete the first two rules. However, *loop detection* always deletes *both rules at the same time*. This is still true if the set $\mathcal{A} = \{q\}$ is used as a reference set for $\mapsto_L$. $\qquad\square$

A normalform w.r.t. the rewriting system $\mapsto_X$ is called a program remainder:

Definition 27 Program Remainder. Let P be a program. Let the program $\hat{P}$ satisfy

1. $ground(P) \mapsto_X^* \hat{P}$,
2. $\hat{P}$ is irreducible w.r.t. $\mapsto_X$, i.e. there is no P' with $\hat{P} \mapsto_X P'$.

Then $\hat{P}$ is called a *program remainder* of P. $\qquad\square$

Lemma 28. *Every program P has a program remainder, i.e. the rewriting system $\mapsto_X$ is terminating.*

Proof. All our transformations strictly reduce the total number of occurring literals. So if $P_0 := ground(P)$ and P_i is any program with $P_{i-1} \mapsto_X P_i$, $i \geq 1$, then we must reach a program P_n in which no further transformation can be applied. This is a program remainder of P. $\qquad\square$

Note that only polynomially many transformations are needed to reach the program remainder, and each of our transformations is computable in polynomial time w.r.t. the size of the EDB, i.e. the number of tuples. As in [29] we exploit the fact, that if the IDB, i.e. the set of rules with non-empty bodies, is assumed to be fixed, the size of the Herbrand base and also the size of the Herbrand instantiation of the program are polynomial in the size of the EDB. Further, all transformations operate on subsets of the Herbrand base (unconditional facts) or on subsets of the Herbrand instantiation (extended conditional facts).

A program remainder is equivalent to the original program under the well-founded and stable model semantics, and, in fact, under a large class of semantics which allow the elementary transformations introduced in Section 4:

Theorem 29 Equivalence of Program Remainder. *Let S be any semantics which allows unfolding, deletion of tautologies, positive and negative reduction, and the deletion of nonminimal rules. Then*

$$
S(\hat{P}) = S(P)
$$

for every program P with remainder $\hat{P}$.

Proof. This follows immediately from the Lemmata 23, 25, and 28. □

A literal A is true in the well-founded model iff A is contained as a fact in the program remainder, $A \in facts(\hat{P})$. Conversely, the well-founded model satisfies **not** A iff A does not appear in any rule head of the program remainder, i.e., $A \notin heads(\hat{P})$. In other words, in the well-founded model exactly the literals of $known_{BASE(P)}(\hat{P})$ (cf. Definition 15) have a definite truth value. All other literals are undefined in the well-founded model. In this respect, the program remainder behaves like the residual program of [6, 7].

Theorem 30 Computation of Well-Founded Semantics.
For every program P and remainder $\hat{P}$, the well-founded model W_P^* of P satisfies exactly those positive and negative literals which are immediately obvious in $\hat{P}$, i.e.

$$W_P^* = known_{BASE(P)}(\hat{P}).$$

Proof. By Theorem 29 and since the well-founded semantics allows the transformations of the rewriting system $\mapsto_X$, P and $\hat{P}$ have the same well-founded model, i.e., $W_P^* = W_{\hat{P}}^*$. Therefore it suffices to show that $W_{\hat{P}}^* = known_{BASE(P)}(\hat{P})$. We do this by executing the the alternating fixpoint procedure on $\hat{P}$.

1. $K_0 = facts(\hat{P})$
   It is clear that at least these facts are contained in K_0, i.e. $facts(\hat{P}) \subseteq K_0$. To show equality assume that

   $$K_0 - facts(\hat{P}) \neq \emptyset$$

   Let

   $$A \leftarrow L_1 \wedge \cdots \wedge L_n$$

   be the first rule with non-empty body applied by the alternating fixpoint procedure. By Definition 2 the L_i are all positive and contained in $facts(\hat{P})$. But then the *success* transformation is applicable to $\hat{P}$. This contradicts the irreducibility of $\hat{P}$.

2. $U_0 = heads(\hat{P})$
   The inclusion

   $$U_0 \subseteq heads(\hat{P})$$

   is trivial. Assume that

   $$U_0 \subset heads(\hat{P})$$

   holds. Let

   $$\mathcal{A} := BASE(P) - U_0$$

We show that *loop detection* w.r.t. $\mathcal{A}$ is applicable to $\hat{P}$, contradicting again the irreducibility of $\hat{P}$. Let

$$A \leftarrow \mathcal{B}$$

be an arbitrary rule of $\hat{P}$ with

$$A \in \mathcal{A}$$

Assume that

$$\mathcal{B} \cap \mathcal{A} = \emptyset$$

Then

$$pos(\mathcal{B}) \subseteq U_0$$

would hold. But then, since $A \in \mathcal{A}$, i.e., $A \notin U_0$, there must be a negative literal **not** $B \in \mathcal{B}$ with $B \in K_0$. In this case negative reduction would be applicable to $\hat{P}$ which is impossible because $\hat{P}$ is irreducible.

3. $K_1 = facts(\hat{P})$

The inclusion

$$facts(\hat{P}) \subseteq K_1$$

is trivial, because the fixpoint

$$K_1 := \text{lfp}(T_{\hat{P}, U_0})$$

(cf. Definition 2) of course contains all facts of $\hat{P}$. To show equality assume that

$$K_1 - facts(\hat{P}) \neq \emptyset$$

Let

$$A \leftarrow L_1 \wedge \cdots \wedge L_n \in \hat{P}$$

be the first rule with non-empty body applied during the computation of K_1. If it contains a positive body literal L_i,

$$L_i \in facts(\hat{P})$$

must hold. But then, *success* is applicable, contradicting the irreducibility of $\hat{P}$. If it contains a negative body literal $L_1 = $ **not** B,

$$B \notin U_0 = heads(\hat{P})$$

must hold. But then, *positive reduction* is applicable, contradicting again the irreducibility of $\hat{P}$.

4. Since $K_1 = K_0$, we also have $U_1 = U_0$, so the fixpoint is reached. $\qquad\square$

From this it is also simple to derive an explicit characterization of the program remainder: From the Herbrand instantiation of the program we obtain the program remainder by

1. deleting every rule instance with a body literal which is false in the well-founded model, and
2. removing from the remaining rule instances the body literals which are true in the well-founded model.

This is a kind of GELFOND/LIFSCHITZ-transformation [19].

Theorem 31 Program Remainder. *Let $\hat{P}$ be a remainder of a program P. The following holds.*

$$\hat{P} = \left\{ A \leftarrow (\mathcal{B} - W_P^*) \mid A \leftarrow \mathcal{B} \in ground(P) \right.$$
$$\left. \text{and for every } B \in \mathcal{B}: \sim B \notin W_P^* \right\}.$$

Thus the remainder of a program is uniquely determined.

Proof. Let us temporarily call the transformation on the right hand side *wred*, i.e. for every program P' let

$$wred(P') := \left\{ A \leftarrow (\mathcal{B} - W_{P'}^*) \mid A \leftarrow \mathcal{B} \in ground(P') \right.$$
$$\left. \text{and for every } B \in \mathcal{B}: \sim B \notin W_{P'}^* \right\}.$$

1. We first show that

$$P_1 \mapsto_X P_2 \implies wred(P_1) = wred(P_2)$$

(a) $P_1 \mapsto_P P_2$: *Positive reduction* removes a negative body literal **not** B from some rule $A \leftarrow \mathcal{B}$, if $B \notin heads(P_1)$. *Positive reduction* does not change the well-founded model. Furthermore **not** B is certainly true in the well-founded model. Thus $\mathcal{B} - W_{P_1}^* = (\mathcal{B} - \{\textbf{not } B\}) - W_{P_2}^*$.

(b) $P_1 \mapsto_N P_2$: *Negative reduction* deletes a rule $A \leftarrow \mathcal{B}$ where $\mathcal{B}$ contains a negative literal **not** B such that $B \in facts(P_1)$. But then B is true in the well-founded model of P_1 and P_2, so the *wred*-transformation will delete this rule anyway.

(c) $P_1 \mapsto_S P_2$: *Success* removes a positive body literal B from some rule $A \leftarrow \mathcal{B}$, if $B \in facts(P_1)$. *Success* does not change the well-founded model, and furthermore B is certainly true in this well-founded model. Thus we can conclude $\mathcal{B} - W_{P_1}^* = (\mathcal{B} - \{B\}) - W_{P_2}^*$.

(d) $P_1 \mapsto_F P_2$: *Failure* deletes a rule $A \leftarrow \mathcal{B}$ where $\mathcal{B}$ contains a positive literal B such that $B \notin heads(P_1)$. But then **not** B is true in the well-founded model of P_1 and P_2, so the *wred*-transformation will delete this rule anyway.

(e) $P_1 \mapsto_L P_2$: *Loop detection* w.r.t. to an unfounded set $\mathcal{A}$ deletes a rule $A \leftarrow \mathcal{B}$ where $\mathcal{B}$ contains a positive literal B such that $B \in \mathcal{A}$. But since all atoms in the unfounded set $\mathcal{A}$ are false in the well-founded model of P_1 and P_2, the *wred*-transformation will delete this rule anyway.

2. Since $ground(P) \mapsto_X^* \hat{P}$, we have

$$wred(ground(P)) = wred(\hat{P})$$

Because the well-founded semantics is instantiation-invariant (cf. Definition 4) the definition of $wred$ implies

$$wred(P) = wred(\hat{P})$$

We now only have to show

$$wred(\hat{P}) = \hat{P}$$

Assume that

$$wred(\hat{P}) \neq \hat{P}$$

Then there is a rule

$$A \leftarrow \mathcal{B} \in \hat{P}$$

such that there is $B \in \mathcal{B}$ and either $A \leftarrow \mathcal{B}$ has been modified by $wred$ because $B \in W_{\hat{P}}^*$ or entirely deleted because $\sim B \in W_{\hat{P}}^*$. But we know by Theorem 30 that

$$W_{\hat{P}}^* = known_{BASE(P)}(\hat{P})$$

We can distinguish the following four cases:

(a) $B \in W_{\hat{P}}^*$.

    i. B is positive. It follows that

$$B \in facts(\hat{P})$$

    But then *success* is applicable, contradicting the irreducibility of $\hat{P}$.

    ii. $B = \mathbf{not}\, C$ is negative. It follows that

$$C \notin heads(\hat{P})$$

    But then *positive reduction* is applicable, again contradicting the irreducibility of $\hat{P}$.

(b) $\sim B \in W_{\hat{P}}^*$.

    i. B is positive. It follows that

$$\mathbf{not}\, B \in W_{\hat{P}}^*$$

    and thus

$$B \notin heads(\hat{P})$$

    But then *failure* is applicable, contradicting the irreducibility of $\hat{P}$.

    ii. $B = \mathbf{not}\, C$ is negative. It follows that

$$C \in W_{\hat{P}}^*$$

    and thus

$$C \in facts(\hat{P})$$

    But then *negative reduction* is applicable, again contradicting the irreducibility of $\hat{P}$.

$\square$

Corollary 32. *The rewriting system $\mapsto_X$ is confluent and the program remainder $\hat{P}$ is the unique normalform of $ground(P)$ w.r.t. $\mapsto_X$.* $\square$

6 Immediate Consequences with Delayed Literals

In the preceding sections, we applied program transformations to $ground(P)$ to derive the program remainder from which we could directly determine the well-founded model. However, the construction of the ground instantiation of P is a very costly operation. In this section we will show that it is sufficient to start the transformation from a subset of $ground(P)$ that can be computed more efficiently.

The key idea is to generate and start from the set of those rule instances of P that do not contain any body literals that are obviously false. We consider a rule instance only if we have reason to believe that all the positive body literals are possibly true. We can start with rule instances without positive body literals. The heads of these rule instances are possibly true, thus further rule instances having these atoms as positive body literals can be derived successively. Further, if we already know an atom A to be true, we should disregard those rule instances having **not** A as negative body literal.

Definition 33 Immediate Consequences with Delayed Literals.
Let P be a normal program. Given a set F of extended conditional facts and a set J of ground atoms, the operator $\bar{T}_{P,J}$ computes the following set of extended conditional facts.

$$\bar{T}_{P,J}(F) := \big\{ A\theta \leftarrow L_1\theta \wedge \cdots \wedge L_n\theta \mid \text{there is a rule } A \leftarrow L_1 \wedge \cdots \wedge L_n \text{ in } P$$

$$\text{and a ground substitution } \theta \text{ for this}$$
$$\text{rule such that for } i = 1, \ldots, n\colon$$
$$L_i \text{ is a positive literal}$$
$$\text{and } L_i\theta \in heads(F), \text{ or}$$
$$L_i \text{ is a negative literal } \textbf{not } B$$
$$\text{and } B\theta \notin J \big\}.$$

□

Remark. Observe that

$$\text{lfp}(\bar{T}_{P,J}) \subseteq \text{lfp}(\bar{T}_{P,\emptyset}) \subseteq ground(P)$$

Further, it is obvious from Definitions 1 and 33 that

$$heads(\text{lfp}(\bar{T}_{P,J})) = \text{lfp}(T_{P,J})$$

□

By an induction on the number of derivation steps we can prove that the derived rule instances contain only constants occurring in the program: Due to range-restriction, every variable occurs in a positive body literal, which in turn is matched with already derived rule instances. But then it is obvious that the set of derived rule instances can be computed in polynomial time w.r.t. to size of the EDB.

We will show that it is correct to start the computation of the program remainder $\hat{P}$ (cf. Section 5) at $\mathrm{lfp}(\bar{T}_{P,\emptyset})$. Assume J to be empty and consider $\mathrm{lfp}(\bar{T}_{P,\emptyset})$. In this case, all negative subgoals are considered true during the iteration. Thus, we generate all rule instances of P whose positive body literals are all possibly true. In other words, we derive all elements of $ground(P)$ except those rule instances having at least one positive body literal that is not derivable, even if all negative subgoals are ignored. This sounds like the specification of the *loop detection*, and in fact, one application of $\mapsto_L$ takes us from $ground(P)$ to $\mathrm{lfp}(\bar{T}_{P,\emptyset})$.

Lemma 34. *Let P be a normal program and let $\bar{T}_{P,\emptyset}$ be defined as above. Then the following holds.*

$$ground(P) \mapsto_L \mathrm{lfp}(\bar{T}_{P,\emptyset})$$

$\square$

Lemma 35. *Let P be a normal logic program. Then the following holds.*

$$\mathrm{lfp}(\bar{T}_{P,\emptyset}) \mapsto_X^* \hat{P}$$

Proof. By Lemma 34 we have

$$ground(P) \mapsto_X^* \mathrm{lfp}(\bar{T}_{P,\emptyset}).$$

The assertion follows, because $\hat{P}$ is the unique normalform of $ground(P)$ w.r.t. $\mapsto_X$ (cf. Corollary 32). $\square$

Proposition 36. *Let S be a semantics which allows unfolding and the deletion of tautologies. Then*

$$S\big(\mathrm{lfp}(\bar{T}_{P,\emptyset})\big) = S(P)$$

holds for every program P.

Proof. By Lemma 25, Lemma 34, and Definition 4. $\square$

To avoid the generation of rule instances having negative body literals that are obviously false, we have to supply a reference set J of facts that are known to be true. Let J be the set of atoms occurring as facts in P and their consequences that can be derived without assuming knowledge about negative subgoals. These definitely true consequences are computed by iterating the standard immediate consequence operator on the set P^+ of definite rules of P. Let $K_0 := \mathrm{lfp}(T_{P^+})$. In the following we will show, that it is correct to start the computation of the program remainder at $\mathrm{lfp}(\bar{T}_{P,K_0})$.

Lemma 37. *Let $K_0 := \mathrm{lfp}(T_{P^+})$. Then the following holds.*

$$\mathrm{lfp}(\bar{T}_{P,\emptyset}) \cup K_0 \mapsto_X^* \mathrm{lfp}(\bar{T}_{P,K_0}) \cup K_0$$

Proof. Let

$$P_1 := K_0 \cup \{(A \leftarrow C) \in \mathrm{lfp}(\bar{T}_{P,\emptyset}) \mid neg(C) \cap K_0 = \emptyset\}$$

It is straightforward to show that

$$\mathrm{lfp}(\bar{T}_{P,\emptyset}) \cup K_0 \mapsto_N^* P_1 \mapsto_L \mathrm{lfp}(\bar{T}_{P,K_0}) \cup K_0$$

holds. □

Theorem 38. *Let K_0 denote the set $\mathrm{lfp}(T_{P+})$. Then $\hat{P}$ is the normalform of $\mathrm{lfp}(\bar{T}_{P,K_0})$ w.r.t. $\mapsto_X$, i.e.*

1. $\mathrm{lfp}(\bar{T}_{P,K_0}) \mapsto_X^* \hat{P}$
2. $\hat{P}$ is irreducible w.r.t. $\mapsto_X$.

Proof. Let

$$K_0 := \mathrm{lfp}(T_{P+})$$

Obviously, all facts of K_0 are true in the well-founded model of P, i.e.,

$$K_0 \subseteq W_P^*$$

From Theorem 30 we know that

$$W_P^* = known_{BASE(P)}(\hat{P})$$

Since K_0 contains only facts, we can conclude that

$$K_0 \subseteq \hat{P}$$

Therefore, by Lemma 35 also

$$\mathrm{lfp}(\bar{T}_{P,\emptyset}) \cup K_0 \mapsto_X^* \hat{P}$$

holds. By Lemma 37 we know that

$$\mathrm{lfp}(\bar{T}_{P,\emptyset}) \cup K_0 \mapsto_X^* \mathrm{lfp}(\bar{T}_{P,K_0}) \cup K_0.$$

Because the rewriting system $\mapsto_X$ is confluent (cf. corollary 32) we can conclude

$$\mathrm{lfp}(\bar{T}_{P,K_0}) \cup K_0 \mapsto_X^* \hat{P}.$$

Let P' denote the normalform of $\mathrm{lfp}(\bar{T}_{P,K_0})$ w.r.t. the rewriting system $\mapsto_X$:

$$\mathrm{lfp}(\bar{T}_{P,K_0}) \mapsto_X^* P'$$

Since during the computation of $\mathrm{lfp}(\bar{T}_{P,K_0})$ in particular all definite rules of P are applied, it is clear that

$$K_0 = \mathrm{lfp}(T_{P+}) \subseteq P'$$

Therefore we have

$$\mathrm{lfp}(\bar{T}_{P,K_0}) \cup K_0 \mapsto_X^* P'$$

Again by confluence it follows that

$$P' = \hat{P}.$$

□

Corollary 39. *Let S be a semantics which allows unfolding, deletion of tautologies, positive and negative reduction, and deletion of nonminimal rules. Let $K_0 := \mathrm{lfp}(T_{P+})$. Then*

$$S\big(\mathrm{lfp}(\bar{T}_{P,K_0})\big) = S(P)$$

holds for every program P. This is in particular true for the well-founded semantics and the stable model semantics.

Proof. Definition 27, Theorem 29, and Theorem 38 □

Remark Efficient Evaluation. Theorem 38 and Corollary 39 indicate that an efficient evaluation method should start the transformation at a relevant subset of $ground(P)$:

1. Compute definitely true facts by $K_0 := \mathrm{lfp}(T_{P+})$.
2. Construct the set $\mathrm{lfp}(\bar{T}_{P,K_0})$ of extended conditional facts.
3. By applying $\mapsto_X$, transform this set into its normalform w.r.t. $\mapsto_X$, i.e., the program remainder $\hat{P}$. □

Example 10 Odd Numbers Revisited. Consider again the program *OddNum* of Example 2. Following Theorem 38, we can start the transformation process at $\mathrm{lfp}(\bar{T}_{OddNum,K_0})$ instead of $ground(OddNum)$. With

$$K_0 = \{succ(0,1), \ldots, succ(n-1,n)\}$$

we have

$$\mathrm{lfp}(\bar{T}_{OddNum,K_0}) = K_0 \cup \{\ odd(1) \leftarrow succ(0,1) \wedge \mathbf{not}\, odd(0),$$
$$\vdots$$
$$odd(n) \leftarrow succ(n-1,n) \wedge \mathbf{not}\, odd(n-1)\}$$

This start set can be constructed by $O(n)$ derivation steps. The following $O(n)$ transformation steps transform the start set into the program remainder of *OddNum*.

$\mathrm{lfp}(\bar{T}_{OddNum,K_0})$
$\qquad \mapsto_S^* K_0 \cup \{\ odd(1) \leftarrow \mathbf{not}\, odd(0), \ldots, odd(n) \leftarrow \mathbf{not}\, odd(n-1)\ \}$
$\qquad \mapsto_P K_0 \cup \{\ odd(1),$
$\qquad\qquad odd(2) \leftarrow \mathbf{not}\, odd(1), \ldots, odd(n) \leftarrow \mathbf{not}\, odd(n-1)\ \}$
$\qquad \mapsto_N K_0 \cup \{\ odd(1),$
$\qquad\qquad odd(3) \leftarrow \mathbf{not}\, odd(2), \ldots, odd(n) \leftarrow \mathbf{not}\, odd(n-1)\ \}$
$\qquad \mapsto_P K_0 \cup \{\ odd(1), odd(3)$
$\qquad\qquad odd(4) \leftarrow \mathbf{not}\, odd(3), \ldots, odd(n) \leftarrow \mathbf{not}\, odd(n-1)\ \}$
$\qquad \mapsto_N K_0 \cup \{\ odd(1), odd(3)$
$\qquad\qquad odd(5) \leftarrow \mathbf{not}\, odd(4), \ldots, odd(n) \leftarrow \mathbf{not}\, odd(n-1)\ \}$

$$\mapsto_P \ K_0 \cup \{\ odd(1), odd(3), odd(5),$$
$$odd(6) \leftarrow \mathbf{not}\ odd(5), \ldots, odd(n) \leftarrow \mathbf{not}\ odd(n-1)\ \}$$

$$\vdots$$

$$\mapsto_X^* \ K_0 \cup \{\ odd(1), odd(3), odd(5), \ldots, odd(n-1)\ \}$$

In summary, the well-founded model of the program $OddNum$ is computed in $O(n)$ derivation/transformation steps. □

7 Relation to Alternating Fixpoint

The computation of the set of all possibly true facts that is needed for the *loop detection* $\mapsto_L$ transformation (cf. Definition 24) is very similar to the computation of possible facts performed in each iteration step of the alternating fixpoint procedure (c.f. Definition 2). There is an even closer correspondence as we will show in this section.

To characterize the computation performed by the alternating fixpoint procedure we define a sequence $(\bar{K}_i, \bar{U}_i)_{i\geq 0}$ where $\bar{K}_i$ and $\bar{U}_i$ are constructed by the program transformations defined in this paper and that is closely related to the sequence $(K_i, U_i)_{i\geq 0}$ computed by the alternating fixpoint procedure (cf. Definition 2).

Definition 40 Alternating Fixpoint by Program Transformations.
Let P be a normal logic program. We define the reductions $\mapsto_{PS} := (\mapsto_P \cup \mapsto_S)$ and $\mapsto_{NL} := (\mapsto_N \cup \mapsto_L)$. The sequence $(\bar{K}_i, \bar{U}_i)_{i\geq 0}$ of sets $\bar{K}_i$ and $\bar{U}_i$ of extended conditional facts is defined by:

$$\bar{K}_0 := \mathrm{lfp}(T_{P+})$$
$$\bar{U}_0 := \mathrm{lfp}(\bar{T}_{P,\bar{K}_0})$$
$$\bar{K}_i \text{ is the normalform of } \bar{U}_{i-1} \text{ w.r.t. } \mapsto_{PS}, \ i > 0$$
$$\bar{U}_i \text{ is the normalform of } \bar{K}_i \text{ w.r.t. } \mapsto_{NL}, \ i > 0$$

The computation halts when the sequence becomes stationary, i.e., when a fixpoint is reached in the sense that

$$(\bar{K}_j, \bar{U}_j) = (\bar{K}_{j+1}, \bar{U}_{j+1})$$

□

Remark. Due to Theorem 38 the sequence $(\bar{K}_i, \bar{U}_i)_{i\geq 0}$ of Definition 40 reaches a fixpoint $(\bar{K}_j, \bar{U}_j)$ and computes the program remainder $\hat{P} = \bar{K}_j = \bar{U}_j$.

- In the first step of the alternating fixpoint procedure, definitely true facts are derived by $K_0 = \mathrm{lfp}(T_{P+})$. Theorem 38 suggests to start also the transformation-based evaluation with $\mathrm{lfp}(T_{P+})$.

- In the second step of the alternating fixpoint procedure, the set of possible facts $U_0 = \text{lfp}(T_{P,K_0})$ is computed by iterating the T_{P,K_0} operator. To be able to apply our program transformations, we have to derive a corresponding set of extended conditional facts. This is done by $\text{lfp}(\bar{T}_{P,K_0})$ that computes the same possible facts, but keeps the rule instances that have been used to derive them.
- For the computation of K_i, $i > 0$, the alternating fixpoint procedure derives more definitely true facts by regarding those negative subgoals as true whose complements are not contained in U_{i-1}. Newly derived true facts are used to derive more true facts by rule applications. At the program transformation side, this corresponds to the *positive reduction* $\mapsto_P$ that deletes negative conditions whose complements are known to be false, i.e. not contained in $heads(\bar{U}_{i-1})$. Facts obtained this way can be used to derive further facts by the *success* $\mapsto_S$ transformation that deletes positive conditions that are now known to be true.
- For the computation of U_i, $i > 0$, those possible facts that are still derivable are recomputed. Rule instances with negative subgoals whose complements are known to be true, i.e. that are contained in K_i, are not used. As a byproduct of this recomputation, the generation of any positive cycles is avoided. Disregarding rule instances with false negative subgoals corresponds to the *negative reduction* $\mapsto_N$. However, by this reduction, positive cycles may be produced. Thus, *loop detection* $\mapsto_L$ has to be applied. Since *loop detection* subsumes the *failure* $\mapsto_F$ transformation, we do not need to apply $\mapsto_F$ separately.

□

The relation between the alternating fixpoint computation and the sequence of program transformations defined above is described by the following theorem.

Theorem 41. *Let P be a normal logic program. Let $(K_i, U_i)_{i \geq 0}$ and $(\bar{K}_i, \bar{U}_i)_{i \geq 0}$ be the sequences given by Definitions 2 and 40, respectively. Then the following holds:*

$$K_i = facts(\bar{K}_i)$$
$$U_i = heads(\bar{U}_i)$$

Proof. The theorem follows from the properties of the alternating fixpoint procedure and the elementary transformations and can be shown by induction on i (see [32]). □

Theorem 41 shows that the program transformation approach will never do more work than the alternating fixpoint procedure. The sets K_0 and $\bar{K}_0$ are equal by definition. Although the set $\bar{U}_0$ contains more elements than U_0, the same number of derivation steps is needed to compute U_0. Consider the case that one possible fact $A \in U_0$ is represented by more than one extended conditional facts $A \leftarrow C$. These conditional facts are the rule instances used to derive the possible fact A.

Then during the computation of U_0, the fact A is derived by the same number of rule instances. Only due to duplicate elimination, the cardinality of U_0 is less than the number of derivation steps needed to compute U_0.

For the computation of the set $\bar{K}_i$, $i > 0$, the same argument holds. Whenever a fact can be derived by the deletion of the body literals of several extended conditional facts, the fact is repeatedly derived in K_i by several rule instances, and the duplicates are eliminated afterwards. Of course, for the derivation of one fact in $\bar{K}_i$, several transformation steps are needed. But analogously, during the iteration of the $T_{P,U_{i-1}}$ operator, also several body literals have to be checked before the head of one rule instance can be derived.

As proposed in [20], the sets K_i do not have to be recomputed in each iteration step, but can be maintained in terms of increments. This optimization is automatically performed by the transformation approach, since extended conditional facts that were transformed into facts by the deletion of their body literals are never changed afterwards.

The most interesting part is the recomputation of the possible facts. Since the alternating fixpoint procedure does not memorize by which rule instances the possible facts in U_{i-1} have been derived, in each iteration step the set U_i has to be recomputed. In the transformation approach, possible facts do not always have to be recomputed. Possible facts that become false can rather be deleted directly if one of their body literals has become false. However, by this reduction, positive cycles can occur and have to be eliminated by the more costly transformation *loop detection*. Although, for many programs the number of applications of *loop detection* can be reduced, for this comparison we have chosen the worst case that in each iteration step the *loop detection* is applied.

For *loop detection*, those facts have to be computed that are still possibly true. *Negative reduction* prevents us from using rule instances with negative body literals already known to be false. Extended conditional facts having positive body literals not derivable anymore are then deleted. Exactly the same is done by the alternating fixpoint procedure by the computation $U_i := \text{lfp}(T_{P,K_i})$. Again, rule instances with negative body literals whose complements are in K_i are excluded.

This comparison illustrates that the computation performed by the alternating fixpoint procedure corresponds to the alternating application of the transformations $\mapsto_{PS}$ and $\mapsto_{NL}$. The *failure* transformation $\mapsto_F$ is not used. It is subsumed by *loop detection* that is applied in every iteration.

However, *loop detection* is a costly operation since it needs a recomputation of all possible facts as it is done by the alternating fixpoint procedure. Instead, the cheaper transformation *failure* should be preferred as long as no *loop detection* is needed. One possibility is to apply *loop detection* only if no application of $\mapsto_{PNSF}$ is possible. This way, many programs can be evaluated more efficiently than by the alternating fixpoint procedure, as illustrated in Examples 1, 2, 3, and 10.

However, in the transformation approach all rule instances that are still relevant are explicitly stored. The alternating fixpoint procedure needs to consider the same rule instances, but generates them on demand without storing them. Thus, while having a (sometimes) better time complexity, the transformation approach is expected to have a space complexity worse than the alternating fixpoint approach.

8 Optimization

We proposed to perform reductions "early", i.e., during the derivation of extended conditional facts. This is simple for reductions depending on the presence of unconditional facts or their consequences derived by definite rules. However, for reductions depending on the absence of extended conditional facts about a literal, we must, of course, be sure that such facts not only are absent *now*, but also cannot be derived later.

A standard method for this is to split the program into components for every group of mutually recursive predicates and locally compute the program remainders for every such component (in any order that is compatible with the predicate dependencies). When evaluating a component, all extended conditional facts about predicates defined in "lower" components are known. Thus reductions for them can be performed immediately.

For instance, if a program is stratified, we can immediately evaluate negative literals (by applying our reductions), and thus never have to delay any positive or negative literals. In this case, we get the standard bottom-up computation of the perfect model.

To evaluate negative subgoals immediately for non-stratified programs, concepts of goal-directedness are needed. For instance, ZUKOWSKI and FREITAG [30] proposed an evaluation method for modularly stratified programs that is based on a combination of magic set transformation and top-down communication. This method always evaluates negative subgoals by separate computations, thus no delaying is required.

The most prominent top-down evaluation method for the full class of normal programs is the SLG-resolution [11, 12, 13]. It tries to completely evaluate a negative subgoal before any of its consequences are derived. Only if this is not possible due to the presence of cyclic negative dependencies, subgoals must be delayed.

Since SLG-resolution is a top-down method, it is of course goal-directed. In bottom-up approaches, goal-directedness is usually added by means of (a form of) magic set transformation. In [20], KEMP et al. show how the magic set transformation can be used to compute the well-founded semantics. MORISHITA [22] as well as DEGERSTEDT and NILSSON [15] propose some optimizations that adapt the magic set transformation to the alternating fixpoint procedure. Another interesting improvement of the magic set method has been presented in [4]. We are planning to extend this approach to normal programs based on the work presented here.

All these approaches use unconditional facts that can lead to many recomputations. In [31], ZUKOWSKI and FREITAG extend the work of [20] to conditional facts. They propose a goal-directed variant of the residual program approach. Currently, this method is being adapted to extended conditional facts as used by the program transformations described in this paper.

Another topic of efficient bottom-up computation is differential or semi-naive evaluation. Again, techniques known for conditional facts [31] have to be adapted to extended conditional facts. Especially, *loop detection* has to be implemented carefully to avoid unnecessary recomputations.

9 Conclusions

We have presented an algorithm for computing the well-founded semantics of function-free programs which is based on the set of elementary program transformations studied by BRASS and DIX [6, 7]. The time complexity of our algorithm is polynomial in the size of the EDB. If we would unfold all positive body literals in the program remainder (and delete tautologies), we would get the residual program plus some non-minimal conditional facts. So the program remainder can be seen as an efficient encoding of the residual program. It is equivalent to the original program under a wide range of semantics. In fact, our rewriting system $\mapsto_X$ is even weaker than the transformations used in [6, 7] because full *unfolding* is not needed to compute the program remainder.

While the computational complexity of the program remainder is decisively lower than that of the residual program, the "intellectual complexity" seems to be higher. One of the strengths of the residual program was its simplicity, and it seems that this has to be partially sacrificed, since we now have to cope with positive loops. But our method still operates on the source program level, and can be understood as a sequence of elementary program transformations.

Obviously, our approach owes much to SLG-resolution developed by CHEN and WARREN [11, 12, 13]. On the other hand we have obtained an important simplification by separating the discussion of the overall evaluation method from the issue of goal-directedness. The latter will have to be investigated in future extensions of our approach.

We have shown that our method never does more work than the alternating fixpoint approach. However, there are examples (such as Example 10), where our method is superior to the alternating fixpoint approach.

The generality of our method gives rise to hope that it can serve as a basis for an integration of the resolution-based, fixpoint-based, and transformation-based evaluation methods.

Acknowledgments

We would like to thank CARL-ALEXANDER WICHERT and JÜRGEN DIX for very helpful discussions.

References

1. C. Aravindan and P. M. Dung. On the correctness of unfold/fold transformation of normal and extended logic programs. *The JLP*, 24(3):201–217, 1995.
2. C. Bell, A. Nerode, R. Ng, and V. S. Subrahmanian. Implementing stable semantics by linear programming. In L. M. Pereira and A. Nerode, editors, *Logic Programming and Non-monotonic Reasoning, Proc. of the Second Int. Workshop (LP-NMR'93)*, pages 23–42. MIT Press, 1993.
3. S. Brass. Bottom-up query evaluation in extended deductive databases. Habilitation thesis, Institut für Informatik, Universität Hannover, 1996.
4. S. Brass. SLDMagic — An improved magic set technique. In B. Novikov and J. W. Schmidt, editors, *Advances in Databases and Information Systems – ADBIS'96*, 1996.
5. S. Brass and J. Dix. Characterizations of the stable semantics by partial evaluation. In A. Nerode, editor, *Logic Programming and Nonmonotonic Reasoning, Proc. of the Third Int. Conf. (LPNMR'95)*, number 928 in LNCS, pages 85–98. Springer, 1995.
6. S. Brass and J. Dix. Disjunctive semantics based upon partial and bottom-up evaluation. In L. Sterling, editor, *Logic Programming, Proc. of the Twelfth Int. Conf. on Logic Programming (ICLP'95)*, pages 199–213. MIT Press, 1995.
7. S. Brass and J. Dix. A general approach to bottom-up computation of disjunctive semantics. In J. Dix, L. M. Pereira, and T. C. Przymusinski, editors, *Non-monotonic Extensions of Logic Programming*, number 927 in LNAI, pages 127–155. Springer, 1995.
8. S. Brass and J. Dix. Characterizing D-WFS: Confluence and iterated GCWA. In *5th European Workshop on Logics in AI (JELIA'96)*, 1996.
9. F. Bry. Logic programming as constructivism: A formalization and its application to databases. In *Proc. of the 8th ACM SIGACT-SIGMOD-SIGART Symposium on Principles of Database Systems (PODS'89)*, pages 34–50, 1989.
10. F. Bry. Negation in logic programming: A formalization in constructive logic. In D. Karagiannis, editor, *Information Systems and Artificial Intelligence: Integration Aspects*, number 474 in LNCS, pages 30–46. Springer, 1990.
11. W. Chen, T. Swift, and D. S. Warren. Efficient top-down computation of queries under the well-founded semantics. *JLP*, 24(3):161–199, 1995.
12. W. Chen and D. S. Warren. Query-evaluation under the well founded semantics. In *Proc. of the Twelfth ACM SIGACT-SIGMOD-SIGART Symposium on Principles of Database Systems (PODS'93)*, pages 168–179, 1993.
13. W. Chen and D. S. Warren. Tabled evaluation with delaying for general logic programs. *JACM*, 43(1):20–74, 1996.
14. P. Cholewiński, V. W. Marek, A. Mikitiuk, and M. Truszczyński. Experimenting with nonmonotonic reasoning. In L. Sterling, editor, *Logic Programming, Proc. of the Twelfth Int. Conf. on Logic Programming (ICLP'95)*, pages 267–281. MIT Press, 1995.
15. L. Degerstedt and U. Nilsson. Magic computation for well-founded semantics. In J. Dix, L. M. Pereira, and T. C. Przymusinski, editors, *Nonmonotonic Extensions of Logic Programming*, number 927 in LNAI, pages 181–204. Springer, 1995.
16. P. M. Dung and K. Kanchansut. A fixpoint approach to declarative semantics of logic programs. In *Proc. North American Conference on Logic Programming (NACLP'89)*, pages 604–625, 1989.

17. P. M. Dung and K. Kanchansut. A natural semantics of logic programs with negation. In *Proc. of the Ninth Conf. on Foundations of Software Technology and Theoretical Computer Science*, pages 70–80, 1989.

18. B. Freitag, H. Schütz, and G. Specht. *LOLA* - a logic language for deductive databases and its implementation. In *Proc. 2nd International Symposium on Database Systems for Advanced Applications (DASFAA '91), Tokyo, Japan, April 2–4, 1991*, pages 216–225, 1991.

19. M. Gelfond and V. Lifschitz. The stable model semantics for logic programming. In R. A. Kowalski and K. A. Bowen, editors, *Logic Programming, Proc. of the 5th Int. Conf. and Symp.*, pages 1070–1080, Cambridge, Mass., 1988. MIT Press.

20. D. B. Kemp, D. Srivastava, and P. J. Stuckey. Bottom-up evaluation and query optimization of well-founded models. *Theoretical Computer Science*, 146:145–184, 1995.

21. W. Marek and M. Truszczynski. Autoepistemic logic. *JACM*, 38(3):588–619, 1991.

22. S. Morishita. An alternating fixpoint tailored to magic programs. In *Proc. of the 12th ACM Symp. on Principles of Database Systems (PODS'93)*, pages 123–134, 1993.

23. K. Sagonas, T. Swift, and D. S. Warren. XSB as an efficient deductive database engine. In R. T. Snodgrass and M. Winslett, editors, *Proc. of the 1994 ACM SIGMOD Int. Conf. on Management of Data (SIGMOD'94)*, pages 442–453, 1994.

24. C. Sakama and H. Seki. Partial deduction of disjunctive logic programs: A declarative approach. In *Fourth Int. Workshop on Logic Program Synthesis and Transformation (LOPSTR'94)*, LNCS. Springer, 1994.

25. H. Seki. Unfold/fold transformation of general logic programs for the well-founded semantics. *JLP*, 16(1):5–23, 1993.

26. V. S. Subrahmanian and C. Zaniolo. Relating stable models and AI planning domains. In L. Sterling, editor, *Logic Programming, Proc. of the Twelfth Int. Conf. on Logic Programming (ICLP'95)*, pages 233–247. MIT Press, 1995.

27. A. Van Gelder. The alternating fixpoint of logic programs with negation. In *Proc. of the Eighth ACM SIGACT-SIGMOD-SIGART Symposium on Principles of Database Systems (PODS'89)*, pages 1–10, 1989.

28. A. Van Gelder. The alternating fixpoint of logic programs with negation. *Journal of Computer and System Sciences*, 47(1):185–221, 1993.

29. A. Van Gelder, K. A. Ross, and J. S. Schlipf. The well-founded semantics for general logic programs. *JACM*, 38:620–650, 1991.

30. U. Zukowski and B. Freitag. Adding flexibility to query evaluation for modularly stratified databases. In *Proc. of the 1996 Joint International Conference and Symposium on Logic Programming (JICSLP'96). September 2 – 6, 1996, Bonn, Germany*, pages 304–319. MIT Press, 1996.

31. U. Zukowski and B. Freitag. The differential fixpoint of general logic programs. In D. Boulanger, U. Geske, F. Giannotti, and D. Seipel, editors, *Proc. of the Workshop DDLP'96 on Deductive Databases and Logic Programming. 4th Workshop in conjunction with JICSLP'96. Bonn, Germany, September 2 – 6, 1996*, volume 295 of *GMD-Studien*, pages 45–56, St. Augustin, Germany, 1996. GMD.

32. U. Zukowski, B. Freitag, and S. Brass. Transformation-based bottom-up computation of the well-founded model. Technical Report MIP-9620, Universität Passau, 1996.

Computation of Non-Ground Disjunctive Well-Founded Semantics with Constraint Logic Programming

Jürgen Dix and Frieder Stolzenburg

University of Koblenz, Department of Computer Science
Rheinau 1, D-56075 Koblenz, Germany
{dix|stolzen}@@informatik.uni-koblenz.de

Abstract. Impressive work has been done in the last years concerning the meaning of negation and disjunction in logic programs, but most of this research concentrated on propositional programs only. While it suffices to consider the propositional case for investigating general properties and the overall behaviour of a semantics, we feel that for real applications and for computational purposes an implementation should be able to handle first-order programs without grounding them.

In this paper we present a theoretical framework by defining a calculus of program transformations that apply directly to rules with variables and function symbols. Our main results are that (1) this calculus is confluent for arbitrary programs, (2) for finite ground programs it is equivalent to a terminating calculus introduced by Brass and Dix (1995), and (3) it approximates a generalisation of D-WFS for arbitrary programs.

We achieve this by transforming program rules into rules with equational constraints thereby using heavily methods and techniques from constraint logic programming. In particular, disconnection-methods play a crucial role. In principle, any constraint theory known from the field of constraint logic programming can be exploited in the context of non-monotonic reasoning, not only equational constraints over the Herbrand domain. However, the respective constraint solver must be able to treat negative constraints of the considered constraint domain.

In summary, this work yields the basis for a general combination of two paradigms: constraint logic programming and non-monotonic reasoning.

Keywords: constraint logic programming, equational constraints, disjunctive logic programming, well-founded semantics, non-monotonic reasoning.

1 Introduction

Recent years have seen an enormous number of different semantics of logic programs with negation. Fewer semantics have been developed for disjunctive programs and nearly all approaches assume "without loss of generality"—as most authors put it—that the underlying programs are *grounded*, i.e. they do not contain variables.

We think that one of the most important advantages of the logic programming paradigm and therefore the success of Prolog is its ability to compute answer-substitutions for a given query. Although semantics for logic programs with negation are undecidable if function symbols and variables are allowed, we are convinced that query answering mechanisms for the non-ground-case have great advantages over the propositional case. Of course, such procedures can only be sound and not complete. But completeness can hold for certain restricted classes of programs as well as for certain queries.

Our approach is essentially based on a calculus of program transformations that has been recently shown to be confluent and terminating for ground programs [BD96]. The most important transformation in this calculus is the partial evaluation property (GPPE) introduced for disjunctive programs independently by [SS95,BD94]. Unfortunately, GPPE is not sound for rules with variables because of the occurrence of unifiable atoms in the heads of rules (see Section 4). In this paper we make GPPE sound—which allows us to use the results of [BD96]—by introducing *inequality constraints*. This immediately leads us to introduce *constraint disjunctive logic programs* and consequently to extend our transformations to this class of programs. Surprisingly, this framework shares the same nice properties as our original calculus. In fact we can lift the results of [BD96] to the non-ground case.

We know the approach [EGLS96] that also considers *non-ground disjunctive* programs. In this approach, the authors define a Gelfond-Lifschitz transformation for first-order programs and consider *instantiation by need* techniques. It is related to [KNS95] where definite non-ground programs are treated. But they only consider normal logic programs, i.e. without disjunctions. In addition, they do not consider the case with function symbols in its full generality. [Stu91] also considers normal logic programs only. He employs *constructive negation* and gives a clean approach to negation in constraint logic programming. Last but not least, we want to mention [AD94,SS95]. These papers present methods based on partial deduction—as also done here—for normal logic programs and disjunctive logic programs, respectively, but both do not aim at incorporating constraint logic programming.

The paper is structured as follows. In Section 2 we introduce the basic notation we will use throughout the paper. In Section 3 we consider ground programs. After introducing our calculus of transformations originally defined in [BD94,BD96], we cite its *confluence* and *termination* for *finite* ground programs: this gives rise to the semantics D-WFS. We then generalise D-WFS to arbitrary infinite ground programs by introducing a *loop-detection rule* and showing that the original calculus still is confluent but does not always terminate.

Our overall framework is introduced in Section 4 where we consider arbitrary first-order programs. We extend program rules by a *constraint theory* and investigate how techniques from *constraint logic programming* apply. In Section 5 we extend our original transformations using the new framework so that they directly apply to programs with variables. We introduce CD-WFS using the new calculus and show how it can be computed and used for *query-answering*. We also show its relation with WFS, GCWA and D-WFS. We conclude with Section 6.

2 Preliminaries

In the first part of this paper we restrict to propositional programs. We also allow that they are infinite, i.e. they are full instantiations of first order programs. Let some fixed finite signature Σ containing the binary connectives $\wedge, \vee, \rightarrow$, the unary connective $\neg$ and the *falsum* $\perp$ be given.

Definition 1 (Logic Program Φ).
A logic program Φ is a (possibly infinite) set of rules of the form

$$A_1 \vee \cdots \vee A_l \leftarrow B_1 \wedge \cdots \wedge B_m \wedge \neg C_1 \wedge \cdots \wedge \neg C_n$$

where the A_i, B_i and C_i are Σ-atoms different from $\perp$, $l \geq 1$, $m \geq 0$, $n \geq 0$. We allow empty conjunctions: they are considered as abbreviations for $\neg\perp$ (the *verum*) which we also denote by $\top$.

We identify such a rule with the triple consisting of the following sets of atoms $\mathcal{A} := \{A_1, \ldots, A_k\}$, $\mathcal{B} := \{B_1, \ldots, B_m\}$, $\mathcal{C} := \{C_1, \ldots, C_n\}$, and write it as $\mathcal{A} \leftarrow \mathcal{B} \wedge \neg\mathcal{C}$. This means, in particular, that we assume the A_i (resp. the B_i, resp. the C_i) to be pairwise distinct.

We write $heads(\Phi)$ for the set of all atoms occurring in rule heads in Φ: these are atoms that are *possibly true*. By *pure* disjunctions we mean disjunctions consisting solely of positive or solely of negative literals. We also want to allow *integrity constraints*, i.e. rules with empty heads ($l = 0$). This will sometimes lead to inconsistent programs of course, i.e. a program Φ may semantically imply both a proposition and its negation.

Definition 2 (Operator $\vdash\!\!\sim$, Semantics $S_{\vdash\!\!\sim}$).
By a semantic operator $\vdash\!\!\sim$ we mean a binary relation between logic programs and pure disjunctions which satisfies the following three arguably obvious conditions:

(1) *Right Weakening:* If $\Phi \vdash\!\!\sim \psi$ and $\psi \subseteq \psi'$ (i.e. ψ is a subdisjunction of ψ'),
then $\Phi \vdash\!\!\sim \psi'$.
(2) *Necessarily True:* If $(\mathcal{A} \leftarrow) \in \Phi$ for a disjunction $\mathcal{A}$, then $\Phi \vdash\!\!\sim \mathcal{A}$.
(3) *Necessarily False:* If $A \notin heads(\Phi)$ for some Σ-ground atom A,
then $\Phi \vdash\!\!\sim \neg A$.

Given such an operator $\vdash\!\!\sim$ and a logic program Φ, by the semantics $S_{\vdash\!\!\sim}(\Phi)$ of Φ determined by $\vdash\!\!\sim$ we mean the set of all pure disjunctions derivable by $\vdash\!\!\sim$ from Φ, i.e. $S_{\vdash\!\!\sim}(\Phi) := \{\psi \mid \Phi \vdash\!\!\sim \psi\}$.

Note that both *model-based* as well as *completion-based* approaches fit well into this framework, because these approaches provide in a natural way a set of *derivable* disjunctions. We simply take the sceptical view: truth in all intended models or in all models of the completion. In this respect, we contribute to the discussion about the usefulness of model theory. On the one hand, our approach is not against model theory. But on the other hand, we do not explicitly need a model theory.

In addition to satisfying the general conditions from Definition 2, we may want a specific semantic operator $\vdash$ to be invariant under certain *natural* program transformations. So, we will give a set of reasonable transformation rules in the sequel.

Definition 3 (Invariance of $\vdash$ under a Transformation).
Suppose that a program transformation *Trans* is given. We view such a transformation as a relation (not necessarily a function) which specifies under what conditions a program Φ is a transformation of another program Φ'. To facilitate notation we also write such a transformation sometimes as a function *Trans* : $\Phi \mapsto Trans(\Phi)$, mapping logic programs into logic programs. In general, however, a particular transformation can be applied in different ways to a program so that $Trans(\Phi)$ is not uniquely defined. We say that the operator $\vdash$ is invariant under *Trans* (or that *Trans* is a $\vdash$-equivalence transformation) iff

$$\Phi \vdash \psi \iff Trans(\Phi) \vdash \psi$$

for any pure disjunction ψ and any program Φ.

Why do we only consider *pure* disjunctions? This is simply because we are interested in the sceptical viewpoint and therefore we can not assume that any semantics is given as a set of models. For example, SLDNF-like semantics usually are given in proof-theoretic terms. In order to be as general as possible—i.e. to cover as many semantics as possible in our framework—, we can only assume that a semantics provides us at least with the notion of deriving arbitrary conjunctions of either positive or either negative literals and of negations of these conjunctions. But these are exactly the pure disjunctions. Some semantics simply do not define what it means to derive a mixed disjunction.

3 D-WFS for ground programs

We now describe several transformations *Trans* which will be later used to define the D-WFS semantics. By abuse of language (and to facilitate reading) we will simply say "$\vdash$ satisfies *Trans*" meaning that "$\vdash$ is invariant under *Trans*". A more complete discussion of our calculus can be found in [BD96,BD97a,BD95b].

3.1 The Calculus of Transformations

We begin with partial evaluation in the sense of the "unfolding" operation. It is the *generalised principle of partial evaluation* (GPPE) [BD94,SS95]:

Definition 4 (GPPE).

A Semantics $S_{\hspace{-2pt}\sim}$ satisfies GPPE iff it is invariant under the following transformation: *Replace a rule $A \leftarrow B \wedge \neg C$ where B contains a distinguished atom B by the rules*

$$A \cup (A_i - \{B\}) \leftarrow (B - \{B\}) \cup B_i \wedge \neg(C \cup C_i) \quad (i = 1, \ldots, k)$$

where $A_i \leftarrow B_i \wedge \neg C_i$ $(i = 1, \ldots, k)$ are *all* the rules with $B \in A_i$.

Note that we are free to select a specific positive occurrence of an atom B and then perform the transformation: this is just to say that the GPPE-transformation is a relation between programs. It is uniquely determined only if we fix a specific occurrence of an atom that we want to replace. The new rules are obtained by replacing B by the bodies of all rules r with head literal B and adding the remaining head atoms of r to the head of the new rule. GPPE also covers the degenerate case when the atom B to be replaced does not appear in any head: then the whole rule is simply deleted.

The next transformation, *elimination of tautologies*, states that tautological clauses like $p \leftarrow p$ do not influence the semantics of a logic program. With the help of *elimination of non-minimal rules* we can get rid of clauses that are subsumed by others.

Definition 5 (Elimination of Tautologies, Non-Minimal Rules).

A semantics $S_{\hspace{-2pt}\sim}$ satisfies the *elimination of tautologies* (TAUT), resp. the *elimination of non-minimal rules* (NMIN) iff $\hspace{-2pt}\sim$ is invariant under the following transformations:

(TAUT) Delete a rule $A \leftarrow B \wedge \neg C$ with $A \cap B \neq \emptyset$.
(NMIN) Delete a rule $A \leftarrow B \wedge \neg C$ if there is another rule $A' \leftarrow B' \wedge \neg C'$ with $A' \subseteq A$, $B' \subseteq B$, and $C' \subseteq C$.

The last two transformations (stated below) allow us to do some simple reductions. We want $\neg L$ to be derivable if L appears in no rule head. Therefore, it should be possible to evaluate the body literal $\neg L$ to true, i.e. to delete $\neg L$ from all rule bodies: this is guaranteed by *positive reduction*. Conversely, if the logic program contains a disjunctive fact $(A_1 \vee \cdots \vee A_k \leftarrow)$, at least one of the atoms occurring in it must be true, so a rule body containing $\neg A_1 \wedge \cdots \wedge \neg A_k$ is surely false, so the entire rule is useless, and it should be possible to delete it: this gives us *negative reduction*.

Definition 6 (Positive and Negative Reduction).

Semantics $S_{\hspace{-2pt}\sim}$ satisfies *positive reduction* (RED$^+$), resp. *negative reduction* (RED$^-$) iff $\hspace{-2pt}\sim$ is invariant under the following transformations:

(RED$^+$) Replace a rule $A \leftarrow B \wedge \neg C$ by $A \leftarrow B \wedge \neg(C \cap heads(\Phi))$.
(RED$^-$) Delete a rule $A \leftarrow B \wedge \neg C$ if there is a rule $(A' \leftarrow)$ with $A' \subseteq C$.

3.2 Finite Ground Programs

If our programs are finite, our calculus has some very nice properties:

Theorem 7 (Confluence and Termination [BD96]).
Our calculus of transformations is confluent and terminating for finite ground programs, i.e. if $\Phi \to^* \Phi'$ and $\Phi \to^* \Phi''$ and both Φ', Φ'' are irreducible, then $\Phi' = \Phi''$. In addition, for any program Φ there is an irreducible Φ' with $\Phi \to^* \Phi'$. We call such irreducible Φ' the residual program $res(\Phi)$ from Φ.

Originally, the semantics D-WFS has been defined as follows:

Theorem 8 (D-WFS [BD97b]).
There exists the weakest semantics $S_{\vdash}$ which is invariant under GPPE, Elimination of Tautologies and Non-Minimal Rules, Positive and Negative Reduction. Moreover, this semantics is consistent (i.e. it does not derive a literal A and its negation $\neg A$) and closed under logical consequences (as a set consisting of pure disjunctions). We call it the Disjunctive Well-Founded Semantics, or, briefly, D-WFS. It coincides with the well-founded semantics WFS for normal and with GCWA for positive disjunctive programs.

With the help of our calculus and the residual program, we can compute D-WFS quite nicely:

Theorem 9 (Completeness of D-WFS wrt. $res(\Phi)$ [BD97b]).
$\Phi \vdash_{D-WFS} \psi \iff$ *there is $A \subseteq \psi$ with $(A \leftarrow) \in res(\Phi)$ or*
there is $\neg A \in \psi$ and $A \notin heads(res(\Phi))$.

This theorem is especially important. It tells us that once the residual program $res(\Phi)$ has been produced, the semantics D-WFS can be immediately determined. In fact, $res(\Phi)$ contains enough information to compute the stable semantics by hyper-resolution (see [BD95a]).

3.3 Infinite Ground Programs

What happens if our programs are infinite? Our transformations are also defined for infinite programs but it is not guaranteed that the calculus always terminates. We consider the program

$$p(x) \leftarrow p(s(x))$$

or the corresponding infinite propositional program P_{loop}

$$p_0 \leftarrow p_1, \; p_1 \leftarrow p_2, \; \dots, p_i \leftarrow p_{i+1}, \dots$$

which can be seen as the full instantiation of the former program. Our GPPE can not "unfold" such an infinite loop and eliminate all these rules. To do this, something like an ω-inference rule is needed which is not a constructive rule. Of course we can try to define a particular *loop detection*—see Definition 10 and the remarks in Subsection 6.1—, but since the general problem is undecidable, there is no constructive solution in general. If the above loop is finite, this can be recognised in a finite number of steps and D-WFS does this.

Although the very definition of D-WFS given in Theorem 8 does not depend on finite programs, we can not just use this formulation for arbitrary programs. This is because the resulting semantics would not extend WFS or GCWA in that case. The weakest such semantics would simply derive nothing from P_{loop}, instead of $\{\neg p_0, \neg p_1, \ldots, \neg p_i, \ldots\}$. The reason is that for infinite programs we can not always get rid of all the positive body atoms—like in P_{loop}. But this was the main achievement of the residual program in Theorem 9: the residual program contains only negative literals in the body.

For infinite ground programs our GPPE is a transformation replacing a rule by a possibly *infinite* set of other rules. It can now happen that infinite applications of GPPE exist or do not exist. Let us shortly illustrate this. We apply GPPE to P_{loop} to replace first p_1 in the first rule. Then we replace p_2 in the second rule and so on (i.e. replacing p_i in the i-th rule). We get a sequence of programs that converges:

$$
\begin{array}{lllll}
P_{loop}: & P_1: & P_2: & P_i: & P_\omega: \\
p_0 \leftarrow p_1 & p_0 \leftarrow p_2 & p_0 \leftarrow p_2 & p_0 \leftarrow p_2 & p_0 \leftarrow p_2 \\
p_1 \leftarrow p_2 & p_1 \leftarrow p_2 & p_1 \leftarrow p_3 & p_1 \leftarrow p_3 & p_1 \leftarrow p_3 \\
p_2 \leftarrow p_3 & p_2 \leftarrow p_3 & p_2 \leftarrow p_3 \quad \cdots & \vdots \quad \cdots & p_2 \leftarrow p_4 \\
\vdots & \vdots & \vdots & p_{i-1} \leftarrow p_{i+1} & \vdots \\
p_i \leftarrow p_{i+1} & p_i \leftarrow p_{i+1} & p_i \leftarrow p_{i+1} & p_i \leftarrow p_{i+1} & p_i \leftarrow p_{i+2} \\
\vdots & \vdots & \vdots & \vdots & \vdots
\end{array}
$$

But if we first replace p_1 in all rules, and then p_2 in all rules and so on (i.e. replacing p_i in the first i rules with i-fold application of GPPE), we get a non-converging series of programs:

$$
\begin{array}{llll}
P_{loop}: & P_1': & P_2': & P_i': \\
p_0 \leftarrow p_1 & p_0 \leftarrow p_2 & p_0 \leftarrow p_3 & p_0 \leftarrow p_i \\
p_1 \leftarrow p_2 & p_1 \leftarrow p_2 & p_1 \leftarrow p_3 & p_1 \leftarrow p_i \\
p_2 \leftarrow p_3 & p_2 \leftarrow p_3 & p_2 \leftarrow p_3 \quad \cdots & \vdots \quad \cdots \\
\vdots & \vdots & \vdots & p_{i-1} \leftarrow p_i \\
p_i \leftarrow p_{i+1} & p_i \leftarrow p_{i+1} & p_i \leftarrow p_{i+1} & p_i \leftarrow p_{i+1} \\
\vdots & \vdots & \vdots & \vdots
\end{array}
$$

Nevertheless we allow the infinite application of our rules, if it leads to a well-defined program. We can now formulate a non-constructive rule which is similar to condition (3) of Definition 2:

Definition 10 (Loop-Detection Rule).
Let A be an atom and Φ be a program. Delete all rules $(A \leftarrow B \land \neg C) \in \Phi$ with

$A \in \mathcal{A}$, if for all Φ' with $\Phi \rightarrow^* \Phi'$ it is $\mathcal{B} \neq \emptyset$ for all $(\mathcal{A}' \leftarrow \mathcal{B}' \wedge \neg \mathcal{C}') \in \Phi'$ with $A \in \mathcal{A}'$.

In the above rule, "$\rightarrow^*$" denotes the transitive closure of the transformations GPPE, TAUT, NMIN, RED$^+$ and RED$^-$. Of course, an application of the loop-detection rule can allow new applications of the other rules. Therefore, we denote with "$\rightarrow^*$" by now the transitive closure of all our rules (including loop-detection).

This rule formalises the intuition that if an atom always (and forever) depends positively on other atoms, then they all should be considered false: this is obviously true for WFS and GCWA. We are now in a position to generalise D-WFS:

Theorem 11 (D-WFS for Infinite Programs).
There exists the weakest semantics $S_{\vdash}$ which is invariant under GPPE, elimination of tautologies and non-minimal rules, positive and negative reduction and satisfies the loop-detection rule. Moreover, this semantics is consistent (i.e. it does not derive a literal A and its negation $\neg A$) and closed under logical consequences (as a set consisting of pure disjunctions). It extends D-WFS from Theorem 9 and is therefore also called D-WFS. It coincides with the well-founded semantics WFS for normal and with GCWA for positive disjunctive programs.

We also have the subsequent confluence result. We will later comment on how approximations of the loop-detection rule can be constructively incorporated in our calculus (see Section 6).

Theorem 12 (Confluence for Infinite Programs).
Our set of transformations is confluent for infinite ground programs, i.e. if $\Phi \rightarrow^* \Phi'$ and $\Phi \rightarrow^* \Phi''$ and both Φ', Φ'' are irreducible, then $\Phi' = \Phi''$. If a program Φ' is irreducible, then D-WFS can be computed by using the characterisation given in Corollary 9.

4 Non-Ground Programs

What are the problems to extend our transformations to first-order programs? One of the main problems is already *built-in* in Definition 1 where we identified a rule with *sets* of atoms: this means that we do not allow for duplicate occurrences. This is not just a technical point: without this restriction, GPPE would not even be a *sound* transformation.

Example 13 (Duplicate Occurrences and GPPE).
In the following program Φ we apply the GPPE and obtain $GPPE_B(\Phi)$.

$$\Phi : A \leftarrow B \qquad GPPE_B(\Phi) : A \vee B \leftarrow$$
$$B \vee B \leftarrow \qquad\qquad\qquad B \vee B \leftarrow$$

$GPPE_B(\Phi)$ is irreducible, or even worse, if $B \vee B$ is identified with B, it reduces to "$B \leftarrow$" only. ("$A \vee B \leftarrow$" is deleted because of NMIN). In any case, if we apply the characterisation given in Corollary 9 we can no more derive A, although this is derivable by D-WFS.

Example 14 (First-Order Program).
In the last example the problem does not occur if we replace $B \vee B$ by B. But similar problems can occur for first-order programs. Suppose we have the program

$$\Phi : \quad \begin{array}{ll} p(x) & \leftarrow q(x) \quad (1) \\ q(x) \vee q(a) \leftarrow & \quad (2) \end{array}$$

and we want to replace $q(x)$ in the first clause. If we do this without taking care of the variables, we get

$$\begin{array}{ll} p(x) \vee q(a) \leftarrow & (1^*) \\ p(a) \vee q(x) \leftarrow & (1^{**}) \\ q(x) \vee q(a) \leftarrow & (2) \end{array}$$

from which $p(a)$ is not derivable, although it should! In order to make the GPPE sound we should split the rule (2) $q(x) \vee q(a) \leftarrow$ into two rules

$$\begin{array}{ll} p(x) & \leftarrow q(x) & (1) \\ q(x) \vee q(a) \leftarrow & / \; x \neq a & (2') \\ q(a) & \leftarrow & (2'') \end{array}$$

such that we now can apply the GPPE in a sound way:

$$\begin{array}{ll} p(x) \vee q(a) \leftarrow & / \; x \neq a & (1') \\ p(a) \vee q(x) \leftarrow & / \; x \neq a & (1'') \\ p(a) & \leftarrow & (1''') \\ q(x) \vee q(a) \leftarrow & / \; x \neq a & (2') \\ q(a) & \leftarrow & (2'') \end{array}$$

Therefore we are forced to generalise our rules by adding *equational constraints*. These constraints are not only equations and their negations as in Prolog II [Col86], but also conjunctions, disjunctions and universally quantified formulae of them (see [Mah88,CL89]). Such constructs arise when we generalise our transformations and take care of the associated constraints. In order to perform the splitting as explained above, we have to introduce a factorisation rule which will be formally defined in Definition 17.

By an extended version of the non-minimal rule (see Definition 24) we can finally reduce Φ to what one may expect, namely:

$$\begin{array}{ll} p(a) \leftarrow & (1''') \\ q(a) \leftarrow & (2'') \end{array}$$

In Subsection 4.1 we extend our framework to disjunctive programs with constraints. In Subsection 4.2 we introduce the *Head Atoms*, the *Factorisation* and add some remarks about *constraint simplification* in general in Section 4.3.

4.1 Constraint Disjunctive Logic Programs

Equational Constraints are introduced and discussed in detail in [Mah88,CL89]. There, it is shown that the satisfiability problem for equational constraints is decidable. [CL89] presents also a complete simplification algorithm for equational constraints, formulated by some rewrite rules. [Mah88] gives a more abstract quantifier elimination procedure.

We will now state the theoretical framework for computing non-ground disjunctive well-founded semantics and start with the definition of the syntax for equational constraints. The equality theory in our context is just syntactical equality.

Definition 15 (Equational Constraints $\mathcal{E}$).
Let V be a set of variables and F a set of function symbols. Then $T(F,V)$ denotes the set of terms over F and V as usual. We define the set of *equational constraints* $\mathcal{E}$ as the smallest set satisfying the following properties:

1. $\perp, \top \in \mathcal{E}$.
2. For all $s, t \in T(F,V)$, $s = t \in \mathcal{E}$.
3. If $R, R' \in \mathcal{E}$ and $x \in V$, then $\neg R, R \wedge R', R \vee R', \exists x R, \forall x R$ are in $\mathcal{E}$.

To facilitate reading, we write $s \neq t$ for $\neg(s = t)$, and $R \to R'$ for $\neg R \vee R'$. We are now able to lift the notion of disjunctive logic program to the non-ground case, by defining a *disjunctive logic program* Φ as a finite set of (not necessarily ground) rules

$$(A_1 \vee \cdots \vee A_l) \leftarrow (B_1 \wedge \cdots \wedge B_m) \wedge (\neg C_1 \wedge \cdots \wedge \neg C_n)$$

where $l \geq 1$ and $m, n \geq 0$. It is often abbreviated as $\mathcal{A} \leftarrow \mathcal{B} \wedge \neg \mathcal{C}$. We will identify $\mathcal{A}$, $\mathcal{B}$ and $\mathcal{C}$ by their sets of atoms $\{A_1, \ldots, A_l\}$, $\{B_1, \ldots, B_m\}$ and $\{C_1, \ldots, C_n\}$, respectively. An atom has the form $p(t_1, \ldots, t_k)$ where $t_1, \ldots, t_k \in T(F,V)$, and p stems from a finite set of predicate symbols.

The next definition introduces a further variant with equational constraints. We always assume that all constraint programs and rules are normalised (see Definition 18). For this, we need the definitions of two transformation rules: elimination of tautologies TAUT and factorisation FACTOR. Both rules are *local*, i.e. they do not refer to the whole rule set. Therefore they can be implemented efficiently. Thus, it makes sense to integrate them into the normalisation process.

Definition 16 (Non-Ground Constraint Disjunctive Logic Program).
A *constraint disjunctive logic program* Φ (or just *constraint program* for short) is a finite set of *rules* of the form

$$L \,/\, R$$

where L is a (not necessarily ground) disjunctive rule but without function symbols occurring in L, and R is an equational constraint.

Definition 17 (TAUT-, FACTOR- and MERGE-rules).
We first introduce elimination of tautologies, factorisation and the MERGE rule. Using these rules we define the normalisations of constraint rules and programs.

(TAUT) We a replace the rule $A \leftarrow \mathcal{B} \wedge \neg \mathcal{C} \ / \ R$ by $A \leftarrow \mathcal{B} \wedge \neg \mathcal{C} \ / \ R \wedge (A \neq B)$ where $A \in \mathcal{A}$ and $B \in \mathcal{B}$ are atoms with the same predicate symbol.

(FACTOR) Let $\mathcal{A} \leftarrow \mathcal{B} \wedge \neg \mathcal{C} \ / \ R$ be a rule, and $A, B \in \mathcal{A}$ atoms with the same predicate symbol, i.e. they have the form $A = p(x_1, \ldots, x_k)$ and $B = p(y_1, \ldots, y_k)$. Then the two rules

$$\mathcal{A} \leftarrow \mathcal{B} \wedge \neg \mathcal{C} \ / \ R \wedge (A \neq B)$$
$$(\mathcal{A} - \{B\}) \leftarrow \mathcal{B} \wedge \neg \mathcal{C} \ / \ R \wedge (A = B)$$

are the *factorisation* of $L \ / \ R$. Here, $A = B$ means $x_1 = y_1 \wedge \cdots \wedge x_k = y_k$, and $A \neq B$ means $x_1 \neq y_1 \vee \cdots \vee x_k \neq y_k$.

(MERGE) Let $\mathcal{A} \leftarrow \mathcal{B} \wedge \neg \mathcal{C} \ / \ R$ and $\mathcal{A}' \leftarrow \mathcal{B}' \wedge \neg \mathcal{C}' \ / \ R'$ be variants of program rules such that $\mathcal{A} = \mathcal{A}'$, $\mathcal{B} = \mathcal{B}'$, and $\mathcal{C} = \mathcal{C}'$. Then we can replace the original program rules by:

$$\mathcal{A} \leftarrow \mathcal{B} \wedge \neg \mathcal{C} \ / \ R \vee R'$$

It is important to notice, that two rules which are merged by the MERGE-rule may be variants of one and the same rule. We need this in order to establish a strong notion of equivalence for irreducible and normalised constraint programs. Two programs Φ and Φ' are called strongly equivalent (written $\Phi \equiv \Phi'$) iff there is a bijection between the respective finite sets of rules such that any corresponding rules are equal. Two rules are called equal iff their corresponding atom sets are variants of each other, and the constraints renamed accordingly are equivalent. Let us consider the two programs

$$\Phi_1 : p(x) \vee p(y) \leftarrow \ / \ (x = a \wedge y = b) \vee (x = c \vee y = d)$$
$$\Phi_2 : p(x) \vee p(y) \leftarrow \ / \ (x = a \wedge y = b) \vee (x = d \wedge y = c)$$

which are not equivalent in the strong sense. This is left as an exercise to the reader. Nevertheless, their ground instantiations are identical, namely

$$\Phi_{ground} = \{p(a) \vee p(b) \leftarrow, \qquad p(c) \vee p(d) \leftarrow \}$$

which means they are equivalent in a weaker sense. However, if we apply MERGE on Φ_1 and Φ_2, respectively, then we get in both cases

$$p(x) \vee p(y) \leftarrow \quad / \ (x = a \wedge y = b) \vee (x = c \wedge y = d) \vee (x = b \wedge y = a) \vee (x = d \wedge y = c)$$

which means $MERGE(\Phi_1) \equiv MERGE(\Phi_2)$.

Definition 18 (Normalisation).
A constraint rule L/R is *normalised* by

1. existentially quantifying all free variables in R not occurring in L with $\exists$,
2. applying TAUT where possible, and
3. performing FACTOR as long as possible.

A constraint program Φ is *normalised* by

1. normalising all rules in the program, and
2. applying the MERGE-rule as long as possible.

We can easily associate to each non-ground constraint disjunctive logic program Φ a possibly infinite ground program. For this, we identify each rule $L \, / \, R$ with all $L\sigma$ where σ is a solution of the constraint R, i.e. a substitution that maps the free variables in R to ground terms. But we also have to think about another problem: how can we translate a non-ground disjunctive logic program to one with constraints? The answer is given by the following definition.

Definition 19 (Variable Abstraction).
We associate with each disjunctive logic program Φ a constraint disjunctive logic program Φ' as follows. For a rule L in Φ, let L' be the result of replacing each argument t of a predicate in L by a fresh variable x. Then Φ' contains the rule

$$L' \, / \, \bigwedge_{x \in var(L')} (x = t)$$

for each rule L in Φ. Here, $var(E)$ denotes the set of all (free) variables occurring in the expression E. In addition, each rule has to be replaced by its normalisation introduced in Definition 17.

Before stating more formal definitions, we illustrate what is going on with the following example.

Example 20 (Running Example).
Consider the program

$$\Phi_0 : \quad \begin{aligned} p(0) &\leftarrow \\ p(x) &\leftarrow \neg p(x) \wedge \neg p(s(x)) \\ p(s(x)) \vee p(s(s(x))) &\leftarrow \\ q(0) &\leftarrow p(x) \wedge \neg q(x) \end{aligned}$$

which is translated into

$$\Phi_1 : \quad \begin{aligned} p(x) &\leftarrow & / \; x = 0 & \quad (1) \\ p(x) &\leftarrow \neg p(x) \wedge \neg p(y) & / \; y = s(x) & \quad (2) \\ p(u) \vee p(v) &\leftarrow & / \; \exists x : u = s(x) \wedge v = s(s(x)) & \quad (3) \\ q(w) &\leftarrow p(x) \wedge \neg q(x) & / \; w = 0 & \quad (4) \end{aligned}$$

by variable abstraction. Note that we will sometimes write rules in a form without variable abstraction in order to keep notation shorter. Our infinite ground program P_{loop} from Subsection 3.3 can now be written easily as

$$\Phi_{loop} : p(x) \leftarrow p(y) \; / \; y = s(x)$$

4.2 Head Atoms and Simplification

One of the most important results of Section 3.2 was the definition of the residual program and Theorem 9. Using these notions we can do query answering by just looking at the *head atoms* of the residual program. In order to define an analogue of $heads(\Phi)$ for constraint programs, we need

Definition 21 (Head-Atoms $heads(\Phi)$).
For a constraint program Φ, we define the *possibly true facts* $heads(\Phi)$ (or *head atoms*) as the smallest set $heads(\Phi)$ satisfying the condition:

If $(A \leftarrow \mathcal{B} \wedge \neg \mathcal{C}) \, / \, R$ is a rule in Φ, and $A \in \mathcal{A}$ then $A \, / \, (\exists \bar{x} \, R)$ where $\bar{x} = var(R) - var(A)$ is also contained in $heads(\Phi)$.

The set of constraint atoms has to be normalised. For all predicate symbols A', not used so far, we add $A'/\bot$.

Note, that $heads(\Phi)$ is finite because Φ is finite. For our example, the possibly true facts are as follows. The constraints are given in an already simplified form here.

$$p(x) \, / \, x = 0 \vee \top \vee \exists z \, x = s(z) \vee \exists z \, x = s(s(z))$$
$$q(y) \, / \, y = 0$$

An important feature while handling constraints is to *simplify* them, i.e. rewriting them into "simpler" ones while preserving equivalence. Since the underlying equational constraint theory is monotonic, simplification can be performed at any time. If a constraint R in a rule reduces to $\bot$, then the respective rule can be discarded. We have to distinguish two cases:

- If the set of function symbols F is infinite, then Clark's axiomatisation of the Herbrand domain yields a satisfaction-complete constraint theory for equational constraints. In this case, basic equational constraints (i.e. unification equations of the form $s = t$, but not general equational constraints) enjoy the independence of negative constraints property:

$$\mathcal{E} \models \exists (R \wedge \neg R_1 \wedge \cdots \wedge \neg R_k) \iff \mathcal{E} \models \exists (R \wedge \neg R_i) \text{ for } 1 \le i \le k$$

This is equivalent to the *very strong completeness* property, i.e. we can restrict to only one derivation while answering any query, provided that we do not have any inequalities. For details, the reader is referred to [Mah93].
- If we assume the set of function symbols F to be finite, then we need the *weak domain closure axiom* in order to make our theory complete [Mah88]:

$$\forall x \bigvee_{f \in F} \exists \bar{z} \, x = f(\bar{z})$$

This case is mainly considered in [CL89]. But this point of view is restricted to Herbrand models only and increases the computational complexity. Because of this we will assume that F is infinite in the sequel.

4.3 Reasoning with Arbitrary Constraint Theories

Until now we only considered equational constraints (Definition 15). But our framework can easily be generalised for arbitrary constraint systems and theories. Thus, we are not restricted to equality constraints over the Herbrand domain. We may consider other domains and other constraints predicates besides $=$. Surprisingly, all definitions (including the transformation rules introduced in Section 5) can also be applied to the general case. Here is the general definition of a constraint system.

Definition 22 (Constraint System).
A *constraint system* (often identified by its constraint theory $\mathcal{T}$, see below) consists of four components:

- a domain D, that is a non-empty set,
- an alphabet Δ, including a set V of variables, the equality symbol $=$ which has to be interpreted by the equality relation on D and the constants $\bot$ and $\top$ with the meaning "false" and "true", respectively,
- a set $\mathcal{R}$ of (open) Δ-formulae, called *constraints*, including all atomic Δ-formulae and closed under all logical connective, i.e. especially negation $\neg$, and
- the constraint theory $\mathcal{T}$; $\mathcal{T}$ should be *satisfaction-complete*, i.e. for all constraint formulae $R \in \mathcal{R}$ either $\mathcal{T} \models R$ or $\mathcal{T} \models \neg R$ holds; therefore we can identify $\mathcal{T}$ with a Δ-interpretation.

The main difference to conventional constraint logic programming is the requirement that the set of constraint-formulae must be closed not only under conjunction $\wedge$, existential quantification $\exists$ and instantiation of variables—as stated in [JM94]—but under all logical connectives. We will see that this is necessary because of the first-order versions of the NMIN, RED$^+$ and RED$^-$ rules in Definition 24. Thus, the respective constraint solvers must be able to treat negative constraints of the considered constraint domain. For example, we could do nonmonotonic reasoning with integer domain constraints. Example 20 can easily be viewed as such a problem:

$$
\begin{array}{lll}
p(x) & \leftarrow & / \ x = 0 & (1) \\
p(x) & \leftarrow \neg p(x) \wedge \neg p(y) & / \ y = x + 1 & (2) \\
p(u) \vee p(v) \leftarrow & / \ u \geq 1 \wedge v = u + 1 & (3) \\
q(w) & \leftarrow p(x) \wedge \neg q(x) & / \ w = 0 & (4)
\end{array}
$$

Now we are also in a position to extend our notion of a semantics for ground programs (Definition 2) straightforwardly to one for constraint disjunctive programs. We say that a constraint disjunctive rule $\mathcal{A} \ / \ R$ subsumes another rule $\mathcal{A}' \ / \ R'$ if there is a variant $\mathcal{A}'' \ / \ R''$ of $\mathcal{A} \ / \ R$ such that $\mathcal{A}'' \subseteq \mathcal{A}'$ and $\forall (R'' \rightarrow R')$.

Definition 23 (Operator $\mathrel{\vdash\!\!\!\sim}$, Semantics $\mathcal{S}_{\mathrel{\vdash\!\!\!\sim}}$).
By a semantic operator $\mathrel{\vdash\!\!\!\sim}$ we mean a binary relation between constraint disjunctive logic programs and pure constraint disjunctions which satisfies the following three conditions:

(1) *Right Weakening:* If $\Phi \mathrel{\vdash\!\!\!\sim} L \mathbin{/} R$ and $L \mathbin{/} R$ subsumes $L' \mathbin{/} R'$,
   then $\Phi \mathrel{\vdash\!\!\!\sim} L' \mathbin{/} R'$.
(2) *Necessarily True:* If $(A \leftarrow \ / R) \in \Phi$ for a constraint disjunction $A \mathbin{/} R$,
   then $\Phi \mathrel{\vdash\!\!\!\sim} A \mathbin{/} R$.
(3) *Necessarily False:* Let $A \mathbin{/} R$ be a constraint atom. If there exists a variant A/R' of an atom in $heads(\Phi)$ and $\forall(R \to \neg R')$ (†), then $\Phi \mathrel{\vdash\!\!\!\sim} \neg A/R$.

   Given such an operator $\mathrel{\vdash\!\!\!\sim}$ and a constraint disjunctive program Φ, by the semantics $\mathcal{S}_{\mathrel{\vdash\!\!\!\sim}}(\Phi)$ of Φ (determined by $\mathrel{\vdash\!\!\!\sim}$) we mean the set of all constraint pure disjunctions derivable by $\mathrel{\vdash\!\!\!\sim}$ from Φ, i.e. $\mathcal{S}_{\mathrel{\vdash\!\!\!\sim}}(\Phi) := \{L \mathbin{/} R \mid \Phi \mathrel{\vdash\!\!\!\sim} L/R\}$.

5   A Calculus for Non-Ground Programs

We have now introduced all necessary machinery to extend our original calculus to constraint programs in Subsection 5.1: Our main results are Theorems 25, 26, 28, 29 and 31. In Subsection 5.2 we consider *query answering* and approximate Theorem 9.

5.1   Extending our Original Transformations

We are now able to state the transformation rules for the new calculus with constraints. We will state the rules in a very abstract way, i.e. without mentioning control of the applicability of the rules. But it is clear that our procedure cannot always terminate because of the undecidability of the underlying problem. Note that our former elimination of tautologies rule will be incorporated into GPPE by normalisation.

Definition 24 (Transformation Rules).
If

$$\mathcal{A} \leftarrow \mathcal{B} \wedge \neg \mathcal{C} \mathbin{/} R$$

is a rule in the constraint program Φ, then it can be replaced by one of the following (sets of) rules. Constraint simplification can be applied immediately on each newly generated rule.

(GPPE) (GPPE plus normalisation of rules)

   Replace the rule $\mathcal{A} \leftarrow \mathcal{B} \wedge \neg \mathcal{C} \mathbin{/} R$ by:

$$\mathcal{A} \cup (\mathcal{A}_1 - \{B\}) \leftarrow (\mathcal{B} - \{B\}) \cup \mathcal{B}_1 \wedge \neg(\mathcal{C} \cup \mathcal{C}_1) \ / \ R \wedge R_1$$
$$\vdots$$
$$\mathcal{A} \cup (\mathcal{A}_k - \{B\}) \leftarrow (\mathcal{B} - \{B\}) \cup \mathcal{B}_k \wedge \neg(\mathcal{C} \cup \mathcal{C}_k) \ / \ R \wedge R_k$$

for all variants of rules $\mathcal{A}_i \leftarrow \mathcal{B}_i \wedge \neg \mathcal{C}_i \ / \ R_i \ (1 \leq i \leq k)$ with $B \in \mathcal{A}_i$ where B is a distinguished atom in $\mathcal{B}$. Each generated rule is replaced immediately by its normalisation. Note, that FACTOR has only to be done with respect to the predicate symbol of B.

(NMIN) (Extended Elimination of Non-Minimal Rules)

Replace the rule $\mathcal{A} \leftarrow \mathcal{B} \wedge \neg \mathcal{C} \ / \ R$ by:

$$\mathcal{A} \leftarrow \mathcal{B} \wedge \neg \mathcal{C} \ / \ R \wedge \neg R'$$

for some variant $\mathcal{A}' \leftarrow \mathcal{B}' \wedge \neg \mathcal{C}' \ / \ R$ of a rule in Φ such that $\mathcal{A}' \subseteq \mathcal{A}$, $\mathcal{B}' \subseteq \mathcal{B}$ and $\mathcal{C}' \subseteq \mathcal{C}$ hold.

(RED$^+$) (Extended Positive Reduction)

Replace the rule $\mathcal{A} \leftarrow \mathcal{B} \wedge \neg \mathcal{C} \ / \ R$ by the two rules:

$$\mathcal{A} \leftarrow \mathcal{B} \wedge \neg \mathcal{C} \ / \ R \wedge R'$$
$$\mathcal{A} \leftarrow \mathcal{B} \wedge \neg(\mathcal{C} - \{C\}) \ / \ R \wedge \neg R'$$

where C is an atom in $\mathcal{C}$ and C'/R' is a variant of a constraint atom in $heads(\Phi)$ such that $C = C'$.

(RED$^-$) (Extended Negative Reduction)

Replace the rule $\mathcal{A} \leftarrow \mathcal{B} \wedge \neg \mathcal{C} \ / \ R$ by:

$$\mathcal{A} \leftarrow \mathcal{B} \wedge \neg \mathcal{C} \ / \ R \wedge \neg R'$$

for some variant $\mathcal{A}' \leftarrow \ / \ R'$ of a rule in Φ such that $\mathcal{A}' \subseteq \mathcal{C}$.

We will now state a derivation for Example 20. We start with RED$^-$ on (2) with clause (3). This causes the replacement of (2) by:

$$p(x) \leftarrow \neg p(x) \wedge \neg p(y) \ / \ y = s(x) \wedge \neg \exists z (x = s(z) \wedge y = s(s(z))) \qquad (2')$$

After applying the non-minimal rule with (1) which is essentially subsumption, the constraint can be simplified to $y = s(x) \wedge x \neq 0 \wedge \forall z \ x \neq s(z)$. This could be further simplified to $\bot$ if we assume that F is finite, i.e. $F = \{0, s\}$.

Since for the predicate q only $q(0)$ is in the set of possibly true facts, we can replace (4) with

$$q(w) \leftarrow p(x) \wedge \neg q(x) \; / \; w = 0 \wedge x = 0 \qquad (4')$$

by RED$^+$. Applying the GPPE on $p(x)$ (where $x = 0$) we get finally:

$$q(w) \leftarrow \neg q(x) \; / \; w = 0 \wedge x = 0 \qquad (4'')$$

When the reader compares Definition 24 with Section 3.1, then we notice that (1) TAUT has been integrated into the GPPE, and (2) RED$^+$ has been turned into a more flexible incremental rule. Especially (1) defines some problems away one may have with the proof of the following important Theorem 25. After that, we can state an analogue of Theorem 8.

Theorem 25 (Confluence).
Let Φ be a constraint disjunctive logic program. The relation $\rightarrow$, given by the transformation rules in Definition 24, is confluent, i.e. $\Phi \rightarrow^* \Phi_1$ and $\Phi \rightarrow^* \Phi_2$ where both Φ_1 and Φ_2 are irreducible implies $\Phi_1 \equiv \Phi_2$. However, there does not always exist an irreducible program Φ' with $\Phi \rightarrow^* \Phi'$.

Theorem 26 (CD-WFS).
For the class of all constraint disjunctive programs Φ that possess an irreducible program Φ' with $\Phi \rightarrow^* \Phi'$, there exists the weakest semantics $S_{\vdash}$ which is invariant under GPPE, elimination of non-minimal rules, positive and negative reduction. We call it the Constraint Disjunctive Well-Founded Semantics, or, briefly, CD-WFS and abbreviate it by $\vdash_{CD-WFS}$.

We could have also defined the semantics on the class of all programs. The reason we did not so is because then the semantics would be too weak compared with WFS or GCWA. For the program Φ_{loop} it would not derive anything, because Φ_{loop} does not have an irreducible program below it (we have not stated a loop-detection rule as we did for infinite ground programs (Definition 10). Of course, we aim to extend our definition to a larger class of programs. CD-WFS can be seen as a constructive approximation of D-WFS (see Theorem 31).

5.2   Residual Program and Query Answering

Now we can define a constructive approximation of D-WFS for non-ground programs. Since our procedure is not guaranteed to terminate we cannot always compute the residual program (see Definition 27). But when it exists, we can do *query answering* similar as in the case of D-WFS (Theorem 9). Before doing so, let us summarise the result of applying the transformation to our example. We end with an irreducible program.

$$
\begin{array}{rll}
res(\Phi): \quad p(x) & \leftarrow & / \; x = 0 \qquad\qquad\qquad\qquad (1) \\
p(x) & \leftarrow \neg p(x) \wedge \neg p(y) & \\
& / \; y = s(x) \wedge x \neq 0 \wedge \forall z \; x \neq s(z) & (2'') \\
p(u) \vee p(v) \leftarrow & & / \; \exists x : u = s(x) \wedge v = s(s(x)) \quad (3) \\
q(w) & \leftarrow \neg q(x) & / \; w = 0 \wedge x = 0 \qquad\qquad (4'')
\end{array}
$$

Definition 27 (Residual Program, Query).
A constraint program Φ is called a *residual program* if no transformation rules are applicable to it, i.e. if it is irreducible. A *query* ψ is a pure disjunction of literals. We identify it with its translation into the rule $L \, / \, R$ by variable abstraction.

Theorem 28 (Computation of CD-WFS).
Let Φ be a (variable abstraction of a disjunctive) program with the residual program $res(\Phi)$, and $\psi = L \, / \, R$ be a pure constraint disjunction. Then

$$\Phi \models_{\text{CD-WFS}} \psi$$

iff one of the following two cases applies

Case 1: *there is a rule $(A \leftarrow) \, / \, R$ in $res(\Phi)$ which subsumes ψ.*
Case 2: *L contains a negative literal $\neg A$ such that the condition (†) from Definition 23 holds.*

In the last theorem we started with checking a statement $\psi = L \, / \, R$ where R is a set of constraints. A more natural setting is given when we ask a query ψ with free variables and try to instantiate these variables in order to find solutions. Such query-answering can also be done.

Theorem 29 (Query Answering).
Let Φ be a (variable abstraction of a disjunctive) program with the residual program $res(\Phi)$, and ψ be a query with variable abstraction $L \, / \, R$. Then

$$\Phi \models_{\text{CD-WFS}} \psi[\delta]$$

iff δ is a solution of one of the following two constraints R^+ and R^-.

Case 1: *There is a rule $(A \leftarrow) \, / \, R$ in $res(\Phi)$, and $A \subseteq L_1 \cup \cdots \cup L_k$ where $L_1 \, / \, R_1, \ldots, L_k \, / \, R_k$ are different variants of $L \, / \, R$ and the constraint $R^+ = (R_1 \wedge \cdots \wedge R_k) \wedge R$ is satisfiable.*
Case 2: *L contains a negative literal $\neg A$ and condition (†) from Definition 23 holds. Then $R^- = R \wedge \neg R'$ is satisfiable.*

The solutions δ of the constraints are called *answers* of the query. If in the former case $k > 0$ holds, then the answer is called *disjunctive* or *indefinite*.

For our example it holds $p(0)$ and $\neg q(s(z))$, but neither $q(0)$ nor $\neg q(0)$ because $(4'')$ is a conditional fact. Sometimes it is not sufficient to look for only one rule while answering queries. For example, the query

$$p(x) \vee p(y) \, / \, (x = 0 \wedge y = 0) \vee \exists z (x = s(z) \wedge y = s(s(z)))$$

fails, although one should expect one positive answer. But we can split the query by factorisation and constraint simplification into:

$$p(x) \vee p(y) \, / \, x = y = 0$$
$$p(x) \vee p(y) \, / \, \exists z (x = s(z) \wedge y = s(s(z))) \wedge x \neq y$$

Then the former query has the answer $x = y = 0$ and the latter $\exists z (x = s(z) \wedge y = s(s(z)))$. Both answers can be combined to the desired disjunctive constraint of the original query. Nevertheless, the MERGE-rule helps us to bundle answers.

Example 30. Consider the program:

$$p(x) \leftarrow \qquad (1)$$
$$p(a) \leftarrow \qquad (2)$$

If we apply NMIN on (1) and variable abstraction on (2) we get:

$$p(x) \leftarrow \ / \ x \neq a \qquad (1')$$
$$p(x) \leftarrow \ / \ x = a \qquad (2')$$

But this would give us two answers for the query $p(z)$. However, the MERGE-rule yields

$$p(x) \leftarrow \ / \ x = a \vee x \neq a$$

which is clearly equivalent to (1) after constraint simplification. This is exactly what one should expect, because (2) can be deleted from the original program by NMIN on (2) with (1). Thus, the query $p(z)$ can now be answered positively by looking at the only remaining rule (1).

Finally we have the following relations of $\vdash_{CD-WFS}$ to other well-known non-monotonic semantics.

Theorem 31 (CD-WFS Related to Other Semantics).
Let Φ be a first-order disjunctive logic program, and ψ be a purely positive or negative clause. We identify Φ with its variable abstracted form, i.e. with its corresponding constraint program. We also assume that $res(\Phi)$ exists. Then the following holds:

1. *Let Φ_{inst} be the possibly infinite instantiation of Φ and ψ_{inst} the set of all ground instances of ψ. Then $\Phi \vdash_{CD-WFS} \psi$ iff $\Phi_{inst} \vdash_{D-WFS} \psi_{inst}$. In particular, if Φ is a ground program (i.e. there are only nullary predicate symbols in Φ), then $\Phi \vdash_{CD-WFS} \psi$ iff $\Phi \vdash_{D-WFS} \psi$).*
2. *If Φ is a positive disjunctive program (i.e. there are no negative literals in the body of any rule in Φ), then $\Phi \vdash_{CD-WFS} \psi$ iff $\Phi \vdash_{GCWA} \psi$.*
3. *If Φ is a normal program (i.e. any rule in Φ contains exactly one literal in its head), then $\Phi \vdash_{CD-WFS} \psi$ iff $\Phi \vdash_{WFS} \psi$.*

6 Conclusions

The careful reader may have noticed that we did not at all incorporate the *loop detection rule* into our framework. The reason is that this rule is essentially the only non-constructive rule that can only be approximated. For example Chen and Warren do such loop detection in their SLG or XSB system [CW95,CSW95,CW96] for non-disjunctive programs (under WFS and STABLE) by *tabling techniques*. However, the main focus of this paper was to introduce the constraint machinery and to combine it with our former calculus. Loop detection is beyond the scope of this paper and we only give some hints in the next subsection.

Another improvement is to apply the *relevance-property* (see [BD97a]). Relevance is the condition that a query does only depend on the subprogram formed by the call-graph below that query. This property holds for D-WFS [BD95a] and therefore, given a query Q we do not have to consider the whole residual program of ϕ, but only the relevant part of it with respect to the query. This often has the effect that this subprogram is much smaller than the original one.

6.1 Explicit Loop Detection

Obviously, by the undecidability of D-WFS, there are always cases where our procedure will not terminate. But sometimes we can overcome this problem. Let us consider the following example:

$$\Phi: \quad p(x) \quad \leftarrow p(s(x))$$
$$p(s(0))) \leftarrow$$

Applying the GPPE and NMIN we get:

$$\Phi': \quad p(x) \quad \leftarrow p(s(s(x))) \; / \; x \neq 0 \wedge x \neq s(0) \quad (*)$$
$$p(s(0)) \leftarrow$$
$$p(0) \quad \leftarrow$$

We notice, that the GPPE rule can be applied on $(*)$ again and again, although it is clear that only $p(0))$ and $p(s(0))$ hold in the D-WFS semantics for this example (and $\neg p(s^i(0))$ for all $i \geq 2$), because both facts cannot be replaced by any of the transformation rules. Here we need a sort of loop detection. As far as we know that GPPE can only be applied to the clause itself and that the corresponding term of the predicate to be replaced gets larger and larger, we can immediately delete such a rule—it will only cause an infinite loop that is not grounded. Such a deletion is in fact nothing but an approximation of the loop detection rule. Finally we get then the following residual program

$$res(\Phi) : p(s(0)) \leftarrow$$
$$p(0) \quad \leftarrow$$

from which D-WFS follows immediately. Of course such approximations need further investigation.

6.2 Outlook

Disjunctive logic programs are natural candidates for e.g. knowledge representation tasks. Often WFS for non-disjunctive programs is too weak. The possibility to explicitly write down disjunctive statements extends the expressive power and makes the formulation of many statements quite naturally. On the other hand, when such information is not needed, our semantics D-WFS coincides with WFS and hence shares its computational advantages. In contrast to the stable semantics, D-WFS is consistent and goal-directed since the GPPE acts top-down. For this, it seems a good idea to make the GPPE more incremental, i.e. to drop the requirement that all definitions of one predicate have to be inserted at once.

A constraint logic programming implementation is currently undertaken in ECLiPSe-Prolog [ECR95] at the University of Koblenz as part of the 4-year project on *Disjunctive Logic Programming* (see [DF96,ADN97] and http://www.uni-koblenz.de/ag-ki/DLP/). We expect to improve efficiency of nonmonotonic systems by exploiting constraint logic programming. For positive disjunctive logic programming, the advantage of such a combination has been shown e.g. in [ST96]. Termination criteria and control are currently elaborated more precisely and are subject of future research. But here for the first time, we have considered a framework for a non-ground disjunctive semantics.

We also mentioned in Subsection 4.3 that our framework can be even more generalised. It is possible to introduce more constraint predicates than just equality "=". But in contrast to usual constraint logic programming, the constraint language must be closed not only under conjunction and existential quantification, but under all logical connectives. In this respect, our work yields the basis for a general combination of two paradigms: constraint logic programming and non-monotonic reasoning. This would lead to a very powerful programming language.

References

[AD94]   Chandrabose Aravindan and Phan Minh Dung. Partial deduction of logic programs wrt well-founded semantics. *New Generation Computing*, 13:45–74, 1994.

[ADN97]   Chandrabose Aravindan, Jürgen Dix, and Ilkka Niemelä. The DisLoP-project. Technical Report TR 1/97, University of Koblenz, Department of Computer Science, Rheinau 1, January 1997.

[BD94]   Stefan Brass and Jürgen Dix. A disjunctive semantics based on unfolding and bottom-up evaluation. In Bernd Wolfinger, editor, *Innovationen bei Rechen- und Kommunikationssystemen*, (IFIP '94-Congress, Workshop FG2: Disjunctive Logic Programming and Disjunctive Databases), pages 83–91, Berlin, 1994. Springer.

[BD95a]   Stefan Brass and Jürgen Dix. A General Approach to Bottom-Up Computation of Disjunctive Semantics. In J. Dix, L. Pereira, and T. Przymusinski, editors, *Nonmonotonic Extensions of Logic Programming*, LNAI 927, pages 127–155. Springer, Berlin, 1995.

[BD95b]   Stefan Brass and Jürgen Dix. Disjunctive Semantics based upon Partial and Bottom-Up Evaluation. In Leon Sterling, editor, *Proceedings of the 12th Int. Conf. on Logic Programming, Tokyo*, pages 199–213. MIT Press, June 1995.

[BD96]   Stefan Brass and Jürgen Dix. Characterizing D-WFS: Confluence and Iterated GCWA. In L.M. Pereira J.J. Alferes and E. Orlowska, editors, *Logics in Artificial Intelligence (JELIA '96)*, LNCS 1126, pages 268–283.

Springer, 1996. (Extended version will appear in the *Journal of Automated Reasoning* in 1997.).

[BD97a] Stefan Brass and Jürgen Dix. Characterizations of the Disjunctive Stable Semantics by Partial Evaluation. *Journal of Logic Programming*, forthcoming, 1997. (Extended abstract appeared in: Characterizations of the Stable Semantics by Partial Evaluation *LPNMR, Proceedings of the Third International Conference, Kentucky*, pages 85–98, 1995. Springer.).

[BD97b] Stefan Brass and Jürgen Dix. Semantics of Disjunctive Logic Programs Based on Partial Evaluation. *Journal of Logic Programming*, accepted for publication, 1997. (Extended abstract appeared in: Disjunctive Semantics Based upon Partial and Bottom-Up Evaluation, *Proceedings of the 12-th International Logic Programming Conference, Tokyo*, pages 199–213, 1995. MIT Press.).

[CL89] Hubert Comon and Pierre Lescanne. Equational problems and disunification. *Journal of Symbolic Computation*, 7:371–425, 1989.

[Col86] Alain Colmerauer. Theoretical model of Prolog II. In Michel van Canegham and David H.D. Warren, editors, *Logic programming and its applications*, pages 3–31. Ablex Publishing Corporation, Norwood, NJ, 1986.

[CSW95] Weidong Chen, Terrance Swift, and David S. Warren. Efficient Top-Down Computation of Queries under the Well-Founded Semantics. *Journal of Logic Programming*, 24(3):219–245, 1995.

[CW95] Weidong Chen and David S. Warren. Computing of Stable Models and its Integration with Logical Query Processing. *IEEE Transactions on Knowledge and Data Engineering*, 17:279–300, 1995.

[CW96] Weidong Chen and David S. Warren. Tabled Evaluation with Delaying for General Logic Programs. *Journal of the ACM*, 43(1):20–74, January 1996.

[DF96] J. Dix and U. Furbach. The DFG-Project DisLoP on Disjunctive Logic Programming. *Computational Logic*, 2:89–90, 1996.

[DLMW96] Jürgen Dix, Donald Loveland, Jack Minker, and David. S. Warren. Disjunctive Logic Programming and databases: Nonmonotonic Aspects. Technical Report Dagstuhl Seminar Report 150, IBFI GmbH, Schloß Dagstuhl, 1996.

[ECR95] ECRC GmbH, München. *ECLiPSe 3.5: User Manual – Extensions User Manual*, 1995.

[EGLS96] T. Eiter, G. Gottlob, J. Lu, and V. S. Subrahmanian. Computing Non-Ground Representations of Stable Models. Technical report, University of Maryland, 1996.

[JM94] Joxan Jaffar and Michael J. Maher. Constraint logic programming: a survey. *Journal of Logic Programming*, 19,20:503–581, 1994.

[KNS95] Vadim Kagan, Anil Nerode, and V. S. Subrahmanian. Computing Minimal Models by Partial Instantiation. *Theoretical Computer Science*, 155:157–177, 1995.

[KSS91] David B. Kemp, Peter J. Stuckey, and Divesh Srivastava. Magic Sets and Bottom-Up Evaluation of Well-Founded Models. In Vijay Saraswat and Kazunori Ueda, editors, *Proceedings of the 1991 Int. Symposium on Logic Programming*, pages 337–351. MIT, June 1991.

[Mah88] Michael J. Maher. Complete axiomatizations of the algebras of finite, rational and infinite trees. In *Proceedings of the 3rd Annual Symposium on Logic in Computer Science*, pages 348–359. Computer Society Press, 1988.

[Mah93]   Michael J. Maher. A logic programming view of CLP. In David S. Warren, editor, *Proceedings of the 10th International Conference on Logic Programming*, pages 737–753. MIT Press, Cambridge, MA, London, England, 1993. Budapest, 1993.

[SS95]   Chiaki Sakama and Hirohisa Seki. Partial Deduction of Disjunctive Logic Programs: A Declarative Approach. In *Logic Program Synthesis and Transformation – Meta Programming in Logic*, LNCS 883, pages 170–182, Berlin, 1995. Springer. Extended version to appear in *Journal of Logic Programming*.

[ST96]   Frieder Stolzenburg and Bernd Thomas. Analysing rule sets for the calculation of banking fees by a theorem prover with constraints. In *Proceedings of the 2nd International Conference on Practical Application of Constraint Technology*, pages 269–282, London, 1996. Practical Application Company.

[Stu91]   Peter J. Stuckey. Constructive negation for constraint logic programming. In *Proceedings of the 6th Annual Symposium on Logic in Computer Science*, pages 328–339, 1991.

Springer
and the
environment

At Springer we firmly believe that an international science publisher has a special obligation to the environment, and our corporate policies consistently reflect this conviction.

We also expect our business partners – paper mills, printers, packaging manufacturers, etc. – to commit themselves to using materials and production processes that do not harm the environment. The paper in this book is made from low- or no-chlorine pulp and is acid free, in conformance with international standards for paper permanency.

 Springer

Lecture Notes in Artificial Intelligence (LNAI)

Lecture Notes in Computer Science